Modern Analytical Techniques

Second Edition

Frank Owen and Ron Jones

PITMAN PUBLISHING
128 Long Acre London WC2B 9AN

© Polytech Publishers Limited 1973
This edition © Longman Group UK Limited

Reprinted 1988, 1989
Second edition 1984
First published in Great Britain 1973

ISBN 0–273–02768–9

Printed and bound in Singapore.

Contents

Computer Programs

A suite of programs to accompany this volume will be available from September 1984. Further details can be obtained from:

> Arrow Software
> 94, Robin Hood Lane
> Helsby
> Warrington, WA6 9NH

Preface to the Second Edition

It has become obvious that, if business is to be controlled effectively, there is a need for both established businessmen and those who are studying for a career in business to obtain an appreciation of the quantitative techniques used to provide a basis for decision taking. We have entered the era when it is necessary for the manager to be numerate. It is unfortunately true that many students starting professional and business studies courses have an imperfect grasp of the mathematical concepts that underpin quantitative analysis. In this book we attempt to explain such concepts step by step as a basis for practical problems encountered in the business world.

In preparing this second edition, we have where possible taken into account the many helpful suggestions made by both teachers and students, and we would like to thank those people who have taken the trouble to write to us offering advice and encouragement. We have removed from this edition many of the statistical concepts as they are now dealt with more fully in our Statistics textbook, and have substituted in their place Input-Output Analysis, Markov Chains, sequencing, replacement strategies, and further applications of networks. We have taken into account the needs of students reading for C.N.A.A. degrees in Business Studies, B/TEC Higher awards, and the Quantitative Analysis papers of the ICMA and Institute of Certified Accountants. At the same time we believe that the practicing businessman who want a clearer understanding of the way his 'specialists' operate, will also find much that is useful.

It is with great sadness that I must report the death of Frank Owen. Frank was a gifted teacher and first class scholar; a man highly respected by his colleagues at Liverpool Polytechnic. To me, Frank was more than a colleague and co-author: he was also a close friend.

Ron Jones.

Chapter One

Graphs and Gradients

Functions

From a very early stage in human history man has been concerned with cause and effect. In fact, many of the most important scientific discoveries have taken place because someone has asked, "What will happen if I do this?". Much of mathematical knowledge is concerned with expressing the relationship between cause and effect in mathematical form. We know, for example, that the distance a body has fallen when dropped depends on the period of time for which it has been falling. The mathematician takes a general statement like this and makes it specific by saying

$$s = \tfrac{1}{2}gt^2$$

where s represents the distance fallen in time t seconds, and g is the gravitational constant, 32.

Now, an expression in this form extends our knowledge in two ways. Firstly, it tells us the exact way in which the distance fallen and the time are related; and secondly, it enables us to calculate the distance fallen if we know for how long the body has been falling. Naturally, if we had been given the distance fallen we could also calculate the time.

If you examine the above expression carefully you will notice one or two things about it. While s and t can take any values, the value of g is given as 32 and cannot change. Thus we may say that

> s and t are *variables*
>
> g is a *constant*

Looking now at the variables s and t we know that the value of s depends on the value of t, and so

> s is the *dependent variable* since its value depends on the value assigned to t
>
> t is the *independent variable* since it may take any value.

When two variables are connected in such a way that the value of one depends on the value of the other we say that the dependent variable is a *function* of the independent variable. Distance fallen is a function of the duration of the fall. Expressed more concisely we can put it that

$$s = f(t) \text{ (s is a function of t)}$$

while the expression $s = \tfrac{1}{2}gt^2$ tells us the precise form of the functional relationship.

Let us examine two such simple functional relationships that you might meet in business. Your transport manager is instructed to hire a car for the use of the company directors. He approaches a car hire firm who quote two different weekly tariffs.

Tariff 1.   A charge of 7.5 pence per mile travelled.
Tariff 2.   A fixed charge of £5 per week with an additional charge of 5 pence per mile travelled.

If we choose the first tariff we know that y (the cost) is a function of x (the distance travelled) and the precise form of the function is

$$y = 7.5x \text{ pence}$$
$$\text{or } y = £0.075x$$

We could draw up a table showing how the weekly charge varies according to mileage like this:

Mileage (x)	0	50	100	150	200	250	300	350
Cost £(y)	0	3.75	7.5	11.25	15	18.75	22.5	26.25

Looking at the table we can see that if 200 miles are covered in the week the charge is £15. We can plot this point on a graph.

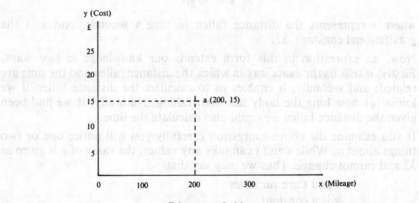

Diagram 1.01.

Having scaled the axes we locate 200 on the x (or horizontal) axis of the graph and imagine a line drawn vertically upwards from this point. This value of x is what we call the x *coordinate*. Now we locate 15 on the y (or vertical) axis and imagine a line drawn horizontally from this point. This value of y is called the y coordinate.

These two lines intersect at the point a, which can be identified by quoting its coordinates (200, 15). Any point on the graph can be identified if we know the coordinates. Thus the point (100, 7.5) is the point representing an x value of 100 and a value of y corresponding to it of 7.5. If we do this for all the remaining points in our table, (0, 0), (50, 3.75), (100, 7.5) . . . etc., we find that it is possible to join all the points by a straight line, and we can read off the weekly charge (y) for any desired mileage (x) up to 350 miles.

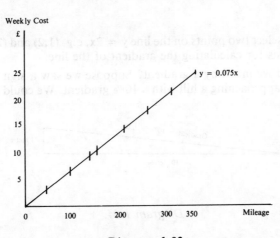

Diagram 1.02.

As we can read off the weekly charge from the graph we can say that the equation of the line we have drawn is the same as the equation describing the function, that is

$$y = 0.075x$$

Now the mileage charge may not be £0.075 per mile but some other value, say £m per mile. The equation of the line then becomes

$$y = mx$$

Any straight line which passes through the origin of the graph, i.e. the point $(0, 0)$, has an equation of the form $y = mx$.

In the diagram below, three such straight lines have been drawn; $y = \frac{1}{2}x$, $y = x$, and $y = 2x$. Notice that the greater is the value of m, the steeper is the slope of the graph. In fact, m measures the *gradient* of the line.

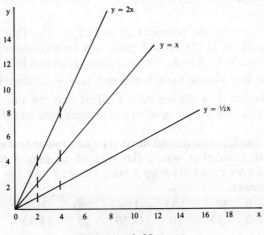

Diagram 1.03.

Gradients

We will now select two points on the line y = 2x, e.g. (1,2) and (2,4) and use them as a basis for calculating the gradient of the line.

Now what do we mean by a gradient? Suppose we saw a sign warning us that we were approaching a hill with a 10% gradient. We could represent it like this:

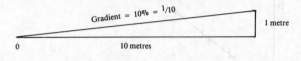

Diagram 1.04.

A mathematician would not, however, call this a 10% gradient; rather would he say that the hill had a gradient of ¹/10. In other words the mathematician calculates the gradient of a line by the formula

$$\frac{\text{vertical distance}}{\text{horizontal distance}}$$

Now if we consider a line drawn on a graph, then clearly the vertical distance is the change in the value of y and the horizontal distance is the change in the value of x. Hence we can state that the gradient of a line joining any two points on a graph is

$$\frac{\text{Change in y}}{\text{Change in x}} \quad \text{or as it is more commonly put} \quad \frac{dy}{dx}$$

Let us now return to the points (1,2) and (2,4). The first point has a y coordinate equal to 2, the second point a y coordinate equal to 4. The change in y, then, is 4 − 2 = 2. Similarly the change in x is 2 − 1 = 1. So the gradient of the line joining these two points is $\frac{2}{1}$ = 2. Since both points lie on the straight line y = 2x we have verified that the line y = 2x has a gradient of 2 and that the value of m does indeed measure the gradient.

We will now consider the second tariff quoted to your transport manager, which you will remember was a flat rate of £5 plus 5 pence per mile travelled. Again we could draw up a table showing how the weekly charge varies with mileage.

Mileage (x)	0	50	100	150	200	250	300	350
Cost £(y)	0	7.50	10	12.50	15	17.50	20	22.50

This information is graphed in Diagram 1.05.

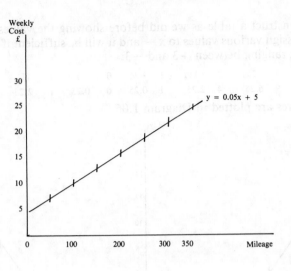

Diagram 1.05.

Again we can read off the weekly charge (y) for any mileage (x) up to 350 miles. For any mileage (x) the weekly charge is

$$y = £(0.05x + 5)$$

We can see that the gradient of this line is 0.05. Select any two points on the line and verify this for yourself.

Suppose that he hire charge was £c and the mileage charge £m per mile. The equation connecting weekly charge and mileage would then be

$$y = mx + c$$

Can you spot the difference between the line y = mx and the line y = mx + c? The first line passes through the origin whereas the second line does not. What then can you conclude about the significance of c when drawing y = mx + c? Surely it is obvious that c determines the point at which the line cuts the y axis.

The gradient of a curve

The straight line has been useful in introducing concepts that we must master and thoroughly understand, and it is of far more use in the business world than many people think. But the functions that result in straight line graphs are only one type of function. The special characteristic of the *linear function* (as it is called) is that the equation contains only terms in which the power of x or y is unity, and constants. Suppose, however, that we are considering equations which contain terms such as x^2 or x^3, or those with terms such as $1/x$ or $2/x^2$. What sort of graph results then? Let us take as an example a situation where y is a function of x such that

$$y = x^2$$

We can construct a table as we did before showing the values taken by y when we assign various values to x — and it will be sufficient if we consider values of x ranging between $+3$ and -3.

x	-3	$-2\frac{1}{2}$	-2	$-1\frac{1}{2}$	-1	$-\frac{1}{2}$	0	$\frac{1}{2}$	1	$1\frac{1}{2}$	2	$2\frac{1}{2}$	3
$y\ (=x^2)$	9	6.25	4	2.25	1	0.25	0	0.25	1	2.25	4	6.25	9

These figures are plotted in Diagram 1.06

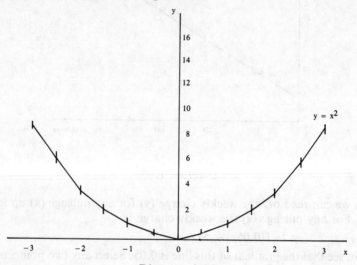

Diagram 1.06.

As you can see this graph is far from a straight line — it results in a U shaped curve which is symmetrical about the y axis. It is what we know as a *parabola*. The gradient of such a curve varies from point to point and we can no longer say that the gradient is measured by m. How then can we measure it?

Let us consider one small section of the parabola $y = x^2$, say between values for x of $\frac{1}{2}$ and $1\frac{1}{2}$. This section of the curve is drawn in diagram 1.07.

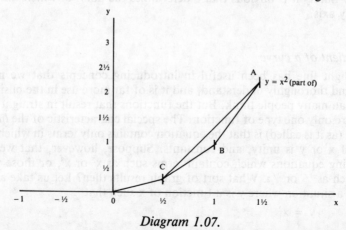

Diagram 1.07.

We will firstly consider the curve between point A (1½,2¼) and point C (½,¼). If we use the same technique as before we find that

$$dy = 2¼ - ¼ = 2 \qquad dx = 1½ - ½ = 1$$

and we obtain a gradient $\dfrac{dy}{dx} = \dfrac{2}{1} = 2$. But this is clearly not the gradient of the curve − it is the gradient of the straight line AC which is a very different thing.

Consider now the point B (1,1) and C (½,¼). The gradient of the straight line BC is $\dfrac{1 - ¼}{1 - ½} = \dfrac{¾}{½} = 1½$. This is still not the gradient of the curve, but it is obvious from the diagram that the gradient of this straight line is much closer to the gradient of the curve than was that of the line AC. In fact, the closer B approaches to A, the more closely does the gradient of the line AB approach that of the curve. If we can allow B to approach so closely to A that the distance between them is infinitely small, the gradient of the line AB will differ from that of the curve by so little that the difference can be ignored. What we have done in fact is to make dx infinitely small so that in effect we are calculating the gradient of the curve at point A rather than between two points. The problem is that we have no means of measuring infinitely small distances by any technique that we have met so far.

The handling of this problem and the calculation of the gradient of a curve at any given point is a matter for differential calculus which we will introduce in a later chapter.

Exercises to Chapter 1

1.1 You decide to have a Spanish holiday and convert your holiday savings into pesetas. The rate of exchange obtainable from your bank is 148 pesetas to the pound. Draw a graph which would enable you to convert pesetas into pounds for amounts up to £5.00. Read off the sterling value of 115 pesetas; 326 pesetas; and 428 pesetas. (answers to the nearest ½ penny). What is the equation of the line?

1.2 Draw the graph of the line $y = -2x + 4$. What do you notice? What is the significance of the sign of m in the equation $y = mx + c$?

1.3 What is the gradient of the line joining the points (3,45) and (7,77)? Can you find the equation of this line?

(Hint: the equation of the line is $y = mx + c$. You have already calculated m, and we know that when $x = 3$, $y = 45$)

1.4 Consider the functions
$$y = 35x + 150$$
$$y = 25x + 200$$

Graph both these functions and hence determine the values of x and y which satisfy both equations.

1.5 Draw the curve of $y = 3x^3 - 9x$ for values of x between $+2$ and -2. For what values of x is the value of y a maximum; a minimum?

1.6 Consider the sketch of the curve $y = x^2$. It is easy to see that the line AB has a gradient of 3. We could allow A to approach B and recalculate the gradient of AB. The results are summarised in the table below where x and y refer to point A, dx is x minus one and dy is y minus one.

x	2	1.5	1.2	1.1	1.01	1.001	1.0001
y	4	2.25	1.44				
dx	1	0.5	0.2				
dy	3	1.25	0.44				
dy/dx	3	2.5	2.2				

Complete the table. What do you notice about the gradient?

1.7 If $y = (x - 1)(x + 5)$ find the values of y when

$x = 2, 1, 0, 9, (a + 1), -5$

1.8 A motorist pays £50 road tax and £130 per year insurance. His car does 20 miles to the gallon and petrol costs £1.40 per gallon. His car is serviced every 3000 miles at a cost of £30. Depreciation per mile increases as mileage increases and can be calculated by multiplying the square of the mileage by 0.001 pence. If he does x miles per year derive an expression for his motoring cost per mile. Graph the expression you have derived and from the graph estimate the mileage that would minimise cost per mile.

Chapter Two

Inequalities

Inequalities

If you come to think about it, one of the most important results of a system of numbers is the ability it gives us to range things in order of magnitude. We know that a man 185cm tall is taller than a man 180cm tall without ever having seen either of them. See how far you can get describing your girl friend (or boy friend) without the use of numbers and you will soon find that, however important the qualitative aspects, a really accurate description soon involves the use of numbers.

Moreover, the number system enables us to measure differences in magnitude. When we say that the man 185cm tall is 5cm taller than the man 180cm tall, we are in fact making a number of mathematical statements such as:

180cm + 5cm = 185cm 185cm − 5cm = 180cm
180cm is less than 185cm 185cm is greater than 180cm

The difference in height is 5cm; and so on.

Now for centuries mathematicians have concentrated on statements such as the first two above, which express the equality of two or more magnitudes. Perhaps this is because it is easier to visualise precisely, things which are the same. But surely the important thing about measurement is the difference between one set of measurements and another. In the last forty years or so a whole new branch of mathematics has been developed based on the fact that quantities are unequal, and it is this that we must first turn our attention to.

To do this you must first understand two basic signs:

(a) >, meaning greater than (e.g. $x > y$, x is greater than y) and its allied ≥, is greater than or equal to (e.g. $x \geq y$, x is greater than or equal to y).

(b) <, is less than (e.g. $y < x$, y is less than x). Can you see the meaning of $y \leq x$?

Suppose we say that $y < 2 < x$. We interpret this as y is less than 2, which is less than x, and can illustrate it in this way.

Now in this example neither x nor y is equal to 2, and so it should be apparent that y must always be less than x.

Is it equally obvious to you that if $x > 2 > y$, then $x > y$. This is really saying the same thing in reverse but it expresses a very important feature of the 'greater than', 'less than' relationship: it is transitive.

Simple Rules of Inequalities

All other relationships are equally simple:

1. Adding a number to both sides of an inequality does not change the sense of the inequality. Thus if $a > b$, $a + 2 > b + 2$; and if $a < b$, $a + 2 < b + 2$.

   You will realise of course that this rule is also true if the number we add is a negative number. If $a > b$, $a + (-1) > b + (-1)$ i.e. $(a-1) > (b-1)$.

2. Multiplying both sides of an inequality by the same positive number does not change the sense of the inequality. Thus if $c > d$. $2c > 2d$. More generally if $c > d$ and $s > 0$, $cs > ds$.

3. Multiplying both sides of an inequality by the same negative number reverses the sign of the inequality. Thus if $a > b$, $-2a < -2b$.

   If you find this one confusing, try it with numbers rather than letters. 5 > 3 but $-2 \times 5 < -2 \times 3$ i.e. $-10 < -5$.

This is all you need to know to go a long way in the mathematics of inequalities.

Simple Linear Inequalities or Linear Inequalities with a Single Variable

Example 1

Suppose we have an equation in the following form.

$2x + 4 > 3x + 2$

Subtracting $2x$ from both sides we have

$4 > 3x - 2x + 2$ or $4 > x + 2$.

Subtracting 2 from both sides

$4 - 2 > x + 2 - 2$ or $2 > x$

More normally we would say $x < 2$.

Now there is no single value of x, but a range of numbers within which the value must fall; but nevertheless the inequality is solved and every value of x which is less than 2 satisfies it.

Graphing and Inequality

Just as it is possible to draw the graph of an equation, so it is possible to draw the graph of an inequality. In this section at least most of the work we do on inequalities will be graphical.

Ordered Pairs

Example 2

Consider the inequality $2x + y > 1$. It describes all combinations of x and y that satisfy the condition $2x + y > 1$.

We know already how to graph $2x + y = 1$. It will be the straight line joining the points $(\frac{1}{2},0)$ $(0,1)$. Remember that every combination of values of x and y on this line will satisfy the equation $2x + y = 1$.

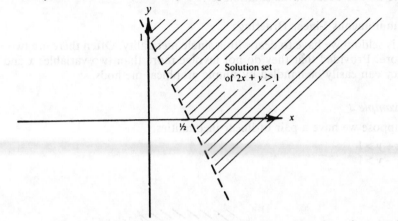

Solution set of $2x + y > 1$

But if the inequality $2x + y > 1$ is to be satisfied, either the value of x must be greater than the value indicated by the graph, or the value of y must. Thus any point lying above the line $2x + y = 1$ gives a pair of value of x and y which will satisfy $2x + y > 1$. We have many such pairs of values, and as a group we may call them the *solution set* of $2x + y > 1$.

Remember however that the solution set does not include any pair of points on the line $2x + y = 1$ — only above it.

Example 3

Let us now depict geometrically the inequality $3x + 2y \leq 6$.

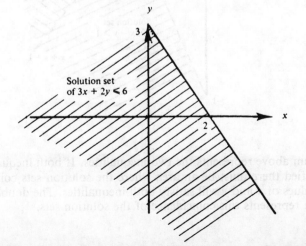

Solution set of $3x + 2y \leq 6$

We proceed exactly as before, graphing the straight line $3x + 2y = 6$.

In this case however the value of $3x + 2y$ must be less than, or equal to 6 and this would be true if the value of x or y were to be less than, or equal to the value shown on the line. In other words, the solution set for $3x + 2y < 6$ consists of all pairs of values of $x + y$ falling on, or below the line $3x + 2y = 6$. Notice that when we graph a 'less than' or 'more than' relationship we use a broken line. If a broken line is drawn, then the combinations on that line do not occur in the solution set.

Simultaneous Linear Orderings

It is seldom we have to deal with a single inequality. Often there are two or more. Provided that they do not involve more than two variables x and y they can easily be handled by simple graphical methods.

Example 4

Suppose we have a pair of linear inequalities.

$$x + y > 1$$
$$2x - y > 1$$

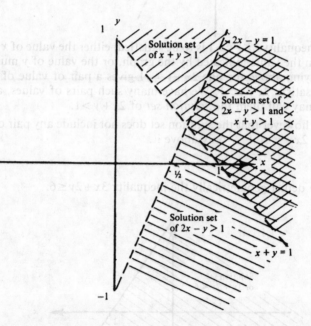

The diagram above represents the two inequalities. If both inequalities are to be satisfied there must be an area where the solution sets coincide i.e. pairs of values of x and y will satisfy both inequalities. The doubly shaded area above represents this coincidence of the solution sets.

Linear Expressions and Linear Programming

Those of you trained in traditional mathematics where the normal relationship is of the type $a = b$ or $2x + 4y + z = 26$ may be wondering why you have had to spend some time mastering expressions which are basically inequalities. Once you begin to try to apply mathematical techniques to problems of production you will not wonder much longer. Most problems you will meet are of the type which involve some *constraints* as a result of having resources limited in quantity or with some limitation on quality attainable. The rest of this chapter is concerned with a simple application of the technique you have just learned to the type of problem the businessman is constantly facing. Possibly without realising it you would have been studying a part of the technique known as 'linear programming'.

This expression is merely management jargon for the technique of reducing a practical problem to a series of linear expressions and then using those expressions to discover the optimal, or best, solution to achieve a given objective. That objective may be the maximisation of profit, the minimisation of cost, or possibly even the best proportions in which to blend Scotch whisky. Whatever the objective, the method tends to be the same.

Of course not all industrial problems are amenable to these methods. There are times when it is quite impossible to·express a given situation in linear form. For these, other, and more complex methods of analysis must be used. But you would be surprised how many problems are capable of being solved by relatively simple techniques.

We will firstly concentrate on the simplest type of problem, those involving only two variables. The reason for this is that such problems are usually capable of simple graphical solution. You will readily appreciate that three variables involve three dimensional graphs which few people really understand, and with more than three variables we enter the realm of graphs which rapidly become unmanageable. For solutions to problems of this type you must wait until a later chapter.

Example 5

Suppose a small tailor is producing two articles only, overcoats and jackets. He has a contract to supply a department store with 10 overcoats and 20 jackets per week. His labour force is limited to five men working a 40 hour week and due to a shortage of working capital he cannot purchase more than 225 yards of cloth per week.

To produce one overcoat takes 5 yards of cloth and 5 hours labour.

To produce one jacket takes 3 yards of cloth and 2 hours labour.

What combination of coats and jackets is it feasible for him to produce?

This is a typical problem that can be expressed mathematically by means of inequalities. We will first examine the *product-mix* that can be produced and then develop the argument to ask what product-mix should be produced.

14

Firstly we state the problem facing the tailor as a series of linear inequalities.

Let x = the number of overcoats produced.
and y = the number of jackets produced.

How does the contract affect his output? He must produce at least 10 overcoats and 20 jackets to meet this contract. Hence

$x \geq 10$ and $y \geq 20$ (These are graphed in diagram 2.1)

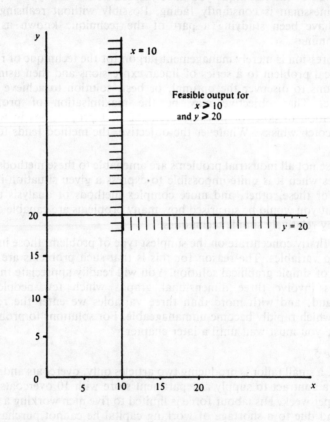

Diagram 2.1 Contract Constraints

There are however constraints imposed on the volume of production by the fact that he has available only 200 hours labour and 225 yards of cloth. Let us consider labour first. If we produce x overcoats per week it will take $5x$ hours of labour. Similarly y jackets will take $2y$ hours of labour.

But we have only 200 hours of labour available so $5x + 2y$ cannot be greater than 200. Thus we may say

$5x + 2y \leq 200$. (The labour constraint is drawn in diagram 2.2)

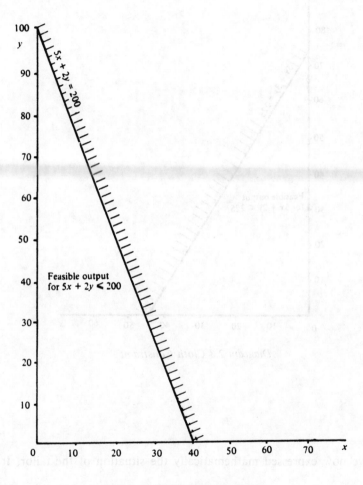

Diagram 2.2 Labour Constraint

Considering now the cloth constraint, we can see that x overcoats take $5x$ yards of cloth, and y jackets take $3y$ yards of cloth. With only 225 yards available it is apparent that

$5x + 3y \leq 225$. (Which is drawn in diagram 2.3)

16

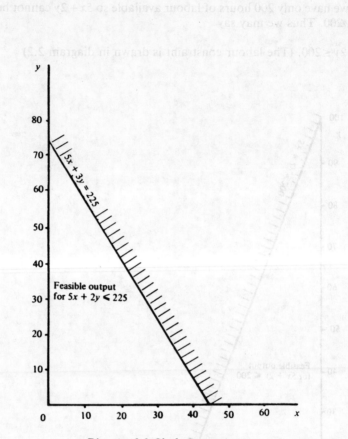

Diagram 2.3 Cloth Constraint

We have now expressed mathematically the situation of the tailor. It is simply:

If he produces x overcoats and y jackets,

$x \geq 10$ $\qquad\qquad$ $y \geq 20$.
$5x + 2y \leq 200$. $\quad$ $5x + 3y \leq 225$.

Before we can go further we must determine the combinations of x and y which are feasible, given the restrictions on labour and raw materials. By far the easiest way of doing this is to sketch the four inequalities, and by examining the solution sets determine what values of x and y satisfy all the inequalities – which we have done in diagram 2.4.

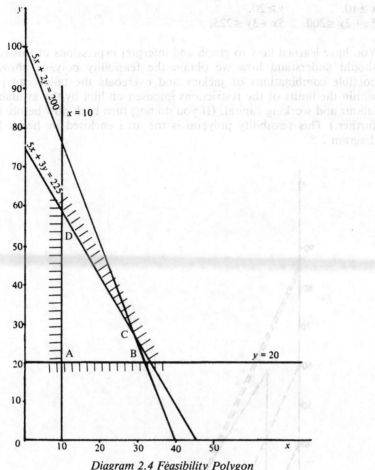

Diagram 2.4 Fèasibility Polygon

In this case we have shaded the combinations of output which are not feasible. It is immediately apparent that there is a polygon ABCD which is unshaded. Within this area production is feasible since neither the contract nor the limited labour force nor the restricted supply of cloth prevents it. This is why such an area is known as feasibility polygon.

We have not yet of course solved any real problem for the tailor. All he has yet is a number of outputs of overcoats and jackets which he knows are possible. It could be 40 jackets and 20 overcoats, or 30 jackets and 25 overcoats. So does the feasibility polygon really help?

Profit Maximisation – Two Dimensional Model

Think once again of the problem we have already partially examined. We have expressed the constraints on his output in the form of linear inequalities viz.

18

$x \geq 10.$ $y \geq 20.$
$5x + 2y \leq 200.$ $5x + 3y \leq 225.$

You have learned how to graph and interpret expressions of this type and should understand how we obtain the feasibility polygon showing all possible combinations of jackets and overcoats the tailor can produce within the limits of the restrictions imposed on him by the availability of labour and working capital. (If you do not, turn back now before reading further.) This feasibility polygon is the area enclosed by heavy lines in diagram 2.5.

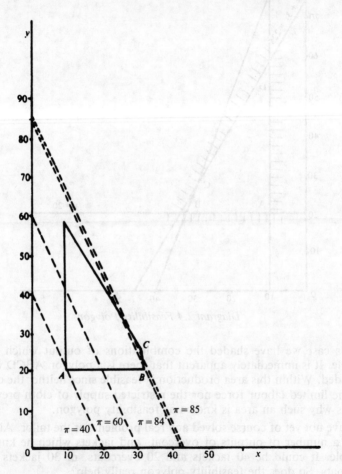

Diagram 2.5 Profit Maximisation

To use what we have obtained we must now consider the objective desired by the tailor. It is highly probable that an important objective will be to maximise his profit and we will concentrate on this. The tailor knows that he makes a profit of £2 on each overcoat he sells and a profit of £1 on each jacket he sells. If, as before, he sells y jackets and x overcoats we may express his total profit as Profit $= y + 2x$ and the problem we are posing is what combination of jackets and overcoats will maximise this profit, and still satisfy the constraints. It is essentially the basic economic problem of how best to use limited resources which are capable of being used in more than one way.

If we state the problem this way: (π is total profit)

Maximise $\pi = y + 2x$
  subject to $\quad x \geq 10 \qquad 2y + 5x \leq 200.$
  $\qquad\qquad\quad y \geq 20 \qquad 3y + 5x \leq 225.$

We have constructed a *mathematical model* of the problem·we wish to solve. Constructing such models is an essential feature of all linear programming problems. The graphical solution is approached like this: firstly we must graph the expressions derived from the constraints and obtain the area of feasibility (which we have already done). (Diagram 2.5). Now we superimpose on this graph a profit line representing $\pi = y + 2x$. To do this we must of course specify some value of π. Suppose we assume that the tailor produces merely to satisfy his contract and nothing else. In this case his output will be 10 overcoats and twenty jackets per week, giving a total profit of £40. (Always approach this problem by assuming minimum possible profit.) If he had not contracted to deliver to a department store minimum possible profit would be zero, and this would result from no production i.e. we would start from the origin of the graph. However, in this case he could not make a smaller profit than £40 He could however make this same profit by producing either 20 overcoats or 40 jackets. If we now join the points representing 40 jackets on the vertical axis and 20 overcoats on the horizontal axis by a straight line, this line will give us all combinations of coats and jackets which will yield a profit of £40. You will readily see that in practice all but one of these combinations are barred to him by the existence of his contract. Graphically this is shown by the fact that our Profit $= £40$ line cuts the feasibility polygon at one point only, the point A, representing a production which just satisfies his contract demand and nothing else.

You should also be able to deduce that the feasibility polygon tells us that he can produce more than this and so increase his profit by producing more overcoats, by producing more jackets, or by producing more of both. In our approach to profit maximisation it seems obvious that he would first produce more overcoats since they yield a greater profit than the jackets. One might assume that he would wish to produce as many overcoats as possible, by moving to point *B* and producing 32 overcoats. This restricted output is determined by the constraint on labour supplies since he is already using 40 hours labour to produce the 20 jackets needed for his contract. There is no doubt that this would increase his profit. It would rise in fact to £84.

Before we consider this alternative however, let us look at one of the intermediate stages in this move — the point at which the tailor can make £60 profit by producing 20 overcoats and 20 jackets, or 10 overcoats and 40 jackets or 15 overcoats and 30 jackets. All these combinations on the profit line $\pi = 60$ are feasible.

If you think carefully about this line, several things are obvious. It does not give a unique solution to the problem we posed, since the profit line gives many different combinations of output all of which lie within the feasibility polygon. Secondly it is immediately apparent that this is not maximum profit. The area of the feasibility polygon lying to the right of the line $\pi = 60$ indicates that we could, with the resources available, produce more of both goods and so raise profit. It is apparent that to obtain a unique solution, the profit line must cut the feasibility polygon at an apex, and also all other combinations of output which give the same profit as this one must lie outside the area of feasibility.

We have then a very limited number of profit lines to consider and since a movement of the profit line to the right implies a rise in total profit the number is still further reduced.

Go back now to the point B and the line $\pi = y + 2x = 84$. this satisfies one of the criteria — it cuts the polygon at an apex — but it is not the solution we are looking for, since several other combinations of output all of which are feasible will give this profit.

We cannot raise profit by producing more overcoats since the output of 32 is restricted by the availability of labour supplies. But there is 5 yards of available material left unused. Is it possible to produce fewer overcoats and use the resources released in such a way as to produce sufficient jackets to raise profit. We will have to produce more than two jackets for every overcoat we sacrifice if we are to succeed.

If we give up one overcoat, we will have available 5 hrs. labour and 10 yards of material. Thus we could produce a theoretical 2½ jackets before our labour force is exhausted. But who will buy half a jacket? The maximum we can produce realistically is 2, and to replace one overcoat by two jackets does not raise profit. We must try producing two overcoats less. This will leave us with 10 hours of labour and 15 yards of cloth, which is enough for 5 jackets. So we can raise profit by £1. We have in fact moved to point C with a profit of £85. Why can be not continue this process, giving up two more overcoats and raising profits further? The possibility of this depended on our having had five yards of cloth unused. Now this has been used up, giving up an overcoat gives us sufficient cloth to produce 1.67 jackets — which is non-profitable.

By the time most of you will be thinking that point C was so 'obvious' in the first place that we could have moved to it immediately. The solution is seldom as obvious as this, and in the exercises you will see that our solution will vary according to the profit ratio of the two articles. Master the general approach and you will never go wrong — well hardly ever.

Cost Minimisation

One of the earliest applications of linear programming was the determination of the most economical use of raw materials to achieve a given objective.

Example 6

Let us suppose that a manufacturer of animal feeding stuffs is asked to supply 40 tons of feed per week to a large farmer. The farmer specifies that the food must contain a minimum of 25% fat and 20% protein, but that the total quantity may otherwise be made up by any bulk feed.

Two convenient raw materials are available, A and B.

A contains 50% fat and 25% protein.
B contains 25% fat and 40% protein.

The manufacturer has in stock 12 tons of A which he wishes to use, but further supplies are readily available. On the other hand he is able to obtain only 20 tons of B per week. The price of both A and B is £25 per ton. In what proportions should he mix A and B in order to satisfy the farmers requirements and minimise his cost of production?

The problem may be expressed mathematically as follows:

1. $A \geq 12$ because of the need to use existing supplies.

2. $B \leq 20$ because of the limitation on supplies. Also $B \geq 0$ as we cannot add a negative quantity.

3. The desired fat content of the mixture is 10 tons (25% of 40 tons) minimum, so 50% of A + 25% of $B \geq 25\%$ of 40. That is $2A + B \geq 40$.

4. The desired protein content is 8 tons (20% of 40 tons) minimum, so 25% of A + 40% of $B \geq 20\%$ of 40. That is $5A + 8B \geq 160$.

5. The restriction on demand is 40 tons per week so $A + B \leq 40$.

6. The cost of the mixture $C = 25A + 25B$.

Our full instructions read:

Minimise $C = 25A + 25B$ subject to
$A \geq 12 \quad 0 \leq B \leq 20 \quad A + B \leq 40$
$2A + B \geq 40 \quad 5A + 8B \geq 160$

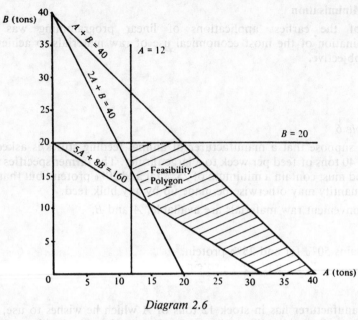

Diagram 2.6

The only one of these constraints that may confuse you is that of the demand constraint. Why do we say $A + B \leq 40$ rather than $A + B = 40$? The point is that we may be able to meet the specification of the feed by using quantities of A and B which total less than 40 tons and make good the difference by using a cheap edible bulk material (sawdust perhaps) rather than the more expensive raw materials.

The production feasibility polygon should now be easy to draw. Draw it and compare your result with diagram 6. Any combination of A and B within the shaded area will satisfy the fat and protein requirements and will not exceed the maximum 40 tons per week which is demanded.

We will approach the problem of minimisation in this way. Let us take an arbitrary cost figure of say £275. This sum is the cost of 11 tons of A, or 11 tons of B, or any combination of $A + B$ on the straight line joining the two points. This cost line is illustrated in Diagram 2.7.

As you can see this cost line does not touch the feasibility polygon at any point at all. What does this mean? Merely that it is not possible to produce the feed to the requested specification at a cost as low as this. So − let us take a different cost level, £750, and add this to our diagram. Certainly at this level of costs there are many combinations of $A + B$ which we can use which will satisfy our needs. We could combine 20 tons of A with 10 of B; or 15 tons of A with 15 of B. But this is not enought − we wish to minimise cost, and the existence of a part of the feasibility polygon to the left of the line $C = $ £750 indicates that we can achieve perfectly satisfactory results at a

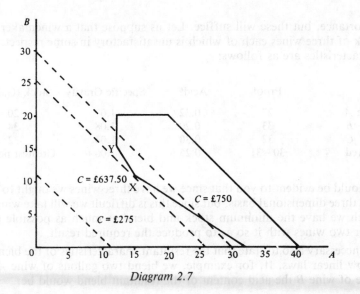

Diagram 2.7

lower cost. We wish the product mix to be as far to the left as it can be. As in profit maximisation the need for a unique solution indicates that the cost line must cut the feasibility polygon at an apex. A study of the polygon and the slope of the cost curve shows that we minimise cost at point X, mixing 14½ tons of A with 11 tons of B at a cost of £637.50 and adding 14½ tons of cheap bulk to make up the required weight of feed.

It might be useful at this point to ask yourself why we rejected the point Y as a minimum cost point, and then ask in what circumstances would we be likely to move to point Y. (Consider relative prices.)

The problem we set ourselves is solved, but please remember you cannot solve such problems without the complete battery of curves. You need to know the slope of the cost curve to determine which apex of the feasibility polygon satisfies the objective.

Blending

Example 7

For our last example in this chapter let us take a problem that those of your who are amateur winemakers may well have met − the problem of blending wines (which in some respect do not meet our requirements) in such proportions that the resultant blend is satisfactory in every respect. This is a problem constantly faced by, for example, the oil companies in attempting to produce a satisfactory commercial product.

As you may know, a good dry table wine should have certain characteristics. It should be about 30 degrees proof to give a satisfactory alcohol content; it should contain at least 0.25% acid, otherwise it is insipid; and its specific gravity should be greater than 1.06. There are probably other characteristics that the experts would consider to be of importance, but these will suffice. Let us suppose that a winemaker has a stock of three wines each of which is unsatisfactory in some respect. Their characteristics are as follows:

	Proof	Acid%	Specific Gravity	Stock (Gallons)
Wine A	27	0.32	1.07	20
B	33	0.20	1.08	34
C	32	0.30	1.04	32
Desired	30 – 31	0.25 +	1.06 +	Greatest possible

It should be evident to you that since we have three wines we ought to graph on a three dimensional basis, but since this is difficult we will take wine A of which we have the minimum stock and blend as much as possible of the other two wines with it so as to produce the required result.

It is necessary also to state that the resultant characteristics of the blend will follow linear laws. If, for example, we blend two gallons of wine A with three of wine B the acid content of the resultant blend would be:

$$\frac{(2 \times 0.32 + (3 \times 0.20)}{2 + 3} = \frac{0.64 + 0.60}{5} = 0.248\%$$

Firstly we will examine the constraints, assuming we blend B gallons of B and C gallons of C with 20 gallons of A.

A. Constraints on Proof

The resultant degrees Proof of such a blend would be

$$\frac{(20 \times 27) + (B \times 33) + (C \times 32)}{20 + B + C}$$

and this must be equal to or greater than 30, and equal to or less than 31. Thus in respect of proof we have two constraints to consider.

Firstly, $\dfrac{540 + 33B + 32C}{20 + B + C} \geq 30$; so $540 + 33B + 32C \geq 600 + 30B + 30C$;

Thus $3B + 2C \geq 60$...Constraint a.

But equally $\dfrac{540 + 33B + 32C}{20 + B + C} \leq 31$; so $540 + 33B + 32C \leq 620 + 31B + 31C$.

Thus $2B + C \leq 80$..Constraint b.

These two restrictions on proof are graphed in Diagram 2.8(a).

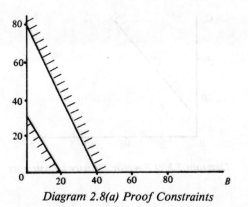

Diagram 2.8(a) Proof Constraints

B. Constraints on Acid Content

We can deal similarly with the constraints on acid content.

i.e. $\dfrac{(20 \times .32) + (.20B) + (.30C)}{20 + B + C} \geq 0.25$

$\therefore 6.4 + .20B + .30C \geq 5.0 + .25B + .25C$

$\therefore -.05B + .05C \geq -1.4$

i.e. $5B - 5C \leq 140$

$B - C \leq 28$

This is graphed in Diagram 2.8(b).

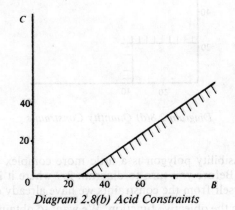

Diagram 2.8(b) Acid Constraints

C. Constraints on Specific Gravity

Likewise the specific gravity constraint is

$\dfrac{(20 \times 1.07) + 1.08B + 1.04C}{20 + B + C} \geq 1.06$

$\therefore 21.4 + 1.08B + 1.04C \geq 21.2 + 1.06B + 1.06C$

$\therefore .02B - .02C \geq -0.2$

or $\qquad C - B \leq 10$

This is graphed in Diagram 2.8(c).

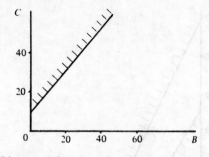

Diagram 2.8(c) Specific Gravity Constraints

D. Quantity Constraints

Finally we have the quantity constraints which can be simply stated as $B \leq 34$ and $C \leq 22$. Remember of course $B \geq 0$ and $C \geq 0$. This is graphed in Diagram 2.8(d).

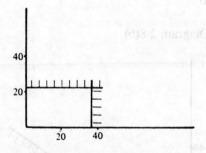

Diagram 2.8(d) Quantity Constraints

The resultant feasibility polygon is a little more complex than those you have met so far. Before you turn to diagram 2.9 where it is drawn, try to obtain it for yourself from the constraints we have already drawn.

Now let us turn to the objective function. We want to obtain as much of the final blend as possible. Remember, however, that our blend is not merely $B + C$. It is (20 gallons of A) + $B + C$. The objective function then is

Maximise $Q = 20 + B + C$

and our instructions read:

maximise $Q = 20 + B + C$

$$\text{Subject to } 3B + 2C \geq 60 \qquad 2B + C \leq 80$$
$$B - C \leq 28 \qquad C - B \leq 10$$
$$0 \leq B \leq 34 \qquad 0 \leq C \leq 22$$

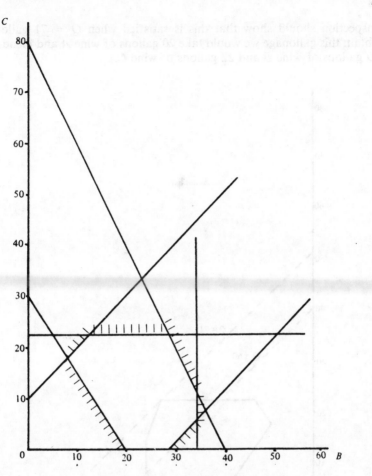

Diagram 2.9 Feasibility Polygon

How do we obtain this objective? Let us take first a given level of our blend, say 60 gallons. This is a blend of 20 gallons of A plus 40 gallons of $(B + C)$. Since A is given we will bother only with $B + C$. The 40 gallons we require may be 40 gallons of B, or 40 gallons of C or any combination of the two totalling 40 gallons. All such combinations are shown on the straight line joining $40B$ and $40C$. In other words this line represents $Q = 60$ gallons. If you look at diagram 2.10 this line passes through the feasibility polygon and there are many combinations of $B + C$ which will blend with A to satisfy us. But equally we could blend more A or more B, or both and still remain within the constraints. (How do we know?) Hence,

$Q = 20 + B + C$ is not maxmised

You will realise that once again we need the line Q to be as far to the right as possible, touching an apex of the polygon but not passing through it.

Inspection should show that this is satisfied when $Q = 71$ gallons. To obtain this gallonage we would take 20 gallons of wine A and blend with it 29 gallons of wine B and 22 gallons of wine C.

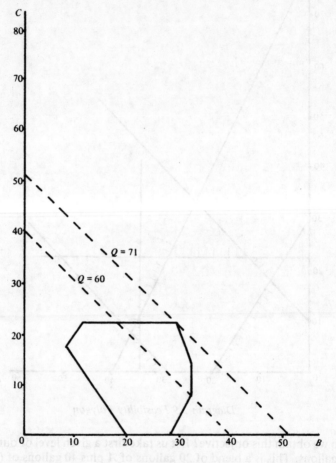

Diagram 2.10

These simple concepts of linear programming have carried us a long way. You can now obtain equalities expressing constraints, set up an objective function, and (so long as we deal in two constraints) obtain a solution.

But how many firms produce only two commodities or have only two inputs? As soon as you try to introduce some realistic problem, simple graphical method breaks down. In the later chapters you will learn how to handle mathematical models involving several variables (although if there are more than three you would be well advised to seek the aid of a computer).

Exercises to Chapter Two

2.1   If $x > 3$ and $y > 4$ find the greatest integer less than $3x + 4y$.

If $x < 3$ and $y > -3$ find the least integer greater than $2x - 3y$.

Show that if $a > b$ then $\dfrac{1}{a} < \dfrac{1}{b}$.

Depict geometrically the solution set of $-x + y > 1$.

Would the solution set be different if $-x + y \geq 1$?

2.2   Sketch the solution sets of the pair of inequalities

$x + y < 1.$
$3x + 2y < 6.$

What would you conclude?

2.3   Sketch the solution set for the triple inequalities,

$x + y \geq 2.$
$x + 4y \leq 4.$
$y > -1.$

2.4   Consider the non linear inequality $x^2 - 6x - 16 < 0$, then $(x + 2)(x - 8) < 0$. If $(x+2) < 0$ what can you conclude about $(x-8)$? Is your conclusion reasonable?

If $(x+2) > 0$ what do you conclude about $(x-8)$? Is your conclusion reasonable?

Deduce the solution to the inequality.

     This question refers to example 5 in the text.

2.5   What output would the tailor produce if the profit was

(a) Overcoats £4   Jackets £1.
(b) Overcoats £1   Jackets £1.

What would be the effect of there being available an addition 5 hours labour?

What would be the effect of an additional 10 yards of material?

Deduce the effect of there being available an additional supply of both 10 yards of cloth and 5 hours of labour.

2.6   A firm is producing two brass ornaments, a standard and a de luxe model. The manufacturing process consists of two machines only

Machine 1	Machine 2
Standard model 1 hour	1 hour
De-luxe model 2 hours	5 hours

There are 20 hours time available on machine 1 and 35 hours on machine 2. The firm makes 50 pence profit on the standard model and £1.50 on the de-luxe,

(a) The first constraint is on machine 1 time and the second on machine 2 time. What is the third?
(b) If the aim is to maximise profit, state the objective function.
(c) Obtain by graphical methods the output which will achieve the objective.

2.7 Suppose that in Example 6 in the text the cost of A was £20 per ton and the cost of B £10 per ton:

(a) Write down the new objective function.

(b) Obtain the optimum solution graphically.

(c) Why is it not possible to obtain a unique solution?

2.8 In Example 7 in the text we have blended wine $B + C$ with 20 gallons of wine A. Would we obtain the same solution if we blended A and C *with 34 gallons of B*. If not, why not?

2.9 Compare Examples 5, 6, 7 in the text.

Suppose we change the objective function in each case to

Example 5.   Maximise $\pi = 2y + 2x$

Example 6.   Minimise $C = 20A + 25B$

Example 7.   Maximise $Q = 30 + B + C$

Is it now possible to obtain optimal solutions?

What changes must you effect to obtain solutions?

In what ways do the changes affect the three types of problems?

2.10 A haulage contractor cwns 6 three ton lorries and 16 thirty hundredweight vans which he is prepared to hire at a charge of £6 per day for a lorry and £4 per day for a van. A manufacturer wishes to transport a minimum of 900 brass casting a day but is unwilling to spend more than £48 a day on hiring transport. A lorry can carry 150 castings and a van can carry 60. Using L to represent lorries and V to represent vans:

(a) Express the above information in the form of a series of in-equalities.

(b) Given that the objective is to minimise cost, what combination of vans and lorries should the manufacturer hire?

(c) List all combinations of vans and lorries which will satisfy the restrictions. What is the largest number of castings that can be carried in one day subject to these restrictions?

2.11 A sports manufacturer produces both tennis rackets and cricket bats. The inputs required for their production are:

	Machine time	Labour time
Bats	1 hour	4 hours
Rackets	2 hours	5 hours

He has available 26 hours of machine time and 92 hours of labour time per day. His sales manager informs him that his maximum daily sales of cricket bats is 20 and of tennis rackets is 11; and that the profit on sale is likely to be £2 on each bat and £3⅓ on each racket. What combination of bats and rackets will maximise profit and what will that profit be?

Should profit change to £1.30 on each bat and £2.60 on each racket, what conclusions could you come to regarding the best product mix?

2.12   A private airline operates two types of aircraft, the Bee and the Wasp, owning 8 of the former and 7 of the latter. The carrying capacities of the two aircraft are:

	Bee	Wasp
Passengers	50	80
Cargo	20 tons	10 tons

Traffic potential is unlimited but the firm has assurances that it will be called upon to carry at least 640 passengers and 190 tons of cargo per day. The estimated cost per journey is £800 for a Bee and £1600 for a Wasp. What is the most economical 'mix' of aircraft?

2.13   A manufacturer is making two products X and Y with the following input requirements.

Product	Raw Materials	Machine Time	Labour
X	4 tons	2 hrs.	1 hr.
Y	1 ton	1 hr.	1 hr.

Inputs are available in the following quantities per week:

90 tons of raw materials
50 hours of machine time
40 hours of labour

The profit is £4 per unit on X and £3 per unit on Y. What product mix will maximise profit?

2.14   Suppose that by law a certain health food must contain at least 3% of Vitamin A and at least 7% of Vitamin B. A manufacturer has stocks of two compounds with the following vitamin content.

	Vitamin A	Vitamin B
Vito	2%	10%
Slam	5%	6%

He wishes to blend Vito and Slam to produce a new product Wow, which meets the minimum vitamin requirements. The sales manager reckons that he can sell up to 60 lbs of Wow per week. If Vito can be produced at £4 profit and Slam at a £5 profit, in what proportions should they be mixed to produce the 60 lbs. of Wow?

2.15   An oil company put additives to petrol to give improved performance and to reduce engine wear. Ideally each 1000 gallons should contain at least 40 mgs. of additive p, 14 mgs. of additive q, and 18 mgs. of additive r. The company can obtain stocks of ingredients which have the following weights of additive per litre:

Ingredient	mgs. p	mgs. q	mgs. r
y	4	2	3
x	5	1	1

Both ingredients cost £1 per litre. The company wishes to know the quantity of each ingredient which will satisfy the conditions and minimise cost.

Chapter Three

Differentiation

We will begin our study of differentiation by summarising what we have learned so far.

1. For any function, $y = f(x)$, say $y = 2x^2$, the value of that function will change as the value of x changes. If $x = 2$, the function has a value of 8; if $x = 3$, the function has a value of 18 and so on.

2. The rate at which the value of the function changes is of great importance in practice and we must learn how to calculate that rate of change.

3. If the function is linear, represented by a straight line graph, the rate of change is uniform, i.e. it is the same whatever the value of x, and we can measure it by measuring the gradient of the line. The gradient is equal to $\dfrac{dy}{dx}$ and this is constant along the line.

4. If the function has a graph which is a curve, we have approximated the gradient of the curve by taking the gradient of the line joining any two points on the curve. Such a line is known as a *chord,* and we obtained better approximations to the gradient by taking successively shorter chords. In question 6 of chapter 1, we asked you to calculate the gradient of a number of such chords, each answer being a closer approximation to the actual rate of change of a function at a point. You have probably realised that if a chord joins two points on the curve which are infinitely close together, so that dx approximates to zero, the chord will be, in fact, the tangent to the curve. The gradient of the curve at any point will be the gradient of the tangent at that point.

In practice, although the gradient can be found by measuring the gradient of the tangent, it is not easy, and for practical purposes, (and for accuracy) an algebraic method is necessary.

Differentiation of x^2

Suppose we have a function $y = x^2$, any point on the resultant curve will have coordinates (x, x^2). Let us now choose a second point on the curve close to this first point such that the x coordinate is increased by a small amount to $x + dx$. The y coordinate will also be increased by a small amount to $y + dy = (x + dx)^2$.

$$y + dy = (x + dx)^2$$
$$= x^2 + 2xdx + (dx)^2$$

We can find dy by subtracting y from both sides.

$$dy = x^2 + 2xdx + (dx)^2 + (-y)$$

Since $y = x^2$

$$dy = x^2 + 2xdx + (dx)^2 - x^2$$
$$= 2xdx + (dx)^2$$

We can obtain the gradient $\dfrac{dy}{dx}$ by dividing both sides by dx

$$\frac{dy}{dx} = \frac{2xdx + (dx)^2}{dx}$$
$$= 2x + dx$$

Now if dx is very small, almost zero, the difference between $2x + dx$ and $2x$ is so small that we can ignore it, and we can say

$$\frac{dy}{dx} = 2x$$

What does this expression mean? Quite simply that if we take any point on the curve, the gradient of the curve at that point is equal to twice the x coordinate. When $x = 3$, that is at the point (3,9), the gradient is 6; when $x = 2$, the point (2,4), the rate of change of the function is 4. In dealing with the gradient of the curve in this way you must remember that $\dfrac{dy}{dx}$ is not a fraction, but merely a convenient way of indicating the gradient of a curve at a point.

Differentiation of 2x³

As before we will increase x by a small amount dx to $x + dx$. Since $y = 2x^3$,

$$y + dy = 2(x + dx)^3$$
$$= 2(x^3 + 3x^2(dx) + 3x(dx)^2 + (dx)^3)$$
$$= 2x^3 + 6x^2(dx) + 6x(dx)^2 + 2(dx)^3$$

Subtracting $y (= 2x^3)$ from both sides, we have

$$dy = 6x^2(dx) + 6x(dx)^2 + 2(dx)^3$$

Now dividing both sides by dx

$$\frac{dy}{dx} = 6x^2 + 6x(dx) + 2(dx)^2$$

If dx is very small $6x(dx)$ and $2(dx)^2$ will be so small they can be ignored and

$$\frac{dy}{dx} = 6x^2$$

A general rule

It would indeed be cumbersome if, every time we wished to differentiate an expression we had to calculate it from first principles in this way. Fortunately if we look at the two results we have we can derive a general method of differentiating.

If $y = x^2$ then $\dfrac{dy}{dx} = 2x$

if $y = 2x^3$ then $\dfrac{dy}{dx} = 6x^2$

If you look carefully at these two expressions you will see that in each case the coefficient of the *derivative* $\dfrac{dy}{dx}$ is equal to the coefficient of x in the original expression multiplied by the index of x in the original expression. For the first expression $1 \times 2 = 2$, and for the second, $2 \times 3 = 6$.

In each case too the index of the derivative is one less than the index of the original expression. So we can deduce the rule:

> To obtain the derivative of an expression multiply the index by the coefficient (giving the coefficient of the derivative,), and subtract one from the index, (giving the index of the derivative).

We can generalise this rule as follows:

> If we have a function $y = mx^n$
>
> The derivative $\dfrac{dy}{dx} = nmx^{n-1}$

Some aspects of differentiation

The above rule holds for all functions, not merely those in which the index is positive.

a) Suppose we are asked to differentiate $y = \frac{1}{x}$

In order to apply the rule we must put this expression into the form $y = mx^n$. We know that

$$\tfrac{1}{x} = x^{-1} \text{ so our expression is } y = x^{-1}$$

and $\dfrac{dy}{dx} = -x^{-2} = \frac{1}{x^2}$

b) In the same way if $y = \sqrt{x}$

$y = x^{\frac{1}{2}}$ and $\dfrac{dy}{dx} = \frac{1}{2}x^{-\frac{1}{2}} = \dfrac{1}{2x^{\frac{1}{2}}} = \dfrac{1}{2\sqrt{x}}$

Thus, provided you can put the expression into the form $y = mx^n$ differentiation will present no problems.

c) Most expressions you will meet are rather more complex than the simple ones we have so far dealt with. A typical algebraic expression would be

$$y = 3x^4 + 2x^3 - 5x^2 + x - 8$$

This more cumbersome expression is no more difficult to differentiate than the easier ones. All we have to do is to take each term of the expression in turn and differentiate that term on its own. The last two terms may however be a little confusing at first glance. Remember that

$$x = 1x^1 \text{ and hence } \frac{dy}{dx} = 1 \times 1x^0 = 1 \times 1 \times 1 = 1$$

and $8 = 8x^0$ and hence $\frac{dy}{dx} = 0 \times 8x^{-1} = 0$

So if we differentiate $y = 3x^4 + 2x^3 - 5x^2 + x - 8$

we get $\frac{dy}{dx} = 12x^3 + 6x^2 - 10x + 1$

We find that in any expression, when we differentiate, the constants disappear. Thus when we differentiate 8, we get the value 0, and this will be true no matter what the constant is.

d) So far we have differentiated only functions in which y is expressed as some function of x, and in which the differential is expressed as $\frac{dy}{dx}$.

You will find, however, that expressions take many forms; e.g. $s = \frac{1}{2}at^2$, where a is a constant. The correct notation for the derivative is, in fact,

$$\frac{d \text{ (the dependent variable)}}{d \text{ (the independent variable)}}$$

so if we were differentiating $s = \frac{1}{2}at^2$

we would say $\frac{ds}{dt} = at$.

In the same way, if we were differentiating $C = \frac{120}{x} + 600x$

we would say $\frac{dC}{dx} = \frac{-120}{x^2} + 600$

e) Sometimes the expression you are asked to differentiate will be the product of two or more other expressions. You might be faced, for example, with something like this:

Differentiate $y = (x^2 + 2)(x - 3)$

Now, there is nothing to stop you from multiplying out this expression and saying that

$$y = x^3 - 3x^2 + 2x - 6$$

and $\frac{dy}{dx} = 3x^2 - 6x + 2$

There will be times though when to multiply out is cumbersome, or even impossible; (for example $y = x^2\sqrt{1-x}$). We need, then, to have a rule for the differentiating products similar to that which we have for differentiating a single expression. That rule is simply this:

> Differentiate one of the factors and multiply by the other. Now differentiate the other factor and multiply by the first. Add the two results and you get $\dfrac{dy}{dx}$.

Generalising, if we call the first factor u and the second factor v, the expression $y = (x^2 + 2)(x - 3)$ becomes $y = uv$

and
$$\frac{dy}{dx} = u\frac{dv}{dx} + v\frac{du}{dx}$$

Apply this rule to the expression

$$y = (x^2 + 2)(x - 3)$$

Let $\quad u = x^2 + 2$

and $\quad v = x - 3$

$$\frac{du}{dx} = 2x \qquad \frac{dv}{dx} = 1$$

$$\frac{dy}{dx} = (x^2 + 2)(1) + (x - 3)(2x)$$

$$= x^2 + 2 + 2x^2 - 6x$$

$$= 3x^2 - 6x + 2$$

which is precisely what we got previously when we multiplied out. This rule may be extended to as many factors as you wish. Suppose we had three factors, u, v and w and are asked to differentiate the expression $y = uvw$

$$\frac{dy}{dx} = vw\frac{du}{dx} + uw\frac{dv}{dx} + uv\frac{dw}{dx}$$

f) Rather similar to this, though perhaps a little more cumbersome, is the situation where the value of y is a quotient such as

$$y = \frac{3x}{x-1} = \frac{u}{v}$$

In this case

$$\frac{dy}{dx} = \frac{v.\dfrac{du}{dx} - u.\dfrac{dv}{dx}}{v^2}$$

This can be stated in words:

> Multiply the denominator by the derivative of the numerator; subtract from it the numerator multiplied by the derivative of the denominator; divide the result by the denominator squared.

Thus if
$$y = \frac{3x}{x-1}$$

$$\frac{dy}{dx} = \frac{(x-1)(3) - (3x)(1)}{(x-1)^2} = \frac{-3}{(x-1)^2}$$

Why Differentiate?

Examine Diagram 3.01. This is the graph of the expression

$$y = 4x^3 + 3x^2 - 36x + 24$$

and, as you can see, the function is plotted between $x = +3$ and $x = -3$.

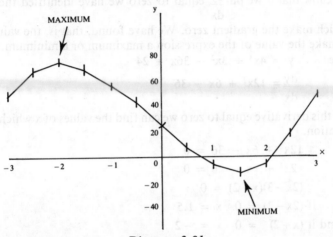

Diagram 3.01.

There is a maximum value of y when $x = -2$ and a minimum of y when x $= +1.5$. Now there are many occasions when we want to know the value of x which makes the expression a maximum or a minimum. Suppose, for example, that we are building a container designed to carry a given volume of liquid. We can find many combinations of length, breadth and height which will give us this volume. But different dimensions to a container involve using differing amounts of material to produce it even though the cubic capacity remains the same. The surface area of a rectangular container, for example is given by:

2 (length × breadth + length × height + height × breadth)

Thus we can build a container of capacity 8 cubic centimetres by building it 8 centimetres long, 1 centimetre high and 1 centimetre wide. The material required would be

2(8 × 1 + 8 × 1 + 1 ×1) square centimetres = 34 square centimetres

We could, alternatively construct our box 4 centimetres long, 2 centimetres wide and 1 centimetre high. In this case the material required would be

2(4 × 2 + 4 × 1 + 2 × 1) square centimetres = 28 square centimetres.

Using the latter dimensions would reduce the material required by 17.6% – an appreciable saving.

The importance of differentiation is that it enables us to identify the value of x which maximises or minimises the value of an expression without having to draw the graph or engage in experiment as we have done above.

Maxima and Minima

Look again at diagram 3.01, this time concentrating on the gradient of the graph. While it is difficult to estimate what the gradient is at any point, we can see that at two points, (where the expression is a maximum and where it is a minimum) the gradient is zero. Now since the gradient is measured by $\frac{dy}{dx}$, we know that if we put $\frac{dy}{dx}$ equal to zero we have identified the values of x which make the gradient zero. We have found, that is, the values of x which make the value of the expression a maximum or a minimum.

Suppose $\qquad y = 4x^3 + 3x^2 - 36x + 24$

$$\frac{dy}{dx} = 12x^2 + 6x - 36$$

Putting this derivative equal to zero we can find the values of x which satisfy the equation.

$$12x^2 + 6x - 36 = 0$$
$$2x^2 + x - 6 = 0$$
$$(2x-3)(x+2) = 0$$
$$\text{If } (2x-3) = 0 \quad x = 1.5$$
$$\text{and if } (x+2) = 0 \quad x = -2$$

There is a snag here, however. We know that when x = 1.5 and when x = -2 there is a maximum or a minimum value. But how can we tell which is which? After all, x = 1.5 could be either a maximum or a minimum value.

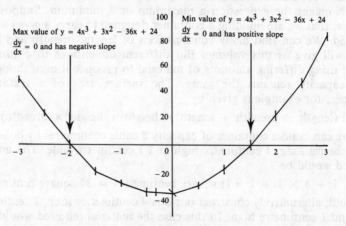

Max value of $y = 4x^3 + 3x^2 - 36x + 24$
$\frac{dy}{dx} = 0$ and has negative slope

Min value of $y = 4x^3 + 3x^2 - 36x + 24$
$\frac{dy}{dx} = 0$ and has positive slope

Diagram 3.02.

The key to discovering which it is lies in an understanding of the behaviour of the derivative. Diagram 3.02 shows the graph of the derivative

$$\frac{dy}{dx} = 12x^2 + 6x - 36$$

As you can see, it is a parabola. If we examine it closely we can see that the value of the derivative is zero when $x = 1.5$ and $x = -2$, which is precisely what we would expect. At these values the gradient of the original expression is zero. More important — when $x = -2$ and the expression is a maximum, the value of the gradient is falling. The curve is falling from left to right, i.e. it has a negative slope. When $x = 1.5$ and the expression is at a minimum value the derivative is increasing and the slope of the graph is positive. This relationship is always true. Whenever the value of the derivative is zero, if the slope of the graph of the derivative at that point is positive the original expression is at a minimum value; whenever it is negative the original expression is at a maximum value.

Now does this mean that to identify which is a maximum and which a minimum we have to draw a graph of the derivative? Of course not. You know that to find the slope of the graph of an expression we differentiate. Although the expression we are considering here is itself a derivative, there is nothing to stop us from differentiating this in its turn. We will then obtain what we know as the second derivative of the original function, indicated by $\frac{d^2y}{dx^2}$. Thus we obtain an expression, the second derivative, which will tell us, for any value of x, the slope of the first derivative.

We now have three expressions:

Original expression $\qquad y = 4x^3 + 3x^2 - 36x + 24$

First derivative $\qquad \dfrac{dy}{dx} = 12x^2 + 6x - 36$

Second derivative $\qquad \dfrac{d^2y}{dx^2} = 24x + 6$

The first derivative identifies for us the point $x = 1.5$ and $x = -2$ at which the original expression is either a maximum or a minimum. The second derivative identifies which is which in the following way.

At the point $x = 1.5$

$$\frac{d^2y}{dx^2} = 24x + 6 = 24 \times 1.5 + 6 = 42$$

The gradient of the first derivative is positive and therefore the original expression is at a minimum value.

At the point $x = -2$

$$\frac{d^2y}{dx^2} = 24x + 6 = 24 \times -2 + 6 = -42$$

For this value of x the gradient of the first derivative is negative and the expression is at a maximum value.

Example

M.A.T. Limited produce bottles of "jabra juice", a drink favoured by the witch doctors of West Africa. At present they are producing variable amounts each week according to the reports of their salesmen. Profits however are low and the managing director instructs his accountants to produce data showing his total revenue and his total costs of production. He then wishes them to determine that level of output which will maximise his firm's profits.

The accountants come up with the following information.

If q is the output of the firm per week in thousands of bottles

Total revenue is given by the expression $23q - \dfrac{q^2}{4}$

Total Cost is given by the expression $36 + 2q + 0.1q^2$

Since profit is total revenue minus total cost it follows that

$$\text{Total Profit} = 23q - \frac{q^2}{4} - 36 - 2q - \frac{q^2}{10}$$

To find the value of q which will maximise total profit we must differentiate this expression.

$$\text{Total Profit} = 21q - \frac{14q^2}{40} - 36$$

$$\frac{d(\text{Profit})}{dq} = 21 - \frac{28q}{40}$$

For profit to be a maximum or a minimum

$\dfrac{d(\text{Profit})}{dq}$ must equal zero i.e.

$$21 - \frac{28q}{40} = 0$$

$$21 = \frac{28q}{40}$$

$$q = \frac{21 \times 40}{28} = 30 \text{ (thousand bottles per week)}$$

But will this maximise or minimise profit? To find out we will take the second derivative.

$$\frac{d^2(\text{Profit})}{dq^2} = \frac{-28}{40}$$

Consider the meaning of this carefully. The slope of the first derivative graph is independent of the value of q. In fact it is constant at $\dfrac{-28}{40}$.

Graphs with a constant gradient are, of course, straight lines, and this is what you would expect from the expression for the first derivative. It is of the form y = mx + c where c = 28 and m = $\dfrac{-28}{40}$. More important from our point of view, the slope of the first derivative is negative, which means that the value of q which we have determined is a value which makes the expression for profits a maximum.

The accountant's response then would be:

"To maximise profits, produce 30,000 bottles of jabra juice each week."

Exercises to Chapter 3

3.1   Differentiate the following functions:

a) $y = 6x^2 + 5x - 7$

b) $y = \dfrac{5}{x} + 4x$

c) $y = 3x^3 + 3x - 1$

d) $y = \dfrac{4}{x^3} + \dfrac{3}{x^2} + \dfrac{2}{x}$

e) $y = (1 + x)^3$

f) $y = (8 - x)(x + 10)$

g) $y = (3x + 1)(2x + 1)$

h) $y = (ax^2 + bx + c)(px + q)$

i) $y = (x^2 + 1)(\frac{1}{2}x + 1)$

j) $y = \dfrac{x + 1}{x + 2}$

k) $y = \dfrac{2x^4}{x^2 - 4}$

l) $y = \dfrac{x^{\frac{1}{2}} + 2}{x^{\frac{1}{2}}}$

3.2   Determine which of the following has a maximum and which a minimum value:

a) $y = mx^2 - c$

b) $y = c - mx^2$

3.3   How many turning points do the following equations have?

a) $y = mx + c$

b) $y = ax^2 + bx + c$

c) $y = ax^3 + bx^2 + cx + d$

3.4   Explain fully each of the following:

a)   A function $y = f(x)$

b)   The first derivative of the function.

c)   The second derivative of the function.

3.5   A motorist pays £50 per year road tax and £130 per year insurance. His car does 25 miles to the gallon and petrol costs £1.40 per gallon. His car is serviced every 6000 miles at a cost of £45. Depreciation increases as mileage increases and can be calculated by multiplying the square of the mileage by 0.0005 pence. If he does x miles per year find the mileage that would minimise cost per mile.

3.6   A manufacturer makes cylindrical containers of 400 cubic centimetres capacity. He wishes to minimise the amount of steel he uses. Find the internal dimensions of the can that would achieve his objective.

3.7 The total revenue of a manufacturer is given as R = x(148 − x) where x is the quantity sold. Find
   a) the sales that would maximise total revenue
   b) the maximum total revenue
   c) the price he would have to charge to maximise total revenue.

3.8 A firm knows that its price (P) and its output (Q) are related by the expression P = 80 − 2Q
   a) Express Q in terms of P
   b) Use this expression to find an expression for total revenue in terms of Q
   c) Find the value of Q which maximises total revenue.

3.9 The costs of production of the same firm are composed of £125 in fixed costs, variable costs of £36 per unit produced and depreciation charges given by the expression £0.05Q^2. Find the level of output which would minimise average cost of production per unit.

3.10 The cost to a supplier of holding goods in stock depends on the amount he orders from the wholesaler. It is found that for John Smith Ltd the annual stockholding costs are

$$\text{Cost} = \frac{50 \times 2000}{q} + \frac{.001q}{4}$$

where q is the quantity ordered from the wholesaler. Find the size of order which will minimise the total cost of holding stock. If the supplier's customers demand 520,000 units a year, how often, on average, will the supplier place an order with his wholesaler?

3.11 A manufacturer knows that his total revenue is given by

$$\text{revenue} = 23Q - \frac{Q^2}{4}$$

   His total cost of production is
   Cost = 36 + 2Q + 0.1Q^2

   where Q is the weekly production in thousands.

   a. Economists define marginal revenue as the rate of change of total revenue. Derive an expression for marginal revenue.

   b. How do you think economists might define "marginal cost"? Derive an expression for marginal cost.

   c. What output will make marginal revenue equal to marginal cost?

   d. Compare your answer with the output of "jabra juice" calculated in the last example in this chapter. What can you deduce?

Chapter Four

Inventories

No firm can operate without holding stocks, even if stock held are small, or they are held for a short period of time..Manufacturers need to hold stocks of raw materials or semi-finished goods in order to maintain a smooth flow of production. They also need to hold stocks of finished goods to meet the requirements of their customers. Moreover, over the last fifty years the trends towards specialisation have intensified. Consider, for example, the motor car manufacturer – apart from the actual shell of the car, his contribution to production is merely to assemble together those components produced by other manufacturers. Clearly, this trend to specialisation has increased the importance of a rational policy towards stock – or as this is sometimes called an 'optimum inventories policy'. The sort of problems we shall consider in this chapter will be the quantity of stock to be ordered, and the time interval between orders. To decide on an optimum inventories policy, however, we need some criterion to enable us to decide that the policy chosen is, in fact, the best policy. Surely, the best policy is the one that involves the lowest inventory costs?

Inventory Costs

It seems appropriate at this point to attempt classification of inventory costs. Firstly, we shall consider *holding costs* which are those costs which arise directly from a decision to hold stocks. How do such costs arise? Well, if stocks are held, it will be necessary to keep them somewhere – perhaps in a warehouse. Thus, holding stocks may involve building or buying premises, and heating and lighting for such premises. It involves paying warehousemen to keep track of the stock, and to move it to where it is needed, when it is needed. Somehow, all such costs must be apportioned to each unit of stock. Fortunately, this is an exercise in cost accountancy, and need not concern us here.

In addition to warehouse costs, there is a second and highly important element in holding costs. Buying inventories ties up a firms capital – and this capital could be used to earn interest. Suppose a firm decides to buy £1,000 worth of spare parts for its machinery. The spare parts are then put into stock until needed. Now instead, the firm could have invested this £1,000 and earned interest. At 10% per annum, this £1,000 would have earned £100 interest in a year. It is reasonable, then, to think of this £100 that the firm could have earned as being an inventory cost – it is money that the firm has foregone through its decision to hold stocks.

Summarising, holding costs comprise storage cost plus cost of capital tied up. Holding costs are expressed as a value "per unit per time period." Suppose, for example, it costs 10p. to store a certain component per month. The component cost £10, and the cost of capital is 15% per year. It costs 10p × 12 to store the component for a year, and additionally the firm has sacrificed 15% of £10 by tying up capital. Thus, the holding cost is 0.1 × 12 + 10 × 0.15 = £2.70 per unit per year.

A second type of inventory cost is *ordering costs* − costs that are incurred each time an order is placed. By far the most obvious element in ordering cost is the clerical cost involved in actually preparing and making the order. There is also the task of ensuring that the best price is being obtained. Ordering costs are expressed as so much 'per order'.

The final element in inventory costs is *stockout costs* i.e. the costs which are incurred when firms actually run out of stock. Sometimes stockout costs are easily calculated − it may be the cost of machines and men being idle through lack of components or raw materials or spare parts. It may be the loss of profit through a failure to fulfil an order. However, running out of stock can cause loss of good will − certainly a cost, but very difficult to evaluate!

An Inventory Model

Tiger Sports Cars produce a high performance, rather expensive sports car. Now most of the components for this car are not produced by Tiger itself but, in common with the volume producers, components are bought from specialist producers. Obviously, Tiger must have stocks of components, and it will be most interesting to examine the factors that determine the size of such stocks. In order to do this, we shall make three assumptions. Firstly, we shall assume that production occurs at a steady rate throughout the year − in other words we are assuming linear demand for components. Secondly, we will assume that any breaks in production are so expensive that the firm would move heaven and earth to ensure that it never runs out of components. Using the mathematicians jargon, we are assuming that stockout costs are infinitely high, and later we will examine the implications of this assumption. Finally, we shall assume that there is no time lag between placing an order for components and receiving delivery (this reinforces the second assumption). This rather artificial assumption enables the firm to reorder when stock runs out, but still avoid stockouts! Armed with these assumptions, we can represent the stock levels held by the firm by diagram 4.1.

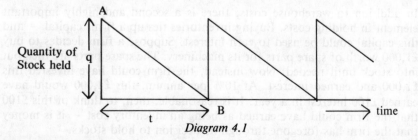

Diagram 4.1

Here, the firm is placing regular orders for q items with its supplier. The straight line AB shows that stock is used up at a steady rate for a time period t, after which the stock is exhausted. (this time period t is called the inventory cycle). Stock is then replenished immediately. The problem we shall be considering is the optimum level of q — i.e. the level of q that minimises inventory costs (the·optimum level of q is frequently called the Economic Ordering Quantity, so you will often find inventory problems referred to as E.O.Q. Models).

To find the optimum batch size to order we need more information. We will need to know how many components are required per time period, and we will need to know the inventory costs. Let us suppose Tiger produces 5,000 vehicles per years and that we are considering an ordering policy for one component — headlights. Clearly, Tiger will require 10,000 headlamps per year. If the firm decides to order in batches of 1,000 headlamps, than $10,000 \div 1,000 = 10$ orders per year must be placed. Again, if the firm orders in batches of 100 then $10,000 \div 100 = 100$ orders per year must be placed. Generalising, if the firm orders batches of q items, then

$$\frac{10,000}{q} \text{ orders per year will be placed}$$

The annual ordering cost can be calculated by multiplying the cost of one order by the number of orders placed per year. Tiger's accountants have calculated that it costs £8 to place an order for headlamps, so

$$\text{ordering costs} = \frac{10,000}{q} \times 8 = \frac{£18,000}{q} \text{ per year}$$

Diagram 4.2 will show clearly the relationship between the batch size ordered and annual ordering costs. In the table below, arbitrary values for the batch size q have been chosen, and the associated annual ordering costs calculated.

If batch size (q) =	50	100	150	200	250	300	350	400
Then ordering costs per annum (£) =	1600	800	533⅓	400	320	266⅔	228.6	200

A glance at diagram 4.2 shows that as we increase the quantity ordered, so we will reduce the annual ordering costs. Now this is precisely what we would expect — larger orders mean fewer orders, and fewer orders means lower annual ordering costs.

So much for ordering costs: we shall now turn our attention to holding costs. The accountants have calculated that it costs £2 per year to store a headlamp. If headlamps cost £10 each, and the cost of capital is 20% per annum then it costs $£10 \times 0.2 = £2$ in tied up capital to hold a headlamp for a year. So the total, annual holding cost per year for one headlamp is £2

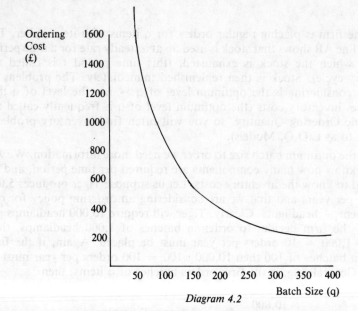

Ordering
Cost
(£)

1600
1400
1200
1000
800
600
400
200

50 100 150 200 250 300 350 400

Batch Size (q)

Diagram 4.2

(storage) + £2 (in tied up capital) = £4. Now as ordering costs are expressed in terms of 'total per year' then it would be advisable to do the same with holding costs. If the firm regularly orders in batches of q items, then the average stock held would be q/2, and the total, annual holding cost would be q/2 × £4 = £2q.

Again, it would be illuminating to draw a diagram, this time showing the relationship between the batch size ordered and the annual holding costs

If the batch size (q)   =   50   100 150 200 250 300 350 400
Then holding costs (£)   =   100   200 300 400 500 600 700 800

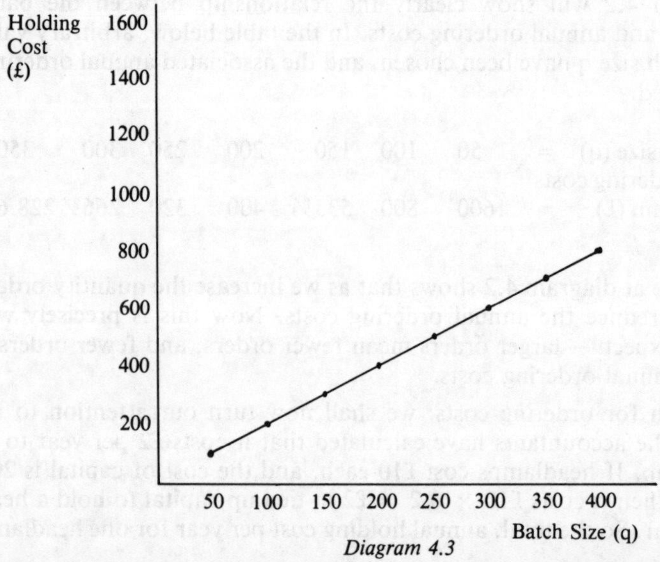

Holding
Cost
(£)

1600
1400
1200
1000
800
600
400
200

50 100 150 200 250 300 350 400

Batch Size (q)

Diagram 4.3

Notice that the smaller the batch size ordered, the lower will be the holding costs, so if we wish to reduce the holding costs, then we would order in small batches – unfortunately this would increase ordering costs! Clearly, then, the problem of selecting the optimum batch size will be to balance ordering cost with holding costs. In fact, we shall now see that *if we choose a batch size that exactly balances ordering costs and holding costs, then total inventory costs would be at a minimum.*

Batch size (q)	50	100	150	200	250	300	350	400
Annual holding cost (£)	100	200	300	400	500	600	700	800
Annual ordering cost (£)	1600	800	533⅓	400	320	266⅔	228.6	200
Total cost	1700	1000	833⅓	800	820	866⅔	928.6	1000

We can see from diagram 4.4 that total inventory costs are minimised at £800, and this can be achieved by ordering batches of 200 items. Notice that if this batch size is ordered, then holding costs and ordering costs are both £400.

We shall now summarise what we have learnt from this particular problem. If Tiger Sports car wishes to minimise the inventory costs associated with holding headlamps, then it will order in batches of 200 headlamps. This will involve the firm with an annual inventory cost of £800, and as 10,000 headlamps per year are required, the firm will order 200 headlamps every week (this is the inventory cycle).

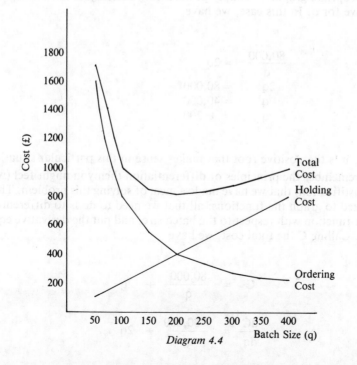

Diagram 4.4

We saw from our graph that inventory costs are at a minimum when ordering costs are equal to holding costs, and it would be as well to check that this is so (after all, perhaps our graph was badly drawn!). If a batch size of 200 gives a minimum level of inventory costs (£800), then any departure from 200 will involve costs greater than £800. Batches of 201 would involve annual inventory costs of

$$\frac{80,000}{201} + 2 \times 201 = £800.00995$$

$$\text{(Ordering)} + \text{(holding)} = \quad \text{(total)}$$

and batches of 199 would involve annual inventory costs of

$$\frac{80,000}{199} + 2 \times 199 = £800.01005$$

So we can see that even marginal changes from our optimum batch size will involve marginal increases in total annual inventory costs.

We have now learnt something extremely useful — to find the optimum batch size for problems like the one facing Tiger, there is no need to draw the appropriate graphs — simply put ordering costs equal to holding costs and solve for q. In this case, we have

$$
\begin{aligned}
\frac{80,000}{q} &= 2q \\
2q^2 &= 80,000 \\
q^2 &= 40,000 \\
q &= \pm\,200
\end{aligned}
$$

Clearly, it is the positive root that makes sense in this particular situation. If you remember the principles of differentiation then you might feel (with some justification) that we have made a meal of solving this problem. There is no need to graph the functions: all that we need to do is to differentiate the cost function with respect to the batch size, and put the derivative equal to zero. Calling C the total cost, we have

$$C = \frac{80,000}{q} + 2q$$

$$\frac{dC}{dq} = \frac{-80,000}{q^2} + 2q$$

For a minimum value of C, $\dfrac{dC}{dq} = 0$, i.e.

$$\dfrac{-80,000}{q^2} + 2 = 0$$

$$2q^2 = 80,000$$

$$q = \pm 200$$

(Notice this is exactly what we got by putting holding costs equal to ordering cost).

Now clearly, we are interested in the positive root (one cannot have a negative batch size!). By taking second derivatives, we can check that q = 200 does indeed give a minimum inventory cost.

$$\dfrac{d_2 y}{dq^2} = \dfrac{160,000}{q^3}$$

and with q = 200, the second derivative will have a positive value i.e.

$$\dfrac{160,000}{(200)^3} > 0$$

so q = 200 does give a minimum inventory cost.

Which method should you use! Well, it's really up to you. We feel that if you have mastered an elimentary knowledge of calculus, then you would be well advised to solve inventory problems using differentiation – after all, it is THE method of solving problems of maxima or minima. Also, if you ever meet more complex inventory problems then you will *have* to use calculus to solve them. If the process off differentiation is a closed book as far as you are concerned, then use the method applied earlier i.e. put ordering costs equal to holding costs and solve for q. But do try to appreciate that by using this method, you appreciation of inventory problems will be somewhat limited.

The Effect of Discounts

We have seen that it is logical for Tiger to order in batches of 200 headlamps. because this minimises inventory costs. However, the supplier of headlamps may not consider this to be a convenient batch size as far as he is concerned. The supplier may well experience economy of handling if only could supply headlamps in larger batches. Regular order of (say) 1000 headlamps might make it worthwhile for the supplier to install mechanised handling facilities (for example, the use of fork-lift trucks). Now one way that the supplier might induce Tiger to order larger batches is to offer a discount for larger orders. Suppose Tiger is offered a 5% discount for orders of 1000 headlamps – should Tiger accept this offer?

Let us firstly recap on order levels of 200 components. This will involve Tiger with inventory costs of £800. In addition to this, however, Tiger must spend $10,000 \times £10 = £100,000$ on actually buying the headlamps, so the total outlay on headlamps would be £100,000 + 800 = £100,800 per year. Clearly, if Tiger is to be induced to accept the supplier's offer, then it must involve Tiger in an annual outlay of less than £100,800 per year.

Suppose Tiger did order batches of 1000 items. Ordering costs would still be £80,000/q, and because the batch size ordered has increased to 1000, ordering costs would fall to 80,000/1,000 = £80 (previously, they were £400). Holding costs would no longer be 2q because the cost of capital tied up will have fallen (Headlamps will now cost £9.50 rather than £10). The holding cost per unit per year would be £2 (storage cost) + 0.2 × £9.50 (cost of capital) = £3.90. So the total holding cost per year would be q/2 × 3.90 = 1.95q, and with batches of 1,000, the annual holding cost would rise to 1000 × 1.95 = £1950 (previously it was £400). So the total inventory cost per year would be £1950 + 80 = £2030. So if batches of 1000 were ordered rather than batches of 200, then total inventory cost would rise by 2030 − 800 = £1230. But we must not forget that by ordering batches of 1,000 Tiger is entitled to a 5% discount − a saving of 50p per headlamp. So the total saving made on the 10,000 headlamps bought in a year would be £5,000. Obviously, Tiger should be advised to take advantage of the discount offered and order batches of 1000 headlamps.

Tiger makes substantial savings − £3770 per year − by increasing the size of batches ordered to 1000 in return for a 5% discount. It would appear that Tiger would have been willing to take up this offer if the discount was less than 5%, and it would be interesting to know what would be the minimum discount that Tiger is prepared to consider. To do this, let us call the discounted price p.

Ordering cost would be $\dfrac{£80,000}{£1,000} = £80$

Storage cost remains at $£2$

Cost of capital tied up is 20% of the discounted price i.e. 0.2p

Average stock held is $\dfrac{1000}{2} = 500,$

So annual holding cost is $500 \times (2 + 0.2p) = 1,000 + 100p$

The total cost of purchasing headlamps is 10,000 p

The total outlay on inventory is

$$80 + 1000 + 100p + 10,000p$$
$$= 1080 + 10100p$$

If Tiger is to take up the discount, then the total cost must be less than the cost associated with a batch of 200 items, so

$$1,080 + 10,100p < 100,800$$
$$10,100p < 99,720$$
$$p < 9.873$$

So it would be reasonable to say that Tiger would order in batches of 1000 if the price was £9.87 or less. This is a discount of $\dfrac{10 - 9.87}{10} \times 100 = 1.3\%$.

Sensitivity Analysis

All of our calculations so far have assumed that we have good data at our disposal. We assumed that demand and costs can be estimated with great precision, but how often will this be the case? We are all familiar with cases where estimates of costs or demand are very wide of the mark indeed! If the estimates of costs and/or demand are wrong, then Tiger will have selected the wrong batch size – it would have ordered in batches of 200 – and a consequence of this will be that inventory costs will be higher than necessary. It would be interesting to see by how much inventory costs will rise due to incorrect estimates – i.e. perform a sensitivity analysis.

We will start by considering what you might consider to be a rather extreme situation. Suppose Tiger gets its production levels wrong. It doesn't produce 5000 vehicles per year, but 7500. – a staggering rise of 50%. This means that 15,000 headlamps per year would be needed, and ordering costs would become

$$\frac{15{,}000}{q} \times 8 = £\frac{120{,}000}{q} \text{ per year}$$

So the total, annual inventory cost would be

$$\frac{120{,}000}{q} + 2q$$

and if batches of 200 are still ordered then annual inventory costs would be

$$\frac{120{,}000}{200} + 2 \times 200 = £1000$$

However, if Tiger had known *in advance* that output would have been 7,500 vehicles, then it would have ordered batches of q items where

$$\frac{120{,}000}{q} = 2q$$

$$q = \sqrt{\frac{120{,}000}{2}}$$

$$= 245,$$

and inventory costs would have been

$$\frac{120{,}000}{245} + 2 \times 245 = £980 \text{ per year}$$

52

Now this is very interesting indeed. Tiger has got its estimate of production levels hopelessly wrong – they turned out to be 50% higher than anticipated. However, inventory costs are a mere $\frac{20}{980} \times 100 = 2\%$ higher than they need have been. A glance at diagram 4.5 shows without doubt that inventory costs are rather *insensitive* to large changes in demand. The same would also be true for changes in the other factors affecting inventory costs (cost of capital, price, ordering costs etc.). This appears to be rather comforting for the person who must decide on the firms inventory policy – large errors in his estimates of data determining inventory policy result in small percentage increases in inventory costs. However, do remember that we have been talking in terms of percentages, and a 2% increase in cost can represent a frighteningly large sum of money!

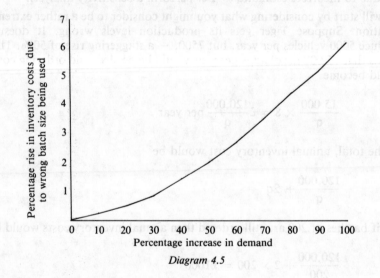

Diagram 4.5

Stockout Costs
The time has now come to introduce stockouts into our basic model.

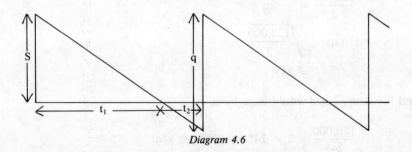

Diagram 4.6

Diagram 4.6 represents what might appear to be rather a strange situation. An order for S items is placed, and stock is used up steadily for a time period t_1 Now instead of reordering immediately, we wait for a time period t_2 before placing an order for a (larger) batch of q items. In other words, for the time period t_2 we have been out of stock, and by the end of this period we have accumulated an unsatisfied demand for (q − s) items. When the batch of q items arrives, we earmark (q − s) to meet the last cycle's demand, so we have only s items to meet the next cycles demand. If we now wait for a time period $t(= t_1 + t_2)$ before making the next order, then again we will be out of stock for a period t_2. An inventory cycle of t, then, will perpetuate stockouts, they will occur at regular intervals.

Seems rather far-fetched, doesn't it? Surely, nobody would deliberately engineer a position in which stockouts would occur, or would they? Let us start by defining some symbols.

q = the optimum batch size
s = the initial inventory level
c_1 = holding cost per unit
c_2 = stockout cost per unit.

Now it can be shown that there is a relationship between s and q, and the form of this relationship is

$$s = \frac{c_2 q}{c_1 + c_2}$$

or $$s = q \times \frac{c_2}{c_1 + c_2}$$

Consider this relationship carefully. If s is less than q, then the initial inventory will be less than the optimum batch size, and stockouts would occur. Surely, s will be less than q if $\frac{c_2}{c_1 + c_2}$ is less than one. Now a glance at this quantity will show that, except in most exceptional circumstances, $\frac{c_2}{c_1 + c_2}$ *must* be less than 1. After all, the denominator must be c_1 more than the numerator! What are these exceptional circumstances?

If $c_1 = 0$, then $\frac{c_2}{c_1 + c_2} = 1$, and s = q. The initial inventory would be equal to the optimum batch size, and we would have reverted to the original model. In these circumstances, then, the firm would not run out of stock. But is it likely that c_1 (the holding cost) would be equal to zero? Surely not − holding stock must cost something as it ties up capital and has to be stored somewhere. This exceptional case can safely be dismissed. The second exceptional case is where c_2 is infinitely large. Again, $\frac{c_2}{c_1 + c_2}$ would equal one, and we would revert to the original model (you may remember that at the beginning of this chapter we assumed that stockout costs were infinitely high). But once more we must question whether this exceptional case could ever be met. Stockout costs may be high, and may be difficult to calculate, but they will be finite!

Let us summarise what we have deduced so far. It will pay a firm to run out of stock as long as $\dfrac{c_2}{c_1 + c_2}$ is less than one. Now except for circumstances that are so unlikely that we must dismiss them, then $\dfrac{c_2}{c_1 + c_2}$ will indeed be less than one. The only conclusion we can draw, then, is that it will always pay firms to run out of stock!

The problem with our conclusion is that although it is analytically sound, it just does not agree with what happens in the real world. Firms do from time-to-time run out of stock, but this is due to accident and not due to design. We shall now attempt to reconcile our conclusions with experience from the real world. Although $\dfrac{c_2}{c_1 + c_2}$ must always be less than one, it could become so near one that there would be no measurable difference between s and q. Suppose q = 1000, and $\dfrac{c^2}{c_1 + c_2} = 0.9999$, then s = 1,000 × 0.9999 = 999.9, and there is no real difference between s and q. Hence, it would not pay the firm to run out of stock. When would $\dfrac{c_2}{c_1 + c_2}$ be very close to one? Surely, when c_2 (stockout cost) are very large in comparison to c_1 (holding cost), and as this is precisely the situation we would expect to meet in the real world then the theory can be reconciled with reality.

We shall conclude this section on stockout costs by considering an example. Tiger cars are now producing the Ferret, an overland army vehicle, at the rate of ten per day. It buys diesel engines to fit into this vehicle and the supplier of diesel engines is only prepared to despatch them in batches of 100. It costs Tiger £10 per day holding costs, and £90 per day stockout costs for diesel engines: what is Tiger's best policy for inventories?

In this case, Tiger has no choice over the batch size − it is fixed at 100. It will be convenient, then, to assume that the value of q is 100. Given this value, we could calculate the value of s.

$$s = \frac{90}{90 + 10} \times 100 = 90.$$

Tiger, then, would ideally like to order an initial batch of 90, and run out of stock to the tune of 10 engines per cycle. But of course, Tiger cannot do this. However, by lengthening the first cycle, Tiger can move into an optimum inventory position. Keep glancing at diagram 4.7 as you read your way through this paragraph. An initial batch of 100 engines is ordered, and this lasts for ten days. Tiger then waits one day before receiving it's next

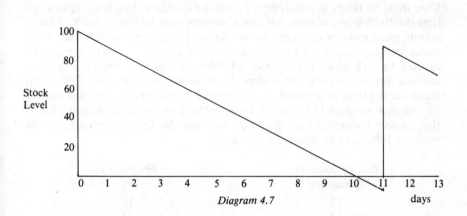

Diagram 4.7

batch of 100 engines. Now ten of this batch is used to satisfy last cycle's production, and the remaining 90 are used for the next cycle's production. If Tiger now receives batches at 10 day intervals it will have moved into an optimum situation after position A.

Random Demand

Perhaps the greatest criticism that can be levelled at the two simple inventory models considered so far is that they assume demand is fixed and known, whereas in practice demand will be subject to variations. At this particular level of study, we cannot hope to deal exhaustively with fluctuating demand, though we can give some idea of his it can be handled under simple, rigidly defined conditions.

Example

At the beginning of each week, a fishmonger places orders for lobsters. Lobsters cost him £1.50 each and he sells tham for £4.50. Lobsters left unsold at the end of the week are unfit for consumption and so destroyed. The fishmonger has noticed that the demand for lobsters varies between 13 and 18 per week. Armed with this information, we can produce a table, showing how much profit he would earn for varying stock levels.

Stock ordered.	Demand					
	13	14	15	16	17	18
13	39	39	39	39	39	39
14	37.5	42	42	42	42	42
15	36	40.5	45	45	45	45
16	34.5	39	43.5	48	48	48
17	33	37.5	42	46.6	51	51
18	31.5	36	40.5	45	49.5	54

Care must be taken in constructing a table like this – you must remember that the fishmonger cannot sell more lobsters than he has in stock. That is why in most rows of the table the maximum is reached and repeated. How many lobsters should the fishmonger order? Surely, it would be sensible to assume he will order the number of lobsters that will yield the greatest *average* profit. Now if he orders 13 lobsters, he will earn £39 profit whatever the level of demand, so his average profit must be £39. But what if he orders more than 13 lobsters? To calculate average profit we must know the relative frequencies of demand. Suppose the fishmonger supplies us with the following additional information.

No. of lobsters demanded	Frequency %
13	10
14	15
15	30
16	25
17	15
18	5
	100.

If the fishmonger placed regular orders for 18 lobsters, he would earn £31.5 on 10% of occasions, £36 on 15% of occasions, £40.5 on 30% of occasions, and so on. So his average profit would be

$$31.5 \times 0.1 + 36 \times 0.15 + 40.5 \times 0.3 + 45 \times 0.25 + 49.5 \times 0.15 + 54 \times 0.05$$
$$= £42.075$$

In a similar fashion, we can calculate the average level of profit for each level of stock ordered.

Lobsters Ordered	Average Profit
13	£39
14	£41.55
15	£43.425
16	£43.95
17	£43.35
18	£42.075

Consulting this table, we can see that it would pay the fishmonger to order 16 lobsters, as this would yield the greatest average profit.

The arithmetic involved in this method is rather tedious – let us attempt a simpler approach. Let us suppose that every unit received but not disposed of in the current period carries a cost c_1, and every unit demanded but not supplied incurrs a loss of profit c_2. Now suppose the firm decides to stock i units. It will make a profit on the ith unit if demand is at least i. Likewise, it will make a loss on that unit if the demand is less than i. If we call $P(D \geq i)$ the proportion of occasions when demand is greater or equal to i, and

$P(D<i)$ the proportion of occasions when demand is less than i, then the average profit earned by the ith unit is

$$c_2 P(D \geq i) - c_1 P(D<i)$$

Obviously, the firm will wish to hold i units only when on average the ith unit makes a profit. In other words

$$c_2 P(D \geq i) - c_1 P(D<i) > 0$$

and as $P(D \geq i) + P(D<i) = 1$

$$c_2(1 - P(D<i)) - c_1 P(D<i) > 0$$
$$-(c_2+c_1) P(D<i) + c_2 > 0$$
$$P(D < i) < \frac{c_2}{c_1+c_2}$$

We can consider $\dfrac{c_2}{c_1+c_2}$ as a critical ratio, stating the conditions necessary for stocking the ith unit. Returning to the fishmonger,

$$c_2 = 1.5, \quad c_2 = 4.5 - 1.5 = 3$$
$$\frac{c_2}{c_1+c_2} = \frac{3}{1.5 + 3} = \frac{2}{3}$$

So we wish to find the number of lobsters i such that $P(D<i) = 2/3$ (or 66⅔%)

Demand less than	% of occasions.
13	0
14	10
15	25
16	55
17	80
18	95
19	100

Consulting the table we see that on 80% of occasions, demand is less than 17 and on 55% of occasions demand is less than 16. As the critical value is 66⅔%, the fishmonger orders 16 lobsters $(55 < 66⅔\%)$. This agrees precisely with the earlier more longwinded method.

Exercises to Chapter Four

4.1   A firm requires 10 components per week, each component costing £15. It costs £1.20 to place an order, and delivery is immediate. Warehousing costs are 75p per unit per year and the cost of capital is 15% per annum. Assuming a 50 week year

   (a) Find an expression for annual inventory costs.

   (b) Find the batch size ordered to minimise inventory costs

   (c) The length of the inventory cycle.

4.2 If a 5% discount is available for orders in excess of 30 items for the component in 4.1, advise the firm.

4.3 A firm requires 4000 components per year, each component costing 40p. It costs £1 to place an order and warehouse costs are 10p per component per year. Cost of capital is 25%.

(a) Find the batch size that minimises inventory costs and the length of the inventory cycle.

(b) Assuming that the firm operates a 5 day week for 50 weeks in the year, and assuming that these is a two day time lag between orders and deliveries, how would this affect your answer to (a).

4.4 Suppose the firm in 4.3 is offered a 1% discount for orders in excess of 500 items or a 5% discount for orders in excess of 2000, which, if either, offer should the firm accept?

4.5 For the firm in 4.3, what is the minimum discount that must be offered to induce the firm to order in batches of 1000 items?

4.6 A certain item costs £20 per unit and firm requires 1350 units per year. Ordering costs are £4 and warehouse costs 60p per unit per year. Cost of capital is 12% per annum. Advise the firm as to its optional inventories policy.

4.7 For the firm in 4.6, find the minimum discount that must be offered to induce the firm to order 500 items.

4.8 The firm in 4.6 can manufacture the item itself for £16 per unit, but this will involve a cost of £3000 in preparing the machinery for a production run. Should the firm produce or buy the item?
(Hint: consider production runs as instantaneous − the £3000 is then similar to an ordering cost).

4.9 A newsagent finds the weekly demand for a magazine varies between 10 and 15 units. He pays the publisher 15p per copy and sells them for 25p per copy. Copies unsold at the end of the week have no value. Prepare a table showing how profit would vary with varying stock levels.

4.10 Suppose that the demand for the magazine in question 4.9 was as follows:

Weekly Demand	10	11	12	13	14	15
Frequency (%)	6%	29%	41%	12%	7%	5%

Find the average profit associated with each possible stock level, and hence deduce the number of magazines the newsagent should order each week.

4.11 Use the critical ratio
$$\frac{c_2}{c_1 + c_2}$$
to verify your answer to question 4.10.

4.12 A wholesaler contracts to supply a manufacturer with 25 components per day. The cost of holding a component is £16 per month, and there is a penalty cost of £10 per component per day for failing to deliver. The wholesaler intends to stock up on components at the beginning of each month. Assuming a 30 day month, find the initial inventory level to minimise inventory costs.

Chapter Five

Matrices

In this chapter, we shall be examining a type of arithmetic that, in all probability, you will not have met before. Some of the concepts used will seem rather strange but their power and flexibility in application warrants their study. Moreover, computers rely heavily on matrices when performing complex caclulations or storing masses of data, so you will never fully appreciate computing without a sound understanding of matrix arithmetic.

What is a Matrix?

Let us suppose that a small firm is considering paying its workers a bonus on all output over a certain weekly level, and thinks that a bonus rate of 10p per unit would be appropriate. The firm wishes to know the weekly cost of this scheme, so the wages manager is instructed to undertake an investigation. He examines the production records of the workers concerned (suppose there are ten of them) and calculates the number of bonus units produced that week:

20	10	15	18	8	3	0	25	22	9

He has obtained what is called a *Set* of data, and it would be easy to calculate the bonus paid i.e.

$$0.1 (20 + 10 + 15 + ...) = £130$$

Of course, we would have obtained the same result if the number of bonus units had been collected in a different order, i.e.

$$0.1 (10 + 18 + 8 + 3 + 25 + 20 + 9 + 22 + 15 + 0) = £130$$

However, if the wages manager wishes to calculate the bonus each worker would receive, then the order of the bonus units would matter. To show that this is so, we would place brackets round the set.

(20	10	15	18	8	3	0	25	22	9)

The set has now become a *Matrix*. A matrix, then is a set of values where the position of the values is important. The implication of the ordering above is that the first worker receives 20 bonus units, the second worker receives 10 bonus units and so on. So if you see a set of numbers enclosed by brackets, always remember that the position of the numbers is important.

Now in this example, the matrix consists of a single row of numbers. It is a special kind of matrix called a *Row Vector*. Quite often, you will see the numbers written in a column like this:

$$\begin{pmatrix} 1 \\ 2 \\ 5 \end{pmatrix}$$

This type of matrix is called a *Column Vector*. If you think carefully, you will realise that if you fill in a football coupon, then you are constructing a column vector. Not only must the results be correctly forecast, but they must be forecast in the correct order — it is no use correctly predicting the total number of home wins, away wins and draws. For example, if you need to forecast the results of six matches, and use the symbols '0' for a draw, '1' for a home win and '2' for an away win then

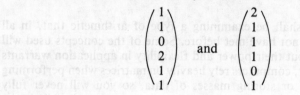

are both the same *set* of results, but are very different predictions. The *actual* results may form the same set i.e.

$$\begin{pmatrix} 2 \\ 0 \\ 1 \\ 1 \\ 1 \\ 1 \end{pmatrix}$$

but neither prediction would win. The sets are the same, but the vectors are different.

Now it would be perfectly possible to have a matrix with more than one row and more than one column. A single row or single column implies that the elements in the set are singly classified — in the case of the column vector above the elements of the matrix were classified according to the order of the matches. However, if a matrix has more than one row and more than one column, then a double classification is implied. For example, a firm may classify its labour force in two ways: by sex or by grade of work.

	Male	Female
Operative	400	100
Clerical	10	50
Executive	5	2

and the matrix

$$\begin{pmatrix} 400 & 100 \\ 10 & 50 \\ 5 & 2 \end{pmatrix}$$

describes the numbers of workers in each category. This matrix has three rows and two columns, and we would call it a (3×2) matrix. Moreover, if we use X to stand for any element in a matrix, then we can identify any particular element in the matrix. The value 5, for example is the element in the third row and the first column, so

$$x_{3,1} = 5$$

Likewise
$$x_{2,2} = 50$$
$$x_{2,1} = 10$$

Let us summarise what we have learnt so far. A matrix is a set where the position as well as the value of each element in the set is significant. If the matrix has a single row or a single column then it is called a vector. We state the dimensions of a matrix as (number of rows × number of columns) – *NEVER* the other way round. In fact this is the golden rule of matrices – everything is considered in a row by column ordering.

Matrix Addition and Subtraction

Suppose a plumbers merchant classifies the taps he holds in stock into bath taps, sink taps and garden taps. He also classifies his taps into imperial and metric sizes. The taps he currently holds in stock are:

	Metric	Imperial
Bath	105	32
Sink	220	45
Garden	96	32

Now the plumbers merchant thinks his stocks are dangerously low, and places an order with his supplier for the following quantities.

	Metric	Imperial
Bath	50	30
Sink	100	50
Garden	40	10

His new level of stock is:

	Metric	Imperial
Bath	155	62
Sink	320	95
Garden	136	42

Let us now suppose that the plumbers merchant receives an order from a plumber as follows:

	Metric	Imperial
Bath	10	5
Sink	20	5
Garden	10	2

The plumbers merchants level of stock is now:

	Metric	Imperial
Bath	145	57
Sink	300	90
Garden	126	40

We could have calculated the change in stock levels using matrices. When the builders merchant orders stock, stock levels increase so we apply matrix addition;

$$\begin{pmatrix} 105 & 32 \\ 220 & 45 \\ 96 & 32 \end{pmatrix} + \begin{pmatrix} 50 & 30 \\ 100 & 50 \\ 40 & 10 \end{pmatrix} = \begin{pmatrix} 155 & 62 \\ 320 & 95 \\ 136 & 42 \end{pmatrix}$$

When the plumber's merchant sells stock, stock levels decrease so we apply matrix subtraction.

$$\begin{pmatrix} 155 & 62 \\ 320 & 95 \\ 136 & 42 \end{pmatrix} - \begin{pmatrix} 10 & 5 \\ 20 & 5 \\ 10 & 2 \end{pmatrix} = \begin{pmatrix} 145 & 57 \\ 300 & 90 \\ 126 & 40 \end{pmatrix}$$

To add, (or subtract) matrices, add (or subtract) the corresponding elements. Addition and subtraction of matrices, then is a very simple process.

However, unlike ordinary arithmetic, not all addition or subtraction of matrices is possible. *It is only possible to add or subtract matrices of the same dimension.* For example, the following operation in matrices would not be possible.

$$\begin{pmatrix} 1 & 2 \\ 2 & 3 \\ 1 & 4 \end{pmatrix} + \begin{pmatrix} 1 & 3 \\ 2 & 2 \end{pmatrix}$$

although

$$\begin{pmatrix} 1 & 2 \\ 2 & 3 \\ 1 & 4 \end{pmatrix} + \begin{pmatrix} 1 & 3 \\ 2 & 2 \\ 0 & 0 \end{pmatrix}$$

is possible.

Matrix Multiplication

Now although addition or subtraction is a straightforward operation, matrix multiplication is not. In fact it is quite difficult to appreciate the logic behind matrix multiplication, and you would be well advised to master the technique first and worry about the logic later. There are two rules of matrix multiplication that you should always follow.

Rule 1.
Take in turn the rows of the first matrix with the columns of the second.
Rule 2.
Find the sum of the products of the corresponding elements.

Let us apply this rule to vectors.

$$A = (2 \quad 1), B = \begin{pmatrix} 2 \\ 3 \end{pmatrix}, \text{ find } AB$$

Now the first matrix has just one row, and the second matrix has just one column, so applying rule 2

$$(2 \times 2) + (1 \times 3) = 7,$$

$$\text{So } (2 \quad 1) \begin{pmatrix} 2 \\ 3 \end{pmatrix} = (7)$$

The result of this multiplication, then, is a single element vector. Notice that we have arrowed the corresponding elements i.e. those elements that must be multiplied together.

Let us see what would happen when we multiply a vector and matrix:

$$A = (2 \quad 1), B = \begin{pmatrix} 2 & 1 \\ 3 & 1 \end{pmatrix} \text{ , find AB}$$

$$AB = (2 \quad 1) \begin{pmatrix} 2 & 1 \\ 3 & 1 \end{pmatrix}$$

In this case, the second matrix has two columns, so we must take the columns of the second matrix in turn —

taking the first column

$$(2 \quad 1) \begin{pmatrix} 2 & 1 \\ 3 & 1 \end{pmatrix}$$

$$(2 \times 2) + (1 \times 3) = 7$$

taking the second column

$$(2 \quad 1) \begin{pmatrix} 2 & 1 \\ 3 & 1 \end{pmatrix}$$

$$(2 \times 1) + (1 \times 1) = 3$$

So

$$(2 \quad 1) \begin{pmatrix} 2 & 1 \\ 3 & 1 \end{pmatrix} = (7 \quad 3)$$

Now you may wonder why the product matrix is a row vector and not a column vector. This results from our final rule of matrix multiplication.

Rule 3

The position of the elements in the product matrix is determined by rule 1: the row position is determined by which row was used in the first matrix and the column position by which column is used in the second matrix.

The product $(3 \times 1) + (1 \times 1) = 3$ used the first (and only) row of the first matrix and the second column of the second matrix, so it takes the position 'first row second column' in the product matrix.

Armed with these three rules, we can now multiply a matrix by a matrix.

$$A = \begin{pmatrix} 2 & 1 \\ 4 & 1 \end{pmatrix} \qquad B = \begin{pmatrix} 2 & 1 \\ 3 & 1 \end{pmatrix} \text{ , find AB}$$

Taking first row with first column.

$$\begin{pmatrix} 2 & 1 \\ 4 & 1 \end{pmatrix}\begin{pmatrix} 2 & 1 \\ 3 & 1 \end{pmatrix}$$

$$(2 \times 1) + (1 \times 3) = 7$$

$$\begin{pmatrix} 2 & 1 \\ 4 & 1 \end{pmatrix}\begin{pmatrix} 2 & 1 \\ 3 & 1 \end{pmatrix} = \begin{pmatrix} 7 \end{pmatrix}$$

Taking first row with second column.

$$\begin{pmatrix} 2 & 1 \\ 4 & 1 \end{pmatrix} \begin{pmatrix} 2 & 1 \\ 3 & 1 \end{pmatrix}$$

$$(2 \times 1) + (1 \times 1) = 3$$

$$\begin{pmatrix} 2 & 1 \\ 4 & 1 \end{pmatrix} \begin{pmatrix} 2 & 1 \\ 3 & 1 \end{pmatrix} = \begin{pmatrix} 7 & 3 \end{pmatrix}$$

Taking second row with first column.

$$\begin{pmatrix} 2 & 1 \\ 4 & 1 \end{pmatrix} \begin{pmatrix} 2 & 1 \\ 3 & 1 \end{pmatrix}$$

$$(4 \times 2) + (1 \times 3) = 11$$

$$\begin{pmatrix} 2 & 1 \\ 4 & 1 \end{pmatrix} \begin{pmatrix} 2 & 1 \\ 3 & 1 \end{pmatrix} = \begin{pmatrix} 7 & 3 \\ 11 \end{pmatrix}$$

Finally, taking second row with second column

$$\begin{pmatrix} 2 & 1 \\ 4 & 1 \end{pmatrix} \begin{pmatrix} 2 & 1 \\ 3 & 1 \end{pmatrix}$$

$$(4 \times 1) + (1 \times 1) = 5$$

$$\begin{pmatrix} 2 & 1 \\ 4 & 1 \end{pmatrix} \begin{pmatrix} 2 & 1 \\ 3 & 1 \end{pmatrix} = \begin{pmatrix} 7 & 3 \\ 11 & 5 \end{pmatrix}$$

We can extend the dimensions of the matrices and still use the same multiplication rules, but beware! Not all matrix multiplications are possible. For example

$$\begin{pmatrix} 1 & 2 & 1 & 1 \\ 3 & 1 & 4 & 2 \\ 5 & 1 & 6 & 3 \end{pmatrix} \begin{pmatrix} 1 & 0 \\ 2 & 1 \\ 1 & 0 \\ 0 & 1 \end{pmatrix}$$

would give a product matrix

$$\begin{pmatrix} 6 & 3 \\ 9 & 3 \\ 13 & 4 \end{pmatrix}$$

but

$$\begin{pmatrix} 1 & 3 & 5 \\ 2 & 1 & 1 \\ 1 & 4 & 6 \\ 1 & 2 & 3 \end{pmatrix} \begin{pmatrix} 1 & 0 \\ 2 & 1 \\ 1 & 0 \\ 0 & 1 \end{pmatrix}$$

has no product matrix. Try to multiply the matrices and you will see that the system of rules breaks down. Taking 'first row with first column' we have

$$(1 \times 1) + (3 \times 2) + (5 \times 1) + \ldots.$$

but there are insufficient elements in the row of the first matrix to complete the procedure: the matrices are not compatible. There is a simple rule for deciding whether matrix multiplication is possible – can you deduce it? There must be the same number of columns in the first matrix as there are rows in the second.

Properties of Matrix Multiplication

In the last section, we used the two matrices

$$A = \begin{pmatrix} 2 & 1 \\ 4 & 1 \end{pmatrix} \quad \text{and B} = \begin{pmatrix} 2 & 1 \\ 3 & 1 \end{pmatrix}$$

and we found that

$$AB = \begin{pmatrix} 2 & 1 \\ 4 & 1 \end{pmatrix} \begin{pmatrix} 2 & 1 \\ 3 & 1 \end{pmatrix} = \begin{pmatrix} 7 & 3 \\ 11 & 5 \end{pmatrix}$$

Suppose that we now reverse the order of the matrices

$$BA = \begin{pmatrix} 2 & 1 \\ 3 & 1 \end{pmatrix} \begin{pmatrix} 2 & 1 \\ 4 & 1 \end{pmatrix} = \begin{pmatrix} 8 & 3 \\ 10 & 4 \end{pmatrix}$$

We can see that matrix multiplication differs fundamentally from algebraic multiplication. In algebra (or ordinary arithmetic) the product AB is identical to the product BA (after all $5 \times 3 = 3 \times 5$) but with matrices the product AB is quite different from the product BA. When multiplying matrices, it is vital that they are put in the right order, and to avoid confusion, mathematicians use the expression 'pre-multiply' and 'post-multiply' – rather than just say multiply. For example, the product matrix AB can be expressed as either 'pre-multiply B by A' or 'post-multiply A by B'. If we have an operation (for example, multiplication) to perform on a number of variables, and it does not matter in which order the variables are placed, then the operation is called *commutative*. Thus, matrix multiplication is non-commutative.

Are there any exceptions to this rule?

$$A = \begin{pmatrix} 2 & 1 \\ 3 & 1 \end{pmatrix} \quad I = \begin{pmatrix} 1 & 0 \\ 0 & 1 \end{pmatrix}$$

$$IA = \begin{pmatrix} 1 & 0 \\ 0 & 1 \end{pmatrix} \begin{pmatrix} 2 & 1 \\ 3 & 1 \end{pmatrix} = \begin{pmatrix} 2 & 1 \\ 3 & 1 \end{pmatrix}$$

$$AI = \begin{pmatrix} 2 & 1 \\ 3 & 1 \end{pmatrix} \begin{pmatrix} 1 & 0 \\ 0 & 1 \end{pmatrix} = \begin{pmatrix} 2 & 1 \\ 3 & 1 \end{pmatrix}$$

Here, then, we have an operation that is commutative. The matrix I is a very special matrix: if the matrix A is either pre-multiplied or post multiplied by I, then A remains unchanged. The matrix I, then, acts in an identical fashion to the number one in ordinary arithmetic: for this reason I is called the *unit matrix* or *identity matrix*. Here, we have shown the identity as a 2 × 2 matrix, but it can have different dimensions to this. For example

$$I = (1), \quad I = \begin{pmatrix} 1 & 0 \\ 0 & 1 \end{pmatrix}, \quad I = \begin{pmatrix} 1 & 0 & 0 \\ 0 & 1 & 0 \\ 0 & 0 & 1 \end{pmatrix}, \quad I = \begin{pmatrix} 1 & 0 & 0 & 0 \\ 0 & 1 & 0 & 0 \\ 0 & 0 & 1 & 0 \\ 0 & 0 & 0 & 1 \end{pmatrix}$$

Notice the common pattern in these examples. Notice also that the identity matrix must be square (i.e. have the same number of rows as it has columns).

Now let us consider the product matrix AA^{-1} where

$$A = \begin{pmatrix} 2 & 1 \\ 3 & 2 \end{pmatrix} \quad \text{and } A^{-1} = \begin{pmatrix} 2 & -1 \\ -3 & 2 \end{pmatrix}$$

$$AA^{-1} = \begin{pmatrix} 2 & 1 \\ 3 & 2 \end{pmatrix} \begin{pmatrix} 2 & -1 \\ -3 & 2 \end{pmatrix} = \begin{pmatrix} 1 & 0 \\ 0 & 1 \end{pmatrix}$$

$$A^{-1}A = \begin{pmatrix} 2 & -1 \\ -3 & 2 \end{pmatrix} \begin{pmatrix} 2 & 1 \\ 3 & 2 \end{pmatrix} = \begin{pmatrix} 1 & 0 \\ 0 & 1 \end{pmatrix}$$

Again, we have a commutative operation: in both cases the product matrix is the identity matrix I. If one of the matrices is called A, then the other, A^{-1}, is called the *inverse* of A. Why is A^{-1} called the inverse? Well, if you remember that the identity matrix is the matrix equivalent of the number one, then a parallel in ordinary arithmetic is

$$5 \times \frac{1}{5} = 1 \qquad \text{or } \frac{2}{9} \times \frac{9}{2} = 1$$

In both cases, the second number is the first number 'inverted'. Also, if you remember that $5^{-1} = 1/5$, you will realise why the inverse of A is A^{-1}.

Now let us consider the three matrices

$$A = \begin{pmatrix} 2 & 1 \\ 3 & 2 \end{pmatrix} \quad B = \begin{pmatrix} 1 & 2 \\ 3 & 1 \end{pmatrix} \quad C = \begin{pmatrix} 2 & 3 \\ 3 & 1 \end{pmatrix}$$

If we wish to find the matrix (AB)C, then we must combine the normal rule of brackets (which specifices the order for an operation) with the non-commutative rule of matrices. First we must find AB, then post-multiply by C

$$AB = \begin{pmatrix} 2 & 1 \\ 3 & 2 \end{pmatrix} \begin{pmatrix} 1 & 2 \\ 3 & 1 \end{pmatrix} = \begin{pmatrix} 5 & 5 \\ 9 & 8 \end{pmatrix}$$

$$(AB)C = \begin{pmatrix} 5 & 5 \\ 9 & 8 \end{pmatrix} \begin{pmatrix} 2 & 3 \\ 3 & 1 \end{pmatrix} = \begin{pmatrix} 25 & 20 \\ 42 & 35 \end{pmatrix}$$

Now let us find A(BC) This time, we must find BC first, then pre-multiply by A

$$BC = \begin{pmatrix} 1 & 2 \\ 3 & 1 \end{pmatrix} \begin{pmatrix} 2 & 3 \\ 3 & 1 \end{pmatrix} = \begin{pmatrix} 8 & 5 \\ 9 & 10 \end{pmatrix}$$

$$A(BC) = \begin{pmatrix} 2 & 1 \\ 3 & 2 \end{pmatrix} \begin{pmatrix} 8 & 5 \\ 9 & 10 \end{pmatrix} = \begin{pmatrix} 25 & 20 \\ 42 & 35 \end{pmatrix}$$

We can conclude that A(BC) = (AB)C or the position of the brackets does not matter in matrix multiplication. Using the jargon, we say that matrix multiplication is *associative*.

Let us now summarise what we have learnt in this section. Generally, matrix multiplication is non-commutative i.e.

$$AB \neq BA$$
$$\text{except that} \quad AI = IA = A$$
$$\text{and} \quad AA^{-1} = A^{-1}A = I$$

Also, matrix multiplication is associative, i.e.

$$A(BC) = (AB)C$$

Row Transformations: Finding the Inverse

If we set up a matrix multiplication sum something like this

$$\begin{pmatrix} 1 & 0 \\ 0 & 1 \end{pmatrix} \begin{pmatrix} 2 & 1 \\ 3 & 2 \end{pmatrix} = \begin{pmatrix} 2 & 1 \\ 3 & 2 \end{pmatrix}$$

then we can alter the rows of two of these matrices and the product matrix will still be correct. We will be performing *row transformations* and there are two rules which govern what we can do.

Rule 1

We can multiply (or divide) any row in the first matrix by a constant as long as we do likewise to the corresponding row in the third matrix.

For example, dividing the top row by 2 gives

$$\begin{pmatrix} \frac{1}{2} & 0 \\ 0 & 1 \end{pmatrix} \begin{pmatrix} 2 & 1 \\ 3 & 2 \end{pmatrix} = \begin{pmatrix} 1 & \frac{1}{2} \\ 3 & 2 \end{pmatrix}$$

You should check that the product matrix is correct

Rule 2

We can add (or subtract) any multiple of one row to any other row in the first matrix as long as we do likewise to the product matrix.

For example, subtracting three times the top row from the bottom row gives.

$$\begin{pmatrix} \frac{1}{2} & 0 \\ -\frac{3}{2} & 1 \end{pmatrix} \begin{pmatrix} 2 & 1 \\ 3 & 2 \end{pmatrix} = \begin{pmatrix} 1 & \frac{1}{2} \\ 0 & \frac{1}{2} \end{pmatrix}$$

Multiplying the bottom row by 2 gives

$$\begin{pmatrix} \frac{1}{2} & 0 \\ -3 & 2 \end{pmatrix} \begin{pmatrix} 2 & 1 \\ 3 & 2 \end{pmatrix} = \begin{pmatrix} 1 & \frac{1}{2} \\ 0 & 1 \end{pmatrix}$$

and subtracting half the bottom row from the top row gives

$$\begin{pmatrix} 2 & -1 \\ -3 & 2 \end{pmatrix} \begin{pmatrix} 2 & 1 \\ 3 & 2 \end{pmatrix} = \begin{pmatrix} 1 & 0 \\ 0 & 1 \end{pmatrix}$$

At each of these stages, you should check that the product matrix is correct.

So we see that the rules for row transformations are indeed correct. So what? Well, if you look carefully at what we have done, you will realise that we have not been performing row transformations haphazardly. Let us define.

$$A = \begin{pmatrix} 2 & 1 \\ 3 & 2 \end{pmatrix}$$

We started with

$$\begin{pmatrix} 1 & 0 \\ 0 & 1 \end{pmatrix} \begin{pmatrix} 2 & 1 \\ 3 & 2 \end{pmatrix} = \begin{pmatrix} 2 & 1 \\ 3 & 2 \end{pmatrix}$$

i.e. $IA = A$

Whereas we ended with

$$\begin{pmatrix} 2 & -1 \\ -3 & 2 \end{pmatrix} \begin{pmatrix} 2 & 1 \\ 3 & 2 \end{pmatrix} = \begin{pmatrix} 1 & 0 \\ 0 & 1 \end{pmatrix}$$

which must be

$$A^{-1}A = I$$

In other words, we have performed row transformations in such a manner as to find the inverse of A! By changing the A on the right hand side of the equals sign into I, we have sympathetically changed the I on the left hand side into the inverse of A.

Let us examine more closely the use of row transformations to find an inverse. You should notice that at no time did the second matrix change, and it seems a waste of effort to restate it after each transformation. To avoid this repetition we can use a *partitioned matrix*. Suppose we wished to find the inverse of $\begin{pmatrix} 2 & 5 \\ 3 & 5 \end{pmatrix}$ Instead of the initial format

$$\begin{pmatrix} 1 & 0 \\ 0 & 1 \end{pmatrix} \begin{pmatrix} 2 & 5 \\ 3 & 5 \end{pmatrix} = \begin{pmatrix} 2 & 5 \\ 3 & 5 \end{pmatrix}$$

we can use the partitioned matrix

$$\left(\begin{array}{cc|cc} 1 & 0 & 2 & 5 \\ 0 & 1 & 3 & 5 \end{array} \right)$$

Can you see that if we transform the right hand side of the partition into the identity matrix $\begin{pmatrix} 1 & 0 \\ 0 & 1 \end{pmatrix}$, then we must transform the left hand side into the required inverse?

$$\left(\begin{array}{cc|cc} 1 & 0 & ② & 5 \\ 0 & 1 & 3 & 5 \end{array} \right)$$

Firstly, we will change the two (ringed) into 1. To do this, divide the top row by 2.

$$\left(\begin{array}{cc|cc} ½ & 0 & 1 & ⁵⁄₂ \\ 0 & 1 & ③ & 5 \end{array} \right)$$

Next, we change the three into zero by subtracting three times the top row from the bottom row

$$\left(\begin{array}{cc|cc} ½ & 0 & 1 & ⑤⁄₂ \\ -³⁄₂ & 1 & 0 & -⁵⁄₂ \end{array} \right)$$

Adding the bottom row to the top row changes ⁵⁄₂ to zero.

$$\left(\begin{array}{cc|cc} -1 & 1 & 1 & 0 \\ -³⁄₂ & 1 & 0 & \overline{-⁵⁄₂} \end{array} \right)$$

Finally, multiplying the bottom row by $-\frac{2}{4}$ changes the $-\frac{5}{2}$ into one

$$\begin{pmatrix} -1 & 1 & | & 1 & 0 \\ \frac{3}{5} & -\frac{2}{5} & | & 0 & 1 \end{pmatrix}$$

So the inverse of $\begin{pmatrix} 2 & 5 \\ 3 & 5 \end{pmatrix}$ is $\begin{pmatrix} -1 & 1 \\ \frac{3}{5} & -\frac{2}{5} \end{pmatrix}$ and we can check that this is correct by multiplying them together. The inverse is correct if the product matrix is the identity.

$$\begin{pmatrix} 2 & 5 \\ 3 & 5 \end{pmatrix} \begin{pmatrix} -1 & 1 \\ \frac{3}{5} & -\frac{2}{5} \end{pmatrix} = \begin{pmatrix} 1 & 0 \\ 0 & 1 \end{pmatrix}$$

If we wish to find the inverse of a 3×3 matrix, then we would use exactly the same method, but this time use a 3×3 identity. For example

$$\begin{pmatrix} 1 & 1 & 1 & | & 1 & 0 & 0 \\ 2 & 1 & 2 & | & 0 & 1 & 0 \\ 1 & 2 & 2 & | & 0 & 0 & 1 \end{pmatrix}$$

Firstly, we will change the first column into $\begin{pmatrix} 1 \\ 0 \\ 0 \end{pmatrix}$ To do this we will

Subtract twice the top row from the middle row and
Subtract the top row from the bottom row.

$$\begin{pmatrix} 1 & 1 & 1 & | & 1 & 0 & 0 \\ 0 & -1 & 0 & | & -2 & 1 & 0 \\ 0 & 1 & 1 & | & -1 & 0 & 1 \end{pmatrix}$$

Now we shall change the second column into $\begin{pmatrix} 0 \\ 1 \\ 0 \end{pmatrix}$ To do this we will

Add the middle row to the top row
Add the middle row to the bottom row and
multiply the middle row by -1

$$\begin{pmatrix} 1 & 0 & 1 & | & -1 & 1 & 0 \\ 0 & 1 & 0 & | & 2 & -1 & 0 \\ 0 & 0 & 1 & | & -3 & 1 & 1 \end{pmatrix}$$

Finally, the third column must be changed to $\begin{pmatrix} 0 \\ 0 \\ 1 \end{pmatrix}$ To do this we must

Subtract the bottom row from the top row

$$\begin{pmatrix} 1 & 0 & 0 & | & 2 & 0 & -1 \\ 0 & 1 & 0 & | & 2 & -1 & 0 \\ 0 & 0 & 1 & | & -3 & 1 & 1 \end{pmatrix}$$

Before completing this section, you should note two important points. Firstly, only square matrices can have inverses (remember the identity must be square). Secondly, even if a matrix is square then it still may not have an inverse: you can show that this is true by trying to find the inverse of

$$\begin{pmatrix} 2 & 1 \\ 4 & 2 \end{pmatrix}$$

Determinants

Finding an inverse can be a cumbersome business. Fortunately there is another method, but at this stage it is only really practical to apply it to a 2 × 2 matrix. Let us examine the matrix

$$A = \begin{pmatrix} a & b \\ c & d \end{pmatrix}$$

The quantity ad − bc is called the *determinant* |d| of the matrix and

$$A^{-1} = \frac{1}{|d|} \begin{pmatrix} d & -b \\ -c & a \end{pmatrix}$$

Notice carefully how the matrix A has been transposed in this expression. We shall now use this method to recalculate the inverse of $A = \begin{pmatrix} 2 & 5 \\ 3 & 5 \end{pmatrix}$

$$|d| = (2 \times 5) - (3 \times 5) = -5$$

$$A^{-1} = \frac{1}{-5} \begin{pmatrix} 5 & -5 \\ -3 & 2 \end{pmatrix}$$

$$= \begin{pmatrix} -1 & 1 \\ 3/5 & -2/5 \end{pmatrix}$$

which gives exactly the same result as we obtained earlier.

At the end of the previous section, we suggested that the matrix $\begin{pmatrix} 2 & 1 \\ 4 & 2 \end{pmatrix}$

did not have an inverse. Notice also that the determinant of this matrix is zero. The two facts are indeed connected − if a matrix is to have an inverse then it cannot have a zero determinant.

Matrix Algebra

Let us now consider a simple algebraic relationship using ordinary numbers.

It is easy to see that

$$ab = c$$

$$a = \frac{c}{b}$$

and that

$$b = \frac{c}{a}$$

If the relationship refers to matrices, however, then re-arranging the relationship is not so straightforward. One reason for this is that the re-arrangement above involves division, and so far we have said nothing about division of matrices. In fact, it is not possible to perform division with matrices, so we are going to have to find another method of re-arranging relationships involving matrices.

Suppose A, B and C are matrices such that

$$AB = C$$

and we wish to change this relationship so that just B is on the left hand side (this is called 'making B the subject of the relationship'). Suppose we multiply both sides by A^{-1}, the inverse of A

$$A^{-1}(AB) = A^{-1}C$$

Now as matrix multiplication is associative,

$$(A^{-1}A) B = A^{-1}C$$

and as $A^{-1}A = I$, the identity,

$$IB = A^{-1}C$$

We also know that IB = B, so

$$B = A^{-1}C$$

So if we know A and C then we can find the matrix B *provided A has an inverse*.

In a similar fashion, we could make A the subject of the relationship. Multiplying both sides by B^{-1}, the inverse of B

$$(AB)B^{-1} = CB^{-1}$$

Notice carefully the position of the inverse: remember that matrix multiplication is non-commutative

$$A(BB^{-1}) = CB^{-1}$$
$$AI = CB^{-1}$$
$$A = CB^{-1}$$

Again, given C and B, we can find A provided that B has an inverse.

Summarising, if AB = C

then $B = A^{-1}C$

and $A = CB^{-1}$

Solutions of Simulataneous Equations

So far, we have spent a lot of time considering matrices without indicating their use. A commonly used application of matrices is in the solution of simultaneous equations. Suppose we wished to solve the equations

$$2x + 5y = 200$$
$$3x + 5y = 225$$

We can write these equations in matrix form like this:

$$\begin{pmatrix} 2 & 5 \\ 3 & 5 \end{pmatrix} \begin{pmatrix} x \\ y \end{pmatrix} = \begin{pmatrix} 200 \\ 225 \end{pmatrix}$$

For convenience sake, let

$$A = \begin{pmatrix} 2 & 5 \\ 3 & 5 \end{pmatrix}, B = \begin{pmatrix} x \\ y \end{pmatrix}, C = \begin{pmatrix} 200 \\ 225 \end{pmatrix}$$

So the equations take the form

$$AB = C$$

And if we can find the vector B then we will have the value of x and the value of y. In the last section, we saw that if

$$AB = C$$
$$\text{then } B = A^{-1}C$$

Also, we found earlier that if

$$A = \begin{pmatrix} 2 & 5 \\ 3 & 5 \end{pmatrix} \text{ then } A^{-1} = \begin{pmatrix} -1 & 1 \\ 3/5 & -2/5 \end{pmatrix}, \text{ so}$$

$$B = \begin{pmatrix} -1 & 1 \\ 3/5 & -2/5 \end{pmatrix} \begin{pmatrix} 200 \\ 225 \end{pmatrix} = \begin{pmatrix} 25 \\ 30 \end{pmatrix}$$

$$\begin{pmatrix} x \\ y \end{pmatrix} = \begin{pmatrix} 25 \\ 30 \end{pmatrix}$$

or x = 25 and y = 30

Taking another example, let us solve

$$2x + y = 7$$
$$3x + 2y = 12$$

$$A = \begin{pmatrix} 2 & 1 \\ 3 & 2 \end{pmatrix}, C = \begin{pmatrix} 7 \\ 12 \end{pmatrix}$$

$$|d| = (2 \times 2) - (3 \times 1) = 1$$

$$A^{-1} = \frac{1}{1}\begin{pmatrix} 2 & -1 \\ -3 & 2 \end{pmatrix} = \begin{pmatrix} 2 & -1 \\ -3 & 2 \end{pmatrix}$$

$$\begin{pmatrix} x \\ y \end{pmatrix} = \begin{pmatrix} 2 & -1 \\ -3 & 2 \end{pmatrix} \begin{pmatrix} 7 \\ 12 \end{pmatrix}$$

$$\begin{pmatrix} x \\ y \end{pmatrix} = \begin{pmatrix} 2 \\ 3 \end{pmatrix}$$

The great advantage of using this method is that frequently in the business world we meet situations where the left hand side of equations remains constant, but the right hand side varies. For example, suppose an engineering firm produces those invaluable products sproggets and widgets. Each sprogget requires 2 hours casting and 1 hour turning, while each widget requires 1 hour casting and 3 hours turning. Suppose we assume that S sproggets and W widgets are produced: this will require

$$2S + W \text{ hours of casting and}$$
$$S + 3W \text{ hours of turning.}$$

Each week the manager of the department producing sproggets and widgets is informed how much turning and casting time has been allocated to him. Suppose that in a particular week he has been allocated 200 hours of casting and 250 hours of turning — how many sproggets and how many widgets should he produce to use the entire allocation?

$$2s + w = 200$$
$$s + 3w = 250$$

$$\begin{pmatrix} 2 & 1 \\ 1 & 3 \end{pmatrix} \begin{pmatrix} s \\ w \end{pmatrix} = \begin{pmatrix} 200 \\ 250 \end{pmatrix}$$

$$|d| = (2 \times 3) - (1 \times 1) = 5$$

$$A^{-1} = \frac{1}{5} \begin{pmatrix} 3 & -1 \\ -1 & 2 \end{pmatrix} = \begin{pmatrix} {}^3\!/\!_5 & -{}^1\!/\!_5 \\ -{}^1\!/\!_5 & {}^2\!/\!_5 \end{pmatrix}$$

$$\begin{pmatrix} s \\ w \end{pmatrix} = \begin{pmatrix} {}^3\!/\!_5 & -{}^1\!/\!_5 \\ -{}^1\!/\!_5 & {}^2\!/\!_5 \end{pmatrix} \begin{pmatrix} 200 \\ 250 \end{pmatrix} = \begin{pmatrix} 70 \\ 60 \end{pmatrix}$$

So 70 sprockets and 60 widgets would be produced.

Now suppose that the manager is informed how much time has been allocated to him over the next 5 weeks.

Week	1	2	3	4	5
Casting	200	250	225	210	200
Turning	250	200	225	260	200

If we do not use matrices, then we would have to solve five sets of simultaneous equations. However, as we already have the inverse, we can put the availabilities (which would form the right hand side of the equations), into a matrix and solve *all* the equations by matrix multiplication.

$$\begin{pmatrix} {}^3\!/\!_5 & -{}^1\!/\!_5 \\ -{}^1\!/\!_5 & {}^2\!/\!_5 \end{pmatrix} \begin{pmatrix} 200 & 250 & 225 & 210 & 200 \\ 250 & 200 & 225 & 260 & 200 \end{pmatrix}$$

$$= \begin{pmatrix} 70 & 110 & 90 & 74 & 80 \\ 60 & 30 & 45 & 62 & 40 \end{pmatrix}$$

For the next 5 weeks then, his production schedule would be

Week	1	2	3	4	5
Sproggets	70	110	90	74	80
Widgets	60	30	45	62	40

Exercises to Chapter 5

5.1 $A = \begin{pmatrix} 2 & -1 & 0 \\ 3 & 1 & 1 \\ 0 & 4 & -2 \end{pmatrix}$ $B = \begin{pmatrix} 1 & 6 & 2 \\ 4 & 0 & -1 \\ -2 & 3 & 1 \end{pmatrix}$

Find
- a) $A + B$
- b) $B + A$
- c) $A - B$
- d) $B - A$
- e) AB
- f) BA

74

5.2 If the elements of the matrix A in question 1 are of the form a_{ij}, and the elements of the B matrix are of the form b_{ij}, which elements are denoted by

a) a_{21} c) b_{13}

b) b_{32} d) a_{22}

5.3 $P = \begin{pmatrix} 4 & 1 \\ 0 & 2 \\ -1 & 3 \end{pmatrix}$ $Q = \begin{pmatrix} 2 & 1 \\ 3 & 5 \end{pmatrix}$ $R = \begin{pmatrix} 6 \\ 3 \end{pmatrix}$

Determine which of the following products are possible and compute their solutions.

a) PQ f) RQ

b) PR g) PQR

c) QP h) PRQ

d) QR i) RPQ

e) RP j) RQP

5.4 Find the inverse of the following matrices.

$A = \begin{pmatrix} 3 & 4 \\ 5 & 1 \end{pmatrix}$ $B = \begin{pmatrix} 4 & 2 \\ 8 & 4 \end{pmatrix}$ $C = \begin{pmatrix} -3 & 5 \\ -1 & -5 \end{pmatrix}$

5.5 Find the inverse of

$$\begin{pmatrix} 3 & 2 & 4 \\ 2 & 1 & 2 \\ 2 & 1 & 4 \end{pmatrix}$$

5.6 Express the following systems of simultaneous equations in matrix form. In each case, find the unknown quantities.

a) $2x + y = 4$ b) $3x + y = 13$ c) $5x + y = 3$

$x + 2y = -1$ $x + 4y = 1$ $6x + 2y = -4$

5.7 Solve the following equations.

(i) $a + b + c = 13$ (ii) $2a + b + c + d = 11$

$2a + b + 2c = 22$ $a + b + 2c + 2d = 17$

$a + 3b + 4c = 39$ $a + 2b + 3c + d = 18$

$2a + 3b + c + 2d = 19$

5.8 To ensure that pigs receive a sufficient vitamin intake, a farmer can mix food additives to pig meal. Three additives are available with the following specifications.

Additive 1. 6 Kg of vitamin A and 4 Kg of vitamin B

Additive 2. 4 Kg of vitamin B, 3 Kg of C and 3 Kg of D

Additive 3. 3 Kg of A, 1 Kg of B. 3 Kg of C and 3 Kg of D.

Put this information into matrix form.

A farmer decides to add 6 containers of additive 1, 8 of additive 2 and 10 of additive 3 to a batch of pigmeal. Put this into an appropriate vector, and deduce the total content of the food.

If a kilo of each vitamin costs £3, £6, £7 and £10 respectively, use an appropriate vector to obtain the cost of each additive, and hence by vector multiplication find the total cost of additives in the batch of feed.

5.9 $x = \begin{pmatrix} \frac{1}{6} & \frac{1}{3} \\ \frac{1}{4} & \frac{1}{2} \end{pmatrix}$ and $A = \begin{pmatrix} 10 \\ 45 \end{pmatrix}$

Given that $XT + A = T$,
find T.

5.10. On a particular occasion a furniture manufacturer has 115 lengths of hardwood and 120 lengths of softwood. This enables him to make 20 chairs and 25 tables. On another occasion he has 120 lengths of hardwood and 110 lengths of softwood. This enables him to make 30 chairs and 20 tables. If we wish to deduce the hardwood and softwood content of each chair and table state the problem in matrix form and solve it.

5.11 A man has a bottle and a decanter, and the matrix

$R = \begin{pmatrix} a & b \\ c & d \end{pmatrix}$ is such that

a is the quantity of gin in the bottle

c is the quantity of vermouth in the bottle

b is the quantity of gin in the decanter

d is the quantity of vermouth in the decanter.

If the bottle contains 240 ml of gin, and the decanter contains 300 ml of vermouth write down the matrix R.

He now pours $\frac{1}{3}$ of the bottle into the decanter. Find the new matrix P that describes the quantities in each container. If Q is the matrix such that

$$QR = P,$$

find the matrix Q.

He tastes the contents of the decanter, and decides the mixture is not strong enough, so he pours half the contents of the decanter back into the bottle. Assuming the quantity tasted is negligible, find the matrix S that describes the quantities in each container.

The mixture in the bottle now suits him perfectly, and he realises that he would like to make more of this mixture in the future. Find the matrix T that describes how to do this, i.e. the matrix T such that

$$TR = S$$

5.12 Mr. Wealthy and Mr. Rich are investors. Both own stakes in their own company, each others company and in Government securities. Mr. Wealthy always keeps $\frac{2}{3}$ of his total wealth invested in his own company (Wealthy Ltd.) and has agreed to keep an amount invested in Mr. Rich's company (Rich Ltd.) equal to $\frac{1}{3}$ of Mr. Rich's wealth. Mr. Rich always keeps $\frac{3}{4}$ of his total wealth invested in his own company, and has agreed to keep an amount invested in Mr. Wealthy's company equal to $\frac{1}{8}$ of Mr. Wealthy's total wealth.

Mr. Wealthy has a total wealth of 240 AMU (i.e. arbitrary monetary units), while Mr. Rich has a total wealth of 180 AMU.

Investment in Investment by	Wealthy Ltd.	Rich Ltd.	Govt. Securities	Total Wealth
Mr. Wealthy				
Mr. Rich				

a)   Complete the matrix above.

b)   What would the matrix above look like if Mr. Wealthy had 30 AMU and Mr. Rich had 20 AMU invested in government securities?

Chapter Six

Linear Programming

When we considered linear programming in Chapter 2, we used graphical methods and so confined our analysis to problems involving two unknown variables. The time has now come to examine a method that can cope with any number of unknown variables. As a preliminary to this analysis, we must examine again the way we used matrices to solve simultaneous equations.

The Detached Coefficient Method

Consider the simultaneous equations

$$x + y = 8$$
$$2x + 3y = 19$$

You should verify for yourself that $x = 5$ and $y = 3$ satisfies both these equations. In the last chapter we saw that the matrix equivalent of these equations was

$$\begin{pmatrix} 1 & 1 \\ 2 & 3 \end{pmatrix} \begin{pmatrix} x \\ y \end{pmatrix} = \begin{pmatrix} 8 \\ 19 \end{pmatrix}$$

and we saw that by using the inverse of the first matrix we could solve these equations. Now in fact there is no need to find the inverse when solving simultaneous equations. The relationship between the matrices will hold if we perform row transformations on the first and the product matrix. Suppose we transform the first matrix into the unit matrix. This would be equivalent to premultiplying the first matrix by its inverse. Now if we perform the same row transformations on the product matrix, then this would be equivalent to premultiplying by the same inverse. In other words, we will solve the equations! The first thing to do is to put the system into a *partitioned matrix* like this

$$\begin{bmatrix} 1 & 1 & \vrule & 8 \\ 2 & 3 & \vrule & 19 \end{bmatrix}$$

The left hand side of the partition gives the coefficients of x and y, and we call this the coefficient matrix. The right hand side of the partition gives the quantities which the equations equal (call this the quantity vector). It follows then that the vertical partitioning line represents the equals sign. We will now change the coefficient matrix into the unit matrix

$$\begin{pmatrix} 1 & 0 \\ 0 & 1 \end{pmatrix}$$

by applying the rules of row transformations to the entire matrix

$$\begin{bmatrix} 1 & 1 & | & 8 \\ 2 & 3 & | & 19 \end{bmatrix}$$

Remember that $x_{2,1}$ stands for the element in the second row and the first column of the matrix. We require that $x_{2,1} = 0$, and this can be achieved by subtracting twice the top row from the bottom row.

$$\begin{bmatrix} 1 & 1 & | & 8 \\ 0 & 1 & | & 3 \end{bmatrix}$$

We also require $x_{1,2}$ to be zero, and this can be achieved by subtracting the bottom row from the top row.

$$\begin{bmatrix} 1 & 0 & | & 5 \\ 0 & 1 & | & 3 \end{bmatrix}$$

Translating the matrix back into equations we have

$$1x + 0y = 5 \text{ i.e. } x = 5$$
$$0x + 1y = 3 \text{ i.e. } y = 3$$

In other words, we have solved the equations. This method can be applied to equations with more than two unknown quantities. For example

$$x + y + z = 5$$
$$2x + y + 2z = 9$$
$$x + 2y + 2z = 8$$

has the matrix equivalent

$$\begin{bmatrix} 1 & 1 & 1 & | & 5 \\ 2 & 1 & 2 & | & 9 \\ 1 & 2 & 2 & | & 8 \end{bmatrix}$$

and we wish to change the coefficient matrix into the unit matrix

$$\begin{pmatrix} 1 & 0 & 0 \\ 0 & 1 & 0 \\ 0 & 0 & 1 \end{pmatrix}$$

Subtracting twice the top row from the centre row changes $x_{2,1}$ to zero.
Subtracting the top row from the bottom row changes $x_{3,1}$ to zero.

$$\left[\begin{array}{ccc|c} 1 & 1 & 1 & 5 \\ 0 & -1 & 0 & -1 \\ 0 & 1 & 1 & 3 \end{array}\right]$$

Subtracting the bottom row from the top row changes $x_{1,3}$ to zero.
Multiplying the centre row by -1 changes $x_{2,2}$ to 1

$$\left[\begin{array}{ccc|c} 1 & 0 & 0 & 2 \\ 0 & 1 & 0 & 1 \\ 0 & 1 & 1 & 3 \end{array}\right]$$

Subtracting the centre row from the bottom row changes $x_{3,2}$ to zero,
completes the transformation and gives the solution matrix.

$$\left[\begin{array}{ccc|c} 1 & 0 & 0 & 2 \\ 0 & 1 & 0 & 1 \\ 0 & 0 & 1 & 2 \end{array}\right]$$

$$1x + 0y + 0z = 2 \text{ i.e. } x = 2$$
$$0x + 1y + 0z = 1 \text{ i.e. } y = 1$$
$$0x + 0y + 1z = 2 \text{ i.e. } z = 2$$

You should now substitute these values for x, y and z in the original
equations to verify the solution.

The method we have used is called the detached coefficient method. Strictly
speaking, it is not necessary to change the coefficient matrix to the unit
matrix using this method. Let us set out step-by-step instructions for using
this method.

Step 1. Select any element in the coefficient matrix
Step 2. Using row transformations, transform this element into unity
Step 3. Using row transformations, detach the remaining coefficients (i.e.
transform them to zero)
Step 4. Select any other element in a row or column not previously chosen.
If no such element exists, stop
Step 5. Go to step 2.

Suppose that we wished to solve

$$3x + 2y + 4z = 19$$
$$2x + y + 2z = 10$$
$$2x + y + 4z = 16$$

Putting this into matrix form

$$\left[\begin{array}{ccc|c} 3 & 2 & 4 & 19 \\ 2 & 1 & ② & 10 \\ 2 & 1 & 4 & 16 \end{array}\right]$$

We arbitrarily select $x_{2,3}$ (ringed). To transform this to 1, we divide the centre row by 2 to give

$$\begin{bmatrix} 1 & \frac{1}{2} & 1 & | & 5 \end{bmatrix}$$

If we subtract 4 times this new centre row from the top and bottom rows, then we detach the other elements in the third column. The matrix now looks like this:

$$\begin{bmatrix} -1 & 0 & 0 & | & -1 \\ 1 & \frac{1}{2} & 1 & | & 5 \\ -2 & -1 & 0 & | & -4 \end{bmatrix}$$

We now select another element, but not in the second row or the third column, and we have chosen $x_{3,1}$. To transform this to 1, divide the third row by -2 to give

$$\begin{bmatrix} 1 & \frac{1}{2} & 0 & | & 2 \end{bmatrix}$$

Adding this new third row to the top row, and subtracting it from the second row detaches the elements in the first column

$$\begin{bmatrix} 0 & \frac{1}{2} & 0 & | & 1 \\ 0 & 0 & 1 & | & 3 \\ 1 & \frac{1}{2} & 0 & | & 2 \end{bmatrix}$$

The only unused row is the first and the only unused column is the second, so we must now transform $x_{1,2}$ to 1. To do this, multiply the first row by 2 to give

$$\begin{bmatrix} 0 & 1 & 0 & | & 2 \end{bmatrix}$$

Subtracting $\frac{1}{2}$ this new top row from the bottom row gives the solution matrix

$$\begin{bmatrix} 0 & 1 & 0 & | & 2 \\ 0 & 0 & 1 & | & 3 \\ 1 & 0 & 0 & | & 1 \end{bmatrix}$$

or
$$0x + 1y + 0z = 2 \text{ i.e. } y = 2$$
$$0x + 0y + 1z = 3 \text{ i.e. } z = 3$$
$$1x + 0y + 0z = 1 \text{ i.e. } x = 1$$

Once again, you should check that the solution is correct by substituting in the equations.

Linear Programming: Simplex Method

Applying detached coefficients to linear programming is called the Simplex Method. Let us start with a maximum profit, two product problem. Suppose a manufacturer is making two products, X and Y with the following input requirements:

Product	Raw materials	Machine time	Labour
Y	4 tons	2 hrs.	1 hr.
Y	1 ton	1 hr.	1 hr.

The inputs are available in the following quantities per week.

90 tons of raw materials
50 hours of machine time
40 hours of labour

The profit is £4 on X and £3 on Y, and the objective is to maximise profit. Assuming the weekly output is x units of X and y units of Y, the following model would describe the problem.

Maximise $\pi = 4x + 3y$
Subject to
$$4x + y \leq 90$$
$$2x + y \leq 50$$
$$x + y \leq 40$$
$$x \geq 0$$
$$y \geq 0$$

Diagram 6.1 shows the mapping of the inequalities and the feasibility polygon. The profit line shows that the solution is at point D, where $x = 10$, $y = 30$ and profit (maximum) is £130.

The detached coefficient method cannot cope with inequalities, so we must transform the model into a system of equations. Consider the first inequality $4x + y \leq 90$, i.e. the raw material inequality. Suppose 10 units of each is produced, then the raw material requirement would be $4 \times 10 + 10 = 50$ tons, and there would be a surplus of 40 tons. What can we deduce about the size of the surplus? If we produce nothing, then the surplus is 90 tons, and if we use all of the raw material then the surplus would be zero. If the surplus is 'a' tons, then

$$0 \leq a \leq 90.$$

It follows from this that the amount used, plus the surplus, must equal 90 tons. Hence

$$4x + y + a = 90$$

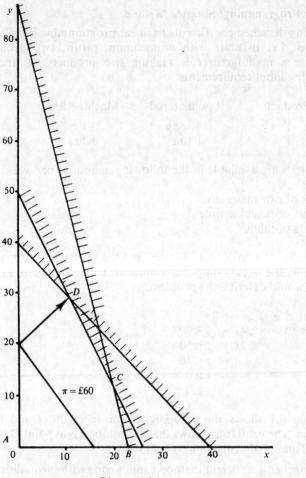

Diagram 6.1

The surplus '*a*' is called *slack variable*. If we call '*b*' the surplus machine time and '*c*' the surplus labour time, then we can rewrite the model as a system of equations

Maximise $\pi = 4x + 3y$
Subject to
$$4x + y + a = 90$$
$$2x + y + b = 50$$
$$x + y + c = 40$$
$$x \geq 0, y \geq 0$$
$$a \geq 0, b \geq 0, c \geq 0$$

Thus, we must satisfy the objective function subject to the constraint equations, and subject to the additional constraint that all variables must be non negative. We can represent the constraint equations in a partitioned matrix.

$$
\begin{bmatrix}
4 & 1 & 1 & 0 & 0 & 90 \\
2 & 1 & 0 & 1 & 0 & 50 \\
1 & 1 & 0 & 0 & 1 & 40
\end{bmatrix}
$$

$$
\begin{array}{cccccc}
\uparrow & \uparrow & \uparrow & \uparrow & \uparrow & \uparrow \\
x & y & a & b & c & \text{Quantity}
\end{array}
$$

Stop for a moment and compare this problem with those considered in the last section. Previously, our problems had the same number of equations as they had variables. But with this problem, while we have 5 variables (x, y, a, b, c) we have only three equations. This difference is reflected in the coefficient matrix which is no longer square. We must conclude then, that this system of equations has no unique solution, but has many solutions. Which solution do we want? Clearly, the one that maximises profit.

Suppose for the moment we ignore the first two columns of this matrix, then we could, perhaps, treat it as a solution matrix. If it is ligitimate to do this, then the solution would be

a = 90 (i.e. 90 tons of raw material are surplus)
b = 50 (i.e. 50 machine hours are surplus)
c = 40 (i.e. 40 hours of labour are surplus)

The solution would correspond to position A in diagram 6.1. Now the implication of this solution is that no inputs are used − so if the solution is to be feasible it follows that nothing is produced and x and y must both equal zero. We are now in a position to formulate rules for interpreting such matrices:

1. Identify the columns that form the solution matrix and read off the corresponding solution.

2. Identify the remaining columns and set the corresponding variables at zero.

We have not yet entered the objective function into our matrix. To do this we use a *double partitioned matrix or Simplex Tableau* and enter the objective function in the last row. As nothing is produced, it follows that profit is zero and so this is entered into the quantity column. Notice that the coefficients of x and y have been entered as negative quantities. The reason for this will become apparent shortly, but for the time being take it to mean that as nothing is produced, the negative quantities in the last row measures profit forgone by not producing x and not producing y.

$$
\left[
\begin{array}{ccccc|c}
4 & 1 & 1 & 0 & 0 & 90 \\
2 & 1 & 0 & 1 & 0 & 50 \\
1 & 1 & 0 & 0 & 1 & 40 \\
\hline
-4 & -3 & 0 & 0 & 0 & 0
\end{array}
\right]
$$

$$
\begin{array}{cccccc}
x & y & a & b & c & Q \\
 & & \uparrow & \uparrow & \uparrow &
\end{array}
$$

Let us now deduce the effect of producing some units of one of the products. It would seem sensible to start with X, as it earns the greatest profit per unit. Suppose we decide to produce as much of X as possible – how many units can be produced? We can answer this problem by considering the x column and the Q column. The first row tells us it takes 4 tons of raw material to produce a unit of x, and 90 tons are available, i.e. there is sufficient raw material to produce $90 \div 4 = 22.5$ units. Reference to the second and third rows tell us there is sufficient machine time to produce $50 \div 2 = 25$ units, and sufficient labour time to produce $40 \div 1 = 40$ units. Raw material supplies restrict the output of x to a maximum of 22.5 units But if we produce 22.5 units of X, we will use all the available raw material, and 'a' would be zero (remember, 'a' is the surplus raw material). Thus x is called the *entering variable,* (it enters the solution matrix) and 'a' the *departing variable* (it departs from the solution matrix). The non-zero variables (marked with an arrow in the matrix above) now become x, b and c.

We start as we did in the last section by dividing the top row by 4

$$\left[\begin{array}{ccccc|c} 1 & \frac{1}{4} & \frac{1}{4} & 0 & 0 & 22\frac{1}{2} \end{array} \right]$$

Now we must detach the remaining coefficients in the x column. The appropriate row transformations would be

Subtract twice the transformed top row from the second row
Subtract the transformed top row from the third row
Add four times the transformed top row to the bottom row:

After completing the transformations, the new matrix would look like this

$$\left[\begin{array}{ccccc|c} 1 & \frac{1}{4} & \frac{1}{4} & 0 & 0 & 22\frac{1}{2} \\ 0 & \frac{1}{2} & -\frac{1}{2} & 1 & 0 & 5 \\ 0 & \frac{3}{4} & -\frac{1}{4} & 0 & 1 & 17\frac{1}{2} \\ \hline 0 & -2 & 1 & 0 & 0 & 90 \end{array} \right]$$

$$\begin{array}{cccccc} x & y & a & b & c & Q \\ \uparrow & & & \uparrow & \uparrow & \end{array}$$

Again, we are interested only in the columns contained in the solution matrix (marked with an arrow). Reading-off this soluion we have

$x = 22\frac{1}{2}$ (produce $22\frac{1}{2}$ units of X)
$b = 5$ (5 hours machine time surplus)
$c = 17\frac{1}{2}$ ($17\frac{1}{2}$ hours of labour surplus)
$a = 0$ (no surplus material)
$y = 0$ (Y is not produced).
$\pi = 90$ (Total profit is £90)

Let us again check the solution to ensure that it is feasible. As X earns £4 per unit profit, $22\frac{1}{2}$ units of X would earn £90. The raw material surplus is

$90 - (4 \times 22\frac{1}{2}) = 0$, the machine time surplus is $50 - (2 \times 22\frac{1}{2}) = 5$ hours and the labour surplus is $40 - (1 \times 22\frac{1}{2}) = 17\frac{1}{2}$ hours. Once again, our solution is feasible and corresponds to point B on the graph.

Now let us produce some units of Y as well as X – how much can we produce? We must use the same method as before i.e. divide the co-efficients in the y column into the quantities in the Q column, and choose the smallest.

Why must we do this? If we do not choose the smallest value, then negative values will occur in the Q vector when we detach the remaining coefficients. You can verify this if you wish by multiplying the top row by 4 (or the third row by $^4/_3$) and detaching the remaining coefficients. We know that negative elements in the Q vector are not feasible. The second row gives the smallest total, so y is the entering variable, and b the departing variable. Multiplying the second row by 2 gives

$$\begin{bmatrix} 0 & 1 & -1 & 2 & 0 & | & 10 \end{bmatrix}$$

To detach the remaining coefficients in the y column, we perform the following row transformations.

Subtract one quarter of the transformed second row from the top row
Subtract three quarters of the transformed second row from the third row
Add twice the transformed second row to the bottom row.

$$\begin{bmatrix} 1 & 0 & \frac{1}{2} & -\frac{1}{2} & 0 & | & 20 \\ 0 & 1 & -1 & 2 & 0 & | & 10 \\ 0 & 0 & \frac{1}{2} & -\frac{3}{2} & 1 & | & 10 \\ \hline 0 & 0 & -1 & 4 & 0 & | & 110 \end{bmatrix}$$

$$\begin{matrix} x & y & a & b & c & Q \end{matrix}$$

x = 20 (produce 20 units of x)
y = 10 (produce 10 units of y)
c = 10 (10 hours of labour surplus)
Profit is £110.
a = 0 (no surplus materials)
b = 0 (no surplus machine time)

This solution corresponds to position C on the graph.

Let us stop for a moment and consider exactly what we have been doing. We have selected an entering variable and performed row transformations to detach the remaining elements in the entering variable column. To detach the element in the objective function row, we have added some multiple of the entering variable row. As we have been adding, *this has caused profit to increase. This gives us a signal as to when we have reached maximum profit.*

If any column in the objective function is negative and we locate the entering variable in that column, then we must add to the objective row to detach the negative coefficient. Hence, profit must increase. If, on the other hand, the coefficient in the objective row and entering variable column is positive, we will detach it by subtracting. This will cause profit to decrease. *Profit is at a maximum, then, when all the coefficients in the objective function cease to be negative.*

Now let us return to the matrix. If we look at the objective function row, we see that there is a negative coefficient in the 'a' column, and if we locate the entering variable in this column we will increase profit. In this column, the second row gives the smallest total, but this cannot be chosen (why?). Instead, we take the third row, and 'c' becomes the departing variable. Multiplying the third row by two gives

$$\begin{bmatrix} 0 & 0 & 1 & -3 & 2 & | & 20 \end{bmatrix}$$

To detach the remaining coefficients in the 'a' column we

Subtract half the transformed third row from the top row
Add the transformed row to the second and fourth row.

$$\left[\begin{array}{ccccc|c} 1 & 0 & 0 & 1 & -1 & 10 \\ 0 & 1 & 0 & -1 & 2 & 30 \\ 0 & 0 & 1 & -3 & 2 & 20 \\ \hline 0 & 0 & 0 & 1 & 2 & 130 \end{array} \right]$$

$$\begin{array}{cccccc} x & y & a & b & c & Q \\ \uparrow & \uparrow & \uparrow & & & \end{array}$$

x = 10 (produce 10 units of X)
y = 30 (produce 30 units of Y)
a = 20 (20 tons of raw material are surplus)
b = 0 (no surplus machine time)
c = 0 (no surplus labour)

The profit is £130.

As there are no negative coefficients in the objective row, this is an optimum solution: profit is at a maximum. You should notice that this corresponds with position D on the graph, and agrees with the graphical method.

Let us check that profit is at a maximum. If we made b the entering variable, can you see that x would have to be the departing variable? To detach the last element in the b column, we would have to subtract the top row from the bottom. Thus the bottom row would become

$$\begin{bmatrix} -1 & 0 & 0 & 0 & 3 & | & 120 \end{bmatrix}.$$

Profit has declined by £10. In a similar fashion, we could show that if c was the incoming variable, then 'a' would be the departing variable, and after detaching the coefficients in the c column profit would decline again by £10.

Working in More Than Two Dimensions

At the beginning of this chapter, we stated that the purpose of introducing the detached coefficient method was to solve linear – programming problems with more than two unknown variables. Such problems are called *multi-dimensional*. Let us consider a problem where more than two products are produced.

A witch-doctor has a healthy business supplying a deadly poison, a mother-in-law repellent spray, an elixir, and a love potion to a seemingly insatiable market. The products are made from the same four ingredients in the following proportions:

Code	Product	Snake oil	Lizards' tongues	Frogs' legs	Bats' wings
X_1	Deadly poison	1 fluid oz.	2	1	3
X_2	Mother-in-law repellent	2 fluid ozs.	1	2	4
X_3	Elixir	2 fluid ozs.	2	1	2
X_4	Love potion	1 fluid oz.	1	2	1

He has been producing 10 units of X_1, 12 units of X_2, 6 units of X_3 and 2 units of X_4 per week at a profit of £4, £6, £4, £3, respectively. Using vector multiplication, his weekly profit is

$$[10 \quad 12 \quad 6 \quad 2] \begin{bmatrix} 4 \\ 6 \\ 4 \\ 3 \end{bmatrix} = £142.$$

The witch-doctor suspects that he is not maximising his weekly profit, and engages our services as management consultants. We learn that the ingredients can be obtained in the following weekly quantities.

70 fluid ozs. of snake oil.
56 lizards tongues.
70 frogs legs.
92 bats wings.

We realise that linear programming would give the product-mix that would maximise profit. If we say X_1, X_2, X_3, and X_4 are the quantities of each product made, and X_5, X_6, X_7 and X_8 are the slack variables, then the mathematical model of his problem would be:

Maximise $\pi = 4X_1 + 6X_2 + 4X_3 + 3X_4$
Subject to
$$X_1 + 2X_2 + 2X_3 + X_4 + X_5 = 70$$
$$2X_1 + X_2 + 2X_3 + X_4 + X_6 = 56$$
$$X_1 + 2X_2 + X_3 + 2X_4 + X_7 = 70$$
$$3X_1 + 4X_2 + 2X_3 + X_4 + X_8 = 92$$
$$X_1 \geq 0, X_2 \geq 0, X_3 \geq 0, X_4 \geq 0$$
$$X_5 \geq 0. \geq X_6 \geq 0, X_7 \geq X_8 \geq 0$$

The first matrix would look like this:

$$
\begin{bmatrix}
1 & 2 & 2 & 1 & 1 & 0 & 0 & 0 & | & 70 \\
2 & 1 & 1 & 0 & 1 & 0 & 0 & & | & 56 \\
1 & 2 & 2 & 2 & 0 & 0 & 1 & 0 & | & 70 \\
3 & 4 & 2 & 1 & 0 & 0 & 0 & 1 & | & 92 \\
-4 & -6 & -4 & -3 & 0 & 0 & 0 & 0 & | & 0
\end{bmatrix}
$$

| X_1 | X_2 | X_3 | X_4 | X_5 | X_6 | X_7 | X_8 | Q |

If we choose X_2 as the entering variable (i.e. the product with the highest rate of profit) then X_8 becomes the departing variable. Performing the necessary row transformations, the second matrix is obtained.

$$
\begin{bmatrix}
-\tfrac{1}{2} & 0 & 1 & \tfrac{1}{2} & 1 & 0 & 0 & -\tfrac{1}{2} & | & 24 \\
\tfrac{5}{4} & 0 & \tfrac{3}{2} & \tfrac{3}{4} & 0 & 1 & 0 & -\tfrac{1}{4} & | & 33 \\
-\tfrac{1}{2} & 0 & 0 & \tfrac{3}{2} & 0 & 0 & 1 & -\tfrac{1}{2} & | & 24 \\
\tfrac{3}{4} & 1 & \tfrac{1}{2} & \tfrac{1}{4} & 0 & 0 & 0 & \tfrac{1}{4} & | & 23 \\
\tfrac{1}{2} & 0 & -1 & -\tfrac{3}{2} & 0 & 0 & 0 & \tfrac{3}{2} & | & 138
\end{bmatrix}
$$

| X_1 | X_2 | X_3 | X_4 | X_5 | X_6 | X_7 | X_8 | Q |
| | ↑ | | | ↑ | ↑ | ↑ | | |

We can continue to perform row transformation until all the negative components in the objective row are detached.

$$
\begin{bmatrix}
-\tfrac{1}{3} & 0 & 1 & 0 & 1 & 0 & -\tfrac{1}{3} & -\tfrac{1}{3} & | & 16 \\
\tfrac{3}{2} & 0 & \tfrac{3}{2} & 0 & 0 & 1 & -\tfrac{1}{2} & 0 & | & 21 \\
-\tfrac{1}{3} & 0 & 0 & 1 & 0 & 0 & \tfrac{2}{3} & -\tfrac{1}{3} & | & 16 \\
\tfrac{5}{6} & 1 & \tfrac{1}{2} & 0 & 0 & 0 & -\tfrac{1}{6} & \tfrac{1}{3} & | & 19 \\
0 & 0 & -1 & 0 & 0 & 0 & 1 & 1 & | & 162
\end{bmatrix}
$$

| X_1 | X_2 | X_3 | X_4 | X_5 | X_6 | X_7 | X_8 | Q |
| | | ↑ | | | | | | |

$$
\begin{bmatrix}
-\tfrac{4}{3} & 0 & 0 & 0 & 1 & 0 & -\tfrac{2}{3} & 0 & -\tfrac{1}{3} & | & 2 \\
1 & 0 & 1 & 0 & 0 & \tfrac{2}{3} & -\tfrac{1}{3} & 0 & | & 14 \\
-\tfrac{1}{3} & 0 & 0 & 1 & 0 & 0 & \tfrac{2}{3} & -\tfrac{1}{3} & | & 16 \\
\tfrac{1}{3} & 1 & 0 & 0 & 0 & -\tfrac{1}{3} & 0 & \tfrac{1}{3} & | & 12 \\
1 & 0 & 0 & 0 & 0 & \tfrac{2}{3} & \tfrac{2}{3} & 1 & | & 176
\end{bmatrix}
$$

| X_1 | X_2 | X_3 | X_4 | X_5 | X_6 | X_7 | X_8 | Q |
| | ↑ | ↑ | ↑ | ↑ | | | | |

This is the optimum solution. Reading from the matrix we have

$X_2 = 12$, make 12 mother-in-law repellent sprays.
$X_3 = 14$, make 14 units of elixir.
$X_4 = 16$, make 16 love potions.
$X_5 = 2$, 2 fluid ozs, of snake oil are surplus.
The profit is £176.

Let us check that the solution is feasible. If the above quantities were produced, the inputs required would be:

$(2 \times 12) + (2 \times 14) + 16$	$= 68$ fluid ozs. of snake oil.
$12 + (2 \times 14) + 16$	$= 56$ lizards tongues.
$(2 \times 12) + 14 + (2 \times 16)$	$= 70$ frogs legs.
$(4 \times 12) + (2 \times 14) + 16$	$= 92$ bats wings.

This agrees the 2 fluid ozs. surplus of smake oil yielded by the matrix.

A Mixed-Inequalities Example

We will state again the tailor problem dealt with in Chapter 2.

Maximise $\pi = \quad y + 2x$
Subject to $\qquad 2y + 5x \leq 200$ (the labour constraint)
$\qquad\qquad 3y + 5x \leq 225$ (the material constraint)
$\qquad\qquad \left.\begin{array}{l} x \geq \;\; 10 \\ y \geq \;\; 20 \end{array}\right\}$ the contract constraints

Adding slack variables to the labour and material constraints presents no problem.

$2y + 5x + a = 200,\ a \geq 0$
$3y + 5x + b = 225,\ b \geq 0$

How can we deal with the contract constraints, which are 'greater than or equal to' ordering? Clearly, it would not make sense to add slack variable, we must subtract them.

$x - d = 10.\quad c \geq 0$
$y - c = 20.\quad d \geq 0$

It should be noted that c and d (which are called artificial variables) are also non-negative. The minus sign does not mean that the variable is negative, it means we must subtract the variable. If, for example $X = 50$, then c must be 40 to satisfy the equation

$x - c = 10$

The first matrix would look like this.

$$
\left[
\begin{array}{cccccc|c}
2 & 5 & 1 & 0 & 0 & 0 & 200 \\
3 & 5 & 0 & 1 & 0 & 0 & 225 \\
1 & 0 & 0 & 0 & -1 & 0 & 20 \\
0 & 1 & 0 & 0 & 0 & -1 & 10 \\
\hline
-1 & -2 & 0 & 0 & 0 & 0 & 0
\end{array}
\right]
$$

$$
\begin{array}{ccccccc}
y & x & a & b & c & d & Q \\
 & & \uparrow & \uparrow & & &
\end{array}
$$

The first solution is to produce nothing, have 200 hours of labour surplus, and 225 yards of cloth surplus. But this is not a feasible solution, as it violates the contract constraints. If we make first x then y the entering variables, we will obtain a feasible solution, but there will be not departing variables.

$$
\left[
\begin{array}{cccccc|c}
2 & 0 & 1 & 0 & 0 & 5 & 150 \\
3 & 0 & 0 & 1 & 0 & 5 & 175 \\
1 & 0 & 0 & 0 & -1 & 0 & 20 \\
0 & 1 & 0 & 0 & 0 & -1 & 10 \\
\hline
-1 & 0 & 0 & 0 & 0 & -2 & 20
\end{array}
\right]
$$

$$
\begin{array}{ccccccc}
y & x & a & b & c & d & Q \\
 & & \uparrow & \uparrow & & &
\end{array}
$$

$$
\left[
\begin{array}{cccccc|c}
0 & 0 & 1 & 0 & 2 & 5 & 110 \\
0 & 0 & 0 & 1 & 3 & 5 & 115 \\
1 & 0 & 0 & 0 & -1 & 0 & 20 \\
0 & 1 & 0 & 0 & 0 & -1 & 10 \\
\hline
0 & 0 & 0 & 0 & -1 & -2 & 40
\end{array}
\right]
$$

$$
\begin{array}{ccccccc}
y & x & a & b & c & d & Q \\
\uparrow & \uparrow & \uparrow & \uparrow & & &
\end{array}
$$

We now have a feasible solution: produce 20 of x, 10 of y and earn £40 profit. This gives us 110 hours of labour, and 115 yards of cloth surplus. Both c and d are zero. We can now proceed in the usual fashion to obtain an optimum solution.

$$
\left[
\begin{array}{cccccc|c}
0 & 0 & 1/5 & 0 & 2/5 & 1 & 22 \\
0 & 0 & -1 & 1 & 1 & 0 & 5 \\
1 & 0 & 0 & 0 & -1 & 0 & 20 \\
0 & 1 & 1/5 & 0 & 2/5 & 0 & 32 \\
\hline
0 & 0 & 2/5 & 0 & -1/5 & 0 & 84
\end{array}
\right]
$$

$$
\begin{array}{ccccccc}
y & x & a & b & c & d & Q \\
\uparrow & \uparrow & & \uparrow & & \uparrow &
\end{array}
$$

$$\left[\begin{array}{cccccc|c}
0 & 0 & 3/5 & -2/5 & 0 & 1 & 20 \\
0 & 0 & -1 & 1 & 1 & 0 & 5 \\
1 & 0 & -1 & 1 & 0 & 0 & 25 \\
0 & 1 & 3/5 & -2/5 & 0 & 0 & 30 \\
\hline
0 & 0 & 1/5 & 1/5 & 0 & 0 & 85
\end{array}\right]$$

$$\begin{array}{ccccccc}
y & x & a & b & c & d & Q \\
\uparrow & \uparrow & & & \uparrow & \uparrow &
\end{array}$$

This is the optimum solution, and reading the variables we have.

y = 25 (make 25 overcoats)

x = 30 (make 30 jackets)

c = 5 (5 jackets made in excess of 20 required to meet the contract)

d = 20 (20 overcoats made in excess of the 10 required to meet the contract)

Labour and material are both fully involved.

Degeneracy: A Blending Example

Let us suppose that by law a certain health food must contain at least 3% of vitamin A, and at least 7% of vitamin B. A manufacturer has stocks of two compounds, with the following vitamin content.

	Vitamin A	Vitamin B
Vito	2%	10%
Slam	5%	6%

He wishes to blend Vito and Slam to produce a new product Wow, that meets the minimum vitamin requirements. The sales manager reckons that he can sell up to 60 lbs. of Wow per week. If Vito can be produced at a £4 profit and Slam at a £5 profit, in what proportions should they be mixed to produce the 60 lbs. of Wow?

As usual, we start by setting up the model. Assuming that x lbs. of Vito and y lbs. of Slam are blended, the objective is

Maximise $\pi = 4x + 5y$

The marketing constraint gives

$x + y \leq 60$

The vitamin A constraint (i.e. at least 3%) gives

$2x + 5y \geq 3(x+y)$

or $2y - x \geq 0$

and the vitamin B constraint gives

$$10x + 6y \geq 7(x+y)$$
$$3x - y \geq 0$$

The mathematical model of the problem is

Maximise π $= 4x + 5y$
Subject to $\quad x + y \leq 60$
$\qquad\qquad 2y - x \geq 0$
$\qquad\qquad 3x - y \geq 0$
$\qquad\qquad x \geq 0, y \geq 0$

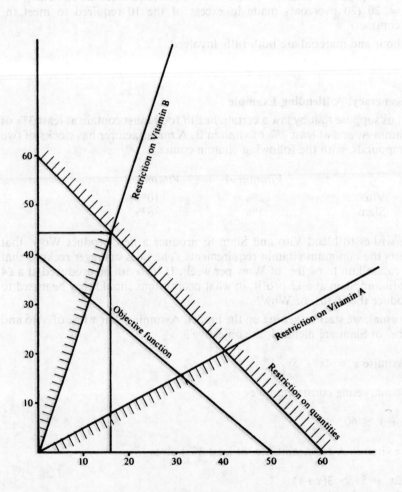

Diagram 6.2

The objective function and constraints are mapped in diagram 6.2. Using the method outlined in Chapter 2, we read off that profit would be maximised when $x = 15$ and $y = 45$, or 15 lbs. of Vito is blended with 45 lbs. of Slam. The profit would be £285. The vitamin A content is

$$\frac{2 \times 15}{100} + \frac{5 \times 45}{100} = \frac{51}{20} \text{ lbs.}$$

or, as a percentage,

$$\frac{51}{20} \times \frac{1}{60} \times \frac{100}{1} = \frac{17}{4} = 4.25\%$$

This is in excess of the minimum requirements. The vitamin B content is

$$\frac{10 \times 15}{100} + \frac{6 \times 45}{100} = 4.2 \text{ lbs.}$$

or, as a percentage,

$$\frac{21}{5} \times \frac{1}{60} \times \frac{100}{1} = 7\%$$

which just meets the minimum requirements.

Now let us solve the same problem using the Simplex method. Notice that two of the inequalities are in a 'greater than or equal to' form, which suggests that an artificial variable should be added. However, if you think back to Chapter 2, you will remember that the inequality sign can be reversed if we multiply throughout by minus one. Hence, instead of writing the vitamin restrictions like this:

$$2y - x \geq 0 \text{ and } 3x - y \geq 0,$$

we can write them like this

$$x - 2y \leq 0, \text{ and } y - 3x \leq 0.$$

We could not do this in the last example – why?

Adding slack variables in the usual way, we can obtain the first matrix

$$
\begin{bmatrix}
1 & 1 & 1 & 0 & 0 & 60 \\
1 & -2 & 0 & 1 & 0 & 0 \\
-3 & 1 & 0 & 0 & 1 & 0 \\
\hline
-4 & -5 & 0 & 0 & 0 & 0
\end{bmatrix}
$$

$$
\begin{array}{cccccc}
x & y & a & b & c & Q \\
 & & \uparrow & \uparrow & \uparrow &
\end{array}
$$

We select y as the entering variable, but which is to be the departing variable? The problem is the presence of the zeros in the quantity column. Such matrices are called *degenerate* and we overcome this problem by adding a small positive amount E to the zeros. The quantity E is so small that it does not affect our final solution.

$$
\begin{bmatrix}
1 & 1 & 1 & 0 & 0 & 60 \\
1 & -2 & 0 & 1 & 0 & E \\
-3 & 1 & 0 & 0 & 1 & E \\
\hline
-4 & -5 & 0 & 0 & 0 & 0
\end{bmatrix}
$$

$$
\begin{array}{cccccc}
x & y & a & b & c & Q \\
 & \uparrow & & \uparrow & \uparrow &
\end{array}
$$

It is now easy to see that if y is the entering variable, then c must be the departing variable.

$$
\begin{bmatrix}
4 & 0 & 1 & 0 & -1 & 60-E \\
-5 & 0 & 0 & 1 & 2 & 3E \\
-3 & 1 & 0 & 0 & 1 & E \\
\hline
-19 & 0 & 0 & 0 & 5 & 5E
\end{bmatrix}
$$

$$
\begin{array}{cccccc}
x & y & a & b & c & Q \\
 & & \uparrow & \uparrow & \uparrow &
\end{array}
$$

Now we make x the entering and a the departing variable

$$
\begin{bmatrix}
1 & 0 & \tfrac{1}{4} & 0 & -\tfrac{1}{4} & 15 - \tfrac{E}{4} \\
0 & 0 & \tfrac{5}{4} & 1 & \tfrac{3}{4} & 75 + \tfrac{7E}{4} \\
0 & 1 & \tfrac{3}{4} & 0 & \tfrac{1}{4} & 45 + \tfrac{E}{4} \\
\hline
0 & 0 & \tfrac{19}{4} & 0 & \tfrac{1}{4} & 285 + \tfrac{E}{4}
\end{bmatrix}
$$

$$
\begin{array}{cccccc}
x & y & a & b & c & Q \\
\uparrow & \uparrow & & \uparrow & &
\end{array}
$$

We now drop the E's from the solution and obtain that £285 profit can be earned by blending 15 lbs. of x with 45 lbs. of y. What do you think the slack variable $b = 75$ means? The slacks a and c are both zero − what do you conclude from this?

Duality

Let us yet again consider the tailor problem, and ask how does the tailor earn his profit. You may think that there is an obvious answer to this question − by producing jackets and overcoats. But we could give a second answer to this question. He earns his profit by combining hours of labour with yards of cloth. If we consider profit from this angle, then we can deduce a considerable amount of information useful ‘to the tailor in addition to the product – mix that maximises profit.

Now suppose the tailor, realising his profit is derived from his inputs of cloth and labour, attempts to assess the relative values of these resources: he is *imputing* his profits to his inputs. He imputes an amount V_1 to each hour of labour, and an amount V_2 to each yard of cloth. Now, we know that it takes 2 hours of labour and 3 yards of cloth to produce a jacket, so the value of inputs in each jacket is

$$2V_1 + 3V_2$$

However, he will want to impute values V_1 and V_2 sufficiently great to account for the profit on jackets (£1). In other words

$$2V_1 + 3V_2 \geq 1 \; : \ldots \ldots \ldots (1)$$

Likewise, as it requires 5 hours labour and 5 yards of cloth to make an overcoat, the values of the inputs would be

$$5V_1 + 5V_2$$

and as the profit is £2 on each overcoat

$$5V_1 + 5V_2 \geq 2 \ldots \ldots \ldots (2)$$

It has been stated that the values V_1 and V_2 must be sufficient to account for the profit on jackets and overcoats. Why, then, state that

$$2V_1 + 3V_2 \geq 1$$

rather than that

$$2V_1 + 3V_2 = 1 \ldots \ldots ?$$

It is possible that the imputed value of inputs used in producing a product exceeds the profit that the product can earn. This would indicate that the resources would be better employed producing some other product. We will return to this point later.

You should realise that there is no unique solution to the simultaneous inequalities (1) and (2). Are there any limits to the values we can place on V_1 and V_2? Well, we know that the tailor has 200 hours of labour and 225 yards of cloth available per week, so the total value of all inputs is

$$A = 200V_1 + 225V_2$$

It might seem reasonable to find the smallest valuation of the *scarce* inputs that would account for all the profits of the outputs. If we did this, then the problem would become

Minimise $A = 200V_1 + 225V_2$
Subject to
$$5V_1 + 5V_2 \geq 2$$
$$2V_1 + 3V_2 \geq 1$$
$$V_1 \geq 0, \quad V_2 \geq 0$$

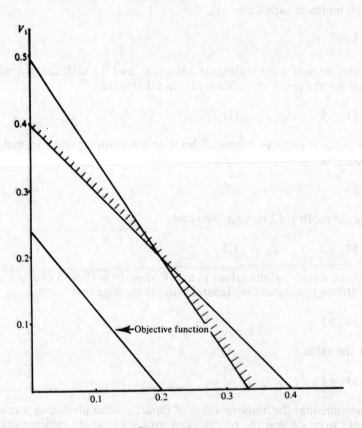

Diagram 6.3

Diagram 6.3 shows the mapping of this model. The objective function itself has not been mapped: this would not be convenient. Instead, the objective function divided by 1000 has been mapped (you should realise that this would not affect its slope). Reading from the graph we see that A is minimised when $V_1 = V_2 = \frac{1}{5}$. Thus 20p is the minimum value we can impute to each hour of labour and each yard of cloth, and still account for all the profit. Now the total imputed value of the inputs is

$$200 \times \frac{1}{5} + 225 \times \frac{1}{5} = £85.$$

Does this ring a bell? The total imputed value is the same as the maximum profit the tailor could earn. *If we choose values for V_1 V_2 . . . V_n that would minimise the total imputed value, we would simultaneously find maximum profit.*

Let us place the linear programming model to maximise profit alongside the previous model.

Maximise $\pi =$	$y + 2x$	Minimise $A =$	$200V_1 + 225V_2$
Subject to	$2y + 5x \le 200$	Subject to	$5V_1 + 5V_2 \ge 2$
	$3y + 5x \le 225$		$2V_1 + 3V_2 \ge 1$
	$y \ge 10.\ x \ge 20$		$V_1 \ge 0.\ V_2 \ge 0.$

It is apparent that there is a strong connection between the two models. Seemingly, if we turn the maximising problem 'inside out' we obtain the minimising problem. What is a column in one becomes a row in the other, the inequality signs are reversed, the coefficients in the quantity column of the first problem become the coefficients of the objective function in the second, and vice versa. Only the non-negative condition for the variables remains unchanged. If the first model is called the primal problem, then the second is called the *dual*. Let us again examine the solution matrix for the primal problem.

$$
\begin{bmatrix}
0 & 0 & 3/5 & -2/5 & 0 & 1 & 20 \\
0 & 0 & -1 & 1 & 1 & 0 & 5 \\
1 & 0 & -1 & 1 & 0 & 0 & 25 \\
0 & 1 & 3/5 & -2/5 & 0 & 0 & 30 \\
0 & 0 & 1/5 & 1/5 & 0 & 0 & 85
\end{bmatrix}
$$

y	x	a	b	c	d	Q
↑	↑	↑	↑	↑	↑	

Dual Variables
V_1 V_2

We identify the columns that form the solution matrix and read off their values from the quantity column. This gives the solution to the primal problem. We then identify the variables outside of the solution matrix and read off their values from the final row. These variables are called the dual variables, and there will be an imputed value for each scarce resource. The solution to the dual problem is that $V_1 = 1/5$ and $V_2 = 1/5$ − which agrees with the values we obtained from the graph. If we solve the primal problem by the Simplex Method we simultaneously solve its dual.

Marginal Revenue Product: Scarcity Values

The objective function in the last problem demands that we find the smallest valuation of the scarce inputs that would account for all the profits of the outputs. You may be wondering why we used the word 'scarce'. If we impute values to scarce resources, then resources that are not scarce will have a zero imputed value. Now of course, businessmen are more interested in resources that are scarce, for they limit the possible output and total profit. Let us again examine the solution matrix for the witch doctor problem.

$$
\begin{bmatrix}
-\tfrac{4}{3} & 0 & 0 & 0 & 1 & -\tfrac{2}{3} & 0 & -\tfrac{1}{3} & 2 \\
1 & 0 & 1 & 0 & 0 & \tfrac{2}{3} & -\tfrac{1}{3} & 0 & 14 \\
-\tfrac{1}{3} & 0 & 0 & 1 & 0 & 0 & \tfrac{2}{3} & -\tfrac{1}{3} & 16 \\
\tfrac{1}{3} & 1 & 0 & 0 & 0 & -\tfrac{1}{3} & 0 & \tfrac{1}{3} & 12 \\
\hline
1 & 0 & 0 & 0 & 0 & \tfrac{2}{3} & \tfrac{2}{3} & 1 & 176
\end{bmatrix}
$$

$$
\begin{array}{cccccccc}
x_1 & x_2 & x_3 & x_4 & x_5 & x_6 & x_7 & x_8 \qquad Q \\
 & & & & \uparrow & \uparrow & \uparrow & \uparrow \\
 & & & & V_1 & V_2 & V_3 & V_4
\end{array}
$$

Suppose we want the imputed values V_1, V_2, V_3 and V_4 that satisfy the dual problem. The values are given in that part of the objective function row that is concerned with the slack variables. Reading from the matrix we obtain

$V_2 = \tfrac{2}{3}$, or the imputed value of lizards tongues is £0.66.
$V_3 = \tfrac{2}{3}$, or the imputed value of frogs legs is £0.66.
$V_4 = 1$, or the imputed value of bats wings is £1.

Notice that $V_1 = 0$, i.e. there is a zero imputed value on snake oil. This is because snake oil is not scarce (there are 2 fluid ozs. surplus).

When we solve the dual problem, we are finding *Scarcity values* for the inputs. Such values are of considerable operational significance. Consider the scarcity value of bats wings: if the restriction on bats wings was lifted so that an extra one was available, then profit would rise by £1. Thus, the scarcity value of an input shows by how much profit would increase if the supply of that resource was increased by one unit. Economists call the scarcity value of an input its *marginal revenue product*.

From any matrix giving an optimal solution to a primal problem we can read values for the dual. This enriches our knowledge of the nature and importance of scarce resources. In the example above, we can deduce that if the supply of lizards tongues or frogs legs was increased by one unit, profit would rise by £0.66, and if the supply of bats wings was increased by one unit, profit would rise by £1. Now suppose the witch-doctor finds an additional, but more expensive, source of supply of bats' wings. How much more can he afford to pay for them? As each extra bats' wing adds £1 to total profit, he could afford to pay anything up to £1 extra for additional supplies, and still increase his profit.

If in a particular week the witch-doctor could obtain an extra 3 bats' wings, we would expect his profit to rise by £3. We could check this by restating the primal problem with the bats' wings constraint as

$$3x_1 + 4x_2 + 2x_3 + x_4 + x_8 = 95$$

rather than

$$3x_1 + 4x_2 + 2x_3 + x_4 + x_8 = 92$$

The Simplex routine could then be reworked. However, exactly the same row transformations as before would be used, and the new solution matrix would be identical with the previous one but for the components in the last column. In fact, there is no need to rework the solution. Let us extract the column vector x_8 from the solution matrix, and identify each row (this is done by identifying each quantity in the Q vector).

$$\begin{bmatrix} -\frac{1}{3} \\ 0 \\ -\frac{1}{3} \\ \frac{1}{3} \\ \hline 1 \end{bmatrix}$$

Snake oil surplus row.
Elixir production row.
Love potion production row.
Mother-in-law repellent production row.
Objective function row.

This column vector tells us precisely what would happen if an extra bats' wing was made available, i.e. the snake oil surplus would fall by $\frac{1}{3}$ of a fluid ounce, love potion production would decline by $\frac{1}{3}$ of a unit, and mother-in-law repellant production would increase by $\frac{1}{3}$ of a unit. Also, profit would increase by £1. In fact, for any input that has a scarcity value we can say that

Column vector × chance in availability of input = change in Q vector.

We are considering an increase of 3 bats' wings

$$\begin{bmatrix} -\frac{1}{3} \\ 0 \\ -\frac{1}{3} \\ \frac{1}{3} \\ \hline 1 \end{bmatrix} \quad [3] \quad = \quad \begin{bmatrix} -1 \\ 0 \\ -1 \\ 1 \\ \hline 3 \end{bmatrix}$$

The snake oil surplus would decline by 1 fluid oz.
The production of elixir would remain unchanged.
One love potion less would be produced.
One extra mother-in-law repellent would be produced.
Profit would rise by £3.

It would seem desirable to check that this new solution is feasible.

	Snake oil	Lizards tongues	Frogs Legs	Bats' Wings	Change in profit
Resources realeased by producing 1 unit less of love potion	1	1	2	1	-3
Resources used by 1 extra repellant	2	1	2	4	+6
Net change	-1	0	0	-3	+3

Producing one love potion less would release 1 fluid oz. of snake oil, 1 lizards tongue, 2 frogs legs and one bats wing. Producing one extra mother-in-law repellent would use 2 fluid ozs. of snake oil, 1 lizards tongue, 2 frogs legs and 4 bats wings. The change in product mix requires an extra fluid oz. of snake oil (i.e. the surplus declines by one) and 3 bats' wings extra (which we assumed were available). Also, as the profit on love potions was £3 each, and £6 each on mother-in-law repellents, the change in product mix would cause profit to rise by £3.

In the original solution, the snake oil surplus was two fluid ozs. An additional 3 bats wings would give a new product mix with a reduction in the snake oil surplus to one fluid oz. If an additional six bats wings were available, then the new product mix would give a zero snake oil surplus. If we considered any increase above six in the availability of bats wings, then the column vector would give a non-feasible solution. For example, 9 extra bats wings would give a change in snake oil surplus of $-\frac{1}{3} \times 9 = -3$, i.e. the new snake oil surplus would be $2 - 3 = -1$. But one cannot have a negative surplus! What can we conclude? Bats' wings have a scarcity value of £1 as long as we do not consider increases in the availability of greater than 6. Why? Because if we increase the availability by greater than 6, snake oil becomes scarce and cannot itself have a zero scarcity value. Can you see that the scarcity value of lizards tongues (£0.66) holds as long as supplies do not increase by more than 3? What is the maximum increase in frogs legs if their scarcity value is to remain at £0.66?

So far, we have considered increases in the availability of scarce resources, but the method holds equally well for decreases. Suppose the availability of bats wings was reduced by 36. Then the new situation would be

$$
\begin{bmatrix} -\frac{1}{3} \\ 0 \\ -\frac{1}{3} \\ \frac{1}{3} \\ 1 \end{bmatrix} \quad [-36] \quad = \quad \begin{bmatrix} 12 \\ 0 \\ 12 \\ -12 \\ -36 \end{bmatrix}
$$

The snake oil surplus would rise by 12 fluid ozs. (to 14).
Elixir production would remain unchanged (at 14).
Love potion production would rise by 12 (to 28).
Mother-in-law repellent production would fall by 12 (to zero).
Profit would fall by £36 (to £140).

Can you see that if the availability of bats wings fell by more than 36, the vector would not give a feasible solution? The scarcity value of bats wings holds as long as its availability does not decline by more than 36, nor increase by more than 6. Finding such limits is called *sensitivity analysis*. There are two simple rules for finding the sensitive limits for a scarce resource, can you find them? What are the sensitive limits for frogs legs and lizards tongues?

Accounting Losses: Opportunity Costs

It was stated earlier that the constraints in the dual problem were by nature of a 'greater than or equal to' form. The time has now come to justify this. First, let us state the dual of the witch-doctors' problem.

Minimise $A = 70V_1 + 56V_2 + 70V_3 + 92V_4$

Subject to
$$V_1 + 2V_2 + V_3 + 3V_4 \geq 4$$
$$2V_1 + V_2 + 2V_3 + 4V_4 \geq 6$$
$$2V_1 + 2V_2 + V_3 + 2V_4 \geq 4$$
$$V_1 + V_2 + 2V_3 + V_4 \geq 3$$
$$V_1 \geq 0, V_2 \geq 0, V_3 \geq 0, V_4 \geq 0$$

Now we know that to solve linear programming problems, we must change inequalities into equations, so artificial variables must be subtracted from the left hand side of each constraint. The first constraint now becomes

$$V_1 + 2V_2 + V_3 + 3V_4 - V_5 = 4$$

Suppose that when we solve this model we find that

$$V_1 + 2V_2 + V_3 + 3V_4 > 4.$$

What does this imply? *It implies that the value of scarce resources used in producing this product exceeds the profit it earns.* Surely, this indicates that the producer would be advised to employ his resources producing something else. Also, there is a second implication: the articificial variable, V_5, will be non-negative. Let us examine both of these implications more clearly.

We know that if the objective function is to be satisfied subject to the constraints, then

$$V_1 = 0. \quad V_2 = \tfrac{2}{3}. \quad V_3 = \tfrac{2}{3}. \quad V_4 = 1.$$

Now we will substitute these values in the first constraint (i.e. the one for deadly poison)

$$1 \times 0 + 2 \times \tfrac{2}{3} + \tfrac{2}{3} + 3 \times 1 = 5, \text{ hence } V_5 = 1.$$

The value of scarce resources used in the production of deadly poison exceeds the profit it can earn. We would not expect the witch-doctor to produce this product (note that the solution to the primal problem tells him not to). What meaning can we attach to the artificial variable? The value of the scarce resources used producing deadly poison exceeds the profit it can earn by £1. Hence $V_5 = 1$ is a measure of the *accounting loss* made on producing this product. In fact, each unit of deadly poison produced costs the witch-doctor £1 in lost profit, and for this reason, economists call the artificial variable the *opportunity cost* of producing the product. If the opportunity cost of producing a good is ≤ 0, then its production is worthwhile. However, if a good has an opportunity cost > 0, then the producer will switch resources away from its production.

Look again at the matrix which gives the solution to the primal problem. The first column refers to x_1, deadly poison. The value of the component in the objective function row of this column is one — the same as the opportunity cost. The column vector containing the opportunity cost demonstrates what would happen to total profit if we could reduce the production of deadly poison by one unit. It also assumes that it is possible to make fractional units of the products

$$
\begin{bmatrix} -\frac{1}{3} \\ 1 \\ -\frac{1}{3} \\ \frac{1}{3} \\ 1 \end{bmatrix}
\begin{array}{l}
\text{snake oil surplus row.} \\
\text{elixir row.} \\
\text{love potion row.} \\
\text{mother-in-law repellent row.} \\
\text{artificial variable row.}
\end{array}
$$

Thus, if it was possible to reduce the production of deadly poison by one unit, this would leave sufficient resources to produce an extra unit of elixir, and $\frac{1}{3}$ of a unit of the mother-in-law repellent, provided that love potion production was also reduced by $\frac{1}{3}$ of a unit. The surplus snake oil would be reduced by $\frac{4}{3}$ fluid ounces. We shall now check if this is feasible.

	Snake oil	Lizards tongues	Frogs legs	Bats wings
Resources released by producing:				
1 unit less of deadly poison	1	2	1	3
$\frac{1}{3}$ units less of love potion	$\frac{1}{3}$	$\frac{1}{3}$	$\frac{2}{3}$	$\frac{1}{3}$
Resources used producing:				
1 extra unit of elixir	2	2	1	2
$\frac{1}{3}$ unit extra of mother-in-law repellent	$\frac{2}{3}$	$\frac{1}{3}$	$\frac{2}{3}$	$\frac{4}{3}$
Difference	$\frac{4}{3}$	0	0	0

Thus the quantities of resources involved are feasible. Now let us check the feasibility of the profit change. The value of the artificial variable tells us that the change in production would cause profit to *increase* by £1

Profit reduction from	
one unit less of deadly poison	£4
$\frac{1}{3}$ unit less of love potion	£1
Profit increase from	
one extra elixir	£4
$\frac{1}{3}$ unit extra of mother-in-law repellent	£2
Net change	£1

The profit change is feasible.

Summary of the Pay-off of the Simplex Method

What has linear programming done for our witch-doctor? It has given him the quantities of each product that must be produced to maximise his profit. It isolates his scarce resources and gives them scarcity values. Hence, the witch-doctor can see how much more he can afford to pay for additional supplies of scarce factors. By using an appropriate column vector, he can deduce his product mix if the availability of one of his scarce factors changes. Finally, he can obtain any accounting losses on his products. For example, let us suppose that the local chief urgently requires a bottle of deadly poison (his mother-in-law is immune to the repellent). Now the accounting loss on deadly poison is £1 – if the chief's order is satisfied profit for that week would decline by £1. Hence, the price of deadly poison must be increased by £1 if profit is to be maintained. The pay-off of the Simplex Method is considerable – is it any wonder that linear programming has made such a considerable impact on industry?

A Minimising Example

We can now examine how the Simplex Method can be used to solve minimising problems. The analysis will be confined to a two dimensional problem so that the Simplex results can be compared with a graphical method. We will use the fact that by maximising a primal problem we simultaneously minimise the dual.

An oil company put additives to petrol to give improved performance and to reduce engine wear. Ideally, each 1000 gallons should contain at least 40 mgs. of additive p, 14 mgs. of additive q and 18 mgs. of additive r. The company can obtain stocks of ingredients which have the following weights of additive per litre.

Ingredient	mgs. p	mgs. q	mgs. r
y	4	2	3
x	5	1	1

Both ingredients cost £1 per litre. The company wishes to know the quantities of each ingredient which will satisfy the conditions at minimum cost i.e.

Minimise $C = y + x$

Subject to
$$4y + 5x \geq 40$$
$$2y + x \geq 14$$
$$3y + x \geq 18$$
$$y \geq 0$$
$$x \geq 0$$

(In deriving these inequalities, we have assumed that the inclusion of the additives does not affect the volume of petrol – any increase in volume would be impossible to detect.)

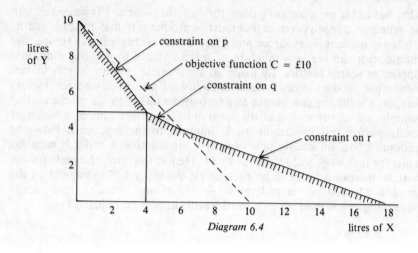

Diagram 6.4

The mapping of the inequalities and objective function is shown in diagram 6.4. We find that $y = 5$ and $x = 4$ and the cost is £9 per 1000 gallons.

Now let us solve this problem by the Simplex Method. We can solve it by considering the dual problem rather than the primal problem. We shall impute a cost V_1 to each mg. of p, V_2 to each mg. of q and V_3 to each mg. of r. Now if we add 1 litre of ingredient y to 1000 gallons of petrol, then the total imputed cost would be

$$4V_1 + 2V_2 + 3V_3$$

Now we use this ingredient solely because it contains additives. Hence, we do not wish the total imputed cost of additives in a litre of ingredient y to exceed its cost to the company. In other words

$$4V_1 + 2V_2 + 3V_3 \leq 1$$

Likewise for each litre of x

$$5V_1 + V_2 + V_3 \leq 1$$

It would be useful to compare these inequalities with those obtained in previous examples of dual problems. Previously, we were considering only scarce resources — what are we considering here? We will impute costs only to those additives that just meet the requirements. If any additive exceeds the requirements, then so much the better. We will give any such additive a zero imputed cost. This is strictly parallel to imputing values to scarce resources only.

If we add slack variables to the left hand side of the inequalities we will transform them into equations.

$$4V_1 + 2V_2 + 3V_3 + V_4 = 1$$
$$5V_1 + V_2 + V_3 + V_5 = 1$$

What meaning can we attach to the slack variables? Now we want the cost of the additives to account for the cost of the ingredient. If this is not the case the slack variable will be non-negative and will again be an accounting loss. It is the opportunity cost of using this ingredient as opposed to another.

If the requirements are to be met, then the total imputed cost of additives will be:

$$40V_1 + 14V_2 + 18V_3$$

Again, comparing with previous examples, we wish to find the very largest valuation on additives that will account for the cost of the ingredients i.e.

Maximise $40V_1 + 14V_2 + 18V_3$
Subject to $2V_1 + 2V_2 + 3V_3 \leq 1$
$\qquad\qquad 5V_1 + V_2 + V_3 \leq 1$
$\qquad\qquad V_1 \geq 0. \ V_2 \geq 0. \ V_3 \geq 0.$

Setting up the matrix in the usual fashion, and performing row transformations we have:

$$
\begin{bmatrix}
4 & 2 & 3 & 1 & 0 & \bigm| & 1 \\
5 & 1 & 1 & 0 & 1 & \bigm| & 1 \\
\hline
-40 & -14 & -18 & 0 & 0 & \bigm| & 0
\end{bmatrix}
$$

$\quad V_1 \qquad V_2 \qquad V_3 \qquad V_4 \qquad V_5 \qquad Q$
$\qquad\qquad\qquad\qquad\qquad\ \uparrow \qquad\ \uparrow$

$$
\begin{bmatrix}
0 & {}^{6}\!/_{5} & {}^{11}\!/_{5} & 1 & -{}^{4}\!/_{5} & \bigm| & {}^{1}\!/_{5} \\
1 & {}^{1}\!/_{5} & {}^{1}\!/_{5} & 0 & {}^{1}\!/_{5} & \bigm| & {}^{1}\!/_{5} \\
\hline
0 & -6 & -10 & 0 & 8 & \bigm| & 8
\end{bmatrix}
$$

$\quad V_1 \qquad V_2 \qquad V_3 \qquad V_4 \qquad V_5 \qquad Q$
$\quad \uparrow \qquad\qquad\qquad\qquad\qquad\qquad \uparrow$

$$
\begin{bmatrix}
0 & 1 & {}^{11}\!/_{6} & {}^{5}\!/_{6} & -{}^{2}\!/_{3} & \bigm| & {}^{1}\!/_{6} \\
1 & 0 & {}^{1}\!/_{60} & -{}^{1}\!/_{6} & {}^{1}\!/_{3} & \bigm| & {}^{1}\!/_{6} \\
\hline
0 & 0 & 1 & 5 & 4 & \bigm| & 9
\end{bmatrix}
$$

$\quad V_1 \qquad V_2 \qquad V_3 \qquad V_4 \qquad V_5 \qquad Q$
$\quad \uparrow \qquad\ \uparrow$

Firstly, let us read off the solution to the maximising problem. The imputed cost of the additives p and q can account entirely for the cost of the ingredients if we impute a cost of £⅙ to each. The very largest valuation on additives that will account for the cost of the ingredients is £9. By analogy with the previous analysis, the largest valuation on additives that will account for the cost of the ingredients will also be the smallest cost for which the ingredients can satisfy the requirements of additive content. Thus, we cannot obtain the desired additive content for less than £9. This agrees with the minimum cost obtained by graphical methods.

Now think back to the last dual problem we examined. The solution to the maximisation problem was given in the quantity column, and the solution to the minimising problem was given in the objective function row. Hence, the values in the V_3, V_4, and V_5 columns of the objective function row must give the solution we require. Let us examine each of these columns in turn. The V_5 column was obtained because a slack variable was added to the coefficients obtained from the quantities of y in the primal problem. Thus V_5 is related to y and we can conclude in our minimising problem $y = 5$. In the same way, we can argue that V_4 is related to x, and $x = 4$. These values agree with the graphical solution. Finally, we notice that $V_3 = 1$. Now the V_3 column was obtained from the coefficients of r, and the value gives the artificial variable subtracted from the inequality giving the desired content of r in 1000 gallons of petrol. Hence, if 5 litres of y and 4 litres of x are added to 1000 gallons of petrol,

the quantity of additive p is $4 \times 5 + 5 \times 4 = 40$ grms.
the quantity of additive q is $2 \times 5 + 4 \quad = 14$ grms.
the quantity of additive r is $3 \times 5 + 4 \quad = 19$ grms. (1 grm. in excess of requirement)
the cost is $5 + 4 = £9$, which is minimum

Appendix: The Use of a Pivot in the Simplex Method

It will be small consolation to you to be told that the linear programming problems we have considered are extremely simple compared with those met in the real world. You have probably found that row transformations are extremely tedious, and sustained arithmetic accuracy is difficult to achieve. However, the point of this chapter has not been to teach you to solve linear programming problems. It is intended to show you that many problems can be solved by such methods. If you can recognise when linear programming is appropriate and if you can interpret a solution matrix, then this chapter will have achieved its purpose. We can with relief leave the actual computation to a computer.

However, many of your will want to work through the stages of the Simplex Method, and may prefer to use a pivot rather than perform row transformations. Let us see how a pivot works.

$$\left[\begin{array}{ccccc|c} 4^* & 1 & 1 & 0 & 0 & 90 \\ 2 & 1 & 0 & 1 & 0 & 50 \\ 1 & 1 & 0 & 0 & 1 & 40 \\ \hline -4 & -3 & 0 & 0 & 0 & 0 \end{array}\right]$$

Firstly, we select the column with the largest digit preceded by a minus sign in the objective row and call this the pivot column. In this case, then, we select the first column. We divide the non-negative components in this column into the components in the quantity column thus

$90 \div 4 = 22.5$
$50 \div 2 = 25$
$40 \div 1 = 40$

The row which gives the smallest result to the division is selected as the pivot row. In this case, the first row is the pivot row. The component in the pivot row *and* pivot column is called the pivot, and this is clearly marked in the matrix by a star.

Next we divide the pivot row by the pivot, and replace the other components in the pivot column with zero. The matrix would now look like this.

1	¼	¼	0	0	22½
0					
0					
0					

We replace the remaining components like this. We imagine a rectangle with the pivot in one corner, and the component we wish to replace in the diagonally opposite corner. We then find the product of the components in the other corners, divide by the pivot, and subtract from the component we are replacing.

Thus, if we wish to replace the third component in the quantity column, the rectangle would be

4*	90
1	40

The product we derive is $1 \times 90 = 90$. Dividing by the pivot we have $90 \div 4 = 22\frac{1}{2}$. Hence, the new value of the component we are replacing is $40 - 22\frac{1}{2} = 17\frac{1}{2}$. The remaining components are treated in exactly the same way.

Exercises to Chapter Six

Use the Simplex Method in each case.

6.1 A manufacturer is prepared to allocate up to 60 hours of labour, 14 machine hours, and 36 kgs of raw materials per week for the production of two products, X and Y. Product X requires 3 hours of labour, 1 machine hour and 3 kgs of raw material, and product Y requires 5 hours of labour, 1 machine hour, and 2 kgs of raw material. The profit on X is £5 per unit and the profit on Y is £4 per unit. The manufacturer wishes to maximise his weekly profit on the production of the two products.

Find the product mix that maximises profit.

6.2 A company manufactures two types of Easter Eggs, A and B, which sell at a profit of 40p and 50p respectively. The eggs are processed through three stages of production, and the average times spent at each stage are

	Blending	Cooking	Packing
A	1 min	5 mins	3 mins
B	2 mins	4 mins	1 min

During a production run, the blending equipment is available for a maximum of 12 machine hours, the cooking equipment for a maximum of 30 machine hours, and the packing equipment for a maximum of 15 machine hours.

(i) Determine how many eggs of each type should be produced in order to maximise profit

(ii) Comment on the utilisation of resources.

6.3 An engineering firm specialises in converting standard trucks and standard vans into mobile caravans. The conversion takes place in two workshops: the assembly shop, where the structural conversion occur, and the finishing shop, where the vehicle is fitted out. At present, the firm has a weekly capacit of 180 man-days in the assembly shop and 135 man-days in the finishing shop. Each truck needs 5 man-days in the assembly shop, but each van only requires 2 man-days. Both vehicles require 3 man-days in the finishing shop. Each converted truck earns £200 profit and each converted van earns £40 profit. The firm has a contract to supply 10 converted trucks per week for export.

(a) Find the weekly output of converted trucks and vans that would maximise profit and find the maximum profit.

(b) By how much would profit increase if

(i) an extra man-day of assembly and

(ii) an extra man-day of finishing was made available?

(c) Comment on the price of converted vans.

6.4 A manufacturer of two commodities has to use three separate materials in their manufacture. The relevant input data is:

	Product		
Material	A	B	Material available
x	3	2	84 units
y	4	5	140 units
z	1	3	63 units

He makes £1 profit on a unit of A, and £2 on a unit of B. What product mix will maximise his profit?

6.5   A manufacturer of electrical equipment produces kettles and irons. The average cost of production is £12 for kettles and £8 for irons. In addition the firm faces transport costs of 40p per kettle and 60p per iron. To maintain its sales the firm has to spend 10p in advertising costs on each item sold. The retail price for kettles and irons are respectively £18 and £11.20. The firms budget allows a maximum of £4,800 on production costs, £240 on transport costs and £500 on advertising costs. Find the output that maximises profit.

6.6   A firm producing three products has a bottleneck in production at a particular point of the productive process involving two machines. It realises there is something wrong with its product mix and wishes to feed into the bottleneck that combination which utilises the available machine time to its fullest extent and is also the most profitable. The relevant data showing the time spent on the production of each product is –

	Product			Time available
	x	y	z	
Machine 1	24 mins.	60 mins.	72 mins.	240 hrs.
Machine 2	60 mins.	72 mins.	48 mins.	240 hrs.
Profit/unit	£1	£2	£2	

State the objective function and the constraints and deduce the optimum product mix. Check that capacity is fully utilised.

6.7   Space travellers colonising Mars discover that it can be made fertile by using a compost containing at least 26% phosphates and 17% nitrates. The compost comes from soils found on Saturn and Venus and is made up in bales of 100 tons by mixing these two soils with inactive soil from Mars. Soil from Saturn contains 60% phosphates and 20% nitrates and cost £8 a ton, while soil from Venus contains 20% phosphates and 40% nitrates and costs £5 per ton.

Set up the initial matrix and hence calculate the quantities of the two soils which must be mixed into each 100 tons bale so as to minimise cost of production. What is the minimum price that must be charged for the compost if the project is to break even?

6.8   A manufacturer wishes to make a certain mixture that contains not more than 5% of sulphur and at least 8% of phosphorus. He intends to mix two compounds with the following specifications

Compound	Sulphur content	Phosphorus content	Cost
A	6%	13%	£1
B	1%	4%	£2

The manufacturer has a budget of £600 to produce this mixture, and he wants to make as much as possible. Formulate an appropriate model and solve it with a matrix.

6.9 A firm makes three products *A B* and *C*. Inputs per unit are

	Machine time	Labour time	Raw materials	Profit
a.	3 hrs.	1 hr.	2 tons	£4
b.	2 hrs.	2 hrs.	1 ton	£6
c.	1 hr.	2 hrs.	3 tons	£5
Available per week	218 hrs.	134 hrs.	150 tons	

He has a contract to supply 10 units of each product per week. Derive a solution matrix which will give maximum profit.

6.10 Let us consider an extension to the tailor problem. A second tailor is producing four products, the input requirement of each being

	Labour	Material	Lining
Coats	5 hrs.	6 yds.	4 yds.
Jackets	4 hrs.	4 yds.	3 yds.
Slacks	2 hrs.	3 yds.	1 yd.
Waistcoats	2 hrs.	1 yd.	1 yd.

His labour force is sufficient to provide 750 hours per week. A wholesaler can supply him with up to 950 yds. of cloth and 560 yds. of lining per week. Labour costs 50p per hour, cloth £1 per yard and lining 25p per yard.

After carefully assessing the prices charged by competitors, he decides to publish the following trade prices.

Coats	£10.10
Jackets	£ 7.25
Slacks	£ 4.65
Waistcoats	£ 2.50

If his objective is to maximise profit, what is the objective function? A department store buying manager sees potential in the tailor's designs, and a contract is arranged to supply 30 coats, 40 jackets, 50 pairs of slacks and 10 waistcoats per week. What are the constraints on the objective function?

Find a solution matrix to satisfy the objective.

6.11 Using the solutions to the primal and dual problem, write a report to the directors of the firm in question 6.10.

6.12 Find you solution matrix for question 6.8. If your solution is correct, you will notice an amount 1600 appears in the quantity vector. What is its significance?

6.13 A farmer has two types of pig meal which he has to combine to produce a satisfactory diet for his pigs.

A kilogram of Swillo contains 32 grams of nutrient A, 4 grams of nutrient B, and 4 grams of nutrient C.

A kilogram of Fillapig contains 16 grams of nutrient A, 8 grams of nutrient B, and 20 grams of nutrient C.

The pigs require at least 12 kilograms of pig meal each day, including a minimum of 256 grams of nutrient A, 56 grams of nutrient B and 80 grams of nutrient C.

(a) Formulate a system of inequalities to represent the information above.

(b) Find the least cost combination of pig meals compatible with the food requirements if a kilogram of Swillo cost £2 and a kilogram of Fillapig costs £3.

(c) If the price of Fillapig rises to £10 per kilogram, the price of Swillo remaining constant, advise the farmer.

6.14   Suppose that ideally a batch of animal food should contain at least 270 units of vitamin A, 100 units of vitamin B and 190 units of vitamin C. The vitamin content is put into the food by adding certain additives. Additive X contains 2 units of each vitamin per gram and costs 5p per gram. Additive Y contains 3 units of vitamin A, and one unit each of vitamins B and C per gram and costs 6p. Additive Z contains 3 of vitamin A, 1 of B and 6 of C, costing 8p per gram. A manufacturer wishes to make a batch of this feed at a minimum cost, how many grams of X, Y and Z should be added?

Chapter Seven

Transportation

When considering linear programming methods, we have so far confined our attention to production problems − maximum profit product − mix, or minimum cost combination for inputs, and blending problems. The time has now come to widen the horizons of linear programming techniques, and introduce various techniques which will simplify the method under certain conditions. Firstly, let us see how linear programming can help the transport manager to solve routing problems. Suppose a firm is producing a certain product in two separate factories. Factory A produces 75 units and factory B 25 units per week. The whole output is sold to three distributors, who take 45, 35 and 20 units per week. The transport manager has calculated the unit cost of moving the output to the distributors as follows:

to distributor

	a	b	c
from factory A	£3	£4	£6
B	£1	£4	£3

Thus it costs £3 to move a unit from factory B to distributor c, £4 to move a unit from Factory A to distributor b etc.

The Simplex Form of the Transportation Problem

Let us suppose amounts X_{11} X_{12} and X_{13} are distributed from factory A to distributors a, b and c respectively. Also that amounts X_{21}, X_{22} and X_{23} are distributed from factory B to each of the three distributors. The *transportation matrix* would look like this.

to distributor

	a	b	c
from factory A	X_{11}	X_{12}	X_{13}
B	X_{21}	X_{22}	X_{23}

Notice the convenience of using suffixes to X when stating a general solution to such problems: X_{13} means the quantity in the first row, third column. Thus the first digit of the suffix locates the row, and the second locates the column.

We can now state that the quantity distributed from Factory A is

$$X_{11} + X_{12} + X_{13}$$

and as we wish the quantity distributed to be the same as the quantity produced

$$X_{11} + X_{12} + X_{13} = 75$$

Likewise, for factory B

$$X_{21} + X_{22} + X_{23} = 25$$

The quantity received by distributor 'a' is

$$X_{11} + X_{21},$$

and as we wish distributor a to receive 45 units

$$X_{11} + X_{21} = 45$$

Finally, from the restriction placed on distributors b and c

$$X_{12} + X_{22} = 35$$
$$\text{and } X_{13} + X_{23} = 20$$

To find the cost of the allocation we note that for each unit sent from factory A to warehouse 'a', a cost of £3 is incurred, so the cost of sending X_{11} units is $3X_{11}$. Using similar arguments for the other quantities, the total allocation cost is

$$3X_{11} + 4X_{12} + 6X_{13} + X_{21} + 4X_{22} + 3X_{23}$$

As the objective is to minimise cost, the problem becomes

Minimise $C = 3X_{11} + 4X_{12} + 6X_{13} + X_{21} + 4X_{22} + 3X_{23}$

Subject to

$$X_{11} + X_{12} + X_{13} = 75 \quad \quad \quad \quad \quad \quad (1)$$
$$X_{21} + X_{22} + X_{23} = 25 \quad \quad \quad \quad \quad \quad (2)$$
$$X_{11} + X_{21} = 45 \quad \quad \quad \quad \quad \quad \quad \quad \quad (3)$$
$$X_{12} + X_{22} = 35 \quad \quad \quad \quad \quad \quad \quad \quad \quad (4)$$
$$X_{13} + X_{23} = 20 \quad \quad \quad \quad \quad \quad \quad \quad \quad (5)$$

All variables ≥ 0

A First Feasible Solution: the 'Northwest Corner' Method

Of course, it would be perfectly possible to solve this problem using methods outlined in the previous chapter, but there is a better way. Firstly, we combine the transportation matrix and the cost matrix like this.

3	4	6
X_{11}	X_{12}	X_{13}
1	4	3
X_{21}	X_{22}	X_{23}

The quantities X are the amounts allocated, and the amounts in the top right-hand corner of each cell represent the allocation costs. Now all linear programming problems that we have investigated involved finding a first feasible solution, and improving on it until an optimum is reached. This method (called the Transportation Method) is no exception. A first feasible solution can be obtained by the 'Northwest Corner' method, so called because we consider the cell in the top left-hand corner first. We then make the amount allocated to this cell (X_{11}) as large as possible. Now we know that

$$X_{11} + X_{12} + X_{13} = 75 \quad \ldots \ldots \ldots \ldots \ldots \quad (1)$$
$$\text{and } X_{11} + X_{21} \qquad = 45 \quad \ldots \ldots \ldots \ldots \ldots \quad (3)$$

As all variables must be non-negative, it follows that it is equation (3) that restrict the size of X_{11} ie $X_{11} \leq 45$. Now if X_{11} is to be as large as possible, then $X_{11} = 45, X_{21} = 0$, and the restrictions now become

$$X_{12} + X_{13} = 30 \quad \ldots \ldots \ldots \ldots \quad (1)$$
$$X_{22} + X_{23} = 25 \quad \ldots \ldots \ldots \quad (2)$$
$$X_{12} + X_{22} = 35 \quad \ldots \ldots \ldots \quad (4)$$
$$X_{13} + X_{23} = 20 \quad \ldots \ldots \ldots \quad (5)$$

We now turn to the second cell in the first row, (X_{12}) and make this quantity as large as possible. From equation (1) we obtain that $X_{12} = 30$, and $X_{13} = 0$ (equation (4) does not restrict the size of X_{12}) and the restrictions now become

$$X_{22} + X_{23} = 25 \quad \ldots \ldots \ldots \ldots \quad (2)$$
$$X_{22} \qquad = 5 \quad \ldots \ldots \ldots \ldots \quad (4)$$
$$X_{23} \qquad = 20 \quad \ldots \ldots \ldots \ldots \quad (5)$$

As the three restrictions are consistent with each other, we now have a feasible solution. The matrix now looks like this

x_{11} 3	x_{12} 4	x_{13} 6
45	30	0
x_{21} 1	x_{22} 4	x_{23} 3
0	5	20

The cost of this solution is $3 \times 45 + 4 \times 30 + 4 \times 5 + 3 \times 20 = £335$.

Finding an Improved Feasible Solution

Returning to our earlier example, we know that the output can be allocated to the distributors at a cost of £335. Let us now see if it is possible to find another allocation at a lower cost. As the system now stands, factory A does not supply any units to distributor c, nor factory B to distributor a. In other words, all the cells are *occupied* except X_{13} and X_{21}. Now X_{21} is the cell with the lowest transport cost: it costs only £1 to supply distributor 'a' from factory B. It would seem sensible then, to let factory B supply distributor a.

Let us investigate the effect on cost of supplying distributor 'a' with one unit from factory B. How will this affect the solution? Cell X_{21} will now become occupied, having one unit. However, factory A will no longer supply distributor 'a' with 45 units, as this would mean that distributor 'a' would be receiving a total of 46 units – one more than he required. Hence cell X_{12} would contain 44 units. This now means that factory A now has a surplus unit, which we can distribute to cell X_{12} (notice that we do not put it in cell X_{13}, the other unoccupied cell – for the moment we are interested only in unoccupied cell X_{21}). If we remove one unit from cell X_{22}, the allocation would be feasible.

Thus we have

$X_{11} = 44$ (saving £3 in transportation costs)
$X_{21} = 1$ (costing £1 more in transportation costs)
$X_{12} = 31$ (costing £4 more in transportation costs)

and

$X_{22} = 4$ (saving £4 in transportation costs)

The net effect on cost, of allocating a unit to cell X_{21} is

$$-3 + 1 + 4 - 4 = -£2$$

i.e. such a move would save £2. We can conclude that every unit we could allocate to cell X_{21} would reduce transport costs by £2, and hence, it would pay us to move as much as possible to that cell.

How much can we allocate to cell X_{21}? For every unit that is allocated to X_{21}, we must remove a unit from both X_{11} and X_{22}. We can remove only 5 units from X_{22} − if we removed more than this we would have a negative (and hence non-feasible) solution. Hence we can move a maximum of 5 units into X_{21}. This would reduce transport costs by £10. (£2 per unit.) The solution would now look like this:

x_{11} 3 40	x_{12} 4 35	x_{13} 6 0
x_{21} 1 5	x_{22} 4 0	x_{23} 3 20

You should satisfy yourself that this solution is feasible. The cost of this allocation is $3 \times 40 + 4 \times 35 + 1 \times 5 + 3 \times 20 = $ £325. This agrees with the predicted cost reduction.

Reallocation Routes

Let us look a little more closely at the problem of allocating into a chosen unoccupied cell, because it can be tricky. Suppose the following allocation had been selected.

x_{11} 77	x_{12}	x_{13}	x_{14} 38	x_{15} +
x_{21} 9 +	x_{22} 35	x_{23}	x_{24}	x_{25} 51 −
x_{31}	x_{32} 39	x_{33} 14	x_{34}	x_{35}
x_{41}	x_{42}	x_{43} 48	x_{44}	x_{45}

Thus there are four factories supplying five distributors. Suppose it was decided that in future factory (1) should supply warehouse 5 i.e. cell X_{15}

should become occupied – how could this be achieved? If distributor 5 is to be supplied from factory 1, he must receive less from factory 2. We mark cell X_{15} with a plus sign, and X_{25}, with a minus. Now if factory (1) is to supply distributor (5) it must reduce its supply to other distributors – otherwise it will be asked to supply more than it can produce. It cannot supply less to distributor (4), as it is distributor (4)'s only supplier, and if we continue to use occupied cells only there would be no method of sympathetically increasing the amount allocated to distributor (4). Hence, it must supply less to distributor (1) and cell X_{11} is marked with a minus. Distributor (1) must now receive more from another factory, and as factory (2) now has surplus output cell X_{21} is marked with a plus. A reallocation route has now been obtained.

Using this route, we see that less is to be allocated to X_{11} and X_{25}. As negative allocations are not permitted, we can remove up to 51 units from both these cells. Thus 51 units is the most that can be allocated into X_{15}. Adding and subtracting 51 units as appropriate we obtain the new allocation. You can check the feasibility of the new solution: the row totals and column totals are the same as the initial allocation.

x_{11} 26	x_{12}	x_{13}	x_{14} 38	x_{15} 51
x_{21} 60	x_{22} 35	x_{23}	x_{24}	x_{25}
x_{31}	x_{32} 39	x_{33} 14	x_{34}	x_{35}
x_{41}	x_{42}	x_{43} 48	x_{44}	x_{45}

Let us now state the rules for finding a reallocation route.

1. Mark the unoccupied cell chosen for allocation with a plus.
2. Examine the row containing the chosen cell, and mark the other occupied cell with a minus. If there are two occupied cells, mark the one which contains another cell within its column.

3. Scan the column containing this cell, and mark the cell that contains another occupied cell within its row with a plus.

4. Continue the process until each row that contains a plus also contains a minus (and vice versa) and until the same conditions apply to columns. A unique reallocation route will then have been found.

5. The most that can be allocated into the chosen unoccupied cell is found by examining those cells containing minus signs. The smallest quantity in these cells is the most that can be moved.

Sometimes the reallocation route is quite involved. If we wanted to allocate into cell X_{45}, then the route would be

x_{11} 26 +	x_{12}	x_{13}	x_{14} 38	x_{15} 51 −
x_{21} 60 −	x_{22} 35 +	x_{23}	x_{24}	x_{25}
x_{31}	x_{32} 39 −	x_{33} 14 +	x_{34}	x_{35}
x_{41}	x_{42}	x_{43} 48 −	x_{44}	x_{45} +

A maximum of 39 units could be moved into cell X_{45}.

If we reallocate using occupied cells only (and we have seen that it is logical to do so as we are interested in one unoccupied cell only) then the Northwest Corner method gives a unique reallocation route. Sometimes it is not possible to use occupied cells only and we shall investigate this later. Finding the reallocation route is of cardinal importance in solving the transportation problem, and exercise 1 at the end of this chapter is designed to help you master the technique.

The Optimum Solution

We left our original problem looking like this:

x_{11} 3
    40
    –
	x_{12} 4
	    35
		x_{13} 6
		
		    +

x_{21} 1
    5
    +
	x_{22} 4	x_{23} 3
		    20
		    –

The 'Northwest Corners' solution was improved upon by allocating into cell X_{21} and clearing cell X_{22}. Can we get an even better solution? The only other solution possible would be to allocated into cell X_{13}. The route for this allocation is marked on the matrix, and we can see that the cost of moving on unit into cell X_{13} would be $+6 + 1 - 3 - 3 = +£1$. Thus, each unit moved into cell X_{13} would increase total cost by £1. Satisfy yourself that this is the case by moving the 5 units into X_{13}, and work out the new total cost. You will find that total cost has increased by £5. As we have now investigated all possible solutions we can see that the second solution was indeed optimal.

Let us now summarise the Transportation Method of Linear Programming. The Transportation Matrix is set up and the 'Northwest Corner' technique used to obtain a first feasible solution. A low cost unoccupied cell is chosen and a route is found for allocating into that cell. The route is costed to see whether reallocation to that cell is worthwhile. The solution is optimal when no further reallocations are worthwhile.

Shadow Costs

You are probably thinking that the method is tedious. It becomes most time consuming to examine the cost of all the alternative solutions, especially as the dimensions of the transportation matrix increase. Can you imagine trying to solve a ten factory, twenty distributor problem? We want a system that will identify immediately which of the alternative solutions will increase and which will decrease the cost of allocation.

To obtain such a system, we will return to the 'Northwest Corner' solution of our original problem:

x_{11} 3	x_{12} 4	x_{13} 6
45	30	
−	+	
x_{21} 1	x_{22} 4	x_{23} 3
	5	20
+	−	

We found that by allocating one unit to cell x_{21}, total cost would change by

$$- 3 + 4 + 1 - 4 = -£2$$

i.e. total cost would decrease by £2, so it is worthwhile moving as many units as possible into this cell. Now let us examine the change in total cost if we allocated one unit to cell x_{13}

x_{11} 3	x_{12} 4	x_{13} 6
45	30	
	−	+
x_{21} 1	x_{22} 4	x_{23} 3
	5	20
	+	−

The change in total cost is

$$+ 6 - 3 + 4 - 4 = £3.$$

As total cost would rise by £3 per unit moved, it would not be worthwhile allocating to cell x_{13}.

We will now attempt to predict these changes in total cost using a method called *fictitious costing*. Such costs have no real meaning, but they do give an efficient method of highlighting those cells that would give a reduction in total cost. We start by supposing that the allocation cost of an *occupied* cell is made up from two components − the dispatch cost incurred by the factory and the reception cost incurred by the distributor. We will enter dispatch costs at the end of each row, and reception costs at the foot of each column.

	I	II	III	Dispatch costs
A	x_{11} 3 45	x_{12} 4 30	x_{13} 6	
B	x_{21} 1	x_{22} 4 5	x_{23} 3 20	
reception costs				

Let us begin by examining the occupied cell x_{11} which has an allocation cost of £3 per unit. We know that

Dispatch cost (for factory A) + Reception cost (for Distributor I) = £3. If we know the reception cost, then we could easily obtain the dispatch cost by subtraction. We will suppose (quite arbitrarily) that Distributor I has a zero reception cost: this means that Factory A's dispatch cost is $3 - 0 = 3$.

	I	II	III	Dispatch costs
A	x_{11} 3 45	x_{12} 4 30	x_{13} 6	3
B	x_{21} 1	x_{22} 4 5	x_{23} 3 20	
reception costs	0			

We can now calculate the remaining dispatch and reception cost. Using cell x_{12}, reception cost for distributors II = $4 - 3 = 1$.

	I	II	III	Dispatch costs
A	x_{11} 3 45	x_{12} 4 30	x_{13} 6	3
B	x_{21} 1	$x_{2\,2}$ 4 5	x_{23} 3 20	
reception costs ➤	0	1		

The next cell to use is x_{22} (We cannot use x_{13} or x_{21} as they are both empty).
Dispatch cost for factory B = $4 - 1 = 3$

	I	II	III	Dispatch costs
A	x_{11} 3 45	x_{12} 4 30	x_{13} 6	3
B	x_{21} 1	$x_{2\,2}$ 4 5	x_{23} 3 20	3
reception costs ➤	0	1		

Finally, using cell x_{23}, reception cost for distributor III = $3 - 3 = 0$.

	I	II	III	Dispatch costs
A	x_{11} 3 45	x_{12} 4 30	x_{13} 6	3
B	x_{21} 1	$x_{2\,2}$ 4 5	x_{23} 3 20	3
reception costs ➤	0	1	0	

Having found all dispatch and reception costs, the next stage is to calculate *shadow* costs. For *empty* cells,

$$\text{Shadow cost} = \text{dispatch cost} + \text{reception cost}$$

For cell x_{21}, shadow cost = $3 + 0 = 3$
For cell x_{13}, shadow cost = $3 + 0 = 3$

The saving in total cost by allocating one unit into each empty cell can now be calculated by subtracting allocation cost from shadow cost. So the saving by allocating one unit to X_{21} is $3 - 1 = £2$, and the saving by allocating one unit to X_{13} is $3 - 6 = -£3$ (i.e. cost would increase). The cost change is entered in the bottom right hand corner of each empty cell

	I	II	III	Dispatch costs
A	x_{11} 3 45	x_{12} 4 30	x_{13} 6 -3	3
B	x_{21} 1 2	x_{22} 4 5	x_{23} 3 20	3
reception costs ➤	0	1	0	

What can we conclude? The cost of not using cell X_{21} is £2, so we would reduce total cost by £2 for every unit that we allocated to that cell. Likewise, the cost of not using cell X_{13} is $-£3$, so we would increase cost by £3 for every unit that we allocated to X_{13}. (Notice that this agrees precisely with our conclusions at the start of this section). *Thus we will allocate to cells where the cost of not using them is positive, and avoid those cells where the cost of not using them is negative. Also we will concern ourselves first with the cell that has the greatest positive cost of remaining unused.* The shadow cost method has the great advantage of finding such costs without the necessity of identifying all the reallocation routes first. In fact we find only one allocation route: the one for the unoccupied cells that reduces cost most. Let us now examine a matrix with greater dimensions

x_{11} 4	x_{12} 5	x_{13} 5	x_{14} 1	x_{15} 2	
90	36 −		+ 1		4
x_{21} 4	x_{22} 4	x_{23} 2	x_{24} 1	x_{25} 2	
	22 +	46 −	0		3
x_{31} 5	x_{32} 6	x_{33} 3	x_{34} 2	x_{35} 3	
		27 +	38 −		4
x_{41} 5	x_{42} 1	x_{43} 5	x_{44} 4	x_{45} 2	
13	5			22	5
0	1	−1	−2	−3	

Reception costs and dispatch costs have been calculated in the usual way, only the positive costs of not using the unoccupied cells have been entered, so that we can see at a glance the cells we should concentrate on. It is easy to decide whether such costs will be positive – if shadow cost exceeds allocation costs, then such costs will indeed be positive. The matrix shows that by allocating into either X_{14} or X_{42} we could reduce costs. It also tells us to concentrate first on X_{42}, as this give the greatest saving per unit allocated. Incidentally, the shadow cost method gives the correct cost of not allocating to an empty cell even when the route is not straight forward. The route for reallocating into X_{14} is marked on the matrix, and the change in cost per unit moved is $+1 - 2 + 3 - 2 + 4 - 5 = -£1$. Hence the cost of not using this route is £1, which agrees with the result obtained by shadow costs.

This enlarged example clearly illustrates the labour saved using the shadow cost method. The method outlined earlier would have involved finding the 12 other routes, and calculating the cost of using each!

Degeneracy

Earlier it was stated that a unique re-allocation route for each unoccupied cell could be found. In fact, this is true only if the number of occupied cells is $n + m - 1$, where n is the number of rows, and m is the number of columns. If the number of occupied cells is less than this, then it may not be possible to find a re-allocation route using occupied cells only. Moreover, it will be impossible to find all the shadow costs. Such matrices are called *degenerate*, and we require a method for dealing with them.

The advantage of the 'Northwest Corner' method is that it avoids degeneracy. Why then, you may ask, should we bother to investigate a method for dealing with it? Well the 'Northwest Corner' method is not a very efficient method of obtaining a first feasible solution – we would be nearer the optimal solution if we allocated to the low allocation cost cells first. But this system of allocation often results in a degenerate matrix. Secondly, it sometimes happens that a non-degenerate matrix goes degenerate after reallocation. Consider the following matrix.

x_{11}	x_{12}
20	30
x_{21}	x_{22}
	20

In this case, $n + m - 1 = 3$, the same as the number of occupied cells. Now suppose it was found to be worthwhile to allocate into cell X_{21}, the resultant matrix would be

x_{11}	x_{12}
	50
x_{21}	x_{22}
20	

which is degenerate.

Let us suppose we were presented with the following feasible solution to a transportation problem. We want to know whether there is a better solution.

x_{11} 1	x_{12} 2	x_{13} 3	
15		30	1
x_{21} 2	x_{22} 5	x_{23} 4	
	35		
x_{31} 1	x_{32} 3	x_{33} 2	
20			1
0		2	

We begin as usual by assigning a zero reception cost to column 1. This gives despatch costs of 1 to rows 1 and 3. Using cell X_{13}, we can obtain a reception cost of 2 for column 3. It is not possible to calculate any other costs as there are insufficient occupied cells. The way out of this problem is to treat one of the unoccupied cells as if it were occupied — which one should we choose? Obviously, we would not choose X_{33} as we already have the dispatch and reception costs relating to that cell. We would choose a cell for which we have either a dispatch cost or a reception cost but not both, and generally, it is better to choose a cell with a low allocation cost. We will treat X_{21} as though it were occupied by allocating to it a small quantity epsilon (ϵ.) Epsilon is so small that it does not affect the feasibility of the solution, nor does it affect the total cost. we can now complete the calculation of dispatch and reception costs

x_{11} 1	x_{12} 2	x_{13} 3	
15	ϵ +	30 −	1
x_{21} 2 2	x_{22} 5 35 −	x_{23} 4 + 2	4
x_{31} 1 20	x_{32} 3	x_{33} 2 1	1
0	1	2	

Allocating 30 units to X_{23} gives

x_{11} 1 15 −	x_{12} 2 $\epsilon+30$ +	x_{13} 3	1
x_{21} 2 + 2	x_{22} 5 5 −	x_{23} 4 30	4
x_{31} 1 20	x_{32} 3	x_{33} 2	1
0	1	0	

This is an optimal solution, though there is a second solution obtained by allocating ... the cost ... solution ... is zero. Note that this second optimal solution is degenerate.

Now allocating 5 units to X_{21}

x_{11} 1 10	x_{12} 2 $\epsilon+35$	x_{13} 3	1
x_{21} 2 5 +	x_{22} 5	x_{23} 4 30 −	2
x_{31} 1 20 −	x_{32} 3	x_{33} 2 + 1	1
0	1	2	

As an optimal solution has been reached this ... is the final solution for distributing the volume of ... the decrease ... by ... solution given above we

Finally, allocating 20 units to X_{33} gives

x_{11} 1
     10
−
	x_{12} 2
	   $\epsilon + 35$
		x_{13} 3
		   + 0
			1

x_{21} 2
   25
+
	x_{22} 5	x_{23} 4
		     10
		−
			2

x_{31} 1	x_{32} 3	x_{33} 2 20	0
0	1	2	

This is an optimal solution, though there is a second solution obtained by allocating to X_{13} (the cost of not using X_{13} is zero). Notice that the second optimal solution is degenerate.

x_{11} 1
     ϵ
	x_{12} 2
	   $\epsilon + 35$
		x_{13} 3
		   10
			1

x_{21} 2
   35
	x_{22} 5	x_{23} 4
		
		     0
			2

x_{31} 1	x_{32} 3	x_{33} 2 20	0
0	1	2	

As an optimal solution can be degenerate, this gives a third reason for mastering the technique of handling degeneracy. In the solutions above, we can drop the epsilon as it is so insignificantly small that it affects neither feasibility nor cost. In practice epsilon is dropped when the matrix ceases to be degenerate.

A Better Method of Obtaining a First Feasible Solution

We noted earlier that we can improve on the Northwest Corner method of finding a first feasible solution. This method involves finding the low cost cells and allocating to them first. This will give a solution nearer to the optimum. Let us examine the following example to see how the method works.

Output of four factories: 110, 80, 60 and 50 units.
Demand of five distributors: 140, 70, 40, 30 and 20 units.
Allocation costs:

	1	2	3	4	5
1	£4	£5	£5	£6	£1
2	£2	£4	£4	£3	£5
3	£3	£2	£4	£5	£5
4	£3	£5	£2	£3	£4

The transportation matrix is presented in the usual form, except for a new first row which gives distributor's demand, and a new first column which gives factory output.

	140̶ 60̶	70̶ 10̶	40̶	30̶ 20̶ 20̶			
110̶ 90̶ 30̶ 20̶	x_{11} 4 60 +	x_{12} 5 10	x_{13} 5	x_{14} 6 20 −	x_{15} 1 20		4
80̶	x_{21} 2 80 −	x_{22} 4	x_{23} 4	x_{24} 3 + 1	x_{25} 5		2
60̶	x_{31} 3	x_{32} 2 60	x_{33} 4	x_{34} 5	x_{35} 5		1
50̶ 10̶	x_{41} 3	x_{42} 5	x_{43} 2 40	x_{44} 3 10	x_{45} 4		1
	0	1	1	2	−3		

The cell with the lowest allocation cost is X_{15}, and we begin by allocating as much as possible to that cell. Now although factory (1) can supply 110 units, distributor (5) can only take 20 units, hence 20 is the most we can allocate to X_{15}. Now we will allow the first row to indicate how much is to be allocated to each distributor, and the column to indicate the amount of output undistributed. Distributor (5) has his full quota, and factory (1) has $110 - 20 = 90$ units undistributed. We show this information at the beginning of column 5 and row 1. We now examine cells with £2 allocation costs (X_{21}, X_{32}, and X_{43}). We allocate as much as possible to these cells, and adjust the row and column headings accordingly. Now we examine cells with £3 allocation costs. We cannot allocate to X_{24} (factory 2's output has all be allocated) nor X_{31} (factory 3's output has all be allocated). We can allocate to either X_{41} or X_{44}. If we do not allocate to X_{41}, then we must allocate to some other cell in row 1. Likewise, if we do not allocate to X_{44} we must allocate to some other cell in column (4). Now as the cells in column (4) have higher allocation costs than column (1), it would seem more logical to allocate to X_{44}. The allocation is now fixed and we have no further choices. The remaining 90 units produced by factory 1 must be allocated as shown. Shadow costs are calculated in the usual fashion, and the only way total cost can be reduced is to allocate into X_{24}. The reallocation route is marked, and allocating 20 units into X_{24} gives:

x_{11} 4 80	x_{12} 5 10	x_{13} 5	x_{14} 6	x_{15} 1 20	4
x_{21} 2 60	x_{22} 4	x_{23} 4	x_{24} 3 20	x_{25} 5	2
x_{31} 3	x_{32} 2 60	x_{33} 4	x_{34} 5	x_{35} 5	1
x_{41} 3	x_{42} 5	x_{43} 2 40	x_{44} 3 10	x_{45} 4	2
0	1	0	1	-3	

This is the optimum allocation.

Solution of Transportation Matrices When Supply and Demand are Not Equal

So far, we have considered examples where supply and demand are matched exactly. This situation is seldom found in practice – shortages of supply or excess capacity are most common. Consider the case where a good is a by-product of some other good – it would be almost impossible to match supply to demand. Let us see how we can deal with such situations.

Output	65,	25,	10
Demand	45,	25,	20

Thus, supply exceeds demand by 10 units. The allocation costs are

£2	£3	£4
£1	£4	£2
£5	£1	£3

We deal with this problem by supposing that the surplus output is put into store; and that the cost of moving the output into store is zero. We introduce an extra column to represent the store and assign to it zero allocation costs. The amount to be allocated to this column is ten units. Allocating according to the 'least cost cell' first method, and calculating shadow costs in the usual fashion we have:

	45̶ 2̶0̶	2̶5̶ 1̶5̶	2̶0̶	1̶0̶	
6̶5̶ 4̶5̶ 3̶0̶ 1̶0̶	x_{11} 2 20 +	x_{12} 3 15 −	x_{13} 4 20	x_{14} 0 10	2
2̶5̶	x_{21} 1 25 −	x_{22} 4	x_{23} 2 + 1	x_{24} 0 2	1
1̶0̶	x_{31} 5	x_{32} 1 10	x_{33} 3	x_{34} 0	0
	0	1	2	−2	

Suppose we had decided not to store the surplus output, but to destroy it. We could then have assigned a very high cost X to each cell of a 'disposal' column – i.e. we would have assumed the high allocation costs represent the loss of revenue. Would this have made any difference to our solution? Try it for yourself – what can you conclude?

If demand exceeds supply, then we use exactly the same method, but this time introducing a false row.

Allocating into cell X_{23} gives

x_{11} 2 40	x_{12} 3 15	x_{13} 4	x_{14} 0 10	2
x_{21} 1 5	x_{22} 4	x_{23} 2 20	x_{24} 0	1
x_{31} 5	x_{32} 1 10	x_{33} 3	x_{34} 0	0
0	1	1	−2	

– the optimum solution.

A Problem Involving Maximisation

Suppose that rather than calculating the cost of allocating the output of a given number of factories to a given number of distributors, a transport manager calculates what would be the profit earned on all the possible allocations. For example, suppose the output of three factories could be sold to four distributors at the following rates of profit

£2	£3	£4	£6
£1	£4	£3	£2
£5	£1	£3	£2

The output of the factories are 65, 25, and 10 units, and the demand of the distributors are 45, 25, 20 and 10 units. The problem is to allocate the output so as to maximise the profit.

Think back to the Simplex Method – it was used to find solutions to objective functions which are to be maximised. If we wished to minimise, we solved the dual problem. Now the transportation method is completely the reverse; if we wish to minimise we solve the primal problem, and if we wish to maximise we solve it dual. Can you remember that we find the dual by turning the primal problem 'inside out'? How can we turn the primal transportation problem inside out? We select the greatest unit profit (in this case it is £6) and subtract all the other profits from this.

$$
\begin{array}{cccc}
4 & 3 & 2 & 0 \\
5 & 2 & 3 & 4 \\
1 & 5 & 3 & 4
\end{array}
$$

Compare the two matrices carefully – the component which had the greatest value in the profit matrix has the least value in the transformed matrix. Also, the component which had the least value in the profit matrix has the greatest value in the transformed matrix. In fact, the order or magnitude of the components has been completely reversed. Now if we minimise the transportation matrix using the transformed components, surely we will be finding that allocation which *maximised* profit. Setting up this matrix in the usual fashion we have:

	~~45~~ ~~35~~	~~25~~	~~20~~	~~10~~	
~~65~~ ~~55~~ ~~35~~	x_{11} 4 35	x_{12} 3	x_{13} 2 20	x_{14} 0 10	4
~~25~~	x_{21} 5 ϵ	x_{22} 2 25	x_{23} 3	x_{24} 4	5
~~10~~	x_{31} 1 10	x_{32} 5	x_{33} 3	x_{34} 4	1
	0	−3	−2	−4	

This is the optimum allocation, and to find the total profit earned by this allocation, we must use the actual profit figures, not the transformed components i.e. $2 \times 35 + 4 \times 20 + 6 \times 10$ etc.

Other Examples of the Transportation Method

The quarterly production of a certain chemical compound is a constant 50 units, but sales vary seasonally. The estimated sales for a particular year are:

Quarter	1	2	3	4
Sales	45	65	60	30

Although output matches demand, there is a marked difference between quarterly production and quarterly sales. The product costs £100 to produce. If, in a particular quarter there is excess output, then the surplus is put into store at a cost of £5 per unit. If a unit is held in store for two quarters, then the storage cost will be £10, but in addition to this it will need filtering at a cost of £10 per unit. If a unit is held for three quarters, then in addition to the £15 storage cost, it will need distilling at a cost of £25 per unit.

The customers of the firm require that the goods be delivered on time, and impose penalties on the firm for late deliveries. If a unit is delivered one quarter late, the price is reduced by £10. If it is delivered two quarters late, the price is reduced by £15, and the price is reduced by £17 if delivery is delayed by three quarters.

Suppose we let the first suffix of X represent the quarter in which the output was produced, and the second suffix represent the quarter in which it was sold. Thus X_{23} represents any units of output that were produced in the second quarter but sold in the third. The total amount produced in the first quarter will be:

$$X_{11} + X_{12} + X_{13} + X_{14}$$

Now, as output matches demand *for the year as a whole,* if follows that the output of the first quarter must be sold at some time during the year, i.e.

$$X_{11} + X_{12} + X_{13} + X_{14} = 50$$

and using the same reasoning

$$X_{21} + X_{22} + X_{23} + X_{24} = 50$$
$$X_{31} + X_{32} + X_{33} + X_{34} = 50$$
$$X_{41} + X_{42} + X_{43} + X_{44} = 50$$

The output that is used for satisfying demand in the first quarter is

$$X_{11} + X_{21} + X_{31} + X_{41}$$

and as the first quarters' orders must be satisfied at some time during the year,

$$X_{11} + X_{21} + X_{31} + X_{41} = 45$$

Similarly

$$X_{12} + X_{22} + X_{32} + X_{42} = 65$$
$$X_{13} + X_{23} + X_{33} + X_{43} = 60$$
$$X_{14} + X_{24} + X_{34} + X_{44} = 30$$

Having obtained the restriction equations, let us find the objective function. Now if both digits in the suffix are the same then this shows that the output was sold in the same quarter that it was produced. The only costs incurred in this case are the production costs of £100 per unit. Thus part of the objective function is

$$100X_{11} + 100X_{22} + 100X_{33} + 100X_{44}$$

If the second suffix of X is one greater than the first then the output of a particular quarter is stored at a cost of £5 i.e.

$$105X_{12} + 105X_{23} + 150X_{34}$$

and using similar arguments, we can obtain

$$120X_{13} + 120X_{24}$$
$$\text{and } 140X_{14}$$

If the second suffix of X is one less than the first, then demand in a particular quarter is satisfied from the next quarters output. This involves a price penalty of £10 per unit or, which is the same thing, costs could be fixed at £110. Thus we have

$$110X_{21} + 110X_{32} + 110X_{43}$$

and again using similar arguments, we can obtain

$$115X_{31} + 115X_{42}$$
$$\text{and } 117X_{41}$$

Solving this problem is the same as

Minimise $C = 100X_{11} + 100X_{22} + 100X_{33} + 100X_{44} + 105X_{12}$
$\qquad\qquad + 105X_{23} + 105X_{34} + 120X_{13} + 120X_{24} + 140X_{14}$
$\qquad\qquad + 110X_{21} + 110X_{32} + 110X_{43} + 115X_{31} + 115X_{42}$
$\qquad\qquad + 117X_{41}$

Subject to the above restrictions. Allocating according to the transportation method, we have:

	~~45~~	~~65~~ ~~15~~ ~~10~~	~~60~~ ~~10~~	~~30~~	
~~50~~ ~~5~~	x_{11} 100 45	x_{12} 105 5	x_{13} 120	x_{14} 140	100
~~50~~	x_{21} 110	x_{22} 100 50	x_{23} 105	x_{24} 120	95
~~50~~	x_{31} 115	x_{32} 110	x_{33} 100 50	x_{34} 105	100
~~50~~ ~~20~~ ~~10~~	x_{41} 117	x_{42} 115 10	x_{43} 110 10	x_{44} 100 30	110
	0	5	0	− 10	

This is the least − cost allocation.

Exercises to Chapter 7

7.1   Suppose an initial allocation is as follows:

x_{11} 77	x_{12}	x_{13}	x_{14} 38	x_{15}
x_{21} 9	x_{22} 35	x_{23}	x_{24}	x_{25} 51
x_{31}	x_{32} 39	x_{33} 14	x_{34}	x_{35}
x_{41}	x_{42}	x_{43} 48	x_{44}	x_{45}

Reallocate to the following cells, performing each operation successively i.e. work reallocation (2) on the matrix resulting from reallocation (1)

(1) X_{42}, (2) X_{41}, (3) X_{23}, (4) X_{32}, (5) X_{35}, (6) X_{34},
(7) X_{43}, (8) X_{41}, (9) X_{15}, (10) X_{22}, (11) X_{43}, (12) X_{34}.

Your final matrix should be:

x_{11} 86	x_{12}	x_{13}	x_{14} 29	x_{15}
x_{21}	x_{22} 30	x_{23} 14	x_{24}	x_{75} 51
x_{31}	x_{32} 44	x_{33}	x_{34} 9	x_{35}
x_{41}	x_{42}	x_{43} 48	x_{44}	x_{45}

7.2   The weekly output of three factories is:

Factory   A   B   C
        139   74   32

The weekly demand from 5 distributors is:

Distributor	a	b	c	d	e
Demand	75	65	55	40	10

and the unit allocation costs are

	a	b	c	d	e
A	£2	£3	£5	£6	£7
B	£3	£6	£5	£2	£1
C	£1	£7	£5	£3	£2

Allocate the output of the factories to the distributors at minimum cost.

7.3   A firm produces a certain product at three factories, and sells the output to four distributors. Output and demand are

Factory	A	B	C
Output (weekly)	65	25	10

Distributor	a	b	c	d
Demand (weekly)	45	25	20	10

The costs of distribution are

	a	b	c	d
A	£2	£3	£4	£6
B	£1	£4	£3	£2
C	£5	£1	£3	£2

If the objective is to minimise cost, form the linear programming model of the problem. Find the least cost of allocation.

7.4   A firm makes a product in five different factories, the weekly output from each being:

Factory	A	B	C	D	E	
	71	26	50	133	76	units

The output is sold to five distributors, with the following weekly demands.

Distributor	a	b	c	d	e
	110	38	52	130	26

The distribution costs per unit (£) are

Distributor	a	b	c	d	e
Factory					
A	7	5	9	4	17
B	12	13	9	10	6
C	4	5	6	5	6
D	6	6	3	5	8
E	4	5	5	7	9

If the objective is to minimise cost, find the objective function and restrictions.

7.5   Under what circumstances can the Transportation Method be used to solve linear programming problems? (Hint: carefully examine the restriction equations in exercise 4).

7,6   Find the least cost allocation for exercise 4. What is the cost of this allocation?

7.7   Suppose an oil company has its refineries sited at Southampton, the Thames estuary, Merseyside and Milford Haven. One of the by-products of refining oil is phenol, which is used by five divisions of the company: Plastics Division of Birmingham, Paints Division of Manchester, Fibres Division of Leeds, Adhesives Division at Bristol, and Drugs Division at Nottingham. The company has its own fleet of vehicles, and it has been calculated that the cost of transporting phenol is 1p per unit per mile. Other relevant information is as follows

Phenol Production	
Southampton	115,000 units
Thames Estuary	95,000 units
Merseyside	53,000 units
Milford Haven	48,000 units
	311,000 units

Phenol Consumption	
Plastics Division	86,000 units
Paints Division	74,000 units
Fibres Division	62,000 units
Adhesives Division	38,000 units
Drugs Division	51,000 units
	311,000 units

Road Distances

	Birmingham	Manchester	Leeds	Bristol	Nottingham
Southampton	128	206	224	75	158
Thames Estuary	110	184	190	116	122
Merseyside	90	35	73	160	97
Milford Haven	167	208	248	146	216

The problem is to allocate phenol to the divisions at minimum cost.

7.8 The Thames refinery is put out of action by a strike, and it is decided to buy phenol from abroad. Assuming it costs more to import phenol than to produce it, find the optimum allocation.

7.9 Find the optimum allocation assuming that Drugs Division is closed, but the Thames refinery strike is over.

7.10 Test whether the following degenerate matrix is optimal (objective is least cost allocation)

	30	20	10	5
35	1 30	1 5	3	4
25	6	3 15	4 10	2
5	3	2	4	5 5

7.11 Assume that the costs in exercise 3 are in fact profits. Find the optimal allocation.

7.12 Assume that the costs in exercise 4 are in fact profits. Find the optimal allocation.

7.13 A manufacturer wishes to make shirts from a large consignment of cloth. He can offer two types of shirt: semi-fitted and fully fitted in four colours: red, blue, green and yellow. He has sufficient dye to product 55 red, 40 blue, 30 green and 20 yellow. His salesman thinks he can sell 85 semi-fitted and 60 fully-fitted shirts of this type. The rate of profit per shirt varies because of differing production costs and differing levels of demand, and the relevant profit figures are:

	Red	Blue	Green	Yellow
Semi-fitted	10p	30p	20p	40p
Fully-fitted	20p	40p	20p	50p

How many shirts of each type should be made to maximise profit?

7.14 A vehicle manufacturer has divided production in the body shop to 45% saloons, 45% vans and 10% convertibles. Each vehicle is capable of taking three different engines − 1000 cc., 1250 cc. and 1500 cc. The sales manager supplies suitable selling prices, and the accountant calculates the profit per vehicle to be as follows

	1000 cc.	1250 cc.	1500 cc.
Saloon	£100	£115	£130
Van	£160	£170	£180
Convertible	£60	£75	£90

If 70% of engines produced at 1000 cc., 10% are 1250 cc. and 20% are 1500 cc., decide which engine should be fitted into which vehicle, and find the proportion of output for each variant. What is the total profit per 100 vehicles sold?

7.15 Suppose that in the last example worked in the text, the estimated demand for the year was

Quarter	1	2	3	4
Quantity	55	65	59	40

Demand exceeds supply by 19 units. In order to keep the customers satisfied, the buying manager is instructed to buy the extra 19 units from an outside firm. He contacts four firms, who quote the following terms:

When goods can be supplied	Price
1st quarter	£140
2nd quarter	£135
3rd quarter	£130
4th quarter	£125

Find the least cost allocation.

Chapter Eight

Assignment and Sequencing

A recruitment officer has five different vacancies to fill, and five men available to fill them. He devises an aptitude test for each vacancy, and administers each test to the applicants. Assessment is on a ten point scale, and a low mark indicates a high aptitude. Thus a score of one would mean the candidate is highly suitable, and a score of ten would indicate that the candidate was most unsuitable. The candidates were assessed as follows:

		Vacancy				
		I	II	III	IV	V
	A	8	7	8	4	1
	B	3	6	2	3	4
Man	C	7	2	1	2	3
	D	4	6	5	5	2
	E	8	8	5	7	1

The objective of the recruitment officer is to allocate men to the tasks in such a fashion that their effectiveness is maximised. It would be possible to solve this problem using the transportation method. If we define x_{ij} as meaning that man i does job j, then clearly either $x_{ij} = 1$ (he does the job) or $x_{ij} = 0$ (someone else does the job). A feasible solution might look like this:

8	7	8	4	1
				1
3	6	2	3	4
		1		
7	2	1	2	3
1				
4	6	5	5	2
	1			
8	8	5	7	1
			1	

The problem is − how will we test this allocation to ensure it is optimal? We could use the method of the last chapter and find dispatch and reception costs, we would need $5 + 5 − 1 = 9$ occupied cells so we would have to allocate epsilon to 4 empty cells. Fortunately, there is a better method of solving such problems.

The Hungarian Method

		Vacancy					row
		I	II	III	IV	V	minima
	A	8	7	8	4	1	1
	B	3	6	2	3	4	2
Man	C	7	2	1	2	3	1
	D	4	6	5	5	2	2
	E	8	8	5	7	1	1

We can deduce from the matrix that man A is best employed at job V, man B is best employed at job III etc. The row minima inserted at the end of the matrix gives the best rating obtained by each man. Suppose we subtract the row minima from all the scores in the corresponding row (i.e. subtract 1 from row 1, 2 from row 2, 1 from row 3 etc), then the resulting zeros would highlight the best job for each man.

		I	II	III	IV	V
	A	7	6	7	3	0
	B	1	4	0	1	2
Man	C	6	1	0	1	2
	D	2	4	3	3	0
	E	7	7	4	6	0

A glance at this matrix confirms that man A, man D and man E are all best suited to job V while man B and man C are best suited to job III. Now let us examine this matrix from the point of view of the vacancies. The column minima gives the best rating obtained at each job. i.e.

$$1 \quad 1 \quad 0 \quad 1 \quad 0$$

and if we subtract the column minima from all the elements in the corresponding columns, then the resulting zeros would again highlight areas of greatest effectiveness.

		Vacancy				
		I	II	III	IV	V
	A	6	5	7	2	0
	B	0	3	0	0	2
Man	C	5	0	0	0	2
	D	1	3	3	2	0
	E	6	6	4	5	0

We will now examine this matrix to see whether the position of the zeros would give a feasible allocation. To do this, we will copy out the matrix again, this time inserting the zeros only.

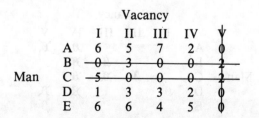

Column I contains only one zero, and so we allocate man B to job I. Now row B indicates that man B would also be efficiently employed at jobs III and IV, but as we have already allocated man B to job I, he cannot also do job III and job IV. Hence, we delete the other zeros in row B. Column II also contains one zero, so we allocate man C to job II, and remove the other two zeros from row C. Row A contains just one zero, so we allocate man A to job V and remove the other two zeros in column V. Unfortunately, we have now used all the zeros either to allocate (indicated by $\emptyset$) or we have eliminated them (indicated by $\cancel{\emptyset}$). However, we have not allocated men to jobs III and IV, so we have not reached an optimal solution. The solution suggested by the zeros is not feasible, not because it contains insufficient zeros, but because the zeros are not distributed in such a fashion to generate a feasible solution. We require a situation where we can allocate to each row and each column at least one unique zero, and the Hungarian method will test whether this is so. It involves drawing the minimum number of straight lines (either horizontally or vertically) so as to cover all the zeros in the matrix. Let us see how this is done. We scan the matrix and find the row or column that contains the most zeros. Column V, row B and row C each contain 3 zeros and we can cover all the zeros with one vertical and two horizontal lines. All of the zeros have now been covered, and it is impossible to cover them all with less than three straight lines. Now this is a five row by five column matrix, and the Hungarian method states that if the minimum number of lines necessary to cover all the zeros is five, then we will have reached a feasible solution.

Vacancy

		I	II	III	IV	V
	A	6	5	7	2	0
	B	0	3	0	0	2
Man	C	5	0	0	0	2
	D	1	3	3	2	0
	E	6	6	4	5	0

As we can cover all the zeros with three straight lines, we must introduce another zero into the matrix. To do this, we first locate the smallest uncovered element in the matrix (which in this case is one) and subtract this from all the uncovered elements. By selecting the smallest element, we have introduced the new zero in the most effective place. This new zero is our entering variable, and as we discovered when looking at the Simplex Method, an entering variable requires a sympathetic departing variable. We achieve this by adding the smallest uncovered element to any element that lies on the intersection of lines covering the zeros. Thus, we add one to the element in row B and column V, and we add one to the element in row C and column V, (Of course, if we do not have a zero at one of the intersections, then we will not have a departing variable.) The matrix now looks like this:

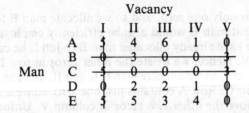

We can cover all the zeros with four lines, so we have not yet reached an optimal solution. We need to introduce another zero into the matrix, and again look for the smallest uncovered element (one). Subtracting one from all the uncovered elements and adding one to the elements at the intersections of the lines gives the next new matrix.

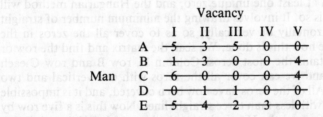

It is impossible to cover all the zeros in the matrix with less than five straight lines, so the position of the zeros indicates the optimum solution.

Vacancy

	I	II	III	IV	V
A				∅	⊗
B			∅	⊗	
Man C		∅	⊗	⊗	
D	∅			⊗	⊗
E					∅

Column (I) contains only one zero, so man D is allocated to job I. Now row D indicates that man D could also fill jobs IV and V, but he cannot do this as we have already allocated him to job I. Hence, we delete the other two zeros in row D as they cannot for part of a feasible solution. Column (II) also contains one zero, so we allocate man C to job II, and eliminate the other two zeros in row C. Now column (III) has one zero, so we allocate man B to task III, and delete the other zero in row B. Column (IV) contains one zero so we allocate man A to job IV and delete the other zero in row A. Allocating man E to job V completes the solution. The men have now been allocated to the jobs in the most effective manner.

Summary of the Hungarian method

Let us now summarise the Hungarian method with a series of simple rules that you can apply to obtain the optimum allocation.

Step 1. Find the smallest element in each row and subtract it from all the elements in that row.

Step 2. Find the smallest element in each column and subtract if from all the elements in that column.

Step 3. Draw the minimum number of horizontal and vertical lines so as to cover all of the zeros. If the number of lines you have drawn is the same as the dimension of the matrix then go to step 7.

Step 4. Find the smallest uncovered element and subtract this number from all the uncovered elements.

Step 5. Add this number to any element at the intersection of two lines.

Step 6. Go to step 3.

Step 7. By examining the position of the zeros, extract from the matrix the optimum allocation.

Perhaps the greatest drawback of the Hungarian method is that it relies on human judgement to decide whether or not the minimum number of lines have been used to cover all the zeros. Sometimes we may think that we have used the minimum number of lines when in fact we could have used less. However, you can rest assured that if you have not used the minimum number of lines, then you will not be able to make an allocation. Consider the matrix below where it appears that five lines are necessary to cover all of the zeros.

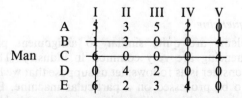

When we attempt an allocation, we find that although we can allocate men to jobs I, II, and III, we have no suggestion to make for job IV and two men available for job V!

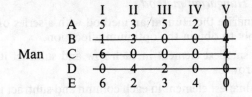

	I	II	III	IV	V
A					0
B			Ø	X	
Man C		X	X	X	
D	Ø			X	X
E					0

The matrix does not generate a solution because we could have covered all the zeros with four lines like this:

	I	II	III	IV	V
A	5	3	5	2	0̶
B	1̶	3̶	0̶	0̶	4̶
Man C	6̶	0̶	0̶	0̶	4̶
D	0̶	4̶	2̶	0̶	0̶
E	6	2	3	4	0̶

Before we leave the Hungarian Method for assignment, it should be noted that we have used the method for minimising, but we could also use it for maximising. To do this, we would find the dual of the problem in the same way as we did when discussing transportation. We would find the largest element in the matrix and subtract all other elements in the matrix from this. So to maximise this:

$$
\begin{array}{ccccc}
8 & 7 & 8 & 4 & 1 \\
3 & 6 & 2 & 3 & 4 \\
7 & 2 & 1 & 2 & 3 \\
4 & 6 & 5 & 5 & 2 \\
8 & 8 & 5 & 7 & 1 \\
\end{array}
$$

we would minimise this:

$$
\begin{array}{ccccc}
0 & 1 & 0 & 4 & 7 \\
5 & 2 & 6 & 5 & 4 \\
1 & 6 & 7 & 6 & 5 \\
4 & 2 & 3 & 3 & 6 \\
0 & 0 & 3 & 1 & 7 \\
\end{array}
$$

A problem of sequencing

Sequencing problems are quite similar to assignment problems, and examples of sequencing are very common in industry. The sequencing problem we will consider is as follows: let us suppose that we have a number of jobs waiting to be processed on a particular machine. Before we can process any job the machine will need preparing, and the cost of this preparation is called the setup cost. Now the setup cost will depend partly on the job itself, and partly on the job previously processed. In many cases, the jobs being processed are so similar that the machinery will require little alteration as we move from job to job, but in some cases, the jobs will be rather dissimilar, and setting up for the next job will be rather complex. The sequencing problem is to decide on the ordering of jobs through the machine in order to minimise the total setup cost.

Let us suppose that we have five jobs to process through a machine and the setup costs involved in moving from job to job are as follows (all costs are in £).

		To				
		A	B	C	D	E
	A	–	8	9	12	5
	B	13	–	6	18	2
From	C	4	15	–	17	3
	D	12	10	4	–	11
	E	18	20	6	11	–

We have a choice of any of the five jobs to be the first in the sequence. However, when we have chosen the first job, there will only be four jobs left to be second in the sequence. Likewise, having chosen the first and second jobs, there will only be three jobs left to be third in the sequence. Arguing in this manner, we can deduce that there are $5 \times 4 \times 3 \times 2 \times 1 = 120$ possible sequences. However, the choice of the first job is quite arbitrary (we will process A first), and this reduces the number of sequences to $120/5 = 24$.

In this case, it would be quite possible to examine all of the sequences and select the sequence with the lowest total setup cost, and the most efficient way to do this is to draw a tree diagram. Examining diagram 8.1 we can see that the optimal sequence is **A,B,E,D,C,A**, and that this sequence would involve a total setup cost of £29.

In this case, it is not difficult to examine all the sequences using a tree diagram, but if we introduce one more job then the number of possible sequences would increase from 24 to 120! We cannot be expected to draw the tree diagram for 120 sequences, so we need some other method of determining the optimum sequence.

Branch and Bounds Method

We will start in a similar fashion to the assignment method. Firstly, we find the row minima and subtract them from all the scores in the corresponding row

		To					Row
		A	B	C	D	E	Minima
	A	–	8	9	12	5	5
	B	13	–	6	18	2	2
From	C	4	15	–	17	3	3
	D	12	10	4	–	11	4
	E	18	20	6	11	–	6

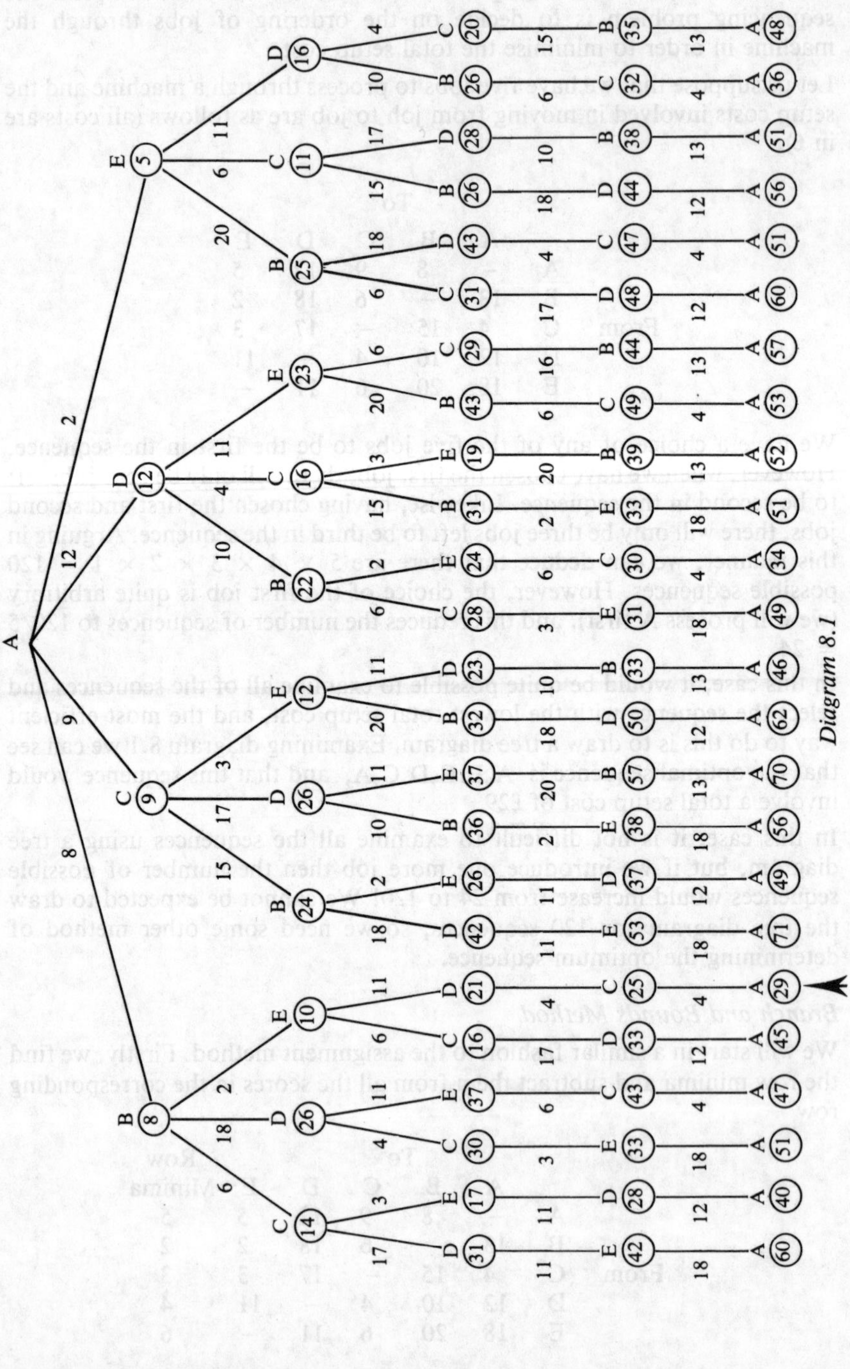

Diagram 8.1

		To			
	A	B	C	D	E
A	–	3	4	7	0
B	11	–	4	16	0
From C	1	12	–	14	0
D	8	6	0	–	7
E	12	14	0	5	–

The sum of the row minima is $5 + 2 + 3 + 4 + 6 = 20$. The column minima are

$$1 \quad 3 \quad 0 \quad 5 \quad 0$$

and subtracting the column minima from corresponding columns gives

		To			
	A	B	C	D	E
A	–	0	4	2	0
B	10	–	4	11	0
From C	0	9	–	9	0
D	7	3	0	–	7
E	11	11	0	0	–

Adding the column minima to the sum of the row minima we have

$$20 + 1 + 3 + 0 + 5 + 0 = 29$$

This figure represents the so-called *lower bound* to our solution: no solution to the sequencing problem could have a set up cost less than £29. (We know from the tree diagram that this is true). Now just as the zero in the assignment method highlights the areas of greatest effectiveness, the zeros in the sequencing matrix show the cheapest way of moving from process to process. Examining the second row of the matrix, we see that it is most efficient to follow process B with process E. If we do not follow process B with process E, then the next best alternative is to follow process B with process C as the would give the smallest cost increase (£4). In other words, if process B is not followed by process E then we will earn a *penalty cost* of £4. For each row, we will find the best sequence, and the penalty cost of not following the best sequence is the cost of the next best alternative. Examining the fourth row, we see that the cost of not following process D with process C (the best alternative) is £3, the cost of following process D with process B (the next best alternative).If a row contains two zeros then there is no penalty cost; take the first row, for example. It does not matter if we follow process A with process B or with process E.

		To					Penalty
		A	B	C	D	E	Cost
	A	–	0	4	2	0	0
	B	10	–	4	11	0	4
From	C	0	9	–	9	0	0
	D	7	3	0	–	7	3
	E	11	11	0	0	–	0

In a similar fashion, we can calculate the penalty cost for each column. Take the first column, for example. We can see that the best course of action is to precede process A by process C. If we do not do this, then the next best alternative is to precede process A by process D. So the penalty cost for the first column is £7. The full set of penalty costs for this matrix is:

		To					Penalty	
		A	B	C	D	E	Cost	
	A	–	0	4	2	0	0	
	B	10	–	4	11	0	4	
From	C	0	9	–	9	0	0	Use sequence
	D	7	3	0	–	7	3	C→A
	E	11	11	0	0	–	0	
penalty cost.		7	3	0	2	0		

Examining the penalty costs, we see that the greatest penalty cost is in the first column. This means that it is most critical to move from process C to process A, and so the sequence C→A must form part of the final optimum sequence. If we go from process C to process A, then we cannot go from process C to any other process, so we remove row C from the matrix. Also, we cannot arrive at process A from any other process, so we remove column A from the matrix. Finally, if we follow process C with process A, we cannot follow process A with process C, so this option is removed from the matrix. So we reduce the matrix like this:

		To					Penalty
		A	B	C	D	E	Cost
	A	–	0	✗	2	0	0
	B	10	–	4	11	0	4
From	C	0	9	–	9	0	0
	D	–	3	0	–	7	3
	E	11	11	0	0	–	0
penalty cost.		7	3	0	2	0	

To this:

		A	B	C	D	E
	A		0		2	0
	B	10	–	4	11	0
	C					
	D		3	0	–	7
	E		11	0	0	–

We now scan the rows and columns of this matrix to ensure that each row and column contains a zero. (Each row and each column does, in fact, contain a zero. If any row or column did not contain a zero, then we would subtract the row or column minimum from the corresponding elements, and add it to the lower bound). The penalty costs are:

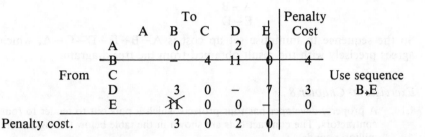

		To					Penalty Cost
		A	B	C	D	E	
	A		0		2	0	0
	B	—		4	11	0	4
From	C						Use sequence
	D		3	0	—	7	3
	E		~~11~~	0	0	—	0
Penalty cost.		3	0	2	0		B,E

The greatest penalty cost is for row B — so we see that it is most critical to follow B with process E. So we remove row B and column E from the matrix. Also, as we cannot now move from process E to process B, we remove this element from the matrix.

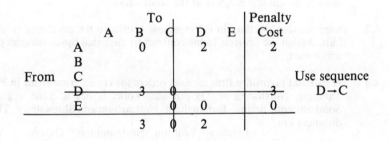

		To					Penalty Cost
		A	B	C	D	E	
	A		0		2		2
	B						
From	C						Use sequence
	D		3	0			3
	E		0	0			0
		3	0	2			D→C

Row D and column B now have the largest penalty costs and we have arbitrarily chosen row D (i.e. follow process D with process C.) So we remove row D and column C from the matrix.

		To					Penalty Cost
		A	B	C	D	E	
	A		0		2		2
	B						
From	D				0		Use sequence
	E				0		A→B
Penalty cost.					2		

152

Examining this matrix, we see that would should follow process A with process B, and process E with process D. We have now reached the optimum sequence, and summarising our results the sequences are:

$$C \rightarrow A$$
$$B \rightarrow E$$
$$D \rightarrow C$$
$$A \rightarrow B$$
$$E \rightarrow D$$

So the sequence to minimise set up cost is $A \rightarrow B \rightarrow E \rightarrow D \rightarrow C \rightarrow A$, which agrees precisely with the result obtained from the tree diagram.

Exercises to Chapter 8

8.1   A property developer has four projects which it puts out to tender to four contractors. The contract bids are shown in the table below (all figures are million pounds).

Contractor	Project			
	I	II	III	IV
A	22	38	33	19
B	26	36	42	14
C	24	42	40	20
D	38	41	37	18

Assume that the developer considers it politic to award one contract to each bidder. Assign the projects to the contractors.

8.2   Suppose that the data in 8.1 represent profits to the developer rather than bids. Assign the projects to the contractors such that the developers profit is maximised.

8.3   A national plant-hire firm receives orders for cranes from firms in Preston, Taunton, Northampton, Oxford and York. It has a crane available in Southampton, Bristol, Birmingham, Nottingham and Shrewsbury. The road distances are

	Preston	Taunton	Northampton	Oxford	York
Southampton	233	87	106	65	236
Bristol	184	43	102	69	214
Birmingham	105	130	50	64	127
Nottingham	100	180	57	94	78
Shrewsbury	82	146	93	104	130

Decide on the allocation of cranes to meet the orders.

8.4   If we use the Hungarian Method, then we will have an optimum allocation for an $N \times N$ matrix when N lines are required to cover all the zeros. Let us return to the examples worked in the text and suppose that it was decided to scrap the last two vacancies. However, five candidates are still available. We now have a 5×3 matrix, but to use the Hungarian method we need a square matrix. We can still solve the problem by introducing two imaginery vacancies and assume that each candidate has a zero rating for these vacancies. Notice that there is no point in subtracting the row minima (they are all zero), so proceed directly to the column minima and find the optimal allocation.

8.5 It is decided to train six astronauts for a flight to Mars. They all receive a general training and then receive aptitude tests for their roles on the mission. The marks awarded were

	Astronaut					
Test for	A	B	C	D	E	F
Flight Commander	21	5	21	15	15	28
Pilot	30	11	16	8	16	4
Navigator	28	2	11	16	25	25
Engineer	19	16	17	15	19	3
Back-up man	26	21	22	28	29	24
Communications	3	21	21	11	26	26

Suggest the crew composition.

8.6 Suppose it was decided to dispense with the back-up man. What should be the composition of the crew?

8.7 Suppose a cost sequencing matrix for five jobs processed through a certain machine are

		To			
		A	B	C	D	E
	A	–	10	7	5	5
	B	11	–	4	6	8
From	C	7	4	–	7	8
	D	5	5	7	–	3
	E	3	8	8	3	–

Determine the optimal sequence.

8.8 Suppose a cost sequencing matrix for four jobs processed through a certain machine are

		To			
		A	B	C	D
	A	–	100	140	200
From	B	500	–	100	130
	C	100	500	–	500
	D	200	500	100	–

Determine the optimal sequence.

8.9 Suppose a cost sequencing matrix for five jobs processed through a certain machine are

		To			
		A	B	C	D	E
	A	–	61	96	68	2
	B	78	–	15	34	16
From	C	74	96	–	57	87
	D	25	7	77	–	18
	E	52	42	60	69	–

Determine the optimal sequence.

8.10   The A.A. Handbook give the following road distances

	Norwich	Dover	Taunton	Hereford
Norwich	–			
Dover	169	–		
Taunton	262	221	–	
Hereford	204	223	95	–

Use the Branch and Bounds method to find the shortest route joining the four towns.

8.11   The A.A. Handbook gives the following road distances.

	Carlisle	Lincoln	Bristol	Cambridge	Preston
Carlisle	–				
Lincoln	180	–			
Bristol	275	166	–		
Cambridge	256	93	154		
Preston	88	123	188	200	–

Use the Branch and Bounds method to find the shortest route joining the five towns.

8.12   The A.A. Handbook gives the following road distances.

	Liverpool	Hereford	Glasgow	Leeds	Cardiff
Liverpool	–				
Hereford	116	–			
Glasgow	221	324	–		
Leeds	72	168	215	–	
Cardiff	200	58	393	236	–

Use the Branch and Bounds method to find the shortest route joining the five towns.

Chapter Nine

Matrices and Economic Models

In this chapter, we will apply our knowledge of matrices to two types of economic model. As this book is an introductory text, the models we shall examine will be essentially simple in nature, though they will increase our understanding of certain economic factors that affect all of us. The first model concerns the structure of an economy and how the component parts are inter-related. We shall see that any change in one part is bound to have repercussions on other parts of the economy. The second model examines how two economies are linked via international trade, how trading imbalances occur, and what can be done to correct them. As we work our way through these models, the power and convenience of using matrices will be well illustrated to us.

Input-Output Analysis

Within any economy, certain industries can be classified as key industries. If those industries are healthy, facing large and bouyant demands, then the economy as a whole is healthy. In most modern, industrial societies, the motor industry is indeed a key industry. Just imagine what would happen if we, as consumers, decided to reduce our demand for motor cars and use alternative forms of transport. The motor industry would soon find itself with stocks of unsold motor vehicles and would have to slim down its labour force. Of course, the effect of the reduction in demand would reach far wider than just the motor industry, as the motor industry would have to reduce its own demand for steel, tyres, power, plastic, glass, components etc.. The motor industry has a number of satelite industries serving it, and the output of these industries is directly related to the output of motor vehicles.

Input-output analysis attempts to predict how the economy would be affected if one or more sectors of the economy are subjected to changes in demand. The government publishes input-output tables, which divide the economy into a large number of sectors (e.g. agriculture, mining and quarrying, motor vehicles etc.) but we will concentrate on a two-sector economy. Also we will assume that the economy is closed i.e. it is not involved in international trade. This will considerably simplify the arithmetic involved, although the method we use could well apply to a multi-sector open economy.

An input-output matrix   (all values in £m.)

OUTPUT Sales by / Input Purchases by	Private Sector	Public Sector	Final Demand	Total
Private sector	120	10	170	300
Public sector	60	30	10	100
Value added	120	60		
Total	300	100		

The table gives input and output details for an economy with 2 sectors — the private sector and the public sector. Reading across the rows tells us how each sector disposes of its output. Examining the first row, the first figure that we meet (£120m) tells us how much the private sector sells to itself. Included in such transactions would be sales of tyres to the motor industry, sales of chemicals to drug manufactures: in fact any sales that involves a firm in the private sector selling raw materials, components or semi-finished goods to other firms in the private sector. The second figure (£10m) tells us how much the private sector sells to the public sector i.e. sales of raw materials, components and finished goods by private sector firms to Government Departments and Nationalised Industries. So, for example, sales of motor vehicles to the Ministry of Defence would fall into this category. The third figure (£170m) is in a column headed final demand and this is the value of sales by the private sector to us as private consumers. Finally, we see that the total value of private sector sales is £300m. — but beware, this is NOT the total value of output of the private sector. You should realise that included in this £300m are goods sold but destined to be resold. For example, tyre sales would be counted twice in this total; once when they are sold to vehicle producers and again when they are sold to us as consumers as part of a motor-vehicles.

Turning to the second row we see that the value of public sector sales to the private sector is £60m. Included in this figure, for example, would be the amount spent on coal, gas and electricity by private industry. The second figure (£30m) tells us how much the public sector sells to itself; sales of coal to the electricity generating authority and sales of gas to hospitals would be examples of such transactions. Finally, the value of sales by the public sector to private consumers was £10m. (included in such transactions would be hospital services, sales of fuel and power).

If we now read down the columns of the matrix, we obtain an analysis of the inputs of each sector. Consider how any firm operates: it buys inputs in the form of raw materials, power, components etc. It then processes the inputs (i.e. "adds value" to them) and sells them as output. Examining the first column we see that the private sector processed £120m worth of inputs generated within the private sector itself, and bought £60m worth of inputs from the public sector. As the total value of sales from the private sector was £300m, it follows that the value added to inputs by the private sector was £120m. Likewise, the total value added to inputs by the public sector was £60m. Consider just how a firm adds value to its inputs – it employs labour to process the inputs (to which it pays wages and salaries), it uses machinery to process the inputs (which is capital and so earns interest), and it pays a profit to itself as a reward for risk taking and organising production. It must follow, then, that the value added by a sector is the incomes earned in that sector, so in our simplified economy £120m is the total income earned in the private sector and £60m is the total income earned in the public sector.

The Technological Matrix

Let us now ask what determines the volume of inter-sector and intra-sector sales. To do this, suppose the sales of electricity increase (assuming electricity generation in undertaken within the public sector). The electricity boards must buy more inputs from private sector firms (oil for example) and also buy more from the public sector (for example, the boards will probably have to buy more coal). So the amount the public sector buys from itself, and the amount the public sector buys from the private sector are both determined by the total sales of the public sector. Generalising, the amount sector i sells to sector j is determined by the total sales of sector j. In fact, it is possible to quantify this relationship with a series of input - output - coefficients, where the coefficient describing the relationship between sector i and sector j is

$$\frac{\text{Volume of sales from sector } i \text{ to sector } j}{\text{Total volume of sales of sector } j.}$$

We would calculate the input/output coefficients for our example like this

		Sales to			
		Private Sector	Public Sector		
Sales from	Private Sector	$\frac{120}{300}$	$\frac{10}{100}$	$= \begin{pmatrix} \frac{4}{10} & \frac{1}{10} \\ \frac{2}{10} & \frac{3}{10} \end{pmatrix}$	
	Public Sector	$\frac{60}{300}$	$\frac{30}{100}$		

This matrix is called the technological matrix (T) and if V is the vector of total sales, then the matrix VT will give inter-sector and intra-sector sales, i.e.

$$VT = \begin{pmatrix} \frac{4}{10} & \frac{1}{10} \\ \frac{2}{10} & \frac{3}{10} \end{pmatrix} \begin{pmatrix} 300 \\ 100 \end{pmatrix} = \begin{pmatrix} 120 + 10 \\ 60 + 30 \end{pmatrix}$$

In fact, if we also put autonomous demand into a vector, then our input-output table can be represented as a series of matrices like this:

$$\begin{pmatrix} \frac{4}{10} & \frac{1}{10} \\ \frac{2}{10} & \frac{3}{10} \end{pmatrix} \begin{pmatrix} 300 \\ 100 \end{pmatrix} + \begin{pmatrix} 170 \\ 10 \end{pmatrix} = \begin{pmatrix} 300 \\ 100 \end{pmatrix}$$

Calling the autonomous demand vector A, then the input-output table could be represented algebraically like this:

$$TV + A = V \dots \dots \dots (1)$$

Changing the level of final demand

We will now attempt to trace the effects of a change in final demand, and in particular we will suppose that the demand for public sector goods falls to £8m.[1] The vector A will become

$$A = \begin{pmatrix} 170 \\ 8 \end{pmatrix}$$

To trace the effects of this change, we must assume that the input/output ratios remain constant (which, in the short run is not an unreasonable assumption). If, then, we assume that the matrix T remains constant, we can calculate the vector of total sales V associated with the new vector of demand A. First we must rearrange equation (1)

$$TV + A = V$$
$$A = V - TV$$
$$A = (I - T) V$$
$$V = (I - T)^{-1} A$$

$$(I - T) = \begin{pmatrix} 1 & 0 \\ 0 & 1 \end{pmatrix} - \begin{pmatrix} \frac{4}{10} & \frac{1}{10} \\ \frac{2}{10} & \frac{3}{10} \end{pmatrix} = \begin{pmatrix} \frac{6}{10} & -\frac{1}{10} \\ -\frac{2}{10} & \frac{7}{10} \end{pmatrix}$$

the determinate $|d| = (\frac{6}{10} \times \frac{7}{10}) - (-\frac{2}{10} \times -\frac{1}{10}) = \frac{4}{10}$

$$(I - T)^{-1} = \frac{10}{4} \begin{pmatrix} \frac{7}{10} & \frac{1}{10} \\ \frac{2}{10} & \frac{6}{10} \end{pmatrix} = \begin{pmatrix} \frac{7}{4} & \frac{1}{4} \\ \frac{2}{4} & \frac{6}{4} \end{pmatrix}$$

$$V = \begin{pmatrix} \frac{7}{4} & \frac{1}{4} \\ \frac{2}{4} & \frac{6}{4} \end{pmatrix} \begin{pmatrix} 170 \\ 8 \end{pmatrix} = \begin{pmatrix} 299.5 \\ 97 \end{pmatrix}$$

---

1. An example of a fall in the demand for public sector goods occured when the U.K. government introduced legislation to make the wearing of seat belts compulsory. The number of accidents requiring major surgery declined quite sharply.

Inter-sector and intra-sector sales are

$$\begin{pmatrix} \tfrac{4}{10} & \tfrac{1}{10} \\ \tfrac{2}{10} & \tfrac{3}{10} \end{pmatrix} \begin{pmatrix} 299.5 \\ 97 \end{pmatrix} = \begin{pmatrix} 119.8 + 9.7 \\ 59.9 + 29.1 \end{pmatrix}$$

The new input-output matrix looks like this

Sales by \ Purchases by	Private Sector	Public Sector	Final Demand	Total
Private Sector	119.8	9.7	170	299.5
Public Sector	59.9	29.1	8	97
Value Added	119.8	58.2		
Total	299.5	97		

Comparing this table with out original table, we see that a fall in demand for public sector goods affects both sectors of the economy. Although demand for public sector goods has fallen by £2m, the fall in the value of public sector sales is £3m. Incomes earned in the private sector fall by £0.2m, and incomes earned in the public sector fall by £1.8m. The value of private sector sales falls by £0.5m. So we can see that even if demand falls for one sector's goods only, other sectors are bound to be affected also. Our example illustrates that economies are comprised of highly interdependent units: changes in demand in one sector cannot be treated in isolation from other sectors of the economy. If the government puts a squeeze on the purchase of public sector goods and services, this is bound to reduce the output of the private sector. Now this raises a rather interesting point: it is becoming fashionable nowadays for governments to restrict public sector output in order to stimulate the private sector. Let us return again to our original input-output matrix

$$\begin{pmatrix} \tfrac{4}{10} & \tfrac{1}{10} \\ \tfrac{2}{10} & \tfrac{3}{10} \end{pmatrix} \begin{pmatrix} 300 \\ 100 \end{pmatrix} + \begin{pmatrix} 170 \\ 10 \end{pmatrix} = \begin{pmatrix} 300 \\ 100 \end{pmatrix}$$

Suppose the government decided to restrict the productive capacity of the public sector to £90m; if we assume that the total volume of private sector sales stays at £300m. then

$$\underset{T}{\begin{pmatrix} \tfrac{4}{10} & \tfrac{1}{10} \\ \tfrac{2}{10} & \tfrac{3}{10} \end{pmatrix}} \underset{V}{\begin{pmatrix} 300 \\ 90 \end{pmatrix}} + \underset{A}{\begin{pmatrix} x \\ y \end{pmatrix}} = \underset{V}{\begin{pmatrix} 300 \\ 90 \end{pmatrix}}$$

Where x is the autonomous demand for private sector output and y is the demand for public sector output. Finding the matrix TV

$$\begin{pmatrix} \frac{4}{10} & \frac{1}{10} \\ \frac{2}{10} & \frac{3}{10} \end{pmatrix} \begin{pmatrix} 300 \\ 90 \end{pmatrix} = \begin{pmatrix} 129 \\ 87 \end{pmatrix}$$

and so

$$\begin{pmatrix} x \\ y \end{pmatrix} = \begin{pmatrix} 300 \\ 90 \end{pmatrix} - \begin{pmatrix} 129 \\ 87 \end{pmatrix} = \begin{pmatrix} 171 \\ 3 \end{pmatrix}$$

In other words, to maintain the private sector value of sales at £300m, the government would have to reduce autonomous demand for public sector goods to £3m. and increase autonomous demand for private sector goods to £171m.

We could easily calculate what the effect would be if the government reduced public sector output without managing private sector autonomous demand. To support an output of £90m, the public sector would have to buy $\frac{1}{10} \times 90 = £9m$ worth of inputs from the private sector. If x is the new volume of sales of the private sector, then we can calculate x from the equation.

$$\frac{4}{10} x + 9 + 170 = x$$
$$179 = 0.6x$$
$$x = £298\tfrac{1}{3}m.$$

The public sector sales to the private sector would be $298\tfrac{1}{3} \times 0.2 = £59\tfrac{2}{3}m$, and to support a total volume of sales of £90m, the public sector would have to supply itself with $90 \times 0.3 = £27m$ of inputs. Hence the public sector could satisfy a level of autonomous demand of

$$80 - 59\tfrac{2}{3} - 27 = £3\tfrac{1}{3}m.$$

The input/output matrix would look like this:

Sales by \ Purchases by	Private Sector	Public Sector	Final Demand	Total
Private sector	$119\tfrac{1}{3}$	9	170	$298\tfrac{1}{3}$
Public sector	$59\tfrac{2}{3}$	27	$3\tfrac{1}{3}$	90
Value added	$119\tfrac{1}{3}$	54		
Total	$298\tfrac{1}{3}$	90		

So we can see that the policy of stimulating the private sector by restricting the public sector has not achieved the desired effect. The total volume of sales and incomes earned in the private sector have both fallen. If the government wishes to stimulate private sector output it must stimulate autonomous demand for private sector goods (which raises output directly) or stimulate demand for public sector goods (which raises private sector output directly).

An International Trade Model

Let us suppose that we are given the task of classifying the kind of expenditure that might be made within an economy – one type of expenditure is the amount private individuals spend on goods and services, and we will call this consumption expenditure (C). A second type of expenditure is when businessmen buy premises and machinery and we will call this investment (I). If we assume that both consumptions and investment involve buying domestically produced goods, then a third type of expenditure would be imports (M). A final classification of expenditure could be the amount spent by the government (G). We have now covered all the possibilities for national expenditure, so

$$\text{National Expenditure} = C + I + M + G$$

It is a basic truth expenditure generates income – every time a motor car is purchased, then income is generated for car dealers, car workers, steel workers, tyre producers etc. If we are examining income from a national viewpoint then consumption, investment and government spending generates income within the country. However, imports create income for foreigners and not for the importing country. Imports generate incomes abroad – it is exports (E) that generate incomes at home, so we can conclude that income earned from foreign trade is $(E - M)$. In algebraic form

$$\text{National Income (Y)} = C + I + (E - M) + G$$
$$\text{or } Y = C + I - M + E + G$$

The amount spent on consumption depends upon the level of income. The greater the level of income, the greater is the level on consumption. If c is the fraction of national income that is spent on consumption then

$$C = cY$$

Using the economist's jargon, c is called the propensity or willingness to consume. In a similar fashion we could argue that the amount imported also depends upon the level of income, and if m is the propensity to import (i.e. the fraction of income spent on imports) then

$$M = mY$$

However, the amount spent by the government and by firms on investment is not directly related to national income, but depends instead on policy decisions. If we call this type of spending autonomous spending A, then we can rewrite our expression for national income like this:

$$Y = cY - mY + E + A \dots \dots \dots (1)$$

Now suppose there are just two countries involved in trade: country i and country j. The amount country i exports to country j depends upon country j's income (Y_j) and country j's propensity to import (m_j): if E_i is country i's exports, then $E_i = m_j Y_j$. So we can formulate that for country i

$$Y_i = c_i Y_i - m_i Y_i + m_j Y_j + A_i$$
$$Y_i = (c_i - m_i)Y_i + m_j Y_j + A_i \dots \dots \dots (2)$$

and for country j,

$$Y_j = (c_j - m_j)Y_j + m_i Y_i + A_j$$
$$\text{or } Y_j = m_i Y_i + (C_j - m_j)Y_j + A_j \dots \dots \dots (3)$$

The matrix equivalent of equations (2) and (3) is

$$\begin{pmatrix} Y_i \\ Y_j \end{pmatrix} = \begin{pmatrix} (c_i - m_i) & m_j \\ m_i & (c_j - m_j) \end{pmatrix} \begin{pmatrix} Y_i \\ Y_j \end{pmatrix} + \begin{pmatrix} A_i \\ A_j \end{pmatrix}$$

$$\text{or} \qquad Y = XY + A \dots \dots \dots (4)$$

So if we know the propensities to consume and import, we can calculate the levels of income and the balance of payments (i.e. the value of exports minus imports) associated with given levels of government expenditure and given levels of investment. To do this, we will have to make Y the subject of equations (4).

$$Y - XY = A$$
$$(I - X)Y = A$$
$$Y = (I - X)^{-1} A$$

If country i has a propensity to consume of 0.8 and a propensity to import of 0.2, then $c_i = 0.8$ and $m_i = 0.2$. If country j has a propensity to consume of 0.6 and a propensity to import of 0.1 then $c_j = 0.6$ and $m_j = 0.1$. The matrix X is

$$X = \begin{pmatrix} 0.8 - 0.2 & 0.1 \\ 0.2 & 0.6 - 0.1 \end{pmatrix} = \begin{pmatrix} 0.6 & 0.1 \\ 0.2 & 0.5 \end{pmatrix}$$

$$(I - X) = \begin{pmatrix} 1 & 0 \\ 0 & 1 \end{pmatrix} - \begin{pmatrix} 0.6 & 0.1 \\ 0.2 & 0.5 \end{pmatrix} = \begin{pmatrix} 0.4 & -0.1 \\ -0.2 & 0.5 \end{pmatrix}$$

the determinate $|d| = (0.4 \times 0.5) - (-0.2 \times -0.1) = 0.18$

$$(I - X)^{-1} = \overset{\frac{1}{0.18}}{} \begin{pmatrix} 0.5 & 0.1 \\ 0.2 & 0.4 \end{pmatrix}$$

$$= \overset{\frac{50}{9}}{} \begin{pmatrix} \frac{5}{10} & \frac{1}{10} \\ \frac{2}{10} & \frac{4}{10} \end{pmatrix}$$

$$= \begin{pmatrix} \frac{25}{9} & \frac{5}{9} \\ \frac{10}{9} & \frac{20}{9} \end{pmatrix}$$

If we know that autonomous spending is £36bn. in country i and £27bn. in country j we can now calculate the national income for each country.

$$\begin{pmatrix} \frac{25}{9} & \frac{5}{9} \\ \frac{10}{9} & \frac{20}{9} \end{pmatrix} \begin{pmatrix} 36 \\ 27 \end{pmatrix} = \begin{pmatrix} 115 \\ 100 \end{pmatrix}$$

Consumption for country i is $0.8 \times 115 = £92$bn. and imports $0.2 \times 115 = £23$bn.

For country j, consumption is $0.6 \times 100 = £60$bn. and imports are $0.1 \times 100 = £10$bn. We can summarise our results in a table like this:

	Consumption	Imports	Exports	Autonomous Spending	Income
Country i.	92	23	10	36	115
Country j.	60	10	23	27	100

Notice that in each case our basic equation is satisfied, i.e.

Income = consumption − imports + exports + autonomous spending.

Notice also that country i has a balance of payments deficit and country j a balance of payments surplus of £13bn.

Correcting a balance of payments deficit

The government of country i will probably want to take some action to eliminate its balance of payments deficit, and one way of doing this would be to reduce the volume of imports while autonomous spending remains unchanged. In other words, the government of country i must take measures to reduce the propensity to import, and we shall now attempt to calculate what the propensity to import should be. Our basic equation for income was

Income = Consumption + Exports − Imports + Autonomous
          spending

  or $Y = C + E - M + A$,

Now if a country's foreign trade is in balance, exports = imports, so it would follow that for country i.

$$Yi = Ci + Ai$$

Now if autonomous spending for country i stays at £36bn, and the propensity to consume remains at 0.8, then

$$Yi = 0.8Yi + 36$$
$$0.2Yi = 36$$
$$Yi = 180.$$

So, if country i is to remove its balance of payments deficit, income must rise to £180bn.

Let us now determine what would be the effects of a balance of payments equilibrium on country j.

$$Yj = Cj + Aj$$

If country j's autonomous spending remains at £27bn, then

$$Yj = 0.6Yj + 27$$
$$0.4Yj = 27$$
$$Yj = 67.5.$$

Also, if country j's propensity to import remains at 0.1, then country j will import $67.5 \times 0.1 = £6.75$bn. from country i. We can now summarise our results in a table.

	Consumption	Imports	Exports	Autonomous Spending	Income
Country i	144	6.75	6.75	36	180
Country j	40.5	6.75	6.75	27	67.5

Country i's propensity to import is $6.75 \div 180 = 0.0375$, and if balance of payments equilibrium is to be achieved while retaining autonomous spending at £36bn, then country i must restrict imports until its propensity to import falls to 0.0375. This could be achieved by imposing import duties or import quotas. Notice that in addition to removing the balance of payments deficit, country i has also experienced a considerable increase in national income (from £115bn to £180bn.), Whereas country j has experienced a considerable fall in income (from £100bn to £67.5bn.). It can be argued with some justification that country i's problems have been 'exported' to country j: country i has solved its balance of payments problems at the expense of country j's living standards. It seems highly likely that country j will retaliate and impose import restrictions of its's own which may lead to both country suffering declines in their living standards in the long run.

An alternative method of solving the balance of payments problems would be for country i to reduce its own income as this is certain to affect the value of its imports. After all, it could be argued that by importing more than it is exporting, country i is living beyond its means. Now probably the easiest way to reduce the level of national income is for the government to reduce its own spending. Now as country i's propensity to import is 0.2, and country j's propensity to import is 0.1, it follows that for balance of payments equilibrium the national income for country j must be twice the national income for country i. Let us suppose that country j maintains its level of autonomous investment at £27bn. We can represent the equilibrium situation like this

$$\begin{pmatrix} \frac{25}{9} & \frac{5}{9} \\ \frac{10}{9} & \frac{20}{9} \end{pmatrix} \begin{pmatrix} Ai \\ 27 \end{pmatrix} = \begin{pmatrix} Y \\ 2Y \end{pmatrix}$$

Multiplying out the matrices

$$\frac{25}{9} Ai + 15 = Y \dots \dots (5)$$
$$\frac{10}{9} Ai + 60 = 2Y \dots \dots (6)$$

Multiplying equation (5) by 18 and equation (6) by 9

$$50\,Ai + 270 = 18Y$$
$$10\,Ai + 540 = 18Y$$

$$\overline{\hspace{2cm}}$$

$$40\,Ai - 270 = 0$$
$$40\,Ai = 270$$
$$Ai = 6.75$$

and using equation (5)

$$Y = \frac{25}{9} \times 6.75 + 15$$
$$Y = 33.75$$

So to achieve a balance of payments equilibrium, country i must undertake a level of autonomous investment of £6.75bn, and this will generate a level of national income of £33.75bn. Consumption in country i would be $0.8 \times 33.75 = £27$bn, and imports would be $0.2 \times 33.75 = £6.75$bn. These actions by country i cause natioanl income in country j to be $2 \times 33.75 = £67.5$bn, consumption would be $0.6 \times 67.5 = £40.5$bn and imports $0.1 \times 67.5 = £6.75$bn.

	Consumption	Imports	Exports	Autonomous Demand	Income
Country i	27	6.75	6.75	6.75	33.75
Country j	40.5	6.75	6.75	27	67.5

Country j's attempt to reduce its balance of payment deficit by reducing government spending has caused a catastrophic decline in its national income. The policy has also had an adverse effect on country j. Clearly, this method of removing an adverse balance of payment would not be acceptable: some combination of both policies (reducing autonomous spending and the propensity to import) would seem to be more desirable.

We stated in the introduction to this chapter that the models examined are essentially simple in nature, both relying heavily on certain assumptions. In the first model, we assumed that the input/output coefficients would remain unchanged, and we have assumed that both sectors were capable of adjusting their output to changes in demand. Adjusting output to a decrease in demand will present few problems, but adjusting to an increase in demand may not be so easy. If the second model, we have assumed that the propensity to consume will fall and the propensity to save rise. Also, it will be no easy task to separate the propensity to import from the propensity to consume. However, the models do give us some insight into the way major economic variables are related.

Exercises to Chapter 9

9.1   In a two-sector economy the input/output matrix for year I is given by: (all figures in $m).

Sales by \ Purchases by	Sector A	Sector B	Autonomous Demand	Total
Sector A	80	16	24	120
Sector B	30	12	6	48
Factor Incomes	10	20		
Total	120	48		

If in year II autonomous demand for sector A is $12m and for sector B is $12m, obtain an input/output matrix for year II.

9.2   The following input/output matrix refers to two industries within an economy

Sales by \ Purchases by	Industry A	Industry B	Autonomous Demand	Total
Industry A	90	300	60	450
Industry B	54	180	366	600
Value Added	306	120		
Total	450	600		

Find the new levels of total output necessary to support a level of autonomous demand of $\begin{pmatrix} 60 \\ 600 \end{pmatrix}$

9.3

Purchases by / Sales by	Sector Civil	Sector Defence	Autonomous Demand	Total
Civil Sector	600	20	280	900
Defence	0	25	75	100
Value Added	300	55		
Total	900	100		

Find the new input/output matrix if autonomous demand is $\begin{pmatrix} 240 \\ 150 \end{pmatrix}$

9.4

Purchases by / Sales by	Sector Private	Sector Public	Autonomous Demand	Total
Private Sector	200	200	200	600
Public	300	225	75	600
Value Added	100	175		
Total	600	600		

Find the new input/output matrix if autonomous demand is $\begin{pmatrix} 100 \\ 150 \end{pmatrix}$

9.5

Purchases by / Sales by	Sector 1	Sector 2	Autonomous Demand	Total
Sector 1	90	5	5	100
Sector 2	8	1	1	10
Value Added	2	4		
Total	100	10		

Find the new input/output matrix if autonomous demand is $\begin{pmatrix} 0 \\ 20 \end{pmatrix}$

9.6   Suppose we are given the following details of two counties

	Consumption	Imports	Exports	Autonomous Spending	Income
Country A	154	11.0	31.5	45.5	220
Country B	189	31.5	11.0	146.5	315

For each country find the marginal propensity to consume and the marginal propensity to import.

9.7   Suppose that autonomous spending rises to 85 in country A and 170 in country B, find the new level of income in each country. What is the balance of payments situation?

9.8   Suppose the level of autonomous spending in 9.7 is maintained. Find the marginal propensity to import for country B that would achieve a balance of payments equilibrium.

9.9   Suppose the marginal propensities in question 9.6 are maintained, and country A maintains autonomous spending at 85. What should be the level of autonomous spending for country B if balance of payments equilibrium is to be achieved.

9.10   Suppose we are given the following details of two countries

	Consumption	Imports	Exports	Autonomous Spending	Income
Country A	750	100	240	110	1000
Country B	720	240	100	620	1200

a)   For each country find the marginal propensity to consume and the marginal propensity to import.

b)   If autonomous spending rises to 152 in country A, and 646 in country B, find the new level of income in each country. What is the balance of payments situation?

9.11   Suppose the level of autonomous spending in 9.10(b) is maintained. Find the marginal propensity to import for country B that would achieve a balance of payments equilibrium.

9.12   Suppose the marginal propensities in 9.10 are maintained and autonomous spending in country A is 152. What should be the level of autonomous spending in country B if balance of payments equilibrium is to be achieved?

Chapter Ten

Probability

If you think carefully, you will realise that much of a statistician's time is spent measuring data and drawing conclusions based on his measurements. Sometimes, all the data is available to the statistician, and the measurements are bound to be accurate. In such circumstances, we can say that he has perfect knowledge of the population he is investigating. Unfortunately, this will not be the usual situation. In most cases, the statistician will not have the details he wants about the entire population, and will be unable to collect all the information he wants because of the cost and labour involved. To take an example; suppose it is required to find the average height of adult males in a particular country; it would not be possible to measure the height of every male. Instead, the statistician would have to make do with the average height of a sample. Now if he is careful about how his sample is drawn, and if the sample is not too small, then the sample average will give a good approximation to the population average. However, because the entire population has not been examined, the statistician can never be completely sure of his results, so when quoting conclusions based on sample evidence it is usual to state just how confident we are of our results.

So you will often see the estimates which are based on sample results quoted "with 95% confidence". Now what, exactly, does this statement mean? Suppose that we are selecting a sample and calculating its average in order to provide an approximation of the population average. To say we are 95% confident cannot mean that the sample we have selected has a 95% probability of being a good or a satisfactory approximation. After all, once we have selected a sample it either gives a good approximation of the population mean or it does not. No, what we mean is that if we were to select a large number of all the possible samples, 95% of them would give us a good approximation. The 95% confidence refers to the probability of our selecting a sample which does this, not the probability that a sample which has already been selected will do so. You may argue, of course, that we are splitting hairs. The difference is not so great as all that. But it is important for probability theory that you get the distinction clear in your own mind.

Some Definitions

Let us suppose that we toss a coin. This experiment can have two outcomes: the coin can land with either heads showing or tails showing. The result of such an experiment is called an *event*. Notice that in this case the events are *mutually exclusive,* that is, if a head occurs, then a tail cannot occur at the same time. Now not all events are mutually exclusive, and we must be careful to recognise when events are mutually exclusive and when they are not. Suppose, for example, we are selecting a card from a pack; and the first event is that the card is red and the second event is that the card is an ace. If we draw the ace of hearts or the ace of diamonds, then both events have occurred simultaneously. Clearly, the events are *not* mutually exclusive. Usually, we use a capital E with a suitable subscript to identify the events in an experiment. We could write the events in the coin-spinning experiment like this:

$$E_1 = \text{the coin shows a head}$$
$$E_2 = \text{the coin shows a tail}$$

Notice to that E_1 and E_2 are *collectively exhaustive:* that is, they account for all the logical possibilities (we treat with contempt the suggestion that the coin lands on its edge!).

Sometimes we will find it convenient to consider the situations when the event would not occur, and we can do this by placing a dash after the symbol for the event. So we could write

$$E_1' = \text{the coin does not show a head}$$

Can you see that in this case E_1' and E_2 are equivalent events? If the coin does not show a head then it must show a tail. We can conclude that if E_1' = E_2, then E_1 and E_2 must be both mutually exclusive and collectively exhaustive.

How we Measure Probability

Let us consider a certain experiment, and list all the possible events; that is, we will ensure that the events are collectively exhaustive. Events that are equally likely will be assigned the same 'weighting'. Suppose, for example, we again consider tossing a coin. We have

$$E_1 = \text{the coin shows a head}$$
$$E_2 = \text{the coin shows a tail}$$

If we make the assumption that the coin is unbiased, then E_1 and E_2 must be equally likely. What we will now do is to assign 'weights' to the events in proportion to the likelihood that they will occur. So we have

	Weight
E_1	1
E_2	1

Now the probability that the event E occurs is

$$P(E) = \frac{\text{Weighting for event E}}{\text{Sum of the weights}}$$

So $\qquad P(E_1) = \frac{1}{2}$ (or 0.5)

and $\qquad P(E_2) = \frac{1}{2}$

So we can see that the probability of obtaining a head with a single throw of a coin is one half. Just what do we mean by this? Well, it is obvious that we cannot demonstrate probability with a single toss of a coin. In fact, the outcome of a single toss depends on the force we exert together with the way the coin was originally facing. It has nothing to do with probability! When we state that the probability of a head is a half, we are surely making some prediction as to the proportion of heads occurring if we repeat this experiment many times. The outcome of each *individual* toss is determined by the forces mentioned earlier, but the outcome of many tosses obeys a law of 'mass behaviour', and it is this 'mass behaviour' that our probability measure is trying to predict. So when we state that the probability of a head is a half, we mean that if the coin is tossed a large number of times, then we would expect heads to occur on 50% of occasions.

Let us now see if we can restate our measure of probability. If an experiment has N *equally likely* outcomes, n of which constitute event E, then we can state that

$$P(E) = \frac{n}{N}$$

Suppose, then, we wished to find the probability of drawing an ace from a well-shuffled pack of cards. Here we have $N = 52$ (there are 52 cards in a pack, all of them having an equal chance of being drawn) and $n = 4$, so

$$P(\text{ace}) = \tfrac{4}{52} = \tfrac{1}{13}$$

Easy, isn't it?

Now suppose that $n = N$. This implies that each and every outcome must constitute event E. In other words, if we perform the experiment we are absolutely certain that event E will occur. Moreover, if $n = N$, then $P(E) = 1$, so we assign a probability measure of 1 to events that are absolutely certain to occur. If the event E cannot possibly occur, then $n = 0$ and $P(E) = 0$, so we assign a zero probability measure to events that are absolutely impossible. As absolute certainty and absolute impossibility are at opposite ends of the spectrum, we have now obtained limits to our measure of probability – $P(E)$ must lie between zero and one. We can write this statement mathematically like this:

$$0 \leq P(E) \leq 1$$

So let this be a warning to you – if you are calculating the probability of an event, and your result is either negative, or greater than one, then you have made a mistake somewhere. We, as examiners, have frequently met solutions to probability problems in the form of (say) $P(E) = 1.5$. Now not only has the candidate obviously performed the calculations incorrectly, but also he has demonstrated that he does not know that $P(E)$ cannot exceed one – you cannot be more certain than absolute certainty! So if you obtain an answer like this in an examination, and you cannot discover where you have gone wrong, please do state that your answer *is* wrong, and state *why* it is wrong!

Earlier, we stated that an experiment has N equally likely outcomes, n of which constitute event E. Hence, it must follow that $N - n$ of the outcomes would *not* constitute event E. We can now formulate that

$$P(E') = \frac{N - n}{N}$$

$$= 1 - \frac{n}{N}$$

So $\qquad P(E') = 1 - P(E)$

We have already discovered that the probability of drawing an ace from a pack of cards is $\frac{1}{13}$, so it must follow that the probability of not drawing an ace is $1 - \frac{1}{13} = \frac{12}{13}$. Later, we will find this formula extremely useful.

The Three Approaches to Probability

Well, we have now seen how to measure probability. However, we have so far been making an assumption without actually spelling it out. We have assumed that we not only know all the possible outcomes of an experiment, but also that we can weight the probability of each outcome in proportion to its likelihood. More importantly, we have assumed we can do both of these things *before the experiment is performed*. In other words, we assume a prior knowledge of the outcomes – we have been using the so-called *a priori* approach to probability. Now although it is true that in many cases we will have the necessary information to use an a priori approach (it is true, for example, when considering games of chance), there are many cases in which an a priori approach cannot be used.

Suppose we have a large case of wood screws, and we wish to find the probability that one screw chosen at random is defective. Clearly, it is possible here to define all the events (the screw is either defective or it isn't) but it is not possible to weight the events in proportion to their likelihood. The only way we can determine probability in this case is to draw a sample of N screws, and count the number of defectives (call this n). We can *estimate* the probability that a randomly chosen screw is defective is $\frac{n}{N}$. This is the so-called *empirical approach* – there is just no way of estimating the probability without drawing that sample!

An appreciation of these two approaches to probability helps to explain a problem that confuses so many students. The problem runs something like this – if I spin a penny 100 times, and on 99 occasions the coin shows heads, what is the probability that it will show heads on the next spin? Some people would argue that the outcome can be either a head or a tail, and the coin has no memory of the 100 previous tosses. So the probability that the coin will show heads on the next spin must be $\frac{1}{2}$. Others would argue that the coin is more likely to show heads than tails, and would estimate the probability of obtaining a head on the next spin to be $\frac{99}{100}$. Well, which approach is the correct one? Surprisingly, the answer is both! In the first case, we are using an a priori approach, reasoning that the experiment has produced a fluke result which does not detract from the fact that the coin is unbiassed. In the second case, we are using an empirical approach, stating that the experimental evidence indicates that the coin is biassed in favour of heads. Now ask yourself this – if you were a gambler, which approach would you prefer to use?

There is a third approach to probability that we must now examine. Suppose we wished to find the probability that a particular horse wins the Derby – clearly we cannot use an a priori approach. Nor can we use an empirical approach, as this would demand that the same race be repeated many times under identical conditions! The only way we can obtain this probability is to give a personal, 'gut feeling' of the horse's chances. This is the so-called *subjective* approach to probability, and it is the method used by bookmakers when fixing odds for a particular horse to win a race. Initially, the odds will be determined by the personal view of the bookmaker, and will be modified as the race approaches according to the collective, subjective views of the punters.

These three distinct approaches to probability raise an interesting philosophical problem. We know that $P(E)$ can never exceed one, but does $P(E) = 1$ imply absolute certainty? It all depends on the approach used. If we use an a priori approach then $P(E) = 1$ means that E *must always* occur. However, using an empirical approach $P(E) = 1$ means that E *has always* occurred – which does not imply that it *must* occur in the future. Likewise, using a subjective approach $P(E) = 1$ means that *we think that E will occur* – which again does not imply that it must occur.

Without doubt, the empirical and subjective approaches are more interesting and more useful than the a priori approach. However, in an introductory book such as this, it is preferable to concentrate our attention on a priori probability, and, unless we state to the contrary, you should assume that an a priori approach is being used.

The Laws of Probability

Let us suppose that we cast two dice, and add the scores of the dice. We could represent all the outcomes in a table like this:

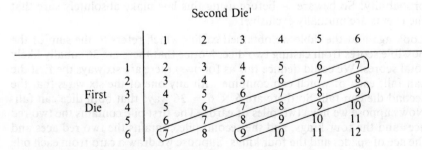

Second Die[1]

		1	2	3	4	5	6
	1	2	3	4	5	6	7
	2	3	4	5	6	7	8
First	3	4	5	6	7	8	9
Die	4	5	6	7	8	9	10
	5	6	7	8	9	10	11
	6	7	8	9	10	11	12

1. Die is the singular, and dice the plural.

The number in front of each row represents the possible scores of the first die, and the number at the head of each column represents the possible scores of the second die. The numbers in the main body of the table represent the sums of the two possible scores. So we see that if we score a total of 11, we must have thrown either a six with the first die and a five with the second, or a five with the first die and a six with the second. We see, then, that there are 36 equally likely total scores ($N = 36$). Let us now define two events.

$$E_1 = \text{the sum of the scores is 7}$$
$$E_2 = \text{the sum of the scores is 9}$$

Now there are 6 ways of scoring a total of 7, so $P(E_1) = \frac{6}{36} = \frac{1}{6}$. Again, there are 4 ways of scoring a total of 9, so $P(E_2) = \frac{4}{36} = \frac{1}{9}$. Now suppose we wished to find the probability that the sum of the scores is *either* 7 *or* 9. We can write the probability symbolically like this:

$$P(E_1 \cup E_2)$$

where $\cup$ is a shorthand way of writing 'either $-$ or'. Consulting the table, we see that there are 10 ways of obtaining a total score of either 7 or 9, so $P(E_1 \cup E_2) = \frac{10}{36} = \frac{5}{18}$. Notice that the 10 ways are obtained by adding the number of ways for E_1 and E_2. This gives us our first law of probability: the so-called addition law.

$$P(E_1 \cup E_2) = P(E_1) + P(E_2)$$

a law which is true only if E_1 and E_2 are mutually exclusive. If the events are not mutually exclusive, then using this law will not yield the correct probability. Suppose we draw a card from a pack, and E_1 is that the card is an ace. So $P(E_1) = \frac{4}{52}$. If E_2 is that the card is a heart, then $P(E_2)$ is $\frac{13}{52}$. If we want to find the probability that the card is either a heart or an ace, we notice that there are 52 equally likely outcomes, 16 of which would be either a heart or an ace (i.e. 13 hearts plus the three other aces). So the probability that the card is either a heart or an ace is $\frac{16}{52}$. Notice that if we had applied the addition law, we would have obtained $\frac{13}{52} + \frac{4}{52} = \frac{17}{52} -$ the wrong probability! So beware $-$ before using this law make absolutely sure that the events are mutually exclusive!

Look again at the table we obtained earlier which refers to the sum of the possible scores from casting two dice. Notice that there are 36 equally likely total scores. We could deduce this as follows: there are six ways the first die can fall, each of which can combine with any one of the six ways that the second die can fall. So there are $6 \times 6 = 36$ ways that both dice can fall. Now suppose we have two piles of cards. The first pile contains the two red aces and the four kings, and the second pile contains the two red aces and the ace of spades and the four kings. Suppose we draw a card from each pile $-$ as there are six cards in the first pile and seven cards in the second, there will be $6 \times 7 = 42$ ways of drawing a pair of cards, one from each pile. We could represent the situation in a table like this:

Second Card

	A♡	A◇	A♠	K♡	K◇	K♠	K♣
A♡	1	2	3	4	5	6	7
A◇	8	9	10	11	12	13	14
First K♡	15	16	17	18	19	20	21
Card K◇	22	23	24	25	26	27	28
K♠	29	30	31	32	33	34	35
K♣	36	37	38	39	40	41	42

In this table we have numbered all the possible 42 combinations of events 1, 2, 3, . . . etc., so combination 25, for example, means drawing the king of diamonds with the first card and the king of hearts with the second. Let us now define two events.

$$E_1 = \text{the first card is an ace, so } P(E_1) = \tfrac{2}{6}$$
$$E_2 = \text{the second card is an ace, so } P(E_2) = \tfrac{3}{7}$$

Suppose we wanted to find the probability that both cards were aces: We could write it symbolically like this

$$P(E_1 \cap E_2)$$

where the symbol $\cap$ is a shorthand form for 'both . . . and'. Notice that there are six ways of obtaining two aces, so $P(E_1 \cap E_2) = \tfrac{6}{42}$. Now we could have obtained this result by multiplying $P(E_1)$ and $P(E_2)$ together ($\tfrac{2}{6} \times \tfrac{3}{7} = \tfrac{6}{42}$). This gives us the second law of probability: the so-called multiplication law.

$$P(E_1 \cap E_2) = P(E_1).P(E_2)$$

a law which applies only if E_1 and E_2 are *independent* (i.e. as long as the outcomes in no way affect each other). We will discuss this point more fully later, but it is worth noting now that independent events cannot be mutually exclusive, and mutually exclusive events cannot be independent.

The second law of probability enables us to modify the first law to take account of events that are not mutually exclusive. A little earlier, we considered the case of drawing a card from a pack, calling E_1 that the event was a heart (so $P(E_1) = \tfrac{4}{52}$), and calling E_2 that the card is an ace (so $P(E_2) = \tfrac{13}{52}$). We stated that the probability that the card is either a heart or an ace $P(E_1 \cup E_2)$ is *not* $\tfrac{4}{52} + \tfrac{13}{52} = \tfrac{17}{52}$. Now why doesn't the addition law work? Surely the fault here is that the card we draw could be the ace of hearts *and we have counted this card twice* − once as a heart and once as an ace. So the probability that the card is either an ace or a heart is $\tfrac{17}{52}$ minus the probability that the card is the ace of hearts. Using the second law, the probability that the card is the ace of hearts is $P(E_1 \cap E_2) = \tfrac{4}{52} \times \tfrac{13}{52} = \tfrac{1}{52}$, so the probability that the card is either an ace or a heart is $\frac{17}{52} - \frac{1}{52} = \frac{16}{52}$ — which agrees precisely with the result we obtained from first principles. We can now restate the addition law to take account of situations when the events are not mutually exclusive:

$$P(E_1 \cup E_2) = P(E_1) + P(E_2) - P(E_1 \cap E_2)$$

This is the so-called *general law of addition,* and it works whether the events are mutually exclusive or not (if the events are mutually exclusive, then they cannot both occur, so $P(E_1 \cap E_2)$ will be zero).

Applications of the Laws of Probability
EXAMPLE 1
Two types of metal A and B, which have been treated with a special coating of paint have probabilities of $\frac{1}{4}$ and $\frac{1}{3}$ respectively of lasting four years without rusting.

If both types of metal are given the special coating on the same day, what is the probability that

(i) both last 4 years without rusting
(ii) at least one of them lasts 4 years without rusting

For part (i), we can use the multiplication law to obtain a probability of $\frac{1}{4} \times \frac{1}{3} = \frac{1}{12}$ that both last for four years. Turning to the second part, we should first notice that four distinct outcomes are possible

(a) both last 4 years   (probability is $\frac{1}{4} \times \frac{1}{3} = \frac{1}{12}$)
(b) A lasts, B doesn't   (probability is $\frac{1}{4} \times \frac{2}{3} = \frac{2}{12}$)
(c) B lasts, A doesn't   (probability is $\frac{3}{4} \times \frac{1}{3} = \frac{3}{12}$)
(d) neither lasts   (probability is $\frac{3}{4} \times \frac{2}{3} = \frac{6}{12}$)

Now any of the outcomes (a), (b) or (c) satisfies the condition that at least one lasts four years, so that probability we require is $\frac{1}{12} + \frac{2}{12} + \frac{3}{12} = \frac{6}{12} = \frac{1}{2}$ Notice that we could have calculated the probability more directly by using the fact that

$$P \text{ (at least one lasts)} = 1 - P \text{ (neither lasts)}$$

This second method can save quite a lot of time, and you should always use it in preference to writing out all the possible outcomes.

EXAMPLE 2
An item is made in three stages. At the first stage, it is formed on one of four machines, *A, B, C* or *D,* with equal probability. At the second stage it is trimmed on one of three machines, *E, F* or *G,* with equal probability. Finally, it is polished on one of two polishers, *H* and *I,* and is twice as likely to be polished on the former as this machine works twice as quickly as the other. Required:
(1) what is the probability that an item is:

(i)   polished on *H?*
(ii) trimmed on either *F* or *G?*
(iii) formed on either *A* or *B,* trimmed on *F* and polished on *H?*
(iv) either formed on *A* and polished on *I,* or formed on *B* and polished on *H?*
(v)   either formed on *A* or trimmed on *F.*

(2) Suppose that items trimmed on *E* or *Ḟ* are susceptible to a particular defect. The defect rates on these machines are 10% and 20% respectively. What is the probability that an item found to have this defect was trimmed on *F?*   (A.C.A.)

First, we shall determine the probabilities for each machine. As the formation stage is equally likely to occur on any one of the four machines, we have

$$P(A) = P(B) = P(C) = P(D) = \tfrac{1}{4}$$

Again, trimming is equally likely to occur on any one of the three machines, so

$$P(E) = P(F) = P(G) = \tfrac{1}{3}$$

Polishing is twice as likely to occur on machine *H* as machine *I,* so

$$P(H) = \tfrac{2}{3}, P(I) = \tfrac{1}{3}$$

(i)   The probability that an item is polished on $H = P(H) = \tfrac{2}{3}$.
(ii) The probability that an item is trimmed on either *F* or *G* $= P(F \cup G)$ $= P(F) + P(G) = \tfrac{2}{3}$.
(iii) Formed on either *A* or *B,* trimmed on *F* and polished on *H*

$$= P(A \cup B) \cap F \cap H$$
$$= [P(A) + P(B)].\, P(F).P(H)$$
$$= (\tfrac{1}{4} + \tfrac{1}{4}) \times \tfrac{1}{3} \times \tfrac{2}{3} = \tfrac{1}{9}$$

(iv) Either formed on *A* and polished on *I* or formed on *B* and polished on *H*

$$= P[(A \cap I) \cup (B \cap H)]$$
$$= [P(A).\, P(I)] + [P(B).P(H)]$$
$$= (\tfrac{1}{4} \times \tfrac{1}{3}) + (\tfrac{1}{4} \times \tfrac{2}{3})$$
$$= \tfrac{1}{4}$$

(v)   Either formed on *A* or trimmed on *F.* These events are *not* mutually exclusive as it is possible to form on *A and* trim on *F,* so we need the general rule of addition, i.e.

$$P(A \cup F) = P(A) + P(F) - P(A \cap F)$$
$$= \tfrac{1}{4} + \tfrac{1}{3} - (\tfrac{1}{4} \times \tfrac{1}{3}) = \tfrac{1}{2}$$

Dealing with the second part of this question, we notice that F is twice as likely to produce a defective item as is machine E. So, given that the item is defective, the probability that it was trimmed on F must be $\frac{2}{3}$.

EXAMPLE 3

In the past, two building contractors, A and B, have competed for twenty building contracts of which ten were awarded to A and six were awarded to B. The remaining four contracts were not awarded to either A or B. Three contracts for buildings of the kind in which they both specialise have been offered for tender.

Assuming that the market has not changed, find the probability that

(a) A will obtain all three contracts;
(b) B will obtain at least one contract;
(c) Two contracts will not be awarded to either A or B;
(d) A will be awarded the first contract, B the second, and A will be awarded the third contract. (I.C.M.A.)

The probability that A gets the contract $P(A) = \frac{10}{20} = \frac{1}{2}$, the probability that B gets the contract is $P(B) = \frac{6}{20} = \frac{3}{10}$, and the probability that neither A nor B gets the contract is $P(A \cup B)' = \frac{4}{20} = \frac{1}{5}$.

(a) The probability that A will obtain all three contracts is $\frac{1}{2} \times \frac{1}{2} \times \frac{1}{2} = \frac{1}{8}$

(b) The probability that B will obtain at least one contract

$$= 1 - P(B \text{ obtains no contracts})$$
$$= 1 - (\tfrac{7}{10} \times \tfrac{7}{10} \times \tfrac{7}{10}) = \tfrac{657}{1000}$$

(c) The probability that a contract is awarded to A or $B = P(A \cup B) = \frac{4}{5}$. We require to know the probability that two contracts will not be awarded to either A or B: this is equivalent to finding the probability that one of the contracts is awarded to either A or B. But the contract awarded to either A or B could be either the first, second or third contract. So the probability we require is

$$\tfrac{4}{5} \times \tfrac{1}{5} \times \tfrac{1}{5} \quad (A \text{ or } B \text{ wins the first contract})$$
plus $\tfrac{1}{5} \times \tfrac{4}{5} \times \tfrac{1}{5} \quad (A \text{ or } B \text{ wins the second contract})$
plus $\tfrac{1}{5} \times \tfrac{1}{5} \times \tfrac{4}{5} \quad (A \text{ or } B \text{ wins the third contract})$
$$= 3 \times \tfrac{4}{5} \times \tfrac{1}{5} \times \tfrac{1}{5} = \tfrac{12}{125}$$

(d) The probability that A is awarded the first contract, B the second and A the third is $\frac{1}{2} \times \frac{3}{10} \times \frac{1}{2} = \frac{3}{40}$.

Tree Diagrams

One of the major problems that occur when dealing with probability is that of ensuring that all logical possibilities are considered. In fact, this is probably the most common student error when dealing with this topic. A tree diagram is a device to help us avoid such errors: it is a diagram which looks something like a tree, each branch of which represents one logical possibility. We shall illustrate tree diagrams by means of an example.

Buggsy Flynn owns 60% of protection rackets and 80% of illegal gambling in Chicago, and he is informed that the police are about to investigate both of these activities. Police records show that 70% of investigations into the protection racket and 90% of investigations into gambling lead to court action. What is the probability that Buggsy will end up in court as a result of the investigations? (You may care to attempt to solve this problem before reading on.)

This problem involves an examination of whether Buggsy is investigated and whether he is charged. We can begin the tree diagram by calculating the probability of an investigation into Buggsy's protection rackets. Since he owns only 60% of the protection in Chicago there is a 0.6 probability that the police investigation will concern him, and the position can be illustrated as:

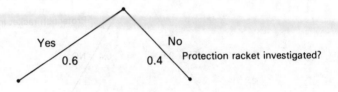

Notice that the probabilities have been inserted on to the diagram. We can now add the possibility of an investigation into illegal gambling on to the diagram.

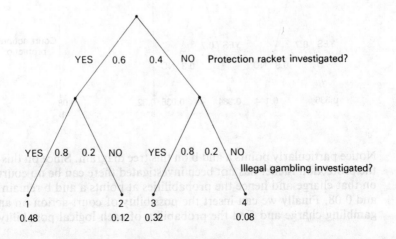

We now have four routes on our tree, and if we multiply the probabilities along each route, then we have deduced the probability of certain events occuring at each point. For example, point 1 represents the situation where Buggsy is investigated on both activities and we find the probability of this happening is 0.48; point 3 is the situation where Buggsy is not investigated on his protection racket but he is investigated on his illegal gambling, and the probability of this is 0.32. Notice that four points cover all the logical possibilities of investigations, so the probabilities must total 1 (0.48 + 0.12 + 0.32 + 0.08 = 1.0).

We will now insert on to the diagram the possibilities of court action resulting from a protection racket investigation.

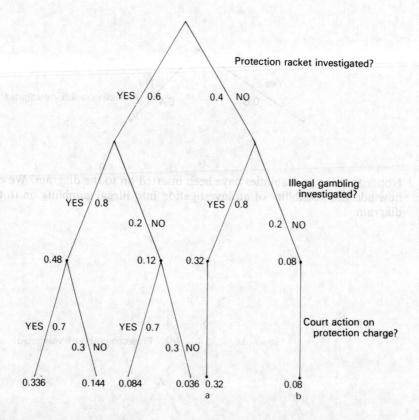

Notice particularly points a and b on this tree diagram. Since on this branch the protection racket has not been investigated there can be no court action on that charge and hence the probabilities at points a and b remain at 0.32 and 0.08. Finally we can insert the possibility of court action on an illegal gambling charge and find the probability of each logical possibility.

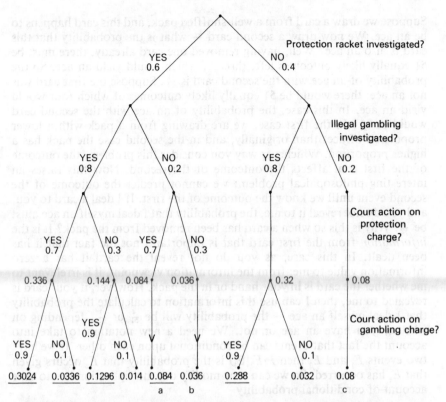

Notice again points a, b and c. In each of these branches there has been no investigation of illegal gambling. Hence there can be no court charge and the probabilities remain as they were at the previous junction.

In the diagram we have underlined every logical possibility that results in Buggsy landing up in court. The probability of his facing a court charge is the sum of the probabilities of all of these, i.e.

$$0.3024 + 0.0336 + 0.1296 + 0.084 + 0.288 = 0.8376$$

Conditional Probability

In the first section, we stated that events cannot bv both mutually exclusive and independent. This should not be taken to mean that if events are not mutually exclusive then they must be independent: there is a third category that we must now examine. When we state that events are independent, we mean that the outcome of one event in no way affects the outcome of the other. Now there are many cases where this is not true: the outcome of the second event is *conditional* on the outcome of the first event. Two examples may clarify this point.

Suppose we draw a card from a well-shuffled pack, and this card happens to be an ace. We now draw a second card — what is the probability that this card is also an ace? Well, having removed one card already, there must be 51 equally likely outcomes left, three of which would yield an ace. So the probability of an ace with the second card is $\frac{3}{51}$. Suppose the first card was not an ace: there would be 51 equally likely outcomes of which four would yield an ace. In this case, the probability of an ace with the second card would be $\frac{4}{51}$. In the first case, we are drawing from a pack with a lower proportion of aces than originally, and in the second case the pack has a higher proportion. Whichever way you consider this problem, the outcome of the first trial affects the outcome of the second. Now this raises an interesting philosophical problem: we cannot predict the outcome of the second event until we know the outcome of the first. If I deal a card to you, and you do not reveal it to me, the probability that I deal myself an ace must be $\frac{4}{52}$. Why is this so when a card has been removed from the pack? It is the *information* from the first card that is important, not the fact that it has been dealt. In this case, as you do not reveal the card it has a zero information value to me: from the information viewpoint, it is irrelevant to me whether the card is in your hand or in the pack. However, if your card is revealed to me, then I can use this information to calculate the probability that I deal myself an ace — the probability will be $\frac{4}{51}$ or $\frac{3}{51}$, depending on whether you have an ace or not. We need a new notation to take into account the fact that events can be conditional upon each other. If we have two events E_1 and E_2 then $P(E_2|E_1)$ is the probability that E_2 occurs given that E_1 has occurred. So we can now modify our multiplication law to take account of conditional probability

$$P(E_1 \cap E_2) = P(E_1) . P(E_2|E_1)$$

If E_1 is draw an ace with the first card, then $P(E_1) = \frac{1}{13}$. If E_2 is draw an ace with the second card, then $P(E_2|E_1) = \frac{3}{51}$. The probability of drawing an ace with both cards is $P(E_1 \cap E_2) = \frac{1}{13} \times \frac{3}{51} = \frac{1}{221}$.

Now let us consider a second example. Suppose we have a box of ten machine parts, three of which are defective. From this we draw a sample of two parts — what is the probability they are both defective? If E_1 is that the first part is defective, and E_2 is the second part is defective, then the events are conditional. $P(E_1) = \frac{3}{10}$, $P(E_2|E_1) = \frac{2}{9}$ and $P(E_1 \cap E_2) = \frac{3}{10} \times \frac{2}{9} = \frac{1}{15}$. Can you see that if we had replaced the first part before drawing the second then E_2 would not be conditional on E_1, and $P(E_2)$ would also be $\frac{3}{10}$? Using the statisticians' jargon, we would say that *sampling without replacement makes the events conditional*. Is this always true? We might have drawn two parts from a very large consignment indeed, and it would seem rather pedantic to state that the consignment is poorer in defectives if the first item drawn is defective. Moreover, the proportion of defectives in a very large consignment can only be an estimate. When sampling from a large population, then E_1 and E_2 can for all intents and purposes be considered independent.

The importance of conditional probability is that it enables us to modify our probability predictions in the light of any additional information that is made available to us.

EXAMPLE 4

When exploration for oil occurs a test hole is drilled. If, as a result of this test drilling it seems likely that really large quantities of oil exist, (a bonanza) then the well is said to have structure. Examination of past records reveals the following information:

Probability (structure and bonanza)	0.20
Probability (structure but no bonanza)	0.15
Probability (no structure but a bonanza)	0.05
Probability (no structure and no bonanza)	0.60

We can put this information into a matrix like this

	Structure	No structure	
Bonanza	0.20	0.05	0.25
No bonanza	0.15	0.60	0.75
	0.35	0.65	1.00

Calculating the row totals and the column totals (often called the marginal probabilities), we can deduce that

$$\text{Probability (Bonanza)} = 0.25$$

since a bonanza can occur either with or without structure. Similarly

Probability (No Bonanza)	=	0.75
Probability (Structure)	=	0.35
Probability (No structure)	=	0.65

Such probabilities are known as prior probabilities – they are obtained from past records. But suppose we are given some additional information – in particular suppose we know that a well has been sunk and structure is revealed. The number of possible outcomes has been reduced to two. We can ignore the "no structure" column of the table and conclude that the weighting for a "bonanza" is 0.2 and the weighting for "no bonanza" is 0.15. So Probability (Bonanza|structure) $= \dfrac{0.2}{0.2+0.15} = 0.571$ and

Probability (No bonanza|structure) $= \dfrac{0.15}{0.2+0.15} = 0.429$

Now suppose we were given the information that the hole does not have structure. We can deduce that

Probability (Bonanza|no structure) $= \dfrac{0.05}{0.65} = 0.077$

and Probability (No bonanza|no structure) $= \dfrac{0.6}{0.65} = 0.923$

184

The probabilities we have just calculated are called posterior probabilities – they cannot be established until after something has happened (i.e. the test hole drilled). The knowledge whether the test hole has structure or not is valuable. Without this knowledge we would estimate the probability of obtaining a bonanza at 0.25, but once the test hole is drilled we can revise our estimates. If the test hole reveals structure then the probability of a bonanza rises to 0.571; if it does not reveal structure the probability of a bonanza falls to 0.077.

Sometimes it is more useful to use tree diagrams to solve conditional probability problems.

EXAMPLE 5

Suppose we have 100 urns. Type 1 urn (of which there are 70) each contains 5 black and 5 white balls. Type 2 urn (which there are 30) each contain 8 black and 2 white balls. An urn is randomly selected and a ball is drawn from that urn. If the ball chosen was black, what is the probability that the ball came from a type 1 urn?

Firstly we notice that

P (urn type 1)	=	0.7
P (urn type 2)	=	0.3
P (Black|type 1)	=	0.5
P (White|type 1)	=	0.5
P (Black|type 2)	=	0.8
P (White|type 2)	=	0.2.

we can now draw the tree diagrams and find the prior probabilities.

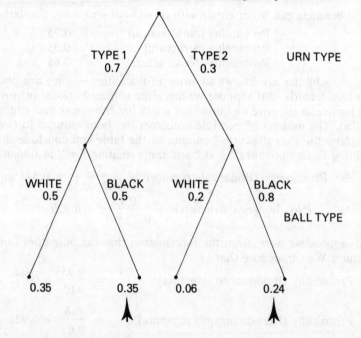

Now given that a black ball was drawn, the logical possibilities of the tree are reduced from four to the two arrowed. So the probability that the ball came from a type 1 urn is $\dfrac{0.35}{0.35 + 0.24} = 0.593$

One of the great difficulties of statistics examiners is the problem of ensuring that the questions they set are not ambiguous. Consider this case.

EXAMPLE 6

Firm A is one of many firms competing for a contract to build a bridge. The probability that Firm A is the first choice is $\frac{1}{9}$; the probability that it is the second choice is $\frac{1}{3}$, and the probability that it is the third choice is $\frac{1}{2}$. What is the probability that Firm A will not be the first, second or third choice?

The ambiguity in this question arises from the precise meaning of the expression "second choice" and "third choice". Are these probabilities joint probabilities, or are they conditional? Suppose we say that the probabilities are conditional – then the $\frac{1}{3}$ probability means that Firm A is the second choice, given that it is not the first choice. The question can then be approached like this.

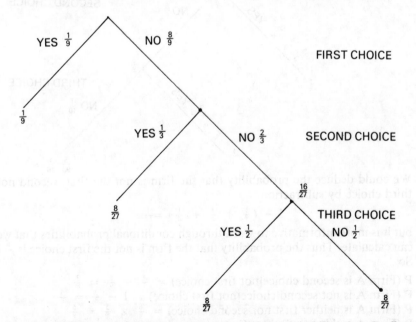

So, assuming the probabilities are conditional, the probability that the firm is neither the first, second nor third choice is $\frac{8}{27}$.

On the other hand, if the probabilities are joint probabilities, the probability of $\frac{1}{3}$ is the probability that the firm is not the first choice but is the second. Think carefully about this distinction. If the probabilities are conditional we say that the probability that the firm is the second choice given that it is not the first is P(not the first) $\times$ P(it is the second) $= \frac{8}{9} \times \frac{1}{3} = \frac{8}{27}$. But if the probabilities are joint we are given the probability that the firm is not the first choice and the probability that it is (both not the first and is the second). That is we now say $\frac{8}{9} \times$ P(it is the second) $= \frac{1}{3}$. The question would be approached like this.

We will calculate the conditional probability that Firm A is the government's second choice, given that it is not the first as follows:

$$P(\text{it is not the first}) \times P(\text{it is the second}|\text{not the first}) =$$
$$P(\text{it is both not the first and is the second})$$

that is $\frac{8}{9} \times$ Conditional probability $= \frac{1}{3}$

Conditional probability $= \frac{1}{3} \times \frac{9}{8} = \frac{3}{8}$

Thus we can build up our tree diagram.

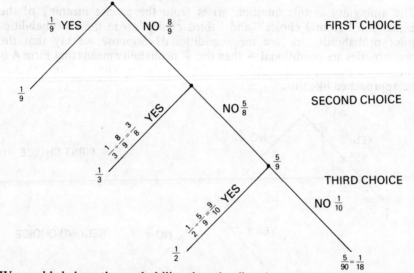

We could deduce the probability that the firm is not the first, second nor third choice by subtraction

$$1 - \left(\frac{1}{9} + \frac{1}{3} + \frac{1}{2} \right) = \frac{1}{18}$$

but it is more informative to work through conditional probabilities that we can calculate. Thus the probability that the firm is not the first choice is $\frac{8}{9}$. So

P (Firm A is second choice|not first choice) $= \frac{1}{3} \div \frac{8}{9} = \frac{3}{8}$

P (Firm A is not second choice|not first choice) $= 1 - \frac{3}{8} = \frac{5}{8}$

P (Firm A is neither first nor second choice) $= \frac{8}{9} \times \frac{5}{8} = \frac{5}{9}$

P (Firm A is third choice|not first or second choice) $= \frac{1}{2} \div \frac{5}{9} = \frac{9}{10}$

P (A is not third choice|neither first not second) $= 1 - \frac{9}{10} = \frac{1}{10}$

P (Firm A is not first nor second nor third choice) $= \frac{1}{10} \times \frac{5}{9} = \frac{1}{18}$

the same answer as before.

Now a few words to conclude this chapter. The concepts underlying probability are extremely easy to understand, and there are very few rules that must be learnt. However, putting these rules (or combinations of these rules) into practice can be very tricky indeed. You would be well advised to re-read the section on the laws of probability to make absolutely sure that you understand them. Also, make certain that you understand the logic employed in the previous examples before you attempt the following exercises. Before you attempt any calculations on the exercises, you should be certain you know the way or ways the desired event can occur (for example, 'at least one' means one or more). Also, you should decide on the relationship between the events – whether they are mutually exclusive, independent, or conditional. Suppose that, after all this, you still cannot cope with probability – what then? Well, at least you can console yourself with the knowledge that although some students find probability a highly stimulating intellectual exercise, by for the bulk of students find probability problems the nearest thing to purgatory! Frequently you will find that although you can see that your answer is wrong, it is extremely difficult to see just where you have gone wrong! Fortunately, a lack of capability at solving probability problems need not hold you up in a statistics course, as a knowledge of what probability means and how it is measured are the important things.

Exercises to Chapter 10

10.1 Explain carefully what is meant by 'the probability of an event'. I.C.A.

10.2 A bag contains nineteen balls, each of which is painted in two colours. Four are red and white, seven are white and black, and eight are black and red. A ball is chosen at random and seen to be partly white. What is it the probability that its other colour is red?

10.3 (a) Explain what is meant by the terms
   (i) mutually exclusive
   (ii) independent
 (b) A manufacturer purchases two machines A and B. The probability that A will last 5 years is $\frac{4}{5}$ and the probability that B will last 5 years is $\frac{3}{4}$. Find the probability that
   (i) both machines will last 5 years
   (ii) only machine A will last 5 years
   (iii) at least one machine will last 5 years

10.4 (a) Explain what you understand by
   (i) independent events
   (ii) conditional probability
 (b) 8% of the items produced in a manufacturing process are known to be faulty. A sample of 5 items is drawn at random. Calculate the probability that the sample
   (i) does not contain any faulty items
   (ii) only contains one faulty item
 (c) Two independent events A and B are such that $P(A) = 0.2$ and $P(B) = 0.4$. Find the values of (i) $P(AB)$, (ii) $P(A + B)$ and (iii) the probability of A occurring given that B has already occurred.

10.5 (a) State the theorems of addition and multiplication of probabilities.

(b) An analysis of the national origins of the employees of a manufacturing company produced the following result:

English	488
Scots	230
Irish	112
Welsh	108
American	30
Other European	16

If two employees of this company are chosen at random, state the probability that

(i) both will be other European

(ii) both will be English

(iii) both will be either Irish or Welsh

(iv) at least one of the two will be a Scot.

10.6 (a) Explain what is meant by (i) mutually exclusive events and (ii) independent events.

(b) (i) What is the chance of throwing a number greater than four with an ordinary die?

(ii) If the probability of throwing a seven with a pair of dice is $\frac{1}{6}$, what is the probability of rolling two sevens in a row?

(iii) If three dice are thrown together, what is the probability of obtaining at least one five?

(iv) Out of 10 steel valve springs 3 are defective. Two springs are chosen at random for testing. What is the probability that both test specimens are:

(a) not defective;

(b) defective?

10.7 The following results were obtained from interviews with 500 people who changed their cars recently, cars being classified as large, medium or small in size, depending on their length.

Previous Car Size	Present Car Size			Total
	Large ($>15'$)	Medium ($13'-15'$)	Small ($<13'$)	
Large	75	47	22	144
Medium	36	75	69	180
Small	11	63	102	176
Total	122	185	193	500

Required:

(1) What proportion of people in the survey changed to:

(i) a smaller car?

(ii) a larger car?

(2) What effect would such car-changing habits have generally on the size of car owned in the future?

(3) What is the probability that a person from the survey selected at random who bought a large car, previously had a small or medium car?

(4) Estimate the average length of car owned at present by the 500 people surveyed, if no owner has a car less than 9 feet or greater than 19 feet.

A.C.A.

10.8   The probability that machine A will be performing a useful function in five years' time is $\frac{1}{4}$ while the probability that machine B will still be operating usefully at the end of the same period is $\frac{1}{3}$.

Find the probability that in five years' time:
- (a) both machines will be performing a useful function;
- (b) neither will be operating;
- (c) only machine B will be operating;
- (d) at least one of the machines will be operating.   I.C.M.A.

10.9   The probability that a man now aged 55 years will be alive in the year 2000 is $\frac{5}{8}$ while the probability that his wife now aged 53 years will be alive in 2000 is $\frac{5}{6}$.

Determine the probability that in 2000:
- (a) both will be alive;
- (b) at least one of them will be alive;
- (c) only the wife will be alive.   I.C.M.A.

10.10   A sub-assembly consists of three components A, B and C. Tests have shown that failures of the sub-assembly were caused by faults in one, two and sometimes all three components. Analysis of 100 sub-assembly failures showed that there were 70 faulty components A, 50 faulty components B, and 30 faulty components C. Of the failures 44 were caused by faults in two components only (i.e. A and B, or A and C, or B and C) and 10 of the 44 faults were in B and C.

If a faulty component is randomly selected, find the probability that it has faults in:
- (a) all three components;
- (b) component A on its own.   I.C.M.A.

10.11   (a) One bag contains 4 white balls and 2 black balls; another contains 3 white balls and 5 black balls. If one ball is drawn from each bag, find the probability that (i) both are white, (ii) both are black, (iii) one is white and one is black.

(b) A purse contains 2 silver coins and 4 copper coins, and a second purse contains 4 silver coins and 3 copper coins. A coin is selected at random from one of the two purses. What is the probability that it is a silver coin?

(c) A box contains M components of which N are defective. Selection occurs without replacement. Find the probability that:
- (i) the first selection is defective;
- (ii) the first two selections consist of one defective and one non-defective;
- (iii) the second selection is defective.   I.C.A.

10.12   An amplifier circuit is made up of three valves. The probabilities that the three valves are defective are $\frac{1}{20}$, $\frac{1}{25}$ and $\frac{1}{50}$ respectively. Calculate the probability that (a) the amplifier workers, (b) that the amplifier has one defective valve.

10.13 In a particular factory, an automatic process identifies defective items produced. Defectives can be classified as lacking strength, incorrect weight or incorrect diameter. A random sample of 1000 items were checked and the following results recorded:

    120 have a strength defect;
    80 have a weight defect;
    60 have a diameter defect;
    22 have strength and weight defects;
    16 have strength and diameter defects;
    20 have weight and diameter defects;
    8 have all three defects.

Find the probability that a randomly chosen item
(i)   is not defectve;
(ii) has exactly two defects.   I.C.A.

10.14 A manufacturer supplies transistors in boxes of 100. A buyer takes a random sample of 5 transistors and if one of them is faulty he rejects the box; otherwise he accepts the box.
(i)   If there are 10 faulty transistors in the box what is the probability that the buyer will accept it?
(ii) What is the probability that he will reject a box which in fact only contains one faulty transistor?

10.15 The table given below shows a frequency distribution of the lifetimes of 500 light bulbs made and tested by ABC Limited:

Lifetime (hours)	Number of light bulbs
400 and less than 500	10
500 and less than 600	16
600 and less than 700	38
700 and less than 800	56
800 and less than 900	63
900 and less than 1000	67
1000 and less than 1100	92
1100 and less than 1200	68
1200 and less than 1300	57
1300 and less than 1400	33
	500

(a) Determine the percentage of light bulbs whose lifetimes are at least 700 hours but less than 1200 hours.
(b) What risk is ABC Limited taking if it guarantees to replace any light bulb which lasts less than 1000 hours?
(c) Instead of guaranteeing the life of the light bulb for 1000 hours, ABC Limited suggests introducing a 100-day money-back guarantee. What is the probability that refunds will be made, assuming the light bulb is in use:
    (i)   7 hours per day;
    (ii) 11 hours per day?   A.C.A.

10.16 A businessman estimates that the probability of gaining an important contract to build a factory is 0.65. If this contract is obtained he will certainly have a probability of gaining a further contract of building an associated computer block – he estimates that this probability is 0.8. If he fails to obtain the contract to build the factory, he will not be asked to deal with the computer block construction. As an alternative to the factory/block contract, there is a probability of 0.35 that the businessman could obtain the contract to build an office block – he could only deal with this if the first set of contracts was not obtained. What is the probability that both factory and computer block contracts will be gained? Also, what is the probability that the businessman will obtain either the computer block contract or the office block contract?   I.C.S.A.

10.17 A company in which the training period for apprentices is five years is considering its intake for the coming year. Information concerning apprentices recruited in previous years is given below:

Year of intake	1963	1964	1965	1966
Number of apprentices recruited	700	500	150	250
Number of apprentices leaving in				
First year	28	18	8	14
Second year	29	18	6	10
Third year	17	8	2	1
Fourth year	13	8	1	2
Fifth year	2	2	1	1

(a) What is the probability that an apprentice will qualify?
(b) What is the probability that an apprentice will stay for longer than two years?
(c) How many apprentices should be recruited in 1971 to provide the company with 300 qualified men in 1976?   I.C.M.A.

10.18 (a) Explain briefly the value of conditional probability calculations to the businessman.

(b)

Firm	Defective Electron Tubes per box of 100 units			
	0	1	2	3 or more
Supplier A	500	200	200	100
Supplier B	320	160	80	40
Supplier C	600	100	50	50

From the data given in the above table, calculate the conditional probabilities for the following questions:

(i) If one box had been selected at random from this universe what are the probabilities that the box would have come from Supplier A; from Supplier B; from Supplier C?

(ii) If a box had been selected at random, what is the probability that it would contain two defective tubes?

(iii) If a box had been selected at random, what is the probability that it would have no defectives and would have come from Supplier A?

(iv) Given that a box selected at random came from Supplier B, what is the probability that it contained one or two defective tubes?

(v) If a box came from Supplier A, what is the probability that the box would have two or less defectives?

(vi) It is known that a box selected at random has two defective tubes. What is the probability that it came from Supplier A; from Supplier B; from Supplier C?   A.C.C.A.

10.19 Two companies A and B regularly bid against each other for building contracts. A has a probability of $\frac{2}{3}$ of winning any given contract while B has a probability of $\frac{1}{3}$. Assuming independence, calculate the probabilities that, of the next two contracts, (i) A wins both (ii) B wins both, (iii) each company wins one.

10.20 (a) If an 'event' is defined as an outcome of an experiment, explain what is meant by
   (i) mutually exclusive events,
   (ii) independent events, and
   (iii) conditional events.
   Give examples of events that would fall into each category.
   (b) To control the quality of output, a sample of ten items is examined each hour and if no defective items are found the process continues, otherwise the process is stopped and adjustments are made. What is the probability that the process will be stopped after a sample is drawn if 10% of the items produced by this process are defective? How large a sample should be drawn to ensure that if 10% of items are defective, then the probability that the process is stopped is at least 99%?

I.C.A.

10.21 A circuit is protected by two fuses, F and G, so arranged that the correct operation of either of them is sufficient to stop the circuit being damaged. The reliability (i.e. the probability that the device operates successfully when required) of the fuses, F and G, is 0.95 and 0.90 respectively. What is the probability that on a given occasion the circuit will not be protected?

10.22 In an experiment the probability of success is $\frac{1}{3}$. If it is performed 6 times, what is the probability of occurrence of (i) 5 successes, (ii) more than 4 successes?

10.23 (a) Explain what are meant by mutually exclusive events, independent events and dependent events.
   (b) A public company holds two accounts: an account A with a government department and an account B with a merchant bank. It has been established that on any given day there is a finite and distinct probability that each account will exceed its overdraft facilities. It may be assumed that the probability that either or both accounts exceed their overdraft facilities is 0.55 whilst the probability that account B exceeds its overdraft facility is 0.25.
      (i) If the fluctuations of the accounts are independent what is the probability that account A exceeds its overdraft facilities on any given day?
      (ii) Had the fluctuations of the accounts been dependent what would have been the probability that account A exceeded its overdraft facilities on any day in which account B also exceeded its overdraft facilities if the probability that both accounts exceeded their overdraft facilities had been 0.12?

I.C.A.

10.24 If three cards are withdrawn from a pack (without replacement) find the probability that they are
  (a) Jack, Queen and King (in that order)
  (b) A Jack a Queen and a King.

10.25 Look again at example 4. Suppose E_1 is that oil is found in commercial quantities and E_2 is that the well has structure. Given that $P(E_1 \cap E_2) = 0.42$, $P(E_1 \cap E'_2) = 0.18$, $P(E'_1 \cap E_2) = 0.28$ and $P(E'_1 \cap E'_2) = 0.12$ what would you conclude?

10.26 A certain mass produced article sometimes has a dimension defect and sometimes a surface defect. Let
  $\quad E_1$ = an article has a dimension defect
  $\quad E_2$ = an article has a surface defect
  $\quad E_3$ = an article is non-defective
  If $P(E_1) = 0.06$, $P(E_2) = 0.07$ and $P(E_3) = 0.9$, what would you conclude?

10.27 Tom, Dick and Harry are candidates for the post of works manager. The managing director will recommend a candidate and the recommendation must be ratified by the board of directors. The probability that the managing director recommends Harry is 60%, with 25% for Dick and 15% for Tom. The probabilities that the board ratifies are 40% for Harry, 35% for Tom, and 25% for Dick
  (a) Find the probability that none of the candidates are appointed.
  (b) Find for each candidate the probability that he is appointed given that the board has ratified the managing directors recommendation.
  N.B. Use a tree diagram to solve this problem.

Chapter Eleven

Decision Criteria

We are all experts in taking decisions. Does this surprise you? Well throughout your life you have had many decisions to take, and the fact that you are alive today, reading this book, indicates that you have taken many decisions correctly. Take a simple problem – the need to get to the other side of a busy road. You have to decide when it is safe to cross. The fact that you have so far taken the correct decision proves that you have carefully weighed up the evidence, and interpreted the evidence correctly. Sometimes the decision will be easy to take; the road might be completely empty and you can cross with safety; and at other times the road will be so busy that to attempt to cross would be suicidal. In other words, we have all the necessary information available to make the correct decision every time. A cautious (and according to Road Safety Officers a sensible) person would obey the following decision rules: Only cross the road when no traffic is in sight. If we obey this rule, then we will always cross the road safely (unless we fall down an uncovered manhole!) Unfortunately, however, it is not always possible to obey this rule, as there are many roads so busy that we could never cross. With normal city centre roads we will seldom find a situation where they are completely empty of traffic, and we must use our judgement to decide when it is safe to cross.

Now of course, the decision taking problems faced by businessmen are much more complex than the decision whether to cross the road. Not only must the businessman decide between many alternatives, but also he often cannot be sure of the consequences of any decision he may make. In this chapter, we shall attempt to discover criteria that may aid the decision taking process.

Decision Criteria

Guy Rope owns a camp site in the Dordogne, and he wishes to develop the site in order to increase his profits. He realises that three options are open to him: he could build a swimming pool and charge the campers for its use, he could build a tennis court and charge for its use, or he could build a restaurant to supply the campers with simple hot meals. He has sufficient funds to undertake just one of the options – what should he do? Obviously, the decision taken by Guy will depend on the profitability of the options, and he realises that the profitability will depend upon the weather. If the summer is too hot, then tennis may prove to be too exhausting; also evening barbecues in the open air will be more popular than restaurant meals. Given a hot summer, then, the swimming pool would be the most profitable option. If the summer is poor, then Guy reckons that his campers would welcome somewhere where they could buy hot meals, and so the restaurant would be the most profitable. People seem to prefer playing tennis when the weather is neither too hot nor too cold, so the tennis court would prove to be the most profitable given an 'average' summer. Armed with these beliefs, Guy estimates the annual profitability of each course of action as follows (all figures in thousand francs).

Table 11.01

		State of Nature		
		Summer is		
		Cool	Average	Hot
	Swimming pool	50	100	150
Strategies	Tennis court	30	180	90
	Restaurant	170	100	40

Notice that the options facing Guy are called *strategies:* a list of strategies is a list of courses of action facing the decision taker who has direct control over which course is chosen. However, Guy has no control whatsoever over the weather (if he had then there would be no problem!). The different types of summer that can occur are called *states of nature;* a list of events outside the control of the decision taker. The table above is usually called a *payoff matrix*. For each strategy it shows the payoff (in this case, the profit) that would result from each state of nature.

What should we advise Guy to do? Unfortunately, mathematics alone cannot help us — we need to know something about Guy's character. What sort of person is he? Is he a gambler, a risk taker who is supremely confident that lady luck is always on his side? If Guy is this type of person, then he would reason as follows — "Lucky me — I am always right. If I build a swimming pool, then the summer will be hot and I will earn 150,000FF. If I build a tennis court, then the summer will be average and I will earn 180,000FF. If I open a restaurant, the summer will be cool and I will earn 170,000FF. The most logical thing for me to do is to go for the greatest profit, so I will build a tennis court".

Table 11.02 summarises Guy's reasoning. For each strategy, he notes the maximum payoff that can result. He then chooses the strategy with the greatest maximum payoff. If Guy acts in this way, then Guy is applying the *maximax criterion:* he is maximising his maximum possible payoff by gambling that the summer will be average.

Table 11.02

	Cool	Average	Hot	Maximum Payoff
Swimming Pool	50	100	150	150
Tennis Court	30	180	90	180 ←
Restaurant	170	100	40	170

Decision takers who practice the maximax criterion must be very rare specimens. If maximax was widely practised, then although we would have a few more millionaires, we would certainly have many more bankruptcies! Lady luck smiles on very few of us indeed! We shall now move to the other end of the spectrum and suppose that Guy is a born pessimist, who always assumes that the states of nature work against him. He would argue something like this: "Suppose I build a swimming pool. Will the summer be hot or even average? No chance! You can bet your bottom dollar that the summer will be cool! Likewise, one sure fire way to ensure a cool summer is for me to build a tennis court. Of course, if I open a restaurant then the summer will be the hottest for years and only a few campers will want feeding. The big money always avoids me. I might as well build a swimming pool as this at least guarantees me 50,000FF. profit. If I build a tennis court I could only be sure of 30,000FF. and opening a restaurant guarantees me no more than 40,000FF. A swimming pool it is, then". Table 11.03 summarises Guy's reasoning.

Table 11.03

	Cool	Average	Hot	Minimum Payoff
Swimming Pool	50	100	150	50
Tennis Court	30	180	90	30
Restaurant	170	100	40	40

For each strategy, he notes the minimum payoff that can result. He then selects the strategy that maximises his minimum payoff. Guy is applying the *maximin criterion;* he is maximising his minimum possible payoff.

So we see that the two criteria are fundamentally different, reflecting quite different states of mind. If Guy adopts the maximax criterion then he is pushing the ceiling on his profits to the highest level (180,000FF.) by building a tennis court. No other strategy could earn this much. However, he is taking a risk: his profit would only be 30,000FF if the summer was cool. On the other hand, if Guy adopts the maximin criterion, then he is raising the floor on his profits to the highest level (50,000FF) by building a swimming pool. No other strategy could guarantee as much as this. However, by building a swimming pool he foregoes the possibility of really large profits (180,000FF from a tennis court or 170,000FF from a restaurant).

There is a third way of analysing the problem facing Guy — a way that neither assumes that Guy is ultra optimistic nor assumes that he is ultra pessimistic. The reasoning is something like this: suppose the summer turns out to be cool — if Guy had opened a restaurant then he would have made the right decision. He would have no 'regret' at all, and earn the maximum possible profit under the circumstances (170,000FF). But suppose he had built a swimming pool – he has made the wrong decision and would certainly regret it. His profit would be 50,000FF, 120,000FF less than it would have been had he made the correct decision. It would seem reasonable, then, to use the 120,000FF as a measure of the extent of his regret. In a similar fashion, if the summer was cool and Guy had built a tennis court, then he would regret the 170,000 – 30,000 = 140,000FF he had foregone. If we use similar reasoning and assume an average summer; then assume a hot summer; we can calculate Guy's regret under all possible circumstances. Our results are summarised in a *regret matrix*. (see table 11.04).

Table 11.04

	Cool	Average	Hot	Maximum Regret
Swimming Pool	120	80	0	120
Tennis Court	140	0	60	140
Restaurant	0	80	110	110

For each strategy, the maximum regret has been identified (for example, had he built a tennis court, then Guy's maximum regret would have been the 140,000FF in profit foregone during a cool summer). Examining the matrix we conclude that Guy should open a restaurant, as this is the strategy that minimises the maximum regret he could experience. If he uses this reasoning as a basis for decision taking, then Guy is applying the *minimax criterion.*

In this section, we have examined three quite distinct criteria for decision taking, and we shall now state a few simple rules to summarise them. The rules will assume that in the payoff matrix the rows refer to the strategies and the columns refer to states of nature.

Rule 1

For each row in the payoff matrix, find the maximum value. If we select the row with the greatest maximum value then we are applying the maximax criterion

	Cool	Average	Hot	Maximum
Swimming Pool	50	100	150	150
Tennis Court	30	180	90	180
Restaurant	170	100	40	170

Rule 2

For each row in the payoff matrix, find the minimum value. If we select the row with the greatest minimum value then we are applying the maximin criterion.

	Cool	Average	Hot	Minimum
Swimming Pool	50	100	150	50
Tennis Court	30	180	90	30
Restaurant	170	100	40	40

◄

Rule 3

Find the maximum value for each column in the payoff matrix, and subtract all the payoffs in each column from their corresponding maximum value. This gives the regret matrix.

Rule 4

For each row in the regret matrix, find the maximum value. If we select the row with the least maximum value, then we are applying the minimax criterion.

	Cool	Average	Hot
Swimming Pool	50	100	150
Tennis Court	30	180	90
Restaurant	170	100	40
Maximum	170	180	150

	Cool	Average	Hot	Maximum Regret
Swimming Pool	120	80	0	120
Tennis Court	140	0	60	140
Restaurant	0	80	110	110

◄

Which Criteria?

We have applied three different criteria to the problem facing Guy. The Maximax criterion suggests he should build a tennis court. The maximin criterion suggests he should build a swimming pool. The minimax criterion suggests he should open a restaurant. Poor Guy must be utterly confused! Which criteria is appropriate to this problem? As we suggested earlier, this is an impossible question to answer as the strategy selected will depend upon Guy's character. However, it is possible to comment generally on the criteria.

1. For the problem facing Guy, each criterion suggested a different strategy, but it frequently happens that different criteria would suggest that we should select the same strategy. For example, if the payoff matrix was

	Cool	Average	Hot
Swimming Pool	30	100	170
Tennis Court	50	180	90
Restaurant	170	100	40

then whatever criterion is applied the strategy selected would be the same — build a tennis court (you should verify for yourself that this is true). This strategy is said to be *dominant,* and no problem of strategy selection exists.

2. The minimax criterion minimises the decision taker's maximum regret, and so it attempts to minimise the consequences of taking the wrong decision. This is an intrinsically satisfying criterion — it seems to be a highly logical method of decision taking. Moreover, this criterion fits in well with economists' ideas of opportunity cost (if you do not know what opportunity cost is, talk to an economist).

3. If we examine the payoff matrix facing Guy, then we notice that whatever strategy he selects and whatever the state of nature, Guy always makes a profit. Because of this, Guy may be tempted to apply the maximax criterion — especially if Guy is what economists call a profit maximiser. He would be following the well quoted 'law' that you must speculate to accumulate. But suppose it was possible for losses to occur: this could well be the case if he opened a restaurant and the summer was hot, or he built a swimming pool and the summer was cool. Surely, Guy would then be strongly tempted to apply the maximin criterion, especially if the losses could threaten his survival as a camp site owner.

4. Guy has a problem selecting the appropriate strategy because he has no control over the states of nature, but if he has *more information* about the states of nature then his decision can be more soundly based. What additional information would help? Well, the states of nature will not be equally likely to occur, so if Guy can assign probabilities to the states of nature this should increase his insight into the problem.

Expected Monetary Value

Suppose that Guy examines the Dordogne weather records over the last 100 years. On 20 occasions the summer was cool, on 70 occasions the summer was average and on 10 occasions the summer was hot. This information enables Guy to deduce the following empirical probabilities

State of Nature	Probability
Cool	0.2
Average	0.7
Hot	0.1

Suppose Guy thinks ahead over the next ten years — using the probability distribution he would predict 2 cool, 7 average and 1 hot summer. So if he was to build a swimming pool he would estimate his earnings (in thousands francs) at

$$2 \times 50 + 7 \times 100 + 1 \times 150 = 950$$

which is an average of $950 \div 10 = 95$ per year. This average earning is called the *expected monetary value* (EMV) of building a swimming pool, and we could calculate it more directly like this:

$$0.2 \times 50 + 0.7 \times 100 + 0.1 \times 150 = 95.0$$

In a similar fashion we could deduce that

EMV (build tennis court) = $0.2 \times 30 + 0.7 \times 180 + 0.1 \times 90 = 141$

EMV (open restaurant) = $0.2 \times 170 + 0.7 \times 100 + 0.1 \times 40 = 108$

We now have another criterion for selecting the appropriate strategy – *select the strategy with the greatest EMV* as this maximises the long run average gains. Guy would be well advised to build a tennis court and earn an average of 141,000FF per year.

Of the four criteria we have examined, EMV has the soundest logical base. Maximising your average long run profits certainly seems a sensible thing to do. However, the criterion does have its drawbacks. We have stated that Guy should build a tennis court because this has the greatest EMV (141,000FF) – but on any particular year he cannot earn this amount. He will earn either 30,000FF or 180,000FF or 90,000FF. Suppose one of these options was a loss, then we would have to enquire whether Guy is capable of shouldering the loss. Sooner or later, losses would be bound to occur, and if they could result in bankruptcy then Guy is clearly using the wrong criterion. The maximin criterion would be more appropriate.

The second problem with using the EMV criterion arises when the term 'long run payoff' makes no sense. In particular, let us suppose that Guy intends to run the camp site for just one summer, obtain the maximum profit he can, then leave the industry (he would be what economists call a 'snatcher'). The EMV of building a tennis court cannot be his long run average profit as there will be no long run! His average profit will be the profit for the year – either 30,000FF or 180,000FF or 90,000FF. But if he stays in the industry then as the years elapse, the closer will his average annual profit move towards 141,000FF. If Guy is a snatcher, must we conclude that the EMV criterion is inappropriate? Not necessarily. If Guy applies the EMV criterion to all the decision problems facing him, however diverse they may be, then he would be maximising his returns over the entire range of problems.

The Value of Perfect Information

For the rest of this problem, we will assume that Guy is a snatcher, basing his decisions on the EMV criterion. He decides to build a tennis court as this has the greatest EMV (141,000FF). Now suppose additional information is available to Guy – in particular let us suppose that a peasant is prepared to predict the weather and that his predictions are always right. In the jargon, we would say that Guy has *perfect information* available to him. This will certainly help the decision taking process. If the peasant predicts a cool summer (and there is a 20% chance that he will) then Guy will open a restaurant. If he predicts an average summer (and there is a 70% chance that he will) then Guy will build a tennis court. If he predicts a hot summer (and there is a 10% chance that he will) Guy will build a swimming pool. Given perfect information, then, Guy will earn either 170,000FF or 180,000FF or 150,000FF. His expected earnings, then, are

$$0.2 \times 170 + 0.7 \times 180 + 0.1 \times 150 = 175,000FF$$

Without this information, Guy's expected earnings were 141,000FF. So the information has a value to Guy of 175,000 − 141,000 = 34,000FF. This 34,000FF is the *expected value of perfect information* (EVPI) Now it is highly likely that the peasant will charge for the information, but the information would certainly be worth buying if its cost was less than EVPI. In other words, if the peasant charges less than 34,000FF for his predictions, then the predictions are worth buying, but if the peasant charges more than 34,000FF then Guy would be advised not to buy a prediction from the peasant and simply apply the EMV criterion.

Multi-stage Decision analysis

We shall now examine a more complex problem, in which the decision taking process is divided into stages. Flint McRae owns the oil prospecting and development rights for a plot of land in California, and a property development company has offered him $50,000 for the plot. Flint must now decide whether to sell the land or to exploit the land as an oilfield. Suppose that Flint decides to exploit the land − he sinks the well but finds no oil. In the jargon of the oil industry, the well is said to be 'dry', and Flint would lose $20,0000. However, the well might yield oil in commercial quantities − a so-called 'wet' well, and this would earn Flint $100,000 in total income. Exceptionally, Flint could obtain a real bonanza from his oilwell − a so-called 'soaking' well, and this would earn $500,000 in total net income. From past experience, Flint knows that there is a 70% chance that the well is 'dry', a 20% chance that it is 'wet' and a 10% chance that it is 'soaking'. If he wishes, Flint can engage a firm of geologists to undertake a seismic survey of the land, and this will cost him $30,000. The geologists supply the following information as to the reliability of such surveys (all figures are prior probabilities).

		Survey report is		
		bad	good	
	dry	0.44	0.26	0.7
true state of the well	wet	0.05	0.15	0.2
	soaking	0.01	0.09	0.1
		0.50	0.50	1.0

If Flint always uses the EMV criterion, what should he do?

In this problem, there are two sets of strategies facing Flint

1) Should he engage the geologist's services?
2) Should he drill or should he sell?

Likewise, there are two sets of states of nature facing Flint

1) The result of the survey (is the report good or bad?)
2) The true state of the well (is it dry, wet or soaking?)

Armed with this information, we can construct a tree diagram of the problem facing Flint. The boxes represent decision points and the circles represent states of nature. So we see that there are four distinct decision points facing Flint.

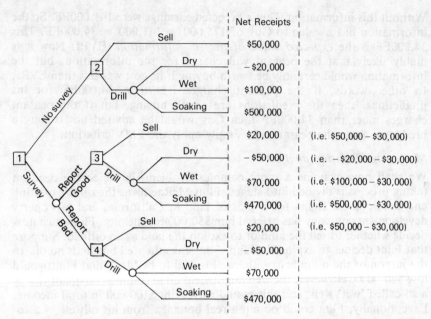

	Net Receipts	
Sell	$50,000	
Dry	– $20,000	
Wet	$100,000	
Soaking	$500,000	
Sell	$20,000	(i.e. $50,000 – $30,000)
Dry	– $50,000	(i.e. – $20,000 – $30,000)
Wet	$70,000	(i.e. $100,000 – $30,000)
Soaking	$470,000	(i.e. $500,000 – $30,000)
Sell	$20,000	(i.e. $50,000 – $30,000)
Dry	– $50,000	
Wet	$70,000	
Soaking	$470,000	

Diagram 11.01

Now before Flint can decide on decision point 1, he must decide on decision points 2, 3 and 4. Hence we will analyse the tree diagram from right to left — a method called the *rollback principle*.

Firstly we shall analyse decision point 2

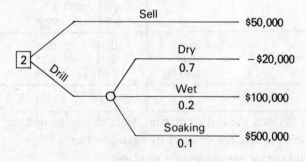

Diagram 11.02

Assuming that Flint reaches decision point 2

EMV (Sell) = $50,000
EMV (Drill) = $0.7 \times -$20,000 + 0.2 \times $100,000 + 0.1 \times $500,000
= $56,000

So we see that if decision point 2 is reached, then Flint will drill. If we now turn to decision point 3, we will need conditional probabilities, ie the probabilities that the well is dry, wet or soaking given a good report from the geologist

P (dry well|good report) $= 0.26 \div 0.5 = 0.52$
P (wet well|good report) $= 0.15 \div 0.5 = 0.30$
P (soaking well|good report) $= 0.09 \div 0.5 = 0.18$

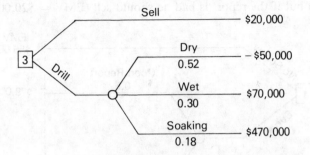

Diagram 11.03

Assuming that Flint reaches decision point 3

EMV (Sell) $= \$20,000$
EMV (Drill) $= 0.52 \times -\$50,000 + 0.3 \times \$70,000 + 0.18 \times \$470,000$
$= \$79,000$

So if decision point 3 is reached, Flint should drill. Turning now to decision point 4

P (dry well|bad report) $= 0.44 \div 0.5 = 0.88$
P (wet well|bad report) $= 0.05 \div 0.5 = 0.10$
P (soaking well|bad report) $= 0.01 \div 0.5 = 0.02$

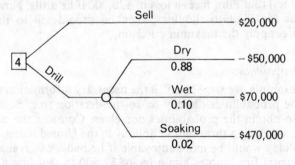

Diagram 11.04

Assuming that Flint reaches decision point 4

EMV (Sell) $= \$20,000$
EMV (Drill) $= 0.88 \times -\$50,000 + 0.1 \times \$70,000 + 0.02 \times \$470,000$
$= -\$27,600$

Clearly, then if decision point 4 is reached, then Flint should sell.

Now that we have evaluated decision points 2, 3 and 4 we can evaluate decision point 1. Before we do this, however, it might be useful to summarise what we have concluded. If Flint does not employ the geologists services, then his best course of action is to drill (EMV = $56,000). If he does employ the geologist's services, then his action will depend upon the geologists report. If the report is good, then Flint should drill (EMV = $79,600) but if the report is bad he should sell (EMV = $20,000)

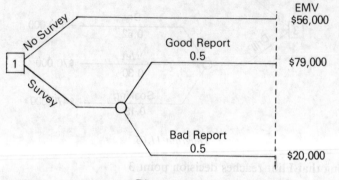

Diagram 11.05

Evaluating decision point 1 we have

EMV (no survey) = $56,000
EMV (survey)   = $79,600 × 0.5 + 20,000 × 0.5 = $49,800

Finally, then, we conclude that Flint should not engage the services of the geologists and drill for oil.

Before leaving this problem, you should notice that there is a chance (a 70% chance, in fact) that Flint faces a loss of $20,000 if he drills. Now if this loss is too great for Flint to shoulder, then he should sell to the property developer i.e. apply the maximin criterion.

Revising Probabilities

In the last example, we were given all the necessary information to enable us to insert the probabilities directly on to the decision tree. Sometimes it is necessary to obtain the probabilities ourselves. Consider the case of John Smith, who is taking a three month holiday in the United States. He realises that his holiday would be more enjoyable if he had a car available to him, and a car rental firm quotes him a fee of $2,500 to rent him a car for the duration of his stay. Alternatively, he could buy a used car of the same type for $3,500, and sell it at the end of his holiday for $2,000. So buying rather than renting would involve John Smith with a net outlay of $1,500. The problem with buying a used car is that the car might breakdown, and while John is perfectly capable of undertaking minor repairs himself at a negligible outlay, he reckons that a major breakdown could involve him with repair charges of $1,500. A friend advises John that the probability that a car of this age and type will breakdown over the next three months is 20%. There is a further alternative facing John Smith: he could persuade his friend to rent the used car for a day for $50. John and his friend could then examine the vehicle, and assess its likelihood of breaking down over the next three months. There is a 90% chance that any prediction they make will be right. What should John Smith do?

Firstly we shall draw the decision tree of the problem, inserting the associated costs (diag. 11.6). We know that the probability of no major fault occuring is 0.8, so we can evaluate decision point 2

Cost if care rented = $2,500

Expected cost if car bought = $1,500 \times 0.8 + 3,000 \times 0.2 = \$1,800$

So if decision point 2 is reached, John Smith would buy the car as this action has the lower expected cost.

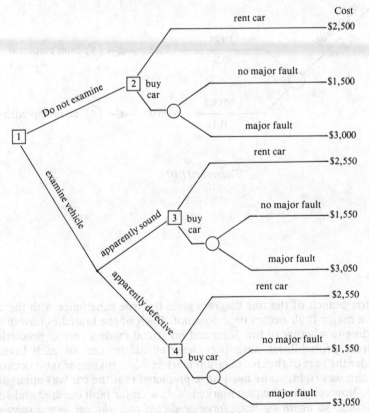

Diagram 11.06.

Evaluation of decision points 3 and 4 is not so straightforward. We need to know the probabilities that the car is apprently sound and apparently defective, and diagram 11.7 illustrates the problem.

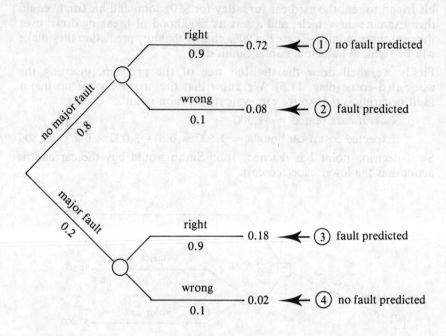

Diagram 11.07

The first branch of the tree diagram gives the true experience with the car: either a major fault occurs or it does not. Each of the branches now divide according to whether or not John and his friend made a correct prediction. The joint probabilities have been inserted at the end of each branch. Consider the part of the tree diagram marked ① : no major fault occurred and John was right, so he must have predicted that the car was apparently sound. Now consider the part marked ④ , a major fault occured and John was wrong, *so again he must have predicted that the car was apparently sound*. So, the probability that John predicts that the car is apparently sound is 0.72 + 0.02 = 0.74, and the probability that he says that the car is apparently defective is 0.08 + 0.18 = 0.26. We can now draw the tree diagram in reverse, insert the probabilities we have deduced, and deduce the remaining probabilities (diagram 11.08).

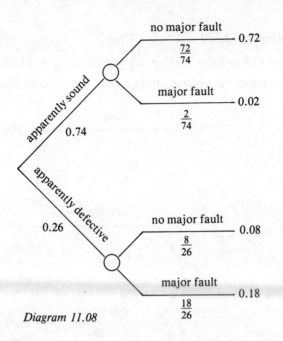

Diagram 11.08

Notice that it is necessary to alter the order of some of the probabilities. We can obtain the conditional probabilities by division − for example, the probability that no major fault occurs given that John thinks the car is sound is $\frac{0.72}{0.74} = \frac{72}{74}$. Likewise, the probability that no major fault occurs given that John thinks the car is defective is $\frac{0.08}{0.26} = \frac{8}{26}$. We can now evaluate the remaining decision points. Taking decision point 3

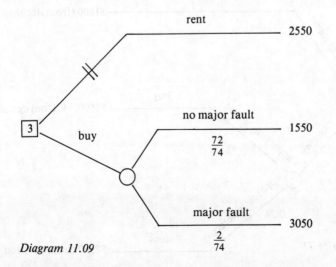

Diagram 11.09

Cost of renting = \$2,550.

Expected cost of buying $= 1550 \times \dfrac{72}{74} + 3050 \times \dfrac{2}{74} = \$1590.54$.

So if decision point 3 is reached, John should buy. Now evaluating decision point 4.

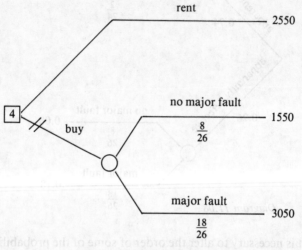

Diagram 11.10

Cost of renting = \$2,550.

Expected cost of buying $= 1550 \times \dfrac{8}{26} + 3050 \times \dfrac{18}{26} = \$2588.46$.

So if decision point 4 is reached, John should rent. Finally, we can evaluate decision point 1.

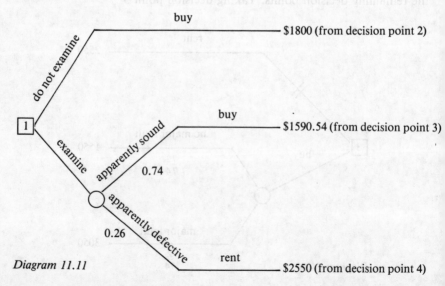

Diagram 11.11

Expected cost if vehicle not examined = $1800.

Expected cost if vehicle examined = 1590.54 × 0.74 + 2550 × 0.26 = $1840. We would advise John to go ahead and buy the vehicle outright, though the decision is very marginal. Should the cost of borrowing the car for a day be less than $50, and/or should John and his friend be more accurate in their prediction, then the alternative course of action might well be chosen.

Exercises to Chapter 11

11.1   An investment trust manager wishes to buy a portfolio of shares and he has sufficient funds to buy either portfolio A, portfolio B or portfolio C. The potential gains from the portfolios will depend upon the level of economic activity in the future, and the following estimates have been made (all figures in £000).

| | | State of Nature | | |
		Expansion	Stability	Contraction
	A	100	50	−50
Portfolio	B	50	100	−25
	C	−50	0	180

Which portfolio should be selected if the manager applies
a)   the maximax criterion?
b)   the maximin criterion?
c)   the minimax criterion?

11.2   Suppose that the investment manager makes the following probability estimates for the states of nature in question 1

Expansion	Stability	Contraction
0.1	0.4	0.5

Which portfolio should the manager buy if he uses the EMV criterion?

11.3   If perfect information is available to the investment manager, how much should he pay for it?

11.4   A newsagent finds the demand for a certain weekly magazine varies between 10 and 16 copies. He pays the publisher 15p per copy and sells them for 25p per copy, but copies unsold at the end of the week have no value as they cannot be returned. Construct the payoff matrix facing the newsagent.

11.5   For the newsagent in question 11.4, how many copies should be held in stock according to
a)   the maximax criterion?
b)   the maximin criterion?
c)   the minimax criterion?

11.6   Suppose the demand for the magazine has the following probabilities

Demand per week	10	11	12	13	14	15	16
Probability	0.05	0.10	0.15	0.25	0.20	0.15	0.1

How many magazines should the newsagent stock according to the EMV criterion?

11.7 Which criterion do you consider the more appropriate to the newsagent in question 11.4.

11.8 Mr. Wealthy has £50,000 invested at 10% per annum compound. He has been given the chance to buy the patent rights for an automatic rifle, and the patent rights will last for 10 years. All rifles made under this patent are sold to the Ministry of Defence, and the contract is worth £10,000 per year. Now it has been hinted that the government is contemplating an increase in defence spending, and should this happen the value of the contract would rise to £40,000 per year. Given that there is a 20% chance of increasing defence spending, and that the patent right would cost £50,000, should Mr. Wealthy buy the patent rights, or should he leave his money invested (NB ignore the income earning capacity of the income from royalties)
Hint: £50,000 invested at 10% per annum compound would grow to 50,000 $\times (1.1)^{10} = £129,687$ in 10 year's time.

11.9 What would have to be the probability of an increase in defence spending to make it just worth while for Mr. Wealthy to buy the patent rights?

11.10 Suppose an official of the Ministry of Defence is prepared to reveal the government's intention on defence expenditure to Mr. Wealthy for a fee of £30,000. Is this information worth buying?

11.11 International Conglometerates Ltd. is considering which of two firms it should purchase. It could buy Allied Dog Foods for £3m. and this could be expected to yield £0.75m per year. However Parliament is considering legislation to restrict the number of dogs. A decision is not expected for two years, but if the number of dogs is restricted, then the annual receipts would fall to £0.1m. Alternatively, Guided Systems Ltd could be bought for £1m, and this would yield a cash flow of £0.5m per year. Within two years, the government must decide whether to replace the present early warning system, and Guided Systems would then have to decide whether or not to expand at a cost of £2m and tender for the replacement system. If the tender is successful, guided Systems cash flow would increase to £0.8m per year, but if the tender is unsuccessful (or if no tender is made) then the cash flow would fall to £0.1m per year. Any decision made now must last for the next ten years.
Draw a tree diagram of the alternative courses of action facing International Conglomerates. Insert the appropriate payoffs and hence decide the best course of action under the maximax and maximin criteria.

11.12 For question 11.11, find the best course of action according to the EMV criterion given the following probabilities
P (Government restricts number of dogs) = 0.4
P (Government replaces early warning system) = 0.7
P (Guided System's tender is successful) = 0.9.

11.13 If an official at the Home Office is prepared to release information on the government's intention towards restricting the number of dogs, how much is this information worth to International Conglomerates?

11.14 A manufacturer has spent £20,000 on developing a product, and must now decide whether to manufacture on a large or small scale. If demand for the product is high, then the expected profit during the product's life would be £700,000 for a high manufacturing level and £150,000 for a low manufacturing level. If the demand is low then the expected profit is £100,000 for a high manufacturing level and £200,000 for a low manufacturing level. The initial indication is a 40% chance of a high demand, but a market research survey could predict the demand with 85% accuracy. How much can the manufacturer afford to spend on market research?

Chapter Twelve

Markov Chains

In this chapter we will bring together what we have learnt about probability and matrices. We shall examine stochastic processes, which we will define as a sequence of events where the outcome of each event depends upon chance elements. We will assume that the process contains a finite number of outcomes which we will call *states*. The probability of the process resulting in a particular state depends primarily on the previous state it was in. You should imagine that the process starts in a particular state, and after a series of step by step movements, the process is either in the original state, or has moved to some other state. If we have sufficient information to calculate the probabilities of moving from state to state (or remaining in a particular state) then such a process is called a Markov Chain. Now you are probably thinking that this is all rather confusing − perhaps an example will clarify just what we mean by a Markov Chain process.

A Market-Share Example

Let us suppose that just two brands of detergent are available to purchasers, and we will call these brands Cleano and Zip. We will also assume that customers buy one packet of detergent per month. When considering which brand should be purchased, the housewife has two choices; she can switch brands (i.e. if she bought Zip last month, then she could buy Cleano this month) or she could stay loyal to the brand purchased last month. Finally, let us suppose that 75% of Cleano's customers and 50% of Zip's customers stay loyal. We could represent the situation with a transition diagram like this:

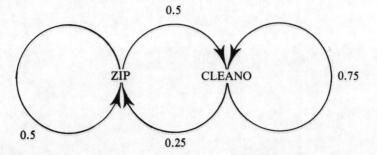

A situation such as this is called a two-state Markov Chain process, and the states are the brands purchased. A better method of presenting the probabilities is in a matrix

		Next Purchase	
		Cleano	Zip
Last purchase	Cleano	$\begin{pmatrix} 0.75 \\ 0.5 \end{pmatrix}$	$\begin{matrix} 0.25 \\ 0.5 \end{matrix} \end{pmatrix}$
	Zip		

A matrix such as this — showing the probabilities of changing states — is called a *transitions matrix,* and it has three important features that you should note. Firstly, the matrix must be square — if it isn't then we will not have covered all the states. After all, if we had two brands to select from on our last purchase then we must have two brands to select from on our next purchase. The second point to note is that as the elements in the matrix are probabilities, it follows that no element can exceed 1 nor be negative. Finally, as the rows of the matrix give the probabilities of either staying in the previous state or switching to another state, it follows that the elements in any row add up to one — you either change or you dont!)

Predicting the Future

We will now set ourselves the task of predicting the share of the market for each brand during next month. To do this we need to know this month's market share, and we will suppose that Cleano has 70% and Zip has 30% of the market. Also we must assume that customer's buying intentions remain fixed, that is, the elements in the transitions matrix remain constant.

Now 70% of the market bought Cleano this month and we know that 75% of them will buy Cleano again next month. This represents $70 \times 0.75 = 52.5\%$ of the market next month. Also, 30% of the market bought Zip this month, and we know that 50% of them will switch to Cleano next month. This represents $30 \times 0.5 = 15\%$ of the market next month. So we would predict Cleano's market share next month to be 52.5% (which it retains) + 15% (which it captures from Zip) = 67.5%, and Zip's market share would be $100 - 67.5 = 32.5\%$ (or 70×0.25 which is captures from Cleano + 30×0.5 which it retains = 32.5%.)

Suppose we put the market shares this month into a row vector (0.7 .0.3) using proportions rather than percentages. We could then predict next month's market shares using matrix multiplication.

$$(0.7 \quad 0.3) \begin{pmatrix} 0.75 & 0.25 \\ 0.5 & 0.5 \end{pmatrix} = (0.675 \quad 0.325)$$

Let us now attempt to generalise. Let P(o) be the initial distribution between the states and P(1) be the distribution after 1 time period. If X is the transitions matrix it follows that

$$P(1) = P(o) X.$$

And if P(2) is the distribution at the end of the second period

$$P(2) = (P_{(0)}X) X$$
$$= P(o)X^2$$

So if P(n) is the distribution after n time periods

$$P(n) = P(o)X^n$$
$$\text{or } P(n) = P(n-1)X$$

The Steady State

Let us now use our general expression to show how the market share changes as time elapses. We know that

$$P(1) = (0.7 \quad 0.3) \begin{pmatrix} 0.75 & 0.25 \\ 0.5 & 0.5 \end{pmatrix} = (0.675 \quad 0.325)$$

$$\text{So } P(2) = (0.675 \quad 0.325) \begin{pmatrix} 0.75 & 0.25 \\ 0.5 & 0.5 \end{pmatrix} = (0.66875 \quad 0.33125)$$

Continuing in this way, we could construct a table showing our results (which have been rounded).

| | % Market Share for | |
Time period	Cleano	Zip
0	70	30
1	67.5	32.5
2	66.875	33.125
4	66.72	33.28
5	66.68	33.32
6	66.67	33.33
7	66.67	33.33

Look carefully at this table and notice how the share of the market is changing. Cleano's share is declining, but the decreases are becoming smaller and smaller. Likewise, Zip's share is rising and the increases are becoming smaller and smaller. In fact, after the six month, the market does not change at all. It appears that the market shares are settling down, with Cleano having ⅔, and Zip ⅓ of the market. We have now reached a *steady state* with fixed market shares.

It may be useful at this stage to enquire just what we mean by a steady state. We mean, in fact, that the number of customers changing from Cleano to Zip is exactly the same as the number of customers changing from Zip to Cleano. This is easily proved: If Cleano has ⅔ of the market, then the proportion of the market changing to Zip is ⅔ × ¼ = ⅙. Likewise, if Zip has ⅓ of the market, the proportion of the market changing to Cleano is ⅓ × ½, which also equals ⅙. So for each product the number of customers lost equals the number of customers gained.

Clearly, being able to predict the ultimate market share is useful. But what is even more interesting is that the ultimate market share is independent of the initial market share. We assumed that initially Cleano had 70% and Zip 20% of the market, but we could have supposed any market share we wished. It would not have affected the ultimate share, which is determined by the transitions matrix and not the initial distribution. Suppose, for example, we assumed that the market initially was evenly split: the table below shows clearly that the ultimate market share would still be ⅔ for Cleano and ⅓ for Zip.

	% Share of market for	
Time Period	Cleano	Zip
0	50	50
1	62.5	37.5
2	65.63	34.37
3	66.41	33.59
4	66.6	33.4
5	66.65	33.35
6	66.66	33.34
7	66.67	33.33
8	66.67	33.33

Solving the Steady State Distribution

We now need a method for finding the steady state without having to perform many matrix multiplications. Suppose that after n periods, the market proportions are π_1 for Cleano and π_2 for Zip. If this represents the steady state, then it must follow that

$$(\pi_1 \quad \pi_2) \begin{pmatrix} \frac{3}{4} & \frac{1}{4} \\ \frac{1}{2} & \frac{1}{2} \end{pmatrix} = (\pi_1 \quad \pi_2)$$

i.e. the proportions do not change, Multiplying out the left hand side we have

$$\frac{3}{4} \pi_1 + \frac{1}{2} \pi_2 = \pi_1 \dots \dots \dots (1)$$
$$\frac{1}{4} \pi_1 + \frac{1}{2} \pi_2 = \pi_2 \dots \dots \dots (2)$$

Apparently, we have two equations containing π_1 and π_2 − but in fact they are both the same equation (you can prove this for yourself). So we cannot use simultaneous equation techniques to solve π_1 and π_2. However, we do know that the proportion buying Cleano plus the proportion buying Zip must equal 1, i.e.

$$\pi_1 + \pi_2 = 1.$$
$$\text{so} \quad \pi_2 = 1 - \pi_1 \dots \dots (3)$$

We can now substitute the value for π_2 obtained in equation (3) either in equation (1) or equation (2) . . . it doesn't matter which one we choose. In this case, we will use equation (1), but first we will remove the fractions by multiplying throughout by 4.

$$3\pi_1 + 2\pi_2 = 4\pi_1$$

but

$$\pi_2 = 1 - \pi_1$$
$$3\pi_1 + 2(1-\pi_1) = 4\pi_1$$
$$3\pi_1 + 2 - 2\pi_1 = 4\pi_1$$
$$3\pi_1 = 2$$
$$\pi_1 = \tfrac{2}{3}$$
$$\pi_2 = \tfrac{1}{3}.$$

This result agrees precisely with the result we obtained earlier.

Now let us see if we can generalise. Suppose the following expression represents a steady state, two state Markov Chain.

$$(\pi_1 \quad \pi_2) \begin{pmatrix} P_{11} & P_{12} \\ P_{21} & P_{22} \end{pmatrix} = (\pi_1 \quad \pi_2)$$

Using the first column of the transitions matrix

$$P_{11}\pi_1 + P_{21}\pi_2 = \pi_1$$
and $\pi_2 = 1 - \pi_1$
so $P_{11}\pi_1 + P_{21}(1 - \pi_1) = \pi_1$
$$\pi_1 - P_{11}\pi_1 + P_{21}\pi_1 = P_{21}$$
$$\pi_1 (1 - P_{11} + P_{21}) = P_{21}$$
$$\pi_1 = \frac{P_{21}}{1 - P_{11} + P_{21}}.$$

In our detergent example, $P_{11} = 0.75$ and $P_{21} = 0.5$, so

$$\pi_1 = \frac{0.5}{1 - 0.75 + 0.5} = \frac{0.5}{0.75} = \frac{2}{3}$$

and $\pi_2 = 1 - \pi_1 = 1 - \tfrac{2}{3} = \tfrac{1}{3}$

Three State Markow Chains

We could find the steady state for a three state Markov Chain process like this:

$$(\pi_1 \quad \pi_2 \quad \pi_3) \begin{pmatrix} P_{11} & P_{12} & P_{13} \\ P_{21} & P_{22} & P_{23} \\ P_{31} & P_{32} & P_{33} \end{pmatrix} = (\pi_1 \quad \pi_2 \quad \pi_3)$$

where $\pi_1 + \pi_2 + \pi_3 = 1$
and so $\pi_3 = 1 - \pi_1 - \pi_2 \ldots \ldots (1)$

Multiplying the vector by the first column of the transitions matrix

$$P_{11}\pi_1 + P_{21}\pi_2 + P_{31}\pi_3 = \pi_1$$

and substituting the value for π_3 in this equation

$$P_{11}\pi_1 + P_{21}\pi_2 + P_{31}(1 - \pi_1 - \pi_2) = \pi_1$$
$$P_{11}\pi_1 + P_{21}\pi_2 + P_{31} - P_{31}\pi_1 - P_{31}\pi_2 = \pi_1$$
$$P_{11}\pi_1 - \pi_1 - P_{31}\pi_1 + P_{21}\pi_2 - P_{31}\pi_2 = -P_{31}$$
$$(P_{11} - 1 - P_{31})\pi_1 - (P_{31} - P_{21})\pi_2 = -P_{31} \ldots . (2)$$

Multiplying the vector by the second column of the transitions matrix

$$P_{12}\pi_1 + P_{22}\pi_2 + P_{32}\pi_3 = \pi_2$$
$$\text{Substituting} \pi_3 = 1 - \pi_1 - \pi_2$$
$$P_{12}\pi_1 + P_{22}\pi_2 + P_{32}(1 - \pi_1 - \pi_2) = \pi_2$$
$$P_{12}\pi_1 + P_{22}\pi_2 + P_{32} - P_{32}\pi_1 - P_{32}\pi_2 = \pi_2$$
$$P_{12}\pi_1 - P_{32}\pi_1 - \pi_2 + P_{22}\pi_2 - P_{32}\pi_2 = -P_{32}$$
$$(P_{12} - P_{32})\pi_1 - (1 - P_{22} + P_{32})\pi_2 = -P_{32} \ldots . (3)$$

We shall now apply these equations to an example. Suppose that in a particular country, three weekly newspapers are published: the Bugle, the Tribune and the Clarion. Of 100 people who bought the Bugle this week, 30 said they would do so again, 40 said they would switch to the Clarion and 30 said they would switch to the Tribune. Of 100 people who bought the Clarion this week, 50 would buy the Clarion again 10 would switch to the Bugle and 40 would switch to the Tribune. Of 100 who bought the Tribune this week, 70 would buy the Tribune again, 20 would switch to the Bugle and 10 would switch to the Clarion. We could summarise the results of our survey in a matrix.

		Next Purchase		
		Bugle	Clarion	Tribune
This Purchase	Bugle	30	40	30
	Clarion	10	50	40
	Tribune	20	10	70

If we assume that the buying intentions expressed by the readers are typical and will continue in the future, then we can find the ultimate market share between the three newspapers. Firstly, we set up the problem using the steady state vector and the transitions matrix.

$$(\pi_1 \quad \pi_2 \quad \pi_3)\begin{pmatrix} .3 & .4 & .3 \\ .1 & .5 & .4 \\ .2 & .1 & .7 \end{pmatrix} = (\pi_1 \quad \pi_2 \quad \pi_3)$$

So $P_{11} = 0.3$, $P_{12} = 0.4$, $P_{21} = 0.1$, $P_{22} = 0.5$, $P_{31} = 0.2$, $P_{32} = 0.1$.

Substituting these values in equation (2)

$$(0.3 - 1 - 0.2)\pi_1 - (0.2 - 0.1)\pi_2 = -0.2$$
$$-0.9\pi_1 - 0.1\pi_2 = -0.2$$

Multiplying by -10

$$9\pi_1 + \pi_2 = 2 \ldots \ldots \ldots \text{(a)}$$

Substituting these values in equation (3)

$$(0.4 - 0.1)\pi_1 - (1 - 0.5 + 0.1)\pi_2 = -0.1$$
$$0.3\pi_1 - 0.6\pi_2 = -0.1$$
$$\text{or } 3\pi_1 - 6\pi_2 = 1 \ldots \ldots \text{(b)}$$

If we multiply equation (b) by 3, it is compatible with equation (a)

$$9\pi_1 - 18\pi_2 = -3$$
$$9\pi_2 + \pi_2 = 2$$

Subtracting

$$-19\pi_1 = -5$$
$$= \frac{5}{19}$$

We can now substitute this value in equation (a)

$$9\pi_1 + \frac{5}{19} = 2$$
$$9\pi_1 = \frac{33}{19}$$
$$= \frac{11}{57}$$

Finally, putting our value for π_1 and π_2 in equation (1)

$$\pi_3 = 1 - \pi_1 - \pi_2$$
$$= 1 - \frac{11}{57} - \frac{5}{19}$$
$$= 1 - \frac{11}{57} - \frac{15}{57}$$
$$= \frac{31}{57}$$

Our results are summarised in the table below.

Newspaper	Predicted Ultimate Market Share
Bugle	11/57
Clarion	15/57
Tribune	31/57

We can check that our answers are correct using matrix multiplication i.e.

$$(11/57 \quad 15/57 \quad 31/57) \begin{pmatrix} .3 & .4 & .3 \\ .1 & .5 & .4 \\ .2 & .1 & .7 \end{pmatrix} = (11/57 \quad 15/57 \quad 31/57)$$

Finding the steady state for a three state Markov Chain is quite a task! If you have a Markov Chain with more than 3 states, you should really seek a computer solution.

Absorbing Markov Chains

If the board of directors of Acme P.L.C. are faced with problems of company strategy, they seek the advice of the company's Management Services Department. When such problems arise, the board briefs Harry, the manager of Management Services, who then opens a file on the problem. Harry then passes the file on to either Tom or Dick for action. There is a 60% chance that Harry will pass the file on to Tom, and a 40% chance he will pass it to Dick. Now both Tom and Dick are wary of recommending a course of action to the board (the board does not suffer fools gladly – and people giving bad advice in the past have been severely dealt with). The alternative to taking a decision is for Tom or Dick to return the file to Harry with a request for more information. The probability that Tom makes such a request is 90%, and the probability that Dick will do so is 80%. If the file is returned to Harry, then Harry supplies more information or advice, then passes the file back to either Tom or Dick. Now just because, say, Dick passes the file back to Harry for advice, it does not follow that Harry returns the file with advice to Dick. There is still a 60% chance of the file going to Tom and a 40% chance of it going to Dick. This situation is the classic 'task shunting' problem – the file is shunting back and forward between Tom, Dick and Harry until eventually a decision is taken. The transition diagram for this problem looks like this.

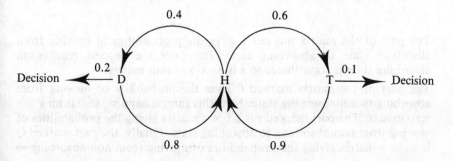

This problem is essentially different from the previous problem. In the previous problem, it was possible to move from any state i to any other state j but in this case, once Tom or Dick make a decision, the process stops. Such problems are called *absorbing Markov Chains or Random Walks*. We shall now identify the states in this problem.

1. Harry has the file
2. Dick has the file
3. Dick closes the file (i.e. makes a decision)
4. Tom has the file
5. Tom closes the file.

States 3 and 5 are called *absorbing states* – if the file moves into this state then the process stops. The other states – 1, 2 and 4 are called non-absorbing states, the file moving freely between them. The transitions matrix is:

		TO				
		1	2	3	4	5
	1	0	0.4	0	0.6	0
	2	0.8	0	0.2	0	0
FROM	3	0	0	1	0	0
	4	0.9	0	0	0	0.1
	5	0	0	0	0	1

When analysing absorbing Markov Chains, it is usual to put the transitions matrix into the so-called *canonical* (or standard) form. This partitions the matrix into s absorbing and t non-absorbing states like this.

$$
\begin{array}{c} s \\ t \end{array}
\left(\begin{array}{c|c} I & O \\ \hline S & Q \end{array} \right)
$$

The part of the matrix marked I gives the probabilities of moving from absorbing state to absorbing state. But once the process reaches an absorbing state it stays there, so I is an s × s unit matrix.

The part of the matrix marked 0 gives the probability of moving from absorbing to nonabsorbing state. Now this cannot happen, so 0 is an s × t zero matrix. The part marked s is a t × s matrix giving the probabilities of moving from non-absorbing to absorbing state. Finally, the part marked Q is a t × t matrix giving the probabilities of moving from non-absorbing to non-absorbing state. The canonical transitions matrix for our task shunting problem is

$$
\begin{array}{c}
 \\
3 \\
5 \\
1 \\
2 \\
4
\end{array}
\begin{array}{ccccc}
3 & 5 & 1 & 2 & 4 \\
\left(\begin{array}{cc|ccc}
1 & 0 & 0 & 0 & 0 \\
0 & 1 & 0 & 0 & 0 \\
\hline
0 & 0 & 0 & 0.4 & 0.6 \\
0.2 & 0 & 0.8 & 0 & 0 \\
0 & 0.1 & 0.9 & 0 & 0
\end{array}\right)
\end{array}
$$

What we shall attempt to do with this problem is to find the average number of times the file is shunted before a decision is taken. We shall also attempt to find the probability that (a) Tom and (b) Dick closes the file.

The Fundamental Matrix

It will be easier to perform the tasks we set ourselves in the last section if we first consider a simpler case. Suppose that in any one year, a firm loses ¾ of its labour force. From the employees viewpoint, this situation is an absorbing Markov Chain with two states – the employee can leave the firm (the absorbing state) or he can stay with the firm (the non-absorbing state.) Let us see if we can determine the average time spent with the firm by an employee. To do this, we will assume that the end of one particular year, a firm has 1024 employees and deduce what would happen to these employees as time elapses. A simple table will show this

Year	Employees left at end of year
1	1024
2	256
3	64
4	16
5	4
6	1
	1365

So we see that by the end of the 6th year, the 1024 men between them completed 1365 years service. Now suppose that the firm could employ a fractional number of men, the series would continue like this: ¼ + ¹/₁₆ + ¹/₆₄ + ... If we keep adding the next term to our total so far, then the total will get very near to 1365⅓. So the average time spent by the employees in this firm is $\dfrac{1365\tfrac{1}{3}}{1024} = 1\tfrac{1}{3}$ years.

In fact, there was no need to write out the table above to find the total number of years service. The series is called a convergent geometric progression – a series where any term is a constant fraction of the previous

222

term. In this case the constant fraction is ¼. We can find the sum of such a series by using the expression

$$\frac{a}{1-r}$$

where a is the first term (in this case 1024) and r is the rate of decrease (¼) So the sum of this series is

$$\frac{1024}{1-¼} = 1365⅓$$

Another point of interest is that we could have deduced the average time spent by considering the probability that an employee stays with the firm for each of n consecutive years.

Year	Probability employee still with firm
1	1
2	¼
3	$(¼)^2 = 1/16$
4	$(¼)^3 = 1/64$
5	$(¼)^4 = 1/256$
.	.
.	.

Again this forms a geometric progression with a first term 1 and constant fraction ¼. Summing this series.

$$\frac{1}{1-¼} = 1⅓$$

– the average time an employee spends with the firm.

Let us now summarise what we have discovered. In a two-state absorbing Markov Chain, if Q is the probability of moving from non-absorbing state to absorbing state, the average number of 'moves' before absorption is given by

$$\frac{1}{1-Q} = (1-Q)^{-1}$$

Now suppose we have more than one non-absorbing states, then Q will be a matrix. Also, we know that the matrix equivalent of 1 is I, the unit matrix, so we must modify the expression above to read

$$(I-Q)^{-1}$$

the inverse of Q. We can now find the average number of moves for our task shunting problem.

$$Q = \begin{pmatrix} 0 & .4 & .6 \\ .8 & 0 & 0 \\ .9 & 0 & 0 \end{pmatrix}$$

$$(I-Q) = \begin{pmatrix} 1 & 0 & 0 \\ 0 & 1 & 0 \\ 0 & 0 & 1 \end{pmatrix} - \begin{pmatrix} 0 & .4 & .6 \\ .8 & 0 & 0 \\ .9 & 0 & 0 \end{pmatrix} = \begin{pmatrix} 1 & -0.4 & -.06 \\ -0.8 & 1 & 0 \\ -0.9 & 0 & 1 \end{pmatrix}$$

Inverting this Matrix.

$$(I-Q)^{-1} = \begin{pmatrix} \dfrac{50}{7} & \dfrac{20}{7} & \dfrac{30}{7} \\[2mm] \dfrac{40}{7} & \dfrac{23}{7} & \dfrac{24}{7} \\[2mm] \dfrac{45}{7} & \dfrac{18}{7} & \dfrac{34}{7} \end{pmatrix}$$

The matrix $(I-Q)^{-1}$ is called the *fundamental matrix,* and its interpretation will be made easier if we insert what the rows and columns mean

			To	
		Harry	Dick	Tom
From	Harry	50/7	20/7	30/7
	Dick	40/7	23/7	24/7
	Tom	45/7	18/7	34/7

We interpret a fundamental matrix as follows: if the process starts with a row state, the elements tell us the average number of times the process is in the column state before absorption. So if the file originates with Harry, it is handled, on average 50/7 times by Harry, 20/7 times by Dick and 30/7 times by Tom before the file is closed. Now in this problem, we have assumed that the file must originate with Harry, so the second and third row have no meaning in the context of this process. Hence, we conclude that the file is shunted 50/7 + 20/7 + 30/7 = 14.3 times within the Management Services Department before the file is closed. Shortly, we will examine a problem where every element in the fundamental matrix has a meaning.

The Probability of Absorption

The second part of our problem was to determine the probability that a) Tom and b) Dick closes the file. Now it is obvious that sooner or later a decision will be taken, so the two probabilities will sum one. Again, it will be easier to examine first our two state problem.

We know that the probability that an employee leaves the firm in any one year is ¾. We can construct a table showing the probability that an employee leaves in any particular year.

Year	Probability employee leaves
1	¾
2	$\frac{1}{4} \times \frac{3}{4}$ (i.e. he stays 1st year and leaves in second)
3	$\frac{1}{4} \times \frac{1}{4} \times \frac{3}{4} = (\frac{1}{4})^2 \times \frac{3}{4}$.
4	$(\frac{1}{4})^3 \times \frac{3}{4}$

Now the employee leaves in either the first, second third etc. . . . . year, so the probability that he leaves is

$$\frac{3}{4} + \frac{1}{4} \times \frac{3}{4} + (\frac{1}{4})^2 \times \frac{3}{4} + (\frac{1}{4})^3 \times \frac{3}{4} + \ldots \ldots \ldots$$
$$= \frac{3}{4}[1 + \frac{1}{4} + (\frac{1}{4})^2 + (\frac{1}{4})^3 \ldots \ldots \ldots \ldots \ldots]$$

Now we already know that the matrix equivalent of the expression in the bracket is the fundamental matrix $(I - Q)^{-1}$. The fraction outside the bracket (¾) is the probability of moving from non-absorbing to absorbing state. Consulting the canonical form of the matrix, we see that the matrix equivalent of this is the matrix s. So the probability of absorption will be given by the matrix B, where,

$$B = (I - Q)^{-1} S$$

We can now find the probability that Tom and Dick close the file.

$$
\begin{pmatrix} \frac{50}{7} & \frac{20}{7} & \frac{30}{7} \\ \frac{40}{7} & \frac{23}{7} & \frac{24}{7} \\ \frac{45}{7} & \frac{18}{7} & \frac{34}{7} \end{pmatrix}
\begin{pmatrix} 0 & 0 \\ \frac{1}{5} & 0 \\ 0 & \frac{1}{10} \end{pmatrix}
=
\begin{pmatrix} \frac{4}{7} & \frac{3}{7} \\ \frac{46}{70} & \frac{24}{70} \\ \frac{36}{70} & \frac{34}{70} \end{pmatrix}
$$

	Dick	Tom
Harry	4/7	3/7
Dick	46/70	24/70
Tom	36/70	34/70

We interpret this matrix as follows: if the process starts in the row state, the elements of the matrix give the probabilities of absorption in the column states. As the file can originate only with Harry, again the last two rows have no meaning. We conclude that the probability that Dick closed the file is 4/7 and the probability that Tom closes the file is 3/7. Notice that the rows of this matrix sum one (which, of course, they must being probabilities).

Steady State Absorbing Markov Chains

Eurofreight moves goods in containers between France, Germany and Italy, and also moves goods within the national boundaries of these countries. From time-to-time, containers are 'lost' i.e. stolen or damaged beyond repair, and the company wishes to analyse the average life of the containers. Let us first define the states in this problem.

State F   –   the container is in France.
State G   –   the container is in Germany.
State I   –   the container is in Italy.
State L   –   the container is lost: this is the absorbing state.

The monthly movement of containers is as follows:

$$
\begin{array}{c}
 \\
 \\
\text{From} \\
 \\
\end{array}
\begin{array}{c}
 \\
F \\
G \\
I \\
\end{array}
\begin{array}{cccc}
\multicolumn{4}{c}{\text{To}} \\
F & G & I & L \\
\left(\begin{array}{cccc}
0.5 & 0.2 & 0.2 & 0.1 \\
0.2 & 0.5 & 0.2 & 0.1 \\
0.1 & 0.3 & 0.4 & 0.2 \\
\end{array}\right)
\end{array}
$$

Firstly, we will put this transitions matrix into canonical form

$$
\begin{array}{c}
 \\
L \\
F \\
G \\
I \\
\end{array}
\begin{array}{cccc}
L & F & G & I \\
\left(\begin{array}{c|ccc}
1 & 0 & 0 & 0 \\
0.1 & 0.5 & 0.2 & 0.2 \\
0.1 & 0.2 & 0.5 & 0.2 \\
0.2 & 0.1 & 0.3 & 0.4 \\
\end{array}\right)
\end{array}
$$

The fundamental matrix is

$$
(I-Q)^{-1} =
\begin{array}{cccc}
F & G & I & \\
\left(\begin{array}{ccc}
24/7 & 18/7 & 2 \\
2 & 4 & 2 \\
11/7 & 17/7 & 3 \\
\end{array}\right)
&
\begin{array}{c}
F \\
G \\
I \\
\end{array}
\end{array}
$$

So we see that a container starting its life in France spends, an average 24/7 months in France 18/7 months in Germany and 2 months in Italy before becoming "lost". So the average life of a container starting in France is $24/7 + 18/7 + 2 = 8$ months, the average life of a container starting in Germany is $2 + 4 + 2 = 8$ months, and the average life of a container introduced in Italy is $11/7 + 17/7 + 3 = 7$ months.

The B matrix for this process is:

$$
\begin{pmatrix}
24/7 & 18/7 & 2 \\
2 & 4 & 2 \\
11/7 & 17/7 & 3 \\
\end{pmatrix}
\begin{pmatrix}
.1 \\
.1 \\
.2 \\
\end{pmatrix}
=
\begin{pmatrix}
1 \\
1 \\
1 \\
\end{pmatrix}
\begin{array}{c}
F \\
G \\
I \\
\end{array}
$$

This shows that all containers are ultimately 'lost'. Now although we know this already, finding the B matrix is still useful — it helps verify our calculations for the fundamental matrix.

This section is headed 'steady state absorbing chains' and we must now examine how this might occur. Let us suppose that Eurofreight introduces 100 containers in each country — at the end of the month the containers will be distributed like this:

$$
(100 \quad 100 \quad 100) \begin{pmatrix} 0.5 & 0.2 & 0.2 \\ 0.2 & 0.5 & 0.2 \\ 0.1 & 0.3 & 0.4 \end{pmatrix} = \begin{matrix} F & I & G \\ (80 & 100 & 80) \end{matrix}
$$

Of the 300 containers introduced 260 remain, so if Eurofreight require 300 containers a month it must introduce 40 new containers per month. We can also see that if Eurofreight requires to maintain the initial distribution of containers (i.e. 100 in each country), then each month it must introduce 20 of these new containers in France and 20 in Italy. The process has now reached a steady state: injections into the system balance leakages from the system. You should note, however, that there is no single steady state with absorbing Markov Chains, rather there will be a steady state for each level of injection. (It is also possible that no steady state exists — and example at the end of this chapter will illustrate this). Given the level of injections, then, it should be possible to calculate the steady state distribution (should one exist). Suppose K gives the steady state distribution for injection J. Leakages from the system in any one time period will be

$$
K - QK
$$

Steady state will occur if leakages equal injections i.e.

$$
\begin{aligned}
K - QK &= J \\
(I - Q)K &= J \\
K &= J(I - Q)^{-1}
\end{aligned}
$$

So if Eurofreight introduce 70 new containers into each country each month, the steady-state distribution will be

$$
(70 \quad 70 \quad 70) \begin{pmatrix} 24/7 & 18/7 & 2 \\ 2 & 4 & 2 \\ 11/7 & 17/7 & 3 \end{pmatrix} = (490 \quad 630 \quad 490)
$$

i.e. 490 each in France and Italy and 630 in Germany.

One final point you should note before we finish this chapter. It is not always possible to achieve a desired steady state. Try, for example to determine the level of injections if the required distribution each month was 80 containers in Germany and 100 containers each in France and Italy.

Exercises to Chapter Twelve

12.1 Suppose that a society of motor traders interview a group of people who buy a new vehicle each year, always buying either a saloon or a hatchback. Of the present owners of saloons, $\frac{2}{3}$ will switch to hatchbacks next year. Of the present owners of hatchbacks, $\frac{1}{4}$ will switch to saloons next year.

Set up the transitions matrix and predict the share of the market between saloons and hatchbacks in the long run.

12.2 A demographic survey of Hong Kong found that, each year 5% of the residents of the ceded territory (i.e. Hong Kong island and Kowloon) moved to the leased territories (i.e. the New Territories), and 2% of residents in the New Territories moved to the ceded territories. Assuming that the total number of people in Hong Kong remains constant (quite an assumption!) determine the long run proportions of residents in the leased and ceded territories.

12.3 An examination of the occupations of fathers and sons yielded the following transitions matrix

		Son's occupation	
		Manual	White collar
Father's Occupation	Manual	$\frac{2}{3}$	$\frac{1}{3}$
	White collar	$\frac{1}{8}$	$\frac{7}{8}$

a) Find the probability that
   i) a white collar worker's grandfather was a manual worker
   ii) a manual worker's grandfather was a white collar worker.
b) Find the ultimate distribution of the labour force.

12.4 When Al Coholic visits a bar, he sometimes buys beer (B) and sometimes buys Gin (G). When deciding which drink to buy next, he takes into account which drink he bought on the last occasion. Suppose that the last 41 orders were as follows

GGGBBGGGBG   BGGBBBBGGB
GBBBBGBBBB   GBGGBGGGGGB

Decide on what proportion of occasions he would buy Gin in the long run.

12.5 In a particular community there are 1,200 registered voters who all participate in yearly elections.

In year 0, 400 votes were cast for the Capitalist Party, 400 votes cast for the Democratic Party and 400 votes cast for the Workers Party.

In past elections a particular pattern has developed. Of the people voting for the Capitalist Party in the last election, 2/3 will do so in the coming election and 1/3 will vote for the Democratic Party.

Of the people voting for the Democratic Party in the last election, 1/2 will do so again in the coming election and 1/2 will transfer their vote to the Workers Party.

Of the people voting for the Workers Party in the last election, 3/4 will vote for the same party in the coming election and 1/4 will vote for the Democratic Party.

(a) How many people will vote for each of the parties in year 1, and year 2?

(b) What proportion of the total votes will each party receive in the long run?

12.6 A group of economists (they are typical so they never agree) are trying to assess the future prospects of an industry. Their opinions polarise into three schools of thought

Group A thinks the industry will expand
Group B thinks the industry will contract
Group C thinks the industry will maintain its present state.

As more information is made available, they change their minds, but they do not change their minds as a group as they put different interpretations on any new information. Economists in group A are equally likely to switch to B or C, but are twice as likely to retain their existing views. Those in group B are less convicted in their views: there is a 50% chance that they will switch to C and a 25% chance that they will switch to A. Group C is the most fickle: only 20% retain their existing views and the rest are equally likely to switch to A or B.

What opinion is held by the majority of economists in the long run?

12.7 Members of a Holiday Club can receive a substantial discount if they take their summer holidays with one of three holiday operators, namely Holitours, Sandseeker and Funtime.

Membership of the club is fixed at 3600, and in its first year of operation each holiday company attracted 1200 members.

When bookings were taken for the second year, 1/2 the members who had booked with Holitours in the first year did so again, but 1/3 booked with Sandseeker and 1/6 booked with Funtime.

Two-thirds of the members who had holidayed with Sandseeker in the first year rebooked with that company in the second year, the remaining 1/3 deciding to holiday with Funtime for the second year.

Funtime had a rebooking success of 75% for the second year but lost 1/4 of its first year customers to Holitours in the second year.

(a) Represent the information above in the form of a transition matrix.

(b) How many members did each of the holiday companies attracted in the second year?

(c) If the same pattern of holiday rebooking and switching occurs every year, determine the number of members booking with each of the companies in:
   (i) the third year.
   (ii) the long run.

12.8 A sample of 3,696 car owners change their car each year, choosing between a Plum, a Mint and a Ray.

Of the 1,056 Plum owners in 1978, ½ bought the same model in 1979 and ¼ bought a Mint.

Of the 528 Mint owners in 1978, ⅓ switched to a Plum in 1979 and ⅙ bought a Ray.

Of the 2,112 Ray owners in 1978, 264 bought a Mint in 1979 but five times as many remained loyal to their 1978 choice and chose another Ray.

(i) Use the information above to derive a transition matrix for this group of car owners.

(ii) Find the number of car owners choosing each model in 1979.

(iii) Stating any assumptions that are necessary for your calculations, find the number of car owners choosing each model:

(a) in 1980

(b) in the long run.

12.9 When a fault occurs in a component, it is sent to the electrical or mechanical department for repair. Of those components arriving in the electrical department, 50% are re-diagnosed as having mechanical faults and so are passed to the mechanical department; and of the remainder 50% are repaired and 50% are scrapped. Of those components arriving in the mechanical department, 30% are re-diagnosed as having electrical faults, and of the remainder ⅔ are repaired and ⅓ are scrapped.

Stating carefully any assumptions that you may make, set up this problem as an absorbing Markov Chain. Find and interpret the fundamental matrix. For each type of fault, find the probability that the component is repaired and the probability that it is scrapped.

12.10 The sales department of a firm classifies its customers accounts as follows:

Type A describes accounts with unpaid debts of age under three months.

Type B describes accounts with unpaid debts with an age between three months and twelve months.

At the end of each month, the first reclassifies each account. If during the month the debt is paid, then the account is cleared (C). If an account contains debts more than 12 months old, then the debt is written off (W). The following transitions matrix has been obtained.

	C	W	A	B
C	1	0	0	0
W	0	1	0	0
A	.6	0	.3	.1
B	.1	.2	.2	.5

i) Explain this matrix in terms of the changes in state.

ii) Find (and interpret) the fundamental matrix.

iii) Find (and interpret) the B matrix.

12.11 Atomics Ltd. make nuclear fuels, and one of the processes involves packing the fuels into lead containers. This is a dangerous occupation because of the risk of exposure to radiation, and so labour turnover is rather high. Further, each month workers are subject to a psychological examination, and if they do not meet the required standards of stability they are moved to less dangerous work. It has been found that on average for any month, 1/8 of the day shift leave the company, and 1/4 are transferred for psychological reasons. The proportions for the nightshift are 1/6 and 1/6 respectively. Although a worker is appointed to a particular shift, as a concession the company will allow him to change shifts at the end of any month. The following behaviour pattern has been observed

		To	
		Day Shift	Night Shift
	Day Shift	$\dfrac{1}{2}$	$\dfrac{1}{8}$
From			
	Night Shift	$\dfrac{1}{6}$	$\dfrac{1}{2}$

Find the fundamental matrix and the B matrix, explaining what information is given by these matrices.

If 48 workers are required for each shift, how many dayworkers and how many nightworkers should be appointed each month?

12.12 A firm classifies its labour force as A (administrative), B (supervisory) and C (clerical and operatives). Each half year it reviews its staff for possible changes in status. The following transitions matrix is available.

	A	B	C
A	0.85	0.05	0
B	0.05	0.75	0.05
C	0	0.05	0.65

Find the fundamental matrix and interpret your results.

Before the next review, some people will leave and some will retire.

Group:	A	B	C
Probability of leaving	0.05	0.1	0.2
Probability of retiring	0.05	0.05	0.1

Find the B matrix and interpret your results.

The firm requires 40 people in group A, 100 in group B and 440 in group C. What should be the firm's half yearly recruiting policy?

Each retiring operative and clerical worker receives a tankard, each retiring supervisor receives a gold watch, and each retiring administrator receives a set of golf clubs. How many presentations of each type would you expect each half year?

Chapter Thirteen

Simulation Techniques

Have you noticed how someone latches on to a particular word or phrase, and then it is picked up by the mass media and hammered at us? War 'escalates', people 'commute' to work, law enforcement officers avoid 'no go' areas. We no longer have spares; we have back-up systems; we no longer spoil the countryside; we pollute the environment. It would be easy to write a long list of such words and phrases. Nowadays, we are all familiar with the word 'simulation' − how did its popularity arise?

During World War II many raw materials were in short supply or not obtainable, and were produced artificially. Such goods were stamped 'imitation', and this proved to be a marketing disaster! 'Imitation' is a highly emotive word. It means 'made in the likeness of', but it did not mean this to potential purchasers! It meant a rather inferior substitute, to be avoided at all costs. If people were to buy such goods then the 'imitation' label would have to be dropped, Thus, 'imitation' silk became 'synthetic' silk, and sales were much healthier. Although the word synthetic was an improvement, it still did not produce the required product image. Now we have 'simulated' fur and 'simulated' suede. Why did the word 'simulated' succeed when 'imitation' and 'synthetic' failed? Probably because 'simulated' is more pleasant sounding, and almost certainly because few people knew what the word meant!

The exploration of space has certainly extended the familiarity of the word similation. To most people, it means a cartoon of an orbital docking or the re-entry of the capsule into the Earth's atmosphere. To N.A.S.A., simulation means a vital part of mission planning and mission control. At the Space Centre in Houston there is a mock-up of the space vehicles in which the astronauts familiarise themselves with layout and control systems. Clearly, it is better to learn in the simulator than to learn in the vehicle. The simulators are not merely used for astronaut training − if something goes wrong during the mission the failure can be reproduced on the simulators and experiments performed to rectify the fault. Again, it is better to experiment on the ground than in the vehicle.

The motives of simulation are clearly indicated by N.A.S.A. A problem is solved by simulation if it is too costly, too dangerous or just impractical to solve directly.

Monte Carlo Methods

In this chapter, we will consider problems that are difficult to solve directly because they contain random elements. However, we will assume that the random elements can be quantified in a probability distribution. Take, for example, the case of a wholesale fishmonger selling boxes of fish. Daily demand will vary, but we will assume that the wholesaler has kept careful records of daily demand – records that can be summarised in a probability distribution. Suppose he faces the following distribution of demand.

No. of boxes demanded per day	Probability
8	¼
9	½
10	¼

The wholesaler, for some reason, wishes to predict a typical chain of demand over the next 12 days. How can he do this?

The essence of simulation techniques is to substitute for the actual probability distribution some other distribution with the same probabilities. We can then use this second distribution to simulate the actual situation. Suppose we spin two coins: the probability distribution below would result.

Result	Probability
Head Head	¼
Head Tail or Tail Head	½
Tail Tail	¼

Now as this second distribution matches perfectly the distribution of demand, we can simulate a chain of daily demand by spinning coins. We could let two heads simulate a demand of 8 boxes, two tails simulate a demand of 10 boxes, and a head and a tail simulate a demand of 9 boxes. A prediction of demand for the next 12 days might look something like this:

Day	Result of spinning two coins	Simulated demand
1	H H	8
2	H H	8
3	H H	8
4	T T	10
5	H T	9
6	T H	9
7	H T	9
8	T T	10
9	H H	8
10	T T	10
11	H H	8
12	T H	9

You should realise that it is necessary to resort to simulation to predict a sequence of demands because probability theory is a statement about long run frequency. We can use probability theory to state that, in the long run, we will experience a daily demand for 8 boxes on 25% of occasions — we cannot use it to predict demand tomorrow, or on any particular day. Incidentally, you should notice that, using the probability distribution we would predict demand to be for 8 boxes on 25% of occasions, whereas in the simulated sequence we experienced a demand for 8 boxes on 5/12 = 41% of occasions. This difference has arisen because we have taken a small sample of just 12 days. The longer the period over which we run the simulation, the closer would the simulated frequencies match the actual frequencies.

Clearly, it will not always be possible to spin coins and use the results as a basis for simulation. Suppose the pattern of demand facing the fishmonger was as follows.

No. of boxes demanded	Probability (%)
0	2
1	17
2	28
3	28
4	15
5	10
	100

Notice that in this case we have used percentage frequency as a measure of probability — it is often convenient to do this. We can use random numbers to obtain a frequency distribution that can form the basis of a simulation. Originally, random numbers were generated by a device rather like a roulette wheel (which explains why simulation is sometimes called 'Monte-Carlo' methods). Nowadays, random numbers are generated by computers. If you ask a computer to generate a string of random numbers for you, then you should not be able to detect any pattern in the string (after all random means "without pattern"). Moreover, we can ask a computer to generate random numbers within certain defined limits (for example we would ask for random numbers in the range 1 to 10, or within the range 20 to 30).

Suppose we ask the computer to generate a random number in the range 00 to 99 inclusive. As there are 100 possibilities for the number generated, then the probability that the computer generates any particular number in this range is 1%. The probability that the number is in the range 00-09 would be 10% (note that 00-09 inclusive is ten numbers not nine). Likewise, the probability that the number generated is within the range 10-39 is 30%. By grouping the random numbers in an appropriate fashion, we can obtain a distribution of random numbers that matches the distribution of demand. We can then use this distribution of random numbers as the basis of our simulation. The probability that the computer generates a random number in the range 00-01 is 2% — the same as the probability that demand is zero. So if the computer generates a random number within the range 00-01, we will let this simulate a zero demand. The probability that the computer generates a random number in the range 02-18 is 17% — the same as the probability that demand is for one box. So if the computer generates a random number within the range 02-18, we will let this simulate a demand for one box. The probability that two boxes are demanded is 28%, and we can use the next 28 random numbers to simulate this, i.e. if the number generated by the computer is in the range 19-46. The complete distribution would look like this:

Random Numbers	Frequency %	Simulates daily demand of
00 – 01	2	0
02 – 18	17	1
19 – 46	28	2
47 – 74	28	3
75 – 89	15	4
90 – 99	10	5

Suppose the computer produces the following list of random numbers

27   89   99   97   03   95   31   50   91   34

Then reading from the table above we see that this simulates the following demand sequence.

2   4   5   5   1   5   2   3   5   2

We shall now extend the example of the fishmonger to illustrate how simulation can be used. Suppose the supply of fish also varies randomly with the following probabilities

No of boxes supplied	0	1	2	3	4	5
Probability (%)	3	19	24	29	20	5

A box of fish costs the fishmonger £12, and the fishmonger sells a box for £23. Any box unsold at the end of the day is sold for cat food at £15 per box. If the fishmonger cannot supply a customer, then there is a loss of goodwill estimated at £5 per box. We will simulate 10 days trading and estimate average daily profit.

We have already simulated 10 days demand, so the first thing we must do, is to simulate 10 days supply. To do this, we need a distribution of random numbers corresponding to the supply frequencies

Random Numbers	Frequency %	Simulates daily Supply of
00 – 02	3	0
03 – 21	19	1
22 – 45	24	2
46 – 74	29	3
75 – 94	20	4
95 – 99	5	5

If the computer produces the following list of random numbers

72,   94,   52,   78,   12,   21,   25,   20,   34,   93

then this simulates the following level of supply

3,   4,   3,   4,   1,   1,   2,   1,   2,   4

Summarising, we have used simulation to make the following predictions

Day	1	2	3	4	5	6	7	8	9	10
Boxes Supplied	3	4	3	4	1	1	2	1	2	4
Boxes Demanded	2	4	5	5	1	5	2	3	5	2

Having simulated demand and supply, we have the necessary information to estimate average daily profit. You should notice that the following rules must apply when estimating the numbers unsold and the level of unsatisfied demand.

1. The number of boxes sold on any day is the number demanded or the number supplied, whichever is the smaller. After all, the fishmonger cannot sell more boxes than he has bought!

2. If, on any particular day, the number of boxes supplied exceeds the number demanded, then the difference represents the quantity unsold.

3. If, on any particular day the number of boxes demanded exceeds the number supplied, then the difference represents the level of unsatisfied demand.

Day	Boxes supplied	Boxes demanded	Boxes Sold	Boxes Unsold	Unsatisfied Demand
1	3	2	2	1	0
2	4	4	4	0	0
3	3	5	3	0	2
4	4	5	4	0	1
5	1	1	1	0	0
6	1	5	1	0	4
7	2	2	2	0	0
8	1	3	1	0	2
9	2	5	2	0	3
10	4	2	2	2	0
	25		22	3	12

Using the totals, we can deduce that

Revenue from sales to customers	= 22 × £23 =	£506	
Revenue from sales for catfood	= 3 × £15 =	£45	
		£551	

Cost of boxes bought	= 25 × £12 = £300		
Loss of goodwill	= 12 × £5 = £60		
Total Cost	= £360		
		£360	

Total Profit earned £191

Average daily profit $= \dfrac{191}{10} =$ £19.10.

A Queueing Model

The final stage in the manufacture of a certain product is inspection and rectification of faults. Previously, this was done by the distributor, but the firm making the product has decided that in future it will perform this operation itself. The production is scheduled such that one product leaves the production line every 20 minutes, but the actual time varies randomly like this:

Minutes late	3	4%
	2	6%
	1	18%
On time		36%
Minutes early	1	21%
	2	9%
	3	6%

Attempting to match production times, the inspector is supplied with sufficient mechanical aids to enable him to complete an inspection and to rectify any faults in 20 mins., on the average. Some products will be relatively free from defects and will pass through inspection in less than 20 mins., while others will take longer. The following distribution of inspection times was obtained

Time	Frequency
18	9%
19	26%
20	32%
21	23%
22	10%

The factory operates for 8 hours each day, so 23 inspections are possible.

The management wishes to derive various measures of performance for the proposed inspection system. In particular, management wishes to know whether the 24 scheduled inspections can be completed on time.

Management might also wish to know for how long during any day the inspector might be idle (which we will call idle time), and for how long products had to wait for inspection (which we will call waiting time).

Firstly, let us find the distribution of random numbers with the same frequencies as production times.

Minutes late	3	4%	00 – 03
	2	6%	04 – 09
	1	18%	10 – 27
On time		36%	28 – 63
Minutes early	1	21%	64 – 84
	2	9%	85 – 93
	3	6%	94 – 99

The production times give the times when the products arrive at the inspection shop. It will be logical to call them 'arrival times' and mark them with a minus when late, a plus when early, and zero when on time. Let us suppose that a product is waiting for inspection at the beginning of the day (it will be the last product produced on the previous day). This means we will require 23 arrival times. The following random numbers were obtained from a computer: 72, 94, 52, 78, 12, 21, 25, 20, 34, 93, 27, 89, 99, 97, 03, 95, 31, 50, 91, 91, 34, 46, 73.

These numbers simulate the following arrival times

$+1, +3, 0, +1, -1, -1, -1, -1, 0, +2, -1, +2, +3, +3, -3, +3, 0, 0, +2, +2, 0, 0, +1$

If we note that the first arrival time refers to the second item produced (the first product is waiting inspection), and arrivals are scheduled at 20 minute intervals, actual arrival times are:

0, 19, 37, 60, 79, 101, 121, 141, 161, 180, 198, 221, 238, 257, 277, 303, 317, 340, 360, 378, 398, 420, 440, 459

Now we require a sequence of inspection times. The distribution of random numbers with the same frequency as the inspection times is:

Time	Frequency	Random pairs
18	9%	00 – 08
19	26%	09 – 34
20	32%	35 – 66
21	23%	67 – 89
22	10%	90 – 99

Obtaining twenty four random numbers will give inspection times.

27, 49, 14, 34, 05, 99, 17, 69, 11, 84, 20, 65, 05, 23, 31, 21, 79, 72, 67, 65, 53, 75, 45, 69

So the inspection times will be (in minutes)

19, 20, 19, 19, 18, 22, 19, 21, 19, 21, 19, 20, 18, 19, 19, 19, 21, 21, 21, 20, 20, 21, 20, 21

There are four rules for this simulated system. The starting time for any inspection will be determined by either the finishing time of the previous inspection or the arrival time of the product; whichever is the later. The finishing time for any inspection will be the starting time plus the inspection time. If the arrival time of any product exceeds the time the previous inspection was finished, then the difference represents the inspector's idle time. If the time at which the inspection starts exceeds the arrival time, then the difference represents the products waiting time.

The simulation shows that on this particular day, the inspector was idle for 11 minutes, and the twenty-four inspections took 7 minutes longer than scheduled. The average waiting time for products was $^{68}/_{24} = 2.83$ mins. This is tolerable as a queue in not forming.

Product Number	Arrival Time	Start	Inspection Time	End	Idle Time	Waiting Time
1	0	0	19	19	0	0
2	19	19	20	39	0	0
3	37	39	19	58	0	2
4	60	60	19	79	2	0
5	79	79	18	97	0	0
6	101	101	22	123	4	0
7	121	123	19	142	0	2
8	141	142	21	163	0	1
9	161	163	19	182	0	2
10	180	182	21	203	0	2
11	198	203	19	222	0	5
12	221	222	20	242	0	1
13	238	242	18	260	0	4
14	257	260	19	279	0	3
15	277	279	19	298	0	2
16	303	303	19	322	5	0
17	317	322	21	343	0	5
18	340	343	21	364	0	3
19	360	364	21	385	0	4
20	378	385	20	405	0	7
21	398	405	20	425	0	7
22	420	425	21	446	0	5
23	440	446	20	466	0	6
24	459	466	21	487	0	7
					11	68

An Inventory Model

Let us use simulation to solve an inventory problem, which in some respects is similar to the inventory model considered in chapter 2. A firm uses 200 components per day at a steady rate. Stock is replaced by purchasing from a supplier. It costs £10 to place an order. Stock holding costs are 0.1p per day. We can find the batch size q that would minimise inventory costs. You should remember that inventory costs (pence per day) will be given by the expression

$$C = \frac{200 \times 1000}{q} + \frac{0.1q}{2}$$

Differentiating C with respect to q

$$\frac{dc}{dq} = \frac{-200000}{q^2} + \frac{0.1}{2}$$

To find the batch size q which minimises inventory costs, the derivative is put equal to zero.

$$\frac{-200000}{q^2} + \frac{0.1}{2} = 0$$

$$q = \sqrt{4000000} = 2000$$

The time interval between orders (the inventory cycle) is $2000 \div 200$ i.e. 10 days.

In previous examples, we have assumed the delivery is immediate, but this is unlikely. Usually, there is a time lag between placing an order and the delivery of the goods. This time lag is called the *lead time*. Now if the lead time is constant, it will not affect the way we have analysed inventories. This will not be the case however, if the lead time is subject to random variations. Suppose in the example above, the lead time was never less than 2 days nor more than 4 days. The lead time distribution might look like this:

Lead Time	Frequency	Lead Time Demand
2 days	29%	400 components
3 days	48%	600 components
4 days	23%	800 components

It will no longer be sufficient to re-order when stock falls to zero. The firm has the choice of selecting three re-order levels: 400, 600 or 800. If a re-order level of 800 components is chosen (i.e. an order is placed when stock falls to 800) then no stockouts will occur. However, stock holding costs will be higher than with re-order levels of 400 or 600. If re-order levels of 400 or 600 are used, then stockouts are inevitable. We shall simulate re-order policy such that an order is placed when the stock level is 600.

Before considering the simulated system, it will be useful to consider some preliminaries. Let us call the stock at the beginning of the cycle the opening stock, and suppose it is 2000 components. This means that with a re-order level of 600 components, an order will be placed at the end of the seventh day. Now the length of the cycle will depend on the lead time. if the lead time is 2 days, the cycle length would be 9 days. Lead times of 3 or 4 days would give cycle lengths of 10 and 11 days respectively. Thus an opening stock of 2000 components could give three different cycle lengths. Must the opening stock be 2000 components? Suppose the opening stock is 2000 and the cycle length is nine days. When the new order arrives there will still be 200 components in stock, so the opening stock for the next cycle will be 2200 components. With an opening stock of 2200 components, stock will be re-ordered at the end of the eighth day and the cycle length would be 10, 11, or 12 days depending on the lead time. Thus there are six possible different cycles: a 2000 or a 2200 component opening stock each with three different cycle lengths.

The stock holding cost will be different for each of the six cycles. Suppose we consider the cycle which has an opening stock of 2000, and a cycle length of 11 days. The average stock held on each of the 11 days would be:

Day	Average Stock	
1	1900	
2	1700	
3	1500	
4	1300	
5	1100	
6	900	⟵ average
7	700	
8	500	⟵ re-order
9	300	
10	100	
11	0	

It can be easily seen that the average stock per day over the cycle is 900 components. The holding cost over the cycle would be

$$900 \times 11 \times 0.1 = £9.90$$

Stock holding costs for other cycles could be calculated in a similar fashion

Opening Stock	Cycle Length	Cost of Cycle
2000	9 days	£9.90
2000	10 days	£10.00
2000	11 days	£9.90
2200	10 days	£12.00
2200	11 days	£12.10
2200	12 days	£12.00

How could a stockout occur? This will happen if the lead time demand exceeds the re-order level. With a re-order level of 600, the lead time demand would have to be 800 for a stockout to occur i.e. if the lead time is four days. Now suppose the lead time was two days. With a re-order level of 600, lead time demand would be 400 and there would be 200 units of inventory held at the end of the cycle (or the cycle has a closing stock of 200 components.)

We can now simulate a re-order level of 600 components. The rules for the simulated system would be as follows:

1. If opening stock is 2000, re-order at the end of the seventh day, and at the end of the 8th day if the opening stock is 2200.

2. Generate a random number. The lead time is determined as follows:

Random digits	Probability	Record lead time of
00 – 28	29%	2 days
29 – 76	48%	3 days
77 – 99	23%	4 days

3. Add the lead time to the re-order day to obtain cycle length.

4. Enter the cost of the cycle from the table obtained earlier.

5. If lead time is 3 days, record a zero closing stock and an opening stock of 2000 for the next cycle.

6. If the lead time is 4 days record a stockout. Also record a zero closing stock and a 2000 opening stock for the next cycle.

7. If the lead time is 2 days, record a closing stock of 200 and an opening stock of 2200 for the next cycle.

If the opening stock for the first cycle is assumed to be 2000 components, the simulation could be like this:

Cycle No.	Opening Stock	Random Number	Lead Time	Cycle Length	Holding Cost	Closing Stock	Stockout
1	2000	43	3	10	10	0	NO
2	2000	40	3	10	10	0	NO
3	2000	45	3	10	10	0	NO
4	2000	86	4	11	9.9	0	YES
5	2000	98	4	11	9.9	0	YES
6	2000	03	2	9	9.9	200	NO
7	2200	92	4	12	12	0	YES
8	2000	18	2	9	9.9	200	NO
9	2200	27	2	10	12	200	NO
10	2200	46	3	11	12.1	0	NO
11	2000	57	3	10	10	0	NO
12	2000	99	4	11	9.9	0	YES
13	2000	16	2	9	9.9	200	NO
14	2200	96	4	12	12	0	YES
15	2000	58	3	10	10	0	NO
16	2000	30	3	10	10	0	NO
17	2000	33	3	10	10	0	NO
18	2000	72	3	10	10	0	NO

19	2000	85	4	11	9.9	0	YES
20	2000	22	2	9	9.9	200	NO
21	2200	84	4	12	12	0	YES
22	2000	64	3	10	10	0	NO
23	2000	38	3	10	10	0	NO
24	2000	56	3	10	10	0	NO
25	2000	90	4	11	9.9	0	YES
					258	259.2	

Now 25 order have been placed at a cost of £10 each. The ordering costs per day are:

$$\frac{250}{258} = \text{£0.968 per day}$$

The daily holding costs are:

$$\frac{259.2}{258} = \text{£1.005}$$

Thus the simulated process gives a daily inventory cost of £1.973, with eight stockouts.

Now let us compare this result with an 800 component re-order level, when stockouts could not occur. You should satisfy yourself that the simulation would be governed by the following rules.

1. The opening stock could be 2000, 2200 or 2400 giving re-orders at the end of the 6th, 7th and 8th day respectively.

2. There are nine possible cycles, the cost of which are:

Opening Stock	Cycle Lengths	Cost
2000	8	£9.6
2000	9	£9.9
2000	10	£10
2200	9	£11.7
2200	10	£12
2200	11	£12.1
2400	10	£14
2400	11	£14.3
2400	12	£14.4

3. A lead time of two days gives a closing stock of 400 and an opening stock of 24000 for the next cycle. Lead times of 3 days and 4 days give closing stock of 200 and zero and opening stocks for the next cycle of 2200 and 2000 respectively.

4. The cycle lengths are obtained in the same way as the previous simulation.

Using the 800 component re-order level, an opening stock of 2000 and the same lead times the simulation would look like this:

Cycle No.	Opening Stock	Lead Time	Cycle Length	Closing Stock	Holding Cost
1	2000	3	9	200	9.9
2	2200	3	10	200	12.0
3	2200	3	10	200	12.0
4	2200	4	11	0	12.1
5	2000	4	10	0	10.0
6	2000	2	8	400	9.6
7	2400	4	12	0	14.4
8	2000	2	8	400	9.6
9	2400	2	10	400	14.0
10	2400	3	11	200	14.3
11	2200	3	10	200	12.0
12	2200	4	11	0	12.1
13	2000	2	8	400	9.6
14	2400	4	12	0	14.4
15	2000	3	9	200	9.9
16	2200	3	10	200	12.0
17	2200	3	10	200	12.0
18	2200	3	10	200	12.0
19	2200	4	11	0	12.1
20	2000	2	8	400	9.6
21	2400	4	12	0	14.4
22	2000	3	9	200	9.9
23	2200	3	10	200	12.0
24	2200	3	10	200	12.0
25	2200	4	11	0	12.1
			250		294.0

Inventory costs are $\dfrac{250}{250} + \dfrac{294.0}{250}$ = £2.176 per day, an increase of £0.203 over the previous model. However, the previous model contained eight stockouts which must also be costed. Suppose that if a stockout occurs, the firm can send its own van to collect the 200 components required for that day. Collection will be on a cash-and-carry basis, and the firm will obtain a discount of £6. However, it costs £10 to send the van so the net cost of cash-and-carry would be £4. Hence, the stockout cost would be £4 plus the cost of holding 1 days inventory, i.e. £4 + 100 × £0.001 = £4.10. Thus the cost of the eight stockouts would be £32.80, which gives a daily stockout cost of

$$\frac{32.80}{258} = £0.127$$

We can summarise the results like this:

Policy 1. Re-order level 800 components, inventory costs £2.176 daily.

Policy 2. Re-order level 600 components, inventory costs £2.100 daily.

On the basis of this simulation, policy 2 would be chosen.

244

Exercises to Chapter 13

13.1 Look again at the fishmonger problem. Suppose that any boxes left over at the end of the day are put into cold storage for sale on the following day. Using the same data for supply and demand, find average daily profit and stock level at the end of the period.

13.2 This question refers to the production model analysed in the text. Suppose that instead of giving a distribution of deviations from scheduled production times, the problem had given *actual* production times. If the actual production times were:

Times (mins.)	17	18	19	20	21	22	23
Frequency %	4	6	18	36	21	9	6

then very different results would have been obtained. Use the same random numbers as used in the text, and rework the simulation using actual production times.

13.3 Consider again the inventory model quoted in the text. Suppose policy 3 is to re-order when the stock falls to 400 components. Find the rules for the system. Using the same lead times as in the text, simulate 25 cycles and find the daily inventory costs. Compare the result with policy 2.

13.4

Lead Time	Frequency	Daily Demand	Frequency
5 days	27%	17 units	7%
6 days	28%	18 units	8%
7 days	35%	19 units	13%
8 days	10%	20 units	43%
		21 units	18%
		22 units	11%

Simulate lead time demand for 10 orders.

Use the following random numbers to determine the lead times

40	85	03	89	17	14	32	13	17	51

Use the following random numbers to determine demand

12	34	79	10	50	40	63	79	71	71
56	66	93	86	79	42	83	60	32	03
86	13	98	80	03	58	63	08	79	59
14	56	96	90	74	55	94	06	93	31
17	97	35	65	30	32	11	36	46	21
15	16	12	74	20	17	45			

13.5 A National Health Service doctor decides to introduce an appointments system for daily consultations. A colleague supplies him with the following information as to patient punctuality.

Minutes early	3	6%
	2	29%
	1	41%
On time		12%
Minutes late	1	7%
	2	5%

The doctor times his consultations over a period, and derives the following frequency distribution:

12 minutes	10%
13 minutes	15%
14 minutes	28%
15 minutes	34%
16 minutes	13%

For convenience, he would like to issue appointments at 15 minutes intervals. He wishes to have an idea of his idle time, the patients waiting time, and whether he can complete his appointments on schedule. Simulate sixteen consultations and derive the required information.

Random Nos for arrivals

17 50 83 94 49 79 43 90 09 40 46 09 95 52 91 15

Random Nos for consultations

14 40 13 08 98 51 74 24 21 12 91 05 44 79 53 16

13.6　The distributions of arrivals and services at a supermarket checkout per time period are given below

Arrivals	Frequency	Services	Frequency
8	8%	7	9%
9	22%	8	19%
10	38%	9	42%
11	26%	10	25%
12	6%	11	5%

Simulate 40 time periods and find the queue length.

Random Nos for arrivals

53	63	35	63	98	02	03	85	58	34
64	62	08	07	01	72	88	45	96	43
50	22	96	31	78	84	36	07	10	55
53	51	35	37	93	02	49	84	18	79

Random Nos for services

98	79	49	32	24	43	84	69	38	37
82	23	28	57	12	86	73	60	68	69
42	58	94	65	90	76	33	30	91	33
53	45	50	01	48	21	47	25	56	92

13.7　In the previous example, the queue will become very long. If the queue exceeds 10, it spills over into the selling area. Under such conditions, it is necessary to open extra checkouts. Find the appropriate time periods when it is necessary to do this.

13.8　Items arriving per time period for servicing at a servicing shop have the following distribution:

Arrivals	0	1	2	3	4	5	6	7	8	9
%	2	7	15	20	20	16	10	6	3	1

Servicing times vary with the complexity of the fault, and the distribution of the number of services completed in each time period is

Services	1	2	3	4	5	6	7	8	9	10
%	4	8	14	18	18	15	10	7	4	2

Simulate 25 time periods and assess the maximum queue length.

Random Numbers for arrivals

09	35	63	35	90	98	47	73	25	35
67	39	92	15	46	45	03	66	08	65
85	15	26	69	45					

Random Numbers for services

51	16	26	46	17	35	46	78	93	79
30	96	95	90	13	52	53	90	56	09
21	13	61	31	86					

13.9 The time it takes a cashier to clear a customer at a supermarket checkout varies according to the number of items purchased. The manager times the cashier, and derives the following frequency distribution.

Time taken to clear customer (secs.)	40	45	50	55	60	65	70
Frequency %		5	8	20	31	22	10	4

He has only one cashier.

The manager notices that during the busiest times, a long queue is forming and overspilling into the selling area. He fears that this is causing people to shop elsewhere. The distribution of 'inter-arrival times' of customers is

Inter-arrival time (secs.)	30	35	40	45	50
Frequency (%)	12	21	29	28	10

Simulate 25 arrivals using random numbers and find the queue length after 25 arrivals.

The manager decides that the maximum queue length allowable before customers go elsewhere is 5. Would a second cashier achieve this?

Random Numbers for Arrivals

40	65	03	89	17	14	32	13	17	51
09	03	78	31	93	88	12	34	79	10
50	40	63	79	71					

Random Numbers for Services

11	36	46	21	15	16	12	74	20	17
45	46	61	30	41	02	65	65	21	

13.10 A manufacturer uses a component at a rate of 50 per day. It costs £6 to place an order, and £0.015 to hold a unit of inventory for a day. Find the batch size q that would minimise inventory costs, on the assumption that delivery is immediate.

Suppose that on 52% of occasions delivery is on the day following the placing of the order, and on 48% of occasions delivery is within two days. Simulate, and cost, 25 cycles for 50 and 100 re-order levels on the assumption that it cost the firm 50p per unit of stock short per day.

Random Numbers for Lead Times

78	93	79	30	96	95	90	13	52	53
90	58	09	21	13	61	31	86	59	32
75	99	59	44	65					

13.11 If the machine breaks down, it costs a firm £30 in lost profit and wages for unemployed operatives if the machine is not repaired immediately. A machine usually breaks down because of the failure of a particular component, so the firm carries a stock of components to effect repairs as quickly as possible. The frequency of weekly failures has been as follows:

No. of failures	Frequency
0	26%
1	42%
2	19%
3	13%

The policy of the firm has been to make the stock of components up to 3 each week. However, the component is very large, and takes up a lot of space. If the firm would be willing to hold one component less it could install another machine which would earn the firm an extra £20 profit per week. Simulate 10 weeks and determine whether it would be worth holding 2 components per week.

R.N. for machine 1

40   88   31   37   73   51   68   23   68   01.

R.N. for machine 2

11   45   50   98   17   88   34   86   59   65.

13.12 In any one day, the price of stock traded on a certain stock exchange can rise, fall or remain unchanged. It is assumed that the direction of the change today depends upon what happened to the stock yesterday. The following probabilities are available:

		Today	
	Up	Unchanged	Down
	Up	.7	.2	.1
Yesterday	Unchanged	.3	.4	.3
	Down	.1	.3	.6

Moreover, if the price changes, it changes by the following amounts:

Amount of change (p)	Probability
½	.30
1	.40
1½	.20
2	.05
2½	.05

Using the random digits below, simulate the next 10 days trading on the assumption that the stock closed yesterday unchanged at 100:

Random numbers for direction of change:

72,   94,   52,   78,   12,   21,   25,   20,   34,   93.

Random numbers for amount of change:

27,   49,   14,   34,   05,   99,   17,   69,   11,   84.

13.13 The following distributions of daily supply and demand for a particular component was recorded as follows:

Daily demand	frequency (%)	Daily Supply	frequency %
8	30	7	5
9	40	8	30
10	20	9	40
11	5	10	20
12	5	11	5

Simulate 10 days trading using the following random numbers:

For demand 21 52 68 33 31 99 91 72 56 90
For supply 94 95 66 78 91 08 52 26 47 01

Obtain a distribution of unsatisfied demand and find the stock level at the end of the period.

13.14 A car hire firm has four cars to rent. The daily distribution of demand for cars is as follows:

No. of cars demanded	frequency
0	10%
1	20%
2	20%
3	25%
4	15%
5	10%

The distribution of the time for which a car is demanded is as follows:

No. of days demanded	frequency
1	15%
2	25%
3	30%
4	20%
5	10%

Rental terms are £15 per day

R.N. for No. of cars demanded

38, 53, 29, 32, 91, 52, 48, 89, 70, 24
06, 31, 48, 09, 06, 60, 24, 42, 08, 08

R.N. for No. of days demanded

51, 94, 37, 01, 49, 51, 59, 63, 88, 17
51, 44, 06, 52, 55, 44, 66, 92, 56, 93 75 83

(a) Using the random numbers above, simulate the demand for vehicles over 20 days.

(b) Write a report advising the car hire firm of your conclusions from running this simulation.

Chapter Fourteen

Compounding and Discounting

At times, all of us find it convenient to save money. Some very fortunate people cannot help but save as their expenditure is less than their income! For most of us, however, saving involves a conscious effort; we must reduce our consumption if we are to save. As saving involves us in sacrificing consumption today, then we must have a motive. We may save to buy a rather expensive item that we cannot at present afford: or for a deposit to buy a house. We may save as insurance against a rainy day, or to supplement a retirement pension. Now if we deposit our savings in a financial institution such as a building society or bank then, in addition to satisfying our motives, savings yield a bonus to us in the form of the interest earned. In fact, some economists would define interest earned as a reward to us for sacrificing consumption today.

Suppose we deposit a certain sum of money in a bank – then the size of that deposit will grow owing to the interest it earns. It would be useful, then, for us to be able to calculate just what sum of money would be available to us in the future.

Simple and Compound Interest

Do you remember the formula

$$I = \frac{P.T.R.}{100}?$$

There can hardly be an adult alive today who did not meet this formula at school. It tells us how much interest (I) we would earn if we deposited £P in a Bank for T years, and if the bank paid interest rate of R% on deposits. If, then, the bank paid 8% per annum on deposits, then a deposit of £250 left in the bank for 4 years would earn

$$I = \frac{250 \times 4 \times 8}{100} = £80$$

Before we examine the implications of this calculation it will be convenient to modify it somewhat. Rather than expressing the rate of interest as a percentage, let us instead express it as a proportion r. To do this, we divide the percentage rate by 100. So, for example if R = 8% then $r = \frac{8}{100}$

= 0.08. Our formula for calculating interest now becomes

$$I = P.T.r.$$

From now on, we shall use r as the rate of interest. Of course, this would in no way affect the result of our calculation:

$$I = 250 \times 4 \times 0.08 = £80$$

Whichever way we express the rate of interest, we still predict that £250 deposited for four years at 8% per annum would earn us £80. But is this figure correct? We would earn £80 only if we *withdrew* the interest each year. Over the four years we would have earned what is called *SIMPLE INTEREST*. But suppose we did not withdraw our interest from the bank. If this is so, then the interest on deposit would itself earn interest. We would then be earning what is called *COMPOUND INTEREST*. Let us now compare the two methods of earning interest on a year by year basis.

	Simple Interest			Compound Interest		
Year	Deposit	Interest		Deposit	Interest	
1	250	$250 \times 0.08 =$	20	250	$250 \quad \times 0.08 =$	20
2	250	$250 \times 0.08 =$	20	270	$270 \quad \times 0.08 =$	21.60
3	250	$250 \times 0.08 =$	20	291.60	$291.6 \quad \times 0.08 =$	23.33
4	250	$250 \times 0.08 =$	20	314.93	$314.93 \times 0.08 =$	25.19
Total interest earned			80			90.12

So we see that there is a considerable difference between the two methods. Compound interest is the method that is invariably used in the business world, and you would be well advised to forget all about simple interest. If we are going to calculate compound interest on a year by year basis, then the calculation will be tedious to say the least. What we require is a formula for compound interest, and to obtain this we shall consider again our example, though this time from a slightly different angle. We shall calculate the value of the deposit at the end of each year if £P is invested at and interest rate r and left for n years.

Value of deposit at end of year = Value of deposit at beginning of year plus interest earned during the year.

Value of deposit at end of first year =

$$P + rP$$

(deposit at start)   (Interest)

$$= P(1+r)$$

Value of deposit at end of 2nd year =

$$P(1+r) + rP(1+r)$$
$$= (1+r)(P+rP)$$
$$= (1+r)P(1+r)$$
$$= P(1+r)^2$$

Value of deposit at end of 3rd year =

$$P(1+r)^2 + rP(1+r)$$
$$= (1+r)^2(P+rP)$$
$$= (1+r)^2 P(1+r)$$
$$= P(1+r)^3$$

So if we call S the value of the deposit (or sum available) after n years.

$$S = P(1+r)^n \qquad \dots\dots\dots\dots\dots(1)$$

and the total interest earned would be

$$P(1+r)^n - P \qquad \dots\dots\dots\dots\dots(2)$$

Example 1

Now let us repeat our earlier calculation

$$P = £250, \ n = 4, \ r, \ = 0.08$$
$$S = 250 \ (1.08)^4.$$

Some of you will have calculators that can calculate the value $(1.08)^4$. Alternatively, the Compounding Table at the back of this book may be used to give

$$(1.08)^4 = 1.3605$$
$$\text{so } S = £250 \times 1.3605$$
$$= £340.125$$

and the interest earned would be

$$£340.125 - £250 = £90.125$$

which agrees with our earlier, long winded method.

At this point, a few words of warning would be appropriate. Compound interest mounts up very quickly, and yields surprisingly large sums. For example, £100 invested at 8% per annum for 20 years would earn

$$100 \ (1.08)^{20} - 100$$
$$= 100 \ (4.6610) - 100$$
$$= £366.10$$

The formula we have derived can also be used to calculate the rate of interest or the number of years, though the calculations are a little more involved.

Example 2

A sum of money is deposited now at 10% per annum. How long will it take for the sum invested to double?

Suppose that the sum invested is P, then after n years we require the sum to be 2P, i.e.

$$P(1+r)^n = 2P$$
$$P(1.1)^n = 2P$$

Dividing both sides by P

$$(1.1)^n = 2$$

We can now search the compounding table to find when $(1.1) = 2$. From this table, we see that

$$(1.1)^7 = 1.9487$$
$$\text{and } (1.1)^8 = 2.1436$$

So although the sum invested would not quite have doubled by 7 years it will have more than doubled after 8 years.

Perhaps those of you well used to logarithms may prefer the following method:

$$\text{If } (1.1)^n = 2$$
$$\text{than n. Log } (1.1) = \text{Log } 2$$
$$\text{and } n = \frac{\text{Log } 2}{\text{Log } (1.1)}$$
$$= \frac{0.3010}{0.0414}$$
$$= 7.27 \text{ years}$$

Example 3

£100 is invested now, and we are prepared to leave it on deposit for 15 years. What rate of interest would it be necessary to earn if the sum invested is to grow to £750?

$$100 \, (1+r)^{15} = 750$$
$$(1+r)^{15} = \frac{750}{100} = 7.5$$

Consulting the compounding tables when $n = 15$, we see that

$$(1.14)^{15} = 7.1379$$
$$\text{and } (1.15)^{15} = 8.1371$$

so we must earn a rate of interest somewhere between 14% and 15%. If we use logarithms, we can obtain a more accurate assessment of the rate of interest.

$$100 \, (1+r)^{15} = 750$$
$$(1+r)^{15} = 7.5$$
$$15. \text{ Log } (1+r) = \text{Log } (7.5)$$
$$\text{Log } (1+r) = \frac{\text{Log } (7.5)}{15}$$
$$\text{Log } (1+r) = 0.0583$$
$$(1+r) = 1.1437$$

So the required rate of interest is 14.37%

Now we could use the formula to find the sum we must deposit to achieve a specified sum in the future.

Example 4

We require £10,000 in 15 years time and we can deposit money at 12% per annum. How much must we invest now to achieve this sum?

$$P(1.12)^{15} = 10,000$$
$$P\,(5.4736) = 10,000$$
$$P = \frac{10,000}{5.4736} = £1,826.95$$

Increasing the sum Invested

So far, we have examined how an initial deposit would grow if it earned compound interest. But suppose we added to the amount deposited at the end of each year. Specifically, suppose we deposited £1000 on the first of January of a certain year, and decided to deposit £100 at the end of each year. If interest is compounded at 10% per annum, then we can use formula (1) to deduce that the

sum on deposit at the end of the first year is
$$1000\,(1 + 0.1) + 100$$

sum on deposit at the end of the second year is
$$1000\,(1 + 0.1)^2 + 100\,(1 + 0.1) + 100$$

sum on deposit at the end of the third year is
$$1000\,(1 + 0.1)^3 + 100\,(1 + 0.1)^2 + 100\,(1 + 0.1) + 100$$

sum on deposit at the end of the nth year is
$$1000\,(1 + 0.1)^n + 100\,(1 + 0.1)^{n-1} + 100\,(1 + 0.1)^{n-2} + \ldots + 100$$

If we generalise the quantities, then we can derive a formula to solve problems like this swiftly and efficiently. If we let P be the initial deposit, r the interest rate and a the amount that we deposit at the end of each year, then after n years the sum available would be

$$S = P\,(1 + r)^n + a(1 + r)^{n-1} + a(1 + r)^{n-2} + \ldots + a$$

Now it can be shown that this expression is equivalent to[1]

---

1. $S = P(1+r)^n + a\,(1+r)^{n-1} + a\,(1+r)^{n-2} + \ldots + a$

Ignore $P(1+r)^n$, then the right hand side forms a geometric progression with a first term $a(1+r)^{n-1}$ and a common ratio $\dfrac{1}{1+r}$, so using the formula to sum a geometric progression

$$S = P(1+r)^n + \frac{a\,(1+r)^{n-1}\,[1 - (\frac{1}{1+r})^n]}{1 - \frac{1}{1+r}}$$

$$S = P(1+r)^n + \frac{a\,(1+r)^{n-1}\,[1 - (\frac{1}{1+r})^n]}{\frac{r}{1+r}}$$

$$S = P(1+r)^n + \frac{a(1+r)^{n-1}\,[1 - (1+r)^{-n}]\,(1+r)}{r}$$

$$S = P(1+r)^n + \frac{a(1+r)^n\,[1 - (1+r)^{-n}]}{r} \qquad S = P(1+r)^n + \frac{a\,(1+r)^n - a}{r}$$

254

$$S = P(1+r)^n + \frac{a(1+r)^n - a}{r} \quad \ldots\ldots (3)$$

So if we initially deposit £1,000, and add £100 to our deposit at the end of each year, and if interest is compounded at 10% per annum then the sum available after four years is

$$S = 1000\,(1.1)^4 + \frac{100\,(1.1)^4 - 100}{0.1}$$

$$= 1000\,(1.4641) + \frac{100\,(1.4641) - 100}{0.1}$$

$$= £1928.20$$

We can also use this formula to calculate the sum left on deposit if we withdraw fixed amounts from the bank each year.

Example 5

Suppose we deposit £20,000 at the beginning of a year at 5% per annum compound. We withdraw £2,000 at the end of each year. What would be the sum available after 4 years?

Here we have

$$P = 20,000$$
$$a = -2,000 \text{ (negative because we withdraw)}$$
$$r = 0.05$$
$$n = 4$$

$$S = P(1+r)^n + \frac{a(1+r)^n - a}{r}$$

$$S = 20,000\,(1.05)^4 + \frac{-2,000(1.05)^4 - (-2000)}{0.05}$$

$$S = 20,000\,(1.2155) + \frac{-2,000(1.2155) + 2000}{0.05}$$

$$S = 24310 - 8620 = £15,690.$$

Formula (3) assumes that a constant amount is added (or withdrawn) from the deposit, and if this amount varies then you must not use the formula. Instead you must use

$$S = P(1+r)^n + a_1(1+r)^{n-1} + a_a(1+r)^{n-2} + \ldots\ldots + a_n \quad \ldots\ldots (4)$$

where a_1 is the sum added after 1 year, a_2 the sum after 2 years and so on.

Example 6

Suppose we have £20,000 deposited at the beginning of a certain year at 9% per annum compound. At the end of the first year we add £1,000 to the deposit, at the end of the second year we add £2,000 and at the end of the third year we add £3,000 and so on. How much would we have on deposit after 4 years?

$$S = 20,000(1.09)^4 + 1000(1.09)^3 + 2000(1.09)^2 + 3000(1.09) + 4,000$$
$$= 20,000(1.4116) + 1000(1.2950) + 2000(1.1881) + 3000(1.09) + 4000$$
$$= 28232 + 1295 + 2376.20 + 3270 + 4,000$$
$$= £39,173.20$$

If we wish to withdraw varying annual amounts, then we would use formula (4) with negative values for a.

Example 7

If the additions in example 6 became withdrawals, then the amount on deposit after four years would be.

$$S = 20,000(1.09)^4 - 1000(1.09)^3 - 2000(1.09)^2 - 3000(1.09) - 4000$$
$$= 20,000 - 28,232 - 1,295 - 2,376.20 - 3,270 - 4,000$$
$$= £17,290.80$$

Sinking Funds

We will now suppose that an accountant is instructed to set aside a sum of money at the end of each year to replace an asset.

Using formula 3 i.e.

$$S = P(1+r)^n + \frac{a(1+r)^n - a}{r}$$

this problem involves a zero initial investment. Putting $P = 0$ in the formula

$$S = \frac{a(1+r)^n - a}{r}$$

If we now make a the subject of this formula, we will have an expression telling us how much we must set aside at the end of each year to achieve a specified sum S

$$rS = a[(1+r)^n - 1]$$

$$\boxed{a = \frac{rS}{(1+r)^n - 1}} \qquad \dots \dots \dots (5)$$

We have derived what is called the *SINKING FUND* formula.

Example 8

Suppose a machine is expected to last 8 years and its replacement price is estimated at £5000. What annual provision must be made to ensure sufficient funds are available if money can be invested at 8% per annum?

Using formula 5.

$$a = \frac{0.08 \times 5000}{(1.08)^8 - 1}$$

$$= \frac{400}{1.8509 - 1}$$

$$= £470.09$$

So £470.09 deposited at the end of each year would be sufficient to yield the required sum. But suppose (as is more likely) the firm wishes to start the fund now and add to it at annual intervals then formula (5) will not do. We will have to use the expression

$$S = a(1+r)^n + a(1+r)^{n-1} + a(1+r)^{n-2} + \ldots + a(1+r)$$

Now it can be shown that this expression is equal to[2]

$$S = a\left[\frac{(1+r)^{n+1} - (1+r)}{r}\right] \ldots (6)$$

and again rearranging this formula to make a the subject.

$$a = \frac{rS}{(1+r)^{n+1} - (1+r)} \ldots (7)$$

Example 9

Repeat example 8, this time assuming that the sum is invested at the beginning of each year. Using formula (7)

$$a = \frac{0.08 \times 5000}{(1.08)^9 - (1.08)}$$

$$= £435.25$$

Trust Funds and Loan Repayments

Let us suppose that we deposit a certain sum of money now, and from this deposit we wish to withdraw at the end of each year a fixed amount. We will continue to withdraw until nothing is left on deposit. In our formula (3) i.e.

$$S = P(1+r)^n + \frac{a(1+r)^n - a}{r}$$

---

2. Writing this expression backwards

$$S = a(1+r) + a(1+r)^2 + a(1+r)^3 + \ldots + a(1+r)^n$$

$$S = a[(1+r) + (1+r)^2 + (1+r)^3 + \ldots + (1+r)^n]$$

The part in the square bracket forms a geometric progression with a first term $(1+r)$ and common ration $(1+r)$ so

$$S = a\left[\frac{(1+r)(1-(1+r)^n)}{1-(1+r)}\right]$$

$$S = a\left[\frac{(1+r)^{n+1} - (1+r)}{r}\right]$$

The terminal sum S would be zero, and because we are withdrawing a would be negative, so

$$P(1+r)^n - \frac{a(1+r)^n + a}{r} = 0$$

$$P(1+r)^n = \frac{a(1+r)^n + a}{r}$$

$$P = \frac{a[(1+r)^n - 1]}{r(1+r)^n}$$

$$\boxed{P = \frac{a[1 - (1+r)^{-n}]}{r}} \quad \ldots\ldots (8)$$

and

$$\boxed{a = \frac{rP}{1 - (1+r)^{-n}}} \quad \ldots\ldots (9)$$

We shall now examine a few applications of the formulae above.

Example 10

You have decided to set up a trust fund for your Aunt Maud. You require the fund to pay her £2,000 per year for the next 10 years. How much will this fund cost you if money can be invested at 10% per annum compound?

This problem involves finding P, the initial investment, so formula 8 is the one required.

$$P = \frac{2000[1 - (1.1)^{-10}]}{0.1}$$

The compounding Tables will not help us here, as we require $(1.1)^{-10}$ and not $(1.1)^{10}$ However, the value required can be found in the Discounting Tables printed at the back of this book (You will soon learn why they are called Discounting Tables). From these tables we learn that

$$(1.1)^{-10} = 0.3855, \text{ so}$$

$$P = \frac{2000[1 - 0.3855]}{0.1}$$

$$= £12,290$$

Example 11

Suppose you borrow £3000 at 14% per annum compound, and you wish to repay this loan in 10 annual instalments. How much must you repay each year?

If you think carefully about this problem, you will realise that it is equivalent to asking how much can be withdrawn at the end of each year if

£3000 is invested now at 14% per annum. So formula 9 is appropriate to this problem.

$$a = \frac{0.14 \times 3000}{1 - (1.14)^{-10}}$$

Using the discounting tables, $(1.14)^{-10} = 0.2697$

$$a = \frac{0.14 \times 3000}{1 - (0.2697)}$$

$$= £575.10$$

The Concept of Present Value

Suppose you were offered the choice of receiving £1000 now or £1000 in twelve month's time — which would you choose? It is almost certain that you would take the money now, even if you had a cast iron guarantee of receiving the money in the future. It would appear that we have a strong preference for holding cash now as against receiving cash in the future, and economists call this preference 'liquidity preference'. Now why is this preference so universally held? Almost certainly, inflation will have something to do with it. After all, if prices are rising then £1000 in 1 year's time will buy less than it will buy now, and so it will have less value than it has now. During inflation, then, it would make sense to take the £1000 now! But suppose (wishful thinking) we had stable prices — we would still almost certainly choose to take the money now. Why?

The great advantage of taking the money now is that it can be invested, earn interest, and grow. Our £1000 invested now at 10% would grow to

£1000 (1.1) = £1100 in one years time.

and to £1000 $(1.1)^2$ = £1210 in two years time.

Given stable prices, then, we should be indifferent between £1000 now, £1100 in one years time and £1210 in two years time. In other words, £1000 receivable today has the same value as £1100 receivable in one year's time and £1210 receivable in 2 year's time. So we can now see why we would prefer the £1000 now: if £1000 now is worth £1100 in one years time, it follows that £1000 in one year's time has a *present value* of less than £1000.

We have introduced a very important concept — that of present value, and this concept needs defining carefully. The present value of a sum of money receivable in the future is the sum you would be prepared to accept now, rather than have to wait for it. We use the interest earning capacity of money to enable us to calculate the present value. As £1000 invested at 10% per annum would grow to £1100 in one year's time we would say that £1100 in one years time has a present value of £1000. We reduce *or discount* the value of a sum receivable in the future to find its present value, and the *discount factor* that we use to do this is the current rate of interest. How can we do this? The first formula we obtained in this chapter was used to calculate how a sum invested now would grow under compound interest.

$$S = P (1+r)^n$$

If S is the sum receivable in the future, then P must be its present value.

$$P = \frac{S}{(1+r)^n}$$

or $$\boxed{P = S (1+r)^{-n}} \dots \dots \ 10$$

The quantity $(1+r)^{-n}$ is the *discounting factor* reducing the value of the sum. (hence the name discounting tables for values of $(1+r)^{-n}$)

Example 12

What is the present value of £1000 receiveable in 2 year's time if money can be invested at 10% per annum compound?

$$S = 1000$$
$$r = 0.1$$
$$n = 2$$
$$P = 1000 \ (1.1)^{-2}$$

Using the Discounting Tables

$$P = 1000 \times 0.8264$$
$$= £826.40$$

So £1000 receivable in 2 year's time has a present value of £826.40 because if we invest £826.40 now at the current interest rate it would grow to £1000 in 2 years. We should be indifferent between receiving £1000 in 2 years time and £826.40 now.

The Present Value of a Stream of Earnings

Let us suppose that we have been promised £1000 in one year, £2000 in two years, £4000 in three years and £3000 in four year's time. We would call this a stream of earnings, and if we wished to find the present value of such a stream we would find the sum of the individual present values. If the current rate of interest is 12%, then the present value would be

$$1000 \ (1.12)^{-1} + 2000 \ (1.12)^{-2} + 4000 \ (1.12)^{-3} + 3000 \ (1.12)^{-4}$$

It is conventional to perform this calculation in a tabular form

Year	Earning	Discount Factor $(1.12)^{-n}$	Present Value
1	1000	0.8930	893.00
2	2000	0.7972	1594.40
3	4000	0.7118	2847.20
4	3000	0.6355	1906.50
			7241.10

So the stream of earnings has a present value of £7241.10. In other words, if we deposited £7241.10 now at 12% per annum then we could draw £1000 at the end of the first year, £2000 at the end of the second year, £4000 at the end of the third year and £3000 at the end of the fourth year. The value of the deposit would then be zero (you should use formula 4 to prove this yourself). So if you were offered an asset which yielded the above stream of earnings and the current interest rate was 12% per annum, then you should be prepared to pay £7241.10 for it.

Now it is perfectly possible to have a constant stream of earnings, and an asset that yields a constant stream is called an *annuity*. We could use the same method as above to calculate the present value of an annuity, but it would be easier to use formula 8, which would give exactly the same results.

Example 13.

You are offered an annuity that would yield £1500 a year for 10 years. How much would you be prepared to pay for it if interest is compounded at 8% per annum?

$$P = \frac{a[1 - (1+r)^{-n}]}{r}$$

$$= \frac{1500[1 - (1.08)^{-10}]}{0.08}$$

$$= £10,065$$

Example 14

Repeat example 13, but this time assume the rate of interest is 12% per annum.

$$P = \frac{1500[1 - (1.12)^{-10}]}{0.12}$$

$$= £8,475$$

The last two examples prove an important point: if the rate of interest rises then the value of a future stream of earnings falls.

Suppose we now consider an annuity that pays a stream of earnings indefinitely – such an asset is called a *perpetual annuity*. How would we find the present value of such an asset? In the formula

$$P = \frac{a[1 - (1+r)^{-n}]}{r}$$

the value of n will be infinity. So $(1+r)^{-n}$ would be zero, and the formula reduces to

$$P = \frac{a}{r}$$

Example 15

An annuity yields £1200 per year for ever. What is its present value if the current rate of interest is 20% per annum?

$$P = \frac{1200}{0.2}$$

$$= £6,000$$

It is easy to see that the present value must be £6000, for if £6000 was invested at 20% per annum then the *simple* interest earned would be £1200 per year. So we could withdraw £1200 per year and leave the capital intact.

Finally, we can use the concept of present value to estimate the market price of fixed interest stock.

Example 16

Ruritanian Transport Stock has a nominal value of £100, and pays a dividend of 7%. Estimate the market price if the stock has eight years to run to maturity, and the current market rate of interest is 10%.

Holding this stock would yield £7 per year for eight years. This has a present value of

$$P = \frac{7 [1 - (1.1)^{-8}]}{0.1} = £37.34$$

Also, the stockholder would receive £100 in eight year's time when the stock matures. This has a present value of

$$100 (1.1)^{-8} = £46.65$$

So the estimated market price is £37.34 + £46.65 = £83.99, because if this sum was invested at current market rates of interest, then the cash flow could be obtained identical to that from the stock.

Exercises to Chapter 14

14.1 If £3250 is invested now at 11% per annum compound, what sum would be available in 7 year's time?

14.2 Complete the table below

	Years required for investment to		
	Double	Treble	Quadruple
Compound Rate			
8%			
12%			
16%			
20%			

14.3 What compound rate would cause £3,265 to grow to £5,776 in six year's time?

14.4 How much must be invested now if you require £12,500 in 5 year's time and if money can be invested at 10% per annum?

14.5 Suppose £9,500 is invested on the first of January of a certain year at 12% compound and £800 is withdrawn at the end of each year. How much would remain after 12 years?

14.6 Suppose £7500 is invested on the 1st of January at 9% per annum compound. Withdrawals are: £1000 at the end of the first year, £1200 at the end of the second year and £2000 at the end of the third year. How much would then remain?

14.7 A machine costing £12,500 now will need replacing in 6 year's time.

   a)   Estimate its replacement price if the rate of inflation is 11% per annum.

   b)   How much must be set aside

   (i) at the end of each year

   (ii) at the beginning of each year

   to replace the machine, if money can be invested at 9% per annum.

14.8 If money can be invested at 9% per annum, how much must be invested now to yield an income of £5000 per year, paid at the end of each year for eight years?

14.9 Suppose £6500 is borrowed at 18% per annum compound. Find the annual repayment necessary to pay off the loan in 12 years.

14.10 Given a discount rate of 14% per annum, find the present value of an annuity which yields

   a)   £650 per year for 8 years

   b)   £650 per year for ever.

14.11 Estimate the market price of a holding of 7% Treasury Stock with a nominal value of £125,000 and 4 years to run to maturity, if the current rate of interest is 10%.

14.12 A machine costs £150,000 and its estimated running costs over its life of 5 years are

year	Running Cost
1	1250
2	2250
3	3000
4	3100
5	3200

Assume all running costs are paid at the end of each year, and that money can be invested at 12% per annum compound.

   a)   How much must be set aside to cover running costs?

   b)   How much must be set aside to cover running costs and replace the machine?

   c)   How much must be set aside to cover running costs and replacement idenfinitely?

Chapter Fifteen

Investment Appraisal

There is little doubt that one of the outstanding features of the last hundred years is the development of new technologies and the application of those technologies to industrial and commercial uses. If you consider such an everyday matter as the passage of information, it could be effected in 1800 only by letter or by personal contact. Today we have a full range of means of communication available to everyone − telephone, telegram, radio, television, telex and many others, most of which did not exist until after 1900. So true is this that many of our major firms now have Communications Sections responsible for developing channels of communication and for choosing those technologies which best meet the communications needs of the firm.

As you can guess, this technological revolution has presented the industrialist with a new set of problems. Not only does he have to decide what to produce, he now has to decide also which of many alternative methods he is going to use. You may, of course, argue that this is not really a new situation. Choice and alternatives have always been with us. The new dimension lies in the number of alternatives and in the cost involved. If you are considering expenditure of only a few hundred pounds, intuition or rule of thumb methods of selection may do little harm. But if expenditure runs into millions of pounds such methods may be catastrophic and lead to bankruptcy.

This, then, is what *investment evaluation* is all about. We have to devise criteria for choice and methods of looking at investment which will enable the business man to decide which of many different investments is best for him − or indeed, if any one of them should be undertaken.

But what criteria should we use? It seems self evident that, since a large expenditure is involved, a financial return will be required, and that the magnitude of that return should be our criterion. Yet, as we saw in the last chapter, we have to be careful. Firstly because two projects yielding different returns may also have involved different capital expenditures and thus are not directly comparable. We cannot offhand say that a project costing £70,000 and yielding a return of £4550 each year is better than one costing £55,000 and yielding an annual return of £3850. In fact, neither is as profitable as putting the money into a Building Society account at 9% interest. It is the rate of return rather than the absolute amount which is important. Secondly, as you know, the timing of the returns is also important. An investment yielding £10,000 a year for three years followed by £2000 a year for three years is very different from one yielding £2000 a year for the first three years and then £10,000 a year for three years.

So it would seem that in developing criteria for investment evaluation, at least three things have to be borne in mind:

a) the financial return
b) the rate of return
c) the timing of the return.

Methods of Investment Appraisal

We will first look at methods of assessing the relative profitability of investment projects which evaluate the returns from the investment but ignore the timing of the returns. There are certain assumptions implicit in using one of these methods:

i) that money received at some future date is worth as much as money received now.

ii) that we can assess with some accuracy both the costs and the net revenues of the different projects.

Furthermore, to keep the analysis fairly simple we will assume that we will not gain by lodging our money on deposit with a bank or a Building Society. Remember, though, that any business-man can do this and assure himself of an income. This income is, then, a minimum below which the cash return from an investment project must not fall.

Given these assumptions, a businessman may decide to adopt as his criterion one of two things:

either i)   how long it will take him to recover his initial outlay, – the payback period.

or   ii)   the relationship between the profits made and his initial outlay – the rate of return.

Payback Period Method

The *payback period* is defined as the number of years it takes the cash proceeds from the investment to equal the initial outlay:

Example:

Omega Engineering is considering its investment programme. It has to assess four different projects each having the same initial capital cost of £10,000. The Financial Director informs the Board that only one of the projects can be financed, and provides the following estimates of potential income. He has taken account of all expenses such as wages and the cost of raw material but has made no provision for depreciation.

Project	Cost	Net Cash Flow Year 1	Year 2	Year 3
	£	£	£	£
A	10000	10000	–	–
B	10000	5000	5000	5000
C	10000	1500	4500	6000
D	10000	6000	8000	5000

Project A is a short term investment. It has a life of one year only, but during that year the net cash flow is just sufficient to cover the initial outlay. Its payback period is, therefore, one year.

Project B returns a steady cash flow of £5000 a year during its life. Two years is sufficient to recover the initial outlay of £10,000 and its payback period is therefore two years.

Project C takes time to build up its potential. During the first two years it earns £6000 in total, £4000 short of the initial cost. If we assume that the £6000 earned in year 3 is earned at an even rate throughout the year, (£500 a month), it takes a further eight months to accumulate this £4000. The payback period is two years eight months, i.e. 2.67 years.

Project D is a high yielding project in its first two years. Again assuming an even flow of earnings the payback period is 1.5 years.

We can now rank the four projects according to the criterion we have adopted – the length of the payback period.

Project	Payback Period (years)	Rank
A	1	1
B	2.0	3
C	2.67	4
D	1.5	2

Project A would be the investment most favoured. Yet, if you think about it, this seems to be an illogical choice. Firstly, we ignore any income received after the payback period. The total income from every other project is greater than that from Project A, yet they are rejected. Thus the method is biassed in favour of those projects with a high cash return in their early years. In times of stringency, when cash flow is important, this is understandable, but very many investments which will ultimately produce a high and steady cash flow for many years take time to yield results. The stability such investments add to a firm's position merits more consideration than this method gives it.

Secondly, we ignore the timing of the cash flow from the point of view of the cost of funds. If the rate of interest is 10%, £10,000 received after one year from project A has a present value of only £9,090.91. Yet we have to invest £10,000 to receive it. It is just not worth while! Put another way, if we lodged £10,000 in a bank at 10% after one year we would have £10,000 $(1 + 0.1) = £11,000$. Investing in project A leaves us with only £10,000 (assuming the machine is worth nothing). Consider now project D. The present value of the cash flows over the three years is

6000(.0991) + 8000(.8264) + 5000(.7513) = 5454.60 + 6611.20 + 3756.50
= £15822.30

and for a cash flow of this present value we sacrifice only £10,000. Serious doubts must be expressed as to whether payback period calculations will lead us to the correct investment decision.

In spite of this, research work carried out by Merritt and Sykes in 1964 showed that 78% of firms here and abroad were using this method. Ten years later an English Institute Research Committee found that it was still the most popular single criterion for investment decisions. Why should this be so?

Well, it is, of course, very easy to understand and apply, and the data it uses is readily available to managers. It seems, too, that in emphasising high early cash flows it satisfies the desire of management for high liquidity. We must admit, and this is something we all tend to forget, that the further we project our potential cash flows into the future, the greater is the risk that the returns we anticipate will not be realised. The manager usually wants to be able to point to a record of success, so he will tend to favour shorter term, low-risk investments in which the initial outlay is recouped quickly.

We cannot help feeling that the continued use of this technique indicates some of the pressures influencing management decisions in the twentieth century, but at the same time it indicates that managers as a body sometimes act in an apparently illogical manner. In view of this might it not be better to look at the total potential income from an investment. We could, then, consider the average annual return as a percentage of cost, either before or after depreciation is allowed for.

Average Annual Rate of Return Techniques

We will firstly consider the concept of gross returns — that is; returns without considering the cost of depreciation. The *gross average annual rate of return* is defined as:

> The average proceeds per year over the whole life of the capital expressed as a percentage of the initial capital cost.

Using the same data that we used to calculate payback period we get the following results:

Project	Capital Cost	Total Cash Flow	Life (years)	Average Cash Flow	% of Capital Cost	Rank
A	10,000	10,000	1	10,000	100	1
B	10,000	15,000	3	5,000	50	3
C	10,000	12,000	3	4,000	40	4
D	10,000	19,000	3	6,333	63.3	2

You will notice that this method has produced exactly the same ranking as the payback period, but this is purely coincidental. If we were to increase the revenue for, say, project B to £11,000 in the third year, it would not affect the payback period, but it would raise the total cash flow to £21,000 and annual average cash flow to £7,000 which is a return of 70% of capital cost. Thus it would be ranked 2.

This method is an improvement. It is still easy to understand, but now it does take account of revenue over the whole life of the asset. Moreover, in using this concept of return on capital employed it is using a yardstick which is familiar to most businessmen and accountants. But it is still a criterion which ignores the critical factor of the timing of the cash flows. It is possible to imagine a firm being forced into liquidation before the very high cash flows anticipated in the future can materialise. We have no indication also of the time span of the returns. A return of 20% for one year only would be equated with a return of 20% each year for five years.

Once again the concept is open to criticism. Yet it is often found in practice – usually as a means of checking the results of more sophisticated techniques. Would we perhaps be better if we were to consider profit rather than cash flow? We will use profit in the normal sense of the net gain to the company after maintaining the value of its assets intact. We will also assume that no investment has any cash value at all once its life has passed. This means that we have to reduce the total cash flow by the cost of capital (£10,000) in order to find the total net cash flow. We will also assume that the depreciation is charged by equal annual instalments.

Project	Cost	Total Cash Flow	Depreciation	Net Cash Flow	Net Average Cash Flow	Annual % of Capital	Rank
A	10,000	10,000	10,000	0	0	0	4
B	10,000	15,000	10,000	5,000	1667	16.67	2
C	10,000	12,000	10,000	2,000	667	6.67	3
D	10,000	19,000	10,000	9,000	3000	30.00	1

Now this is much better. At last we have a ranking indicative of benefit to the firm. Project A which only just recovers its cost is no longer first choice. In fact, it is last choice, and is shown as not being profitable. But are we being fair? Because the project lasts for one year only we are charging the whole cost of capital against that years income. The longer the life of capital the lower is the average annual depreciation charge and the more likely it is that the average annual net cash flow will be positive. Many people argue that the very basis of our calculation is wrong. If we charge depreciation against the cash flow we ought not to calculate that cash flow as a percentage of initial capital cost. Since reinvestment of the depreciation provision makes the capital self-liquidating we should express the average annual net cash flow as a percentage of the average capital employed. In this case that would be as a percentage of £5,000.

Whatever may be the merits of these arguments, all the methods we have looked at so far suffer from one glaring defect – they ignore the timing of the cash flows. They assume that, say, £5,000 received in five years time has the same value to the industrialist as £5,000 received next year. As we have seen, this is most certainly not so. It is to this concept that we must now turn our attention.

Discounted Cash Flow Techniques

As we saw in the last chapter money received now is preferred to money received in the future, and interest is paid to overcome this time preference. We developed a method of calculating the present value of a sum of money receivable in the future. If you think back you will remember that the present value of such future receipts depends on two factors:

a) the time period involved. The longer the interval before receipt of the cash, the lower is the present value.

b) the rate of interest. The higher the rate of interest, the lower will be the present value.

We developed the formula for calculating present value — the present value of £a receivable in n years is:

$$\text{Present Value} = a(1+r)^{-n}$$

$$\text{where } r = \text{the rate of interest}$$

So that you will not have the cumbersome task of calculating $(1+r)^{-n}$ the discount tables at the back of the book give you the present value of £1 for values of n up to 20 years and values of r up to .35.

Now if you think about it this problem of present value is precisely the problem the businessman is facing. In investing he is spending money *now* in order to receive a flow of cash at various times *in the future*. This too is the weakness of all the methods in the previous sections. It is futile to argue that if an investment has returned £5,000 at the end of year one and a further £5,000 at the end of year two the businessman has recouped the capital cost of £10,000. He has, in fact, recouped only the present value of the two cash payments, namely, given a rate of interest of 14%

$$5000(.8772) + 5000(.7695) = £8233.50$$

In considering an investment we may find ourselves in two completely different positions. We may have ample funds for investment and merely wish to know if a particular project will yield a rate of return equal to the cost of providing funds. In such cases we will use a technique usually known as the *Net Present Value Method*. Often, however, funds are limited, and we are faced by a number of projects competing for limited funds. We wish to invest in that project yielding the highest rate of return. To solve this problem we will use a technique referred to as the *Internal Rate of Return Method*.

Net Present Value Method

You will remember that in the last chapter you learned how to calculate the present value of a sum of money receivable at some date in the future. You will understand, too, that no manufacturer is going to use his money to buy capital equipment unless there is every prospect that the return on that capital will be at least equal to the return he could get by putting his money into a building society or bank account. Let us bring these two concepts together to see how they enable a businessman to make an investment decision.

Example:

Mr. Arnold White, a market gardener is considering whether to buy a new cultivator to help him in his business. The cultivator would cost him £6,000 but would enable him to undertake contracts which he estimates will be worth £3,000 a year after all expenses have been paid. Unfortunately the cultivator has a life of only three years and will have no scrap value at the end of that time. The current rate of interest is 12%. Should he undertake the investment?

Here Mr. White has several problems to consider. It is not just a question of the income he will receive. Obviously £3,000 a year is a much higher income than he would receive if he put his money on deposit at 12% – or even 20%. But against this is the fact that if he places his cash on deposit he will still have his £6,000 at the end of three years, whereas if he buys the cultivator, he will be left with only a worthless machine. If the investment is to be worthwhile then, he must consider not only the annual income, but also whether he can recoup the capital cost of the machine. The best way of assessing this is to calculate the present value of the annual cash flows.

End of Year	Cash Flow	Discount Factor $(1+.12)^{-n}$	Present Value
1	3000	.8929	2678.70
2	3000	.7972	2391.60
3	3000	.7118	2135.40
			£7205.70

Thus the cash flows have a total present value of £7205.70. How can you interpret this? Well, on buying the machine we are in fact buying an annuity which will yield an income of £3000 a year for three years. You could use your annuity formula to calculate the cost of such an annuity if the rate of interest were 12%. But this is what we have calculated when we have calculated the present value of the cash flows. So we obtain an annuity worth £7205.70 by spending £6000 on the cultivator. This is quite a bargain by any standards.

The investment has a net present value of £7205.70 less the cost of the cultivator.

$$\text{Net Present Value} = £7205.70 - £6000 = £1205.70$$

Now if you think about it, it is obvious that the net present value of an investment will depend on what you think the net profit will be year by year. If costs are rising and hence profits are falling, net present value is reduced. Profit figures for the future are in fact only estimates and can be materially affected by the optimisms or pessimism of the businessman.

Example:

Shortly before he buys the cultivator Arnold White is shocked to discover that his annual wage bill has risen by £500 due to a wage award. Being a pessimist he believes that the wage bill will continue to rise year by year, and that he will be able to cover only a part of these increased costs by price increases. He revises his ideas and comes up with the following forecast of earnings:

Year 1   £2500   Year 2   £2400   Year 3   £2350

He wonders if he should really buy the cultivator in these circumstances.

Year	Earnings	$(1+.12)^{-n}$	Present Value
1	2500	.8929	2232.25
2	2400	.7972	1913.28
3	2350	.7118	1672.73
		Present Value =	5818.26
		Less	6000.00
		Net Present Value =	$-£\ 181.74$

The Net Present Value is negative. White is being asked to pay £6000 for an income which to him is worth only £5818.26 today. He would do better to hang on to his money and deposit it in a bank.

Net Present Value can also be affected by changes in the rate of interest. This should be obvious if you remember that the value of our discount factor $(1+r)^{-n}$ depends on the value of r. Let us see how changes in r will affect the investment decision.

Example:

Just as he is getting desperate Arnold White is told that the rate of interest is about to fall from 12% to 9%. Does this affect his decision not to buy the cultivator?

His calculations now appear as follows:

Year	Earnings	$(1+.09)^{-n}$	Present Value
1	2500	.9174	2293.50
2	2400	.8417	2020.08
3	2350	.7722	1814.67
			6128.25
		Less	6000.00
		Net Present Value	£ 128.25

As you can see, the fall in the rate of interest has raised the present value of the cash flows and the investment again becomes worth while. It is logical that this should be so. With the fall in the rate of interest, the alternative use of money (putting it in a bank or building society) yields a lower return. The investment is, therefore, relatively more profitable.

Although Arnold White is only a small market gardener he has taught us a great deal. Summarising what we have learned so far:

a) Net Present Value = Present Value of the cash flows less the cost of the investment.

b) Net Present Value may be positive or negative. If it is positive the investment is worthwhile; if it is negative the investment should not be undertaken.

c) A fall in interest rates or a rise in net earnings will increase net present value. A rise in interest rates or a fall in net earnings will reduce net present value.

As you will probably have appreciated already, this method can be used to compare the relative merits of several investments.

Example:

A salesman calls in to see Arnold White. He hopes to be able to sell to him a bigger and better cultivator. There is one on the market costing £8000, which, because it does the job more quickly should ensure that returns are higher. Arnold does a quick estimate and comes up with the following figures:

	Machine A	Machine B
Cost	6000	8000
Earnings:		
Year 1	4000	4800
2	4000	6400
3	4000	4000

He wonders which cultivator he should buy. It is no use his buying both. The current rate of interest is 10%.

		Project A		Project B	
Year	$(1+.1)^{-n}$	Cash Flow	Present Value	Cash Flow	Present Value
1	.9091	4000	3636.40	4800	4363.68
2	.8264	4000	3305.60	6400	5288.96
3	.7513	4000	3005.20	4000	3005.20
			9947.20		12657.84
Less Cost of Capital			6000.00		8000.00
Net Present Value			£3947.20		£4657.84

We now face a tricky problem. Both machines are profitable but we have not considered any criterion to help us decide which is the better. Many people would say that all they are interested in is contribution to profit. If this is so, machine B certainly adds more to profit than does n achine A. We could make the choice by a direct ranking of the net present value. But is this really correct? Perhaps we should be interested in the efficiency of the capital we employ and look at the percentage return. Direct comparison will give us this only if the cost of capital were the same in both cases. Since it is not, we must turn the net present value into a profitability ratio index by expressing it as a proportion of the cost of capital. Thus:

	Machine A	*Machine B*
Capital Cost	6000	8000
Net Present Value	3947.20	4657.84

$$\text{Index} = \frac{3947.20}{6000.00} = .658 \qquad \frac{4657.84}{8000.00} = .582$$

Now the boot is on the other foot. In terms of present value, each pound spent on machine A contributes 65.8 pence to profits, whereas each pound spent on machine B contributes only 58.2 pence.

We will not try to tell you which of these two criteria is the better. Each firm will have its own policy and will have laid down its own criteria. Provided they have done so for logical reasons and are consistent in their policies, there is little more to be said.

Internal Rate of Return Method

If you think back over the methods of investment evaluation we have considered, you will quickly see that one thing is missing. Nowhere have we actually calculated the *rate* of return. Net present value measures the contribution to profits: the profitability index measures the contribution of each pound of capital invested; even the so-called rate of return measures only the level of profits as a percentage of capital cost. As yet we have not measured the rate of return in terms of interest.

This is precisely what the internal rate of return does. Many firms find the method suitable because they are not only interested in an investment being profitable — they want to know how profitable. Thus the internal rate of return is an extremely useful way of comparing several investments when we can afford to finance only one of them. There is more than this however. In all our examples we have been given a rate of interest to enable us to calculate the discount factor. Now there are times when an appropriate rate of discount cannot be determined. When this is so, the only way we can judge whether an investment is worthwhile is by assessing its rate of profit as compared with some predetermined standard.

In principle the technique is very easy to understand. We attempt to determine the rate of discount which will equate the present value of future cash flows with the capital cost of the investment. In practice it is not so easy. To find the true discount rate we have to proceed by trial and error until we come across it. Let us see how it works:

Example:

Arnold White has bought his cultivator for £6000 and believes that his returns for the next three years will be £2500, £3000 and £2000. Evaluate this investment by calculating the internal rate of return.

One way of tackling the problem would be to calculate the present value of the three cash flows using every rate of discount from 1% upwards, until we find one that equates present value with capital cost. It is not a method we recommend! Surely it would be better to try to estimate the rate of return and start our search with that estimated figure. So we proceed as follows. The total cash flow over the life of the project is £2500 + £3000 + £2000 = £7500. Since the cultivator cost £6000 this leaves us with a surplus of £1500, i.e. $\frac{1500}{6000} \times 100 = 25\%$ of capital cost. Quite simply this could be looked on as 8.33% a year. It would be better to start our search here rather than at 1% or by pure guesswork. We know, however, that calculating the rate of return in this way *underestimates* the internal rate of return so we might as well allow for this. A good working rule is to increase this estimate by about a third to a half. So we could estimate the internal rate of return to be somewhere in the region of 8.33 × 1.33 to 8.33 × 1.5 or between 11.1 and 12.5. So we will start our search for the true internal rate of return using a rate of discount of 11%.

| | | $r = .11$ | | | $r = .12$ | | | $r = .13$ | |
Year	Cash Flow	$(1+.11)^{-n}$	P.V.	$(1+.12)^{-n}$	P.V.	$(1+.13)^{-n}$	P.V.
1	2500	.9009	2252.25	.8929	2232.25	.8850	2212.50
2	3000	.8116	2434.80	.7972	2391.60	.7831	2349.30
3	2000	.7312	1462.40	.7118	1423.60	.6931	1386.20
Present value			6149.45		6047.45		5948.00

Trying r = .11 first we find the present value to be £6149.45, too high a figure. So the rate of discount we have chosen is too low. When we increase r to .12 the present value falls to £6047.45, still too high but we are getting very close. Moving to r = .13 we find the present value is £5948 − too low. So the true internal rate of return lies between 12% and 13%. For most purposes this would suffice but we can find the exact figure if we wish by interpolation. The technique is simple:

$$\text{Internal rate of return} = 12\% + \frac{(\text{P.V. when } r = .12) - (\text{capital cost})}{(\text{P.V. when } r = .12) - (\text{P.V. when } r = .13)}$$

$$\text{I.R.R.} = 12\% + \frac{6047.45 - 6000}{6047.45 - 5948.00}$$

$$= 12 + \frac{47.45}{99.45} = 12.477\%$$

We can easily prove that this is the true internal rate of return by calculating the discount factors for r = .12477. (These, of course are not in your printed tables, but can easily be obtained on your calculator).

Year	Cash Flow	$(1.12477)^{-n}$	Present Value
1	2500	.88907	2222.675
2	3000	.79045	2371.35
3	2000	.70276	1405.52
			£5999.55

There is a 45 pence error due to approximating the discount factor to five decimal places and because of our approximating the rate of return to three decimal places.

274

On the surface 12.477% may seem a high rate of return. After all, you will say, profits are only £1500 and if we invested £6000 at only 9% we would earn £1620 at simple interest and £1770 at compound interest in three years. What is wrong then. Well, if you argue like this, what is wrong is your understanding of what we are doing. Look at it like this.

If we invest £6000 at 12.477%, at the end of the first year we have £6000 × 1.12477 = £6748.62. We now withdraw £2500 leaving £4248.62. By the end of the second year interest has increased this to £4248.62 × 1.12477 = £4778.72. We now withdraw £3000 leaving £1778.72. At the end of the next year this will amount to £2000.65 when we withdraw £2000 closing the account. Again we get a slight error due to rounding. It is this type of situation we are considering when we calculate the internal rate of return. We are in fact calculating the rate of interest which will make the present value of an annuity yielding unequal cash flows equal to a predetermined sum.

Let us conclude this chapter by examining the results produced by the various methods we have discussed.

Example:

The board of M.A.T. Ltd are considering three alternative investment policies presented to them by their planning team.

Project A costs £25000 and has a life of ten years. The estimated cash flows are £5000 in year 1, rising by £500 a year to £7000. Returns then remain steady for the life of the asset.

Project B costs £8000 but has a life of only 4 years. It yields £4000 during each of the first two years, £2000 in year 3 and £1000 in year 4. It is estimated, however, that it will have a scrap value of £1000.

Project C costs £10000, also lasts for 4 years and it is believed that it will yield £5000 in year 1, £4000 in year 2, and £3000 in each of the remaining two years.

The Board has no set policy but wishes each project to be evaluated and ranked in order of preference using

a) Payback period   c) Profitability Index
b) Net Present Value (N.P.V.)   d) Internal rate of return (I.R.R.)

The rate of interest is 10%.

Payback Period

Project	Cost	Payback Period	Rank
A	25000	4.29	3
B	8000	2.00	1
C	10000	2.33	2

Net Present Value

Project A

Year	Cash Flow	$(1 + .1)^{-n}$	Present Value
1	5000	.9091	4545.50
2	5500	.8264	4545.20
3	6000	.7513	4507.80
4	6500	.6830	4439.50
5	7000	.6209	4346.30
6	7000	.5645	3951.50
7	7000	.5312	3592.40
8	7000	.4665	3265.50
9	7000	.4241	2968.70
10	7000	.3855	2698.50
			38860.90
	Less		25000.00
	Net Present Value		£13860.90

Project B

Year	Cash Flow	$(1 + .1)^{-n}$	Present Value
1	4000	.9091	3636.40
2	4000	.8264	3305.60
3	2000	.7513	1502.60
4	2000	.6830	1366.00
			9810.60
	Less		8000.00
	Net Present Value		£1810.60

Project C

Year	Cash Flow	$(1 + .1)^{-n}$	Present Value
1	5000	.9091	4545.50
2	4000	.8264	3305.60
3	3000	.7513	2253.90
4	3000	.6830	2049.00
			12154.00
	Less		10000.00
	Net Present Value		£2154.00

Summary of Net Present Value

Project	N.P.V. (£)	Rank
A	13860.90	1
B	1810.60	3
C	2154.00	2

Profitability Index

Project	Cost	N.P.V.	Index = $\dfrac{\text{N.P.V.}}{\text{Cost}}$	Rank
A	25000	13860.90	.554	1
B	8000	1810.60	.226	2
C	10000	2154.00	.215	3

Internal Rate of Return

Project A

Year	Cash Flow	$r = .20$		$r = .21$	
		$(1 + .2)^{-n}$	P.V.	$(1 + .21)^{-n}$	P.V.
1	5000	.8333	4166.50	.8264	4132.00
2	5500	.6944	3819.20	.6830	3756.50
3	6000	.5787	3472.20	.5645	3387.00
4	6500	.4823	3134.95	.4665	3032.25
5	7000	.4019	2813.30	.3855	2698.50
6	7000	.3349	2344.30	.3186	2230.20
7	7000	.2791	1953.70	.2633	1843.10
8	7000	.2326	1628.20	.2176	1523.20
9	7000	.1938	1356.60	.1799	1259.30
10	7000	.1615	1130.50	.1486	1040.20
			25819.45		24902.25

$$\text{I.R.R.} = 20 + \frac{819.45}{25819.45 - 24902.25} = 20.89\%$$

Project B

Year	Cash Flow	$r = .21$		$r = .22$	
		$(1 + .21)^{-n}$	P.V.	$(1 + .22)^{-n}$	P.V.
1	4000	.8264	3305.60	.8197	3278.80
2	4000	.6830	2732.00	.6719	2687.60
3	2000	.5645	1129.00	.5507	1101.40
4	2000	.4665	933.00	.4514	902.80
			8099.60		7970.60

$$\text{I.R.R.} = 21 + \frac{99.60}{8099.60 - 7970.60} = 21.77\%$$

Project C

Year	Cash Flow	$r = .20$		$r = .21$	
		$(1 + .2)^{-n}$	P.V.	$(1 + .21)^{-n}$	P.V.
1	5000	.8333	4166.50	.8264	4132.00
2	4000	.6944	2777.60	.6830	2732.00
3	3000	.5787	1736.10	.5645	1693.50
4	3000	.4823	1446.90	.4665	1399.50
			10127.10		9957.00

$$\text{I.R.R.} = 20 + \frac{127.10}{10127.10 - 9957.00} = 20.75$$

Summary of I.R.R.

Project	I.R.R.	Ranking
A	20.89	2
B	21.77	1
C	20.75	3

Summary of Rankings

Project	Cost	Payback Period	N.P.V.	Profitability Index	I.R.R.
A	25000	3	1	1	2
B	8000	1	3	2	1
C	10000	2	2	3	3

Well, what do you make of that? Depending on the method you use each project is ranked last and each project is ranked second. The only thing that one can say with certainty is that no method of calculation we have used ranks project C first. It is generally inferior to the other two and should not be considered. The advice we would offer you is to consider carefully all the implications of the choice you make. Remember what each method tells you and what you lose when you do make a choice. You are unlikely to change company policy, but policies followed for years may be out of date and a periodic review of all current methods of evaluation could yield surprising conclusions.

Exercises to Chapter 15.

15.1 Given that the current rate of interest on deposits is 10% would you prefer to buy a television set for £200 cash now, or by making a deposit of £100 now and paying a second instalment of £120 in one years time.

Would your answer be different is the second instalment were to be fixed at

a) £115.

b) £108.

15.2 A piece of equipment costing £1000 has an expected life of 5 years. It is estimated that the cash flow resulting from the use of the machine will be £400 a year. The rate of return expected from capital of this type is 15%.

Calculate   a)   the pay back period

            b)   the net present value

            c)   the internal rate of return of the capital.

15.3 A firm is faced by two alternative investment plans. Plan A will cost £750 and plan B £950. Both plans involve the purchase of equipment the life of which is four years, and it is estimated that the cash flows during that time will be:-

Year

Plan	1	2	3	4
A	300	400	300	200
B	500	400	300	300

A minimum return of 20% on cost of capital is required. What advice would you give the firm?

15.4 a) Explain what is meant by
   i) the internal rate of return and
   ii) the net present value of an investment project.

   b) In each case indicate how the concept can be used to determine the viability of an investment project.

   c) Use the present value method to determine whether a firm should borrow money at 14% interest per annum to undertake a project costing £10,000 but yielding a return of £3000 a year for 6 years.

15.5 A firm can purchase a machine for £12,000 which will save £5,000 a year in labour costs. The machine has running costs of £1000 in the first year of operation rising by £500 a year thereafter. The machine has to be overhauled after four years at an additional cost of £500 and can be sold at the end of its useful life of seven years for £800.

Should the firm buy this machine if it is borrowing funds at a rate of interest of 9%?

15.6 A firm is offered four methods of paying for a piece of capital equipment, viz:
   i) a single payment of £12,000 immediately
   ii) no initial payment but £5,500 at the end of each year for three years
   iii) a payment of £4,000 immediately plus payments of £3,000 at the start of each year of the next four years
   iv) a payment of £7000 at the end of the year and a similar payment after a further four years.

The firm will meet any expenditure from a sum of £20,000 lodged in a bank account earning interest of 12% per annum.

Which method of payment would you recommend the firm to adopt?

15.7 The directors of Lambskin Ltd are considering three investment projects, Project A costs £3,000, Project B £3,500 and Project C £4,000.

The expected cash flows are

year	A	B	C
1	800	1000	600
2	1000	1200	1400
3	2000	1800	1800
4	1500	1800	2200

which project would you recommend to the directors?

15.8 A manufacturer has £5,600 available to purchase a new plant. His accountant recommends that equipment should not be installed unless it yields an internal rate of return of at least 12%. He expects to make £600 net profits in the first year of operation, £800 in the second year and £1,000 a year thereafter. The expected life of the plant is ten years and it has a scrap value of £500.

What would you advise?

15.9 Discuss the problems a manufacturer is likely to encounter if he is attempting to divide between different investment opportunities if he decides to use
   a) the payback period criterion
   b) net present value
which do you prefer and why?

15.10 The returns anticipated on a machine costing £850 are

year	1	£300
	2	£400
	3	£300
	4	£200

The current rate of return on capital is expected to be 20%.

a) Is the investment viable?

b) If the machine has a scrap value of £200 at the end of its four year life does this affect the investment decision?

c) The firm is liable to pay tax at the rate of 40% of the previous years receipts. What is now the position

    i) ignoring scrap values

    ii) allowing for scrap values.

d) From your calculations what would you conclude about the effect of taxation on the investment decision?

Chapter Sixteen

Replacement

In the last chapter, we used discounted cash flow techniques to decide whether or not the purchase of a piece of capital equipment was viable. Now sooner or later, the equipment will need replacing, and it is the function of this chapter to examine optimum replacement strategies. Of course, replacement strategies are not relevant just to the business world − we as consumers have possessions that will need replacing (for example, motor cars, domestic electrical appliances) the theory developed will apply equally well to replacing consumer goods. We shall derive replacement strategies in such a fashion that the cost of replacement is minimised, though you should note that such strategies need not be optimal. I may, for example, know that replacing my motor car every six years makes sound economic sense, though I may change it every three years because I enjoy the prestige of owning a new vehicle. It would be very difficult to place some monetary value on the satisfaction derived from owning a new vehicle.

Before we examine replacement models, we should note that there are basically two types of asset or goods that will need replacing. One type of asset will continue to give excellent service for a period of time, and then fail completely. Such an asset requires little or no maintenance, but once it fails it is useless as it cannot be repaired. Electric light bulbs and certain electronic components are good examples of this type of good. Components used in the motor industry are tending nowadays to fall into this category: it is becomming more usual to replace a defective component than it is to repair it. A second category of asset is the type that tends not to fail completely but to deteriorate with time − motor vehicles and most types of machinery would fall into this category. Such assets have associated running costs, and these costs tend to increase over time. Sooner or later, the running costs will be at such a level that replacement becomes economically necessary.

Items that fail completely

We will use electric light bulbs as our example of items that fail completely because such an example enables us to make certain simplifying assumptions without departing from reality to too great an extent. Let us suppose that over a very long period, the length of life of electric bulbs used in the warehouse of a certain factory has been observed, and the following data obtained.

	Proportion of bulbs installed at
Week	*beginning of week 1 that fail*
(W)	*during week W.*
1	0.2
2	0.3
3	0.4
4	0.1
	1.0

Table 16.1

Examining the table, we see that no bulb has a life of more than 4 weeks, so a bulb that has lasted 3 weeks is sure to fail during the fourth week.

The warehouse has 1000 of these bulbs, and at the end of each week, the caretaker replaces any bulb that has failed. Replacing bulbs in this way (i.e. as they fail) is called an individual replacement strategy. It would be possible for the caretaker to replace *all* the light bulbs at the end of the week whether they have failed or not and this is called group replacement strategy. Now the replacement cost per bulb is likely to be less with group replacement than with individual replacement. With group replacement, there is no need to look for the failed bulbs. Also, suppose the bulbs are in covered fittings, each containing (say) twenty bulbs. The caretaker must position his ladder and remove the cover no matter how many he replaces. Positioning the ladder and removing the cover are fixed costs and, within any fitting, do not depend upon the number of bulbs replaced. Let us suppose that the replacement cost per bulb (i.e. price of bulb plus labour) is 50p for group replacement and 75p per week for individual replacement. It is easy to see that the total cost of group replacement would be $0.5 \times 1000 = £500$ per week.

In order to calculate the cost of individual replacement, we need to know the number of bulbs failing each week, and to do this we will assume that at the beginning of week 1 all the bulbs were new. We can expect these bulbs to fail as follows:

| Week | 1 | 2 | 3 | 4 |
| No. of failures. | $1000 \times 0.2 = 200$ | $1000 \times 0.3 = 300$ | $1000 \times 0.4 = 400$ | $1000 \times 0.1 = 100$ |

At the end of the first week, 200 bulbs will need replacing, and these bulbs will fail as follows

| Week | 2 | 3 | 4 | 5 |
| No. of failures | $200 \times 0.2 = 40$ | $200 \times 0.3 = 60$ | $200 \times 0.4 = 80$ | $200 \times 0.1 = 20$ |

At the end of the second week, 300 of the original bulbs and 40 of those replaced in week 1 = 340 will need replacing, and these will fail as follows

| Week | 3 | 4 | 5 | 6 |
| No. of failures | $340 \times 0.2 = 68$ | $340 \times 0.3 = 102$ | $340 \times 0.4 = 136$ | $340 \times 0.1 = 34$ |

At the end of the third week $68 + 60 + 400 = 528$ will need replacing. Continuing in this way we can determine the number of bulbs replaced each week. It would be convenient to summarise our results, and this is done in table 16.2.

Age of failing bulbs

Week	1 Week	2 Weeks	3 Weeks	4 Weeks	No. Replaced	Cost of Replacement
0					1000	£750
1	200				200	£150
2	40	300			340	£255
3	68	60	400		528	£396
4	106	102	80	100	388	£291
5	78	158	136	20	392	£294
6	78	116	211	34	439	£329

Table 16.2

Notice how table 16.2 is constructed: to obtain the numbers of failing bulbs on any diagonal line in the table we multiply the number replaced in the week preceding the diagonal by the proportion failing in successive weeks. For example, the data in the marked diagonal is obtained like this:

$$340 \times 0.2, \qquad 340 \times 0.3, \qquad 340 \times 0.4, \qquad 340 \times 0.1$$

The number replaced is obtained by taking the sum of the number of failing bulbs in that week. So, for example, the number failing in week 5 is $78 + 158 + 136 + 20 = 392$; and as it costs 75p to replace a bulb the replacement cost is £294.

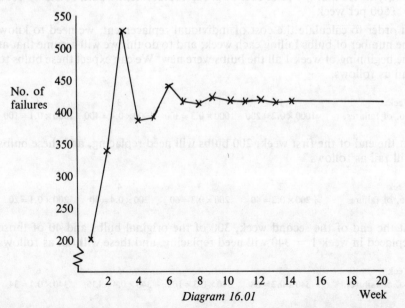

Diagram 16.01

The number of bulbs replaced is graphed in diagram 16.1. Notice that the number of replacements rises and falls, but the oscillations peter out until eventually a steady state is reached (from about week 14 onwards) with 417 bulbs replaced each week. We can obtain the steady-state replacement level without having to calculate replacement on a week-by-week basis if we use the expression

$$\text{No. of failures in steady state} = \frac{\text{Total number of bulbs}}{\text{Average life of bulbs}}$$

The average life of bulbs is calculated as follows

Life (weeks)	No. of Bulbs	Total Life
1	200	200
2	300	600
3	400	1200
4	100	400
		2400

Average life = $\dfrac{2400}{1000}$ = 2.4 weeks.

No. of failures $\dfrac{1000}{2.4}$ = 416⅔

Average cost of individual replacement = 416⅔ × 0.15 = £312.50. As the cost of group weekly replacement is £500, then individual replacement is to be preferred.

Mixed Strategies

So far, we have examined and costed group replacement and individual replacement strategies: we shall now look at a mixture between the two strategies. What we mean by this is that failures will be replaced at the end of each week for n weeks, then at the end of the next week all the bulbs will be replaced. Suppose, for example, it is decided to replace all the bulbs at the end of the third week. From table 16.2, we obtain that the cost of replacing failed bulbs at the end of the first week is £150, and cost of replacement at the end of the second week is £255. As it costs £500 to replace all the bulbs it follows that the total cost of a three week replacement cycle is 150 + 255 + 500 = £905, which represents an average weekly cost of £301.66 per week. Notice that this cost is less than the cost of an individual replacement strategy (£312.50). Table 16.3 shows how the average weekly cost of a mixed strategy varies for different replacement cycles.

284

Replacement Cycle	Group Replacement Cost	Cost of replacing failures in						Total Cost	Average Cost
		1	2	3	4	5	6		
1	500							500	500.00
2	500	150						650	325.00
3	500	150	255					905	301.66
4	500	150	255	396				1390	325.25
5	500	150	255	396	291			1592	318.40
6	500	150	255	296	291	294		1886	314.66
7	500	150	255	296	291	294	329.25	2215.25	316.00

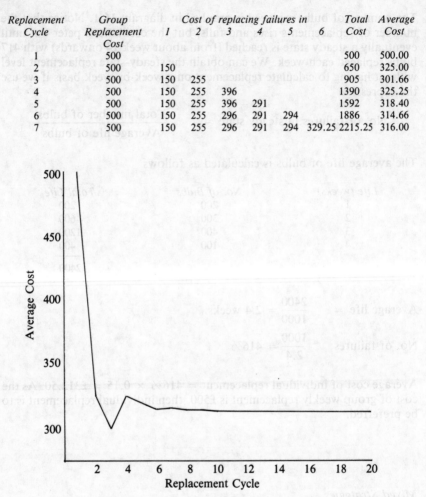

Diagram 16.02

Diagram 16.2 shows how the cost of the mixed strategy fluctuates according to the replacement cycle. Notice that once again the average cost tends to stabilise (at about £314). Notice also that the minimum average cost occurs with a 3 week replacement cycle. The results of the three replacement strategies are summarised in table 16.4.

Strategy	Weekly Cost
Group	£500
Individual	£312.50
Mixed on a Three week cycle.	£301.60

Table 16.4

We would conclude, then, that the optimum strategy would be a mixed one, replacing failures at the end of each week, and replacing all the bulbs at the end of each third week.

Before we leave this problem, a few comments must be made. Firstly, we have assumed that any bulb that fails is not replaced until the end of the week. Had we assumed that failed bulbs were replaced immediately, then the mathematics involved in this problem would have been much more complex (and it is doubtful whether the result would have been affected significantly). It is because of this assumption that light bulbs were chosen as our example – not changing light bulbs until the end of the week would not stop the operation of the warehouse (though it may affects its efficiency). However, had we chosen electronic components as our example then failing to replace them immediately would probably result in a complete system breakdown. A second point is that we have measured failure rate against time, but in many cases it may not be sensible to do this. Suppose, for example, we are considering the failure rate of clutches on motor vehicles; then it would be sensible to measure the failure rate against mileage rather than against time. Finally, you should note that replacement before failure is often an intuitive practice – if a repair job on a car involves removing the engine or gearbox, then it often makes sense to replace the clutch, even though it has not failed.

Assets that deteriorate with time

Now let us examine the other type of asset – the type that does not fail suddenly and completely but which deteriorates with time. Machinery and motor vehicles fall into this category. Now there are two distinct types of cost associated with this type of asset. Firstly, there is running cost – the cost associated with operating the asset. For example, if the asset is a motor vehicle, then the running costs would be road fund, insurance, petrol costs, servicing and repairs. It is a feature of such assets that as they age, so the running costs become greater. With motor vehicles, this would not be true with all the components making up running costs – and road fund and insurance are not dependent upon the age of the vehicle, though we would expect that, for a given annual mileage, the greater the age of the vehicle, the more will be spent on servicing, petrol and repairs. The second type of cost is the replacement or capital cost, which we calculate by subtracting the resale price of the asset from the cost of replacing it. Suppose for example, a new car costs £6,000, and we are offered £2000 for our existing vehicle, then the replacement cost would be 6000 − 2000 = £4000.

In order to investigate how we would deal with this type of asset, let us suppose that a firm has a fleet of vehicles for which it wishes to determine the optimum replacement policy. A replacement vehicle costs £6,000 and if we examine the motoring journals, we could obtain details of the resale value of the vehicles. Suppose we obtained the following data

Age of vehicle (years)	1	2	3	4	5	6	7	8	9	10
Resale Value (£)	4500	3300	2300	1700	1400	1200	1000	900	850	800

Subtracting the resale values from £6,000 will give us the cost of replacing the vehicle in each year.

Age of vehicle (years)	1	2	3	4	5	6	7	8	9	10
Replacement cost (£)	1500	2700	3700	4300	4600	4800	5000	5100	5150	5200

To find the optimum replacement period we need running cost for the vehicles, and to simplify the analysis we will suppose that all running costs are met at the end of the year.

Year	1	2	3	4	5	6	7	8	9	10
Running costs	1000	1050	1150	1300	1500	1750	2050	2400	2800	3250

Suppose the firm decides to keep the vehicle 4 years, then it would have incurred running costs of 1000 + 1050 + 1150 + 1300 = £4500, and it will need £4300 to replace the vehicle. So the total cost of keeping the vehicle 4 years and then replacing it is 4500 + 4300 = £8800, which is an average cost of $\frac{8800}{4}$ = £2200 per year. We could calculate the average cost per year if the vehicle was replaced after 1,2,3 etc. years, and this has been done in table 16.5.

Year	Running Cost	Cumulative Running Cost	Capital Cost	Total Cost	Average Cost
1	1000	1000	1500	2500	2500
2	1050	2050	2700	4740	2375
3	1150	3200	3700	6900	2300
4	1300	4500	4300	8800	2200
5	1500	6000	4600	10600	2120
6	1750	7750	4800	12550	2092
7	2050	9800	5000	14800	2114
8	2400	12200	5100	17300	2163
9	2800	15000	5150	20150	2238
10	3250	18250	5200	23450	2345

Table 16.5

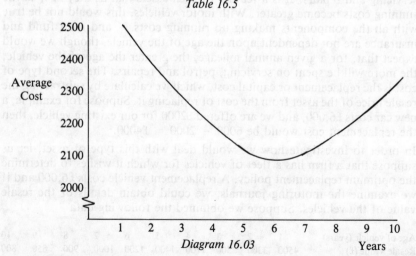

Diagram 16.03

It would appear to make sense to replace the fleet of vehicles after six years, because this is the replacement cycle that would minimise average cost. Diagram 16.3 shows how average cost changes with the replacement period. Notice how the curve flattens out around its lowest point — this implies that if the firm wishes to put off replacement to year 7, or bring replacement forward to year 5, then average cost would not change greatly. This 'insensitive' nature of average costs to small movements away from the optimum replacement period is a common phenomemon, and can have important implications. Suppose, for example it is considered bad for the company image to operate 'old' vehicles, and so it is decided to replace the vehicles when they are 4 years old rather than the optimum six years — average cost would only be £108 above optimum, an increase of $\frac{108}{2092} \times 100$

$= 5.16\%$.

Discounting and Replacement

The problem with the method that we have just used is that it ignores the time value of money. When we looked at compounding and discounting, we saw that if we were examining money over time then we should discount the cash flow and obtain its present value. Rather than looking at actual running cost and replacement cost we should really be examining the present value of such costs. If we assume that the firm earns 10% on its capital employed, then we can use this figure as a basis for discounting the costs.

Table 16.6 shows running costs and replacement costs discounted at 10% per annum. Notice that discounted total cost is constantly rising, and so in itself is no indicator of the optimum replacement period. Now of course, it would not be legitimate to divide by the number of years and so obtain average cost, because once again we would be ignoring the time value of money.

Year	$(1.1)^{-n}$	Capital Cost	Discounted Capital Cost	Running Cost	Discounted Running Cost	Discounted Total Cost
1	0.9091	1500	1364	1000	909	2273
2	0.8264	2700	2231	1050	868	4008
3	0.7513	3700	2780	1150	864	5421
4	0.6830	4300	2937	1300	888	6466
5	0.6209	4600	2856	1500	931	7316
6	0.5645	4800	2710	1750	988	8157
7	0.5132	5000	2566	2050	1052	9066
8	0.4665	5100	2379	2400	1120	9999
9	0.4241	5150	2184	2800	1187	10991
10	0.3855	5200	2005	3250	1253	12065

Table 16.6

To find the optimum replacement period, we need some method of "averaging out" the discounted total cost, and probably the best way to do this is to set up a *perpetual replacement fund* for each replacement period. A perpetual replacement fund is a fund that can meet all the running costs incurred during the vehicles life, replace the vhicles, have an amount left in

288

the fund to do likewise for the replacement vehicle, and so on for ever. Of course, the calculation of this fund assumes that the running costs and replacement costs remain fixed. In order to illustrate the perpetual replacement fund, suppose we decide to replace the vehicle after 3 years. The perpetual replacement fund £x would have to yield sufficient income when invested at 10% per annum to meet the following costs.

	Year	Cost	
	1	1000	running costs
	2	1050	
Vehicle replaced →	3	4850	(i.e. running and replacement costs.)
	4	1000	
	5	1050	
Vehicle replaced →	6	4850	
	7	1000	
	8	1050	
Vehicle replaced →	9	4850	
	10	1000	

We must imagine this 3 year cost-cycle continuing forever.

Consider the cost incurred during the first cycle. We have already calculated that the present value of these costs are

$$1000 \times 0.9091 + 1050 \times 0.8264 + 4850 \times 0.7513 = £5421$$

So if we invest £5421 now at 10% p.a. the fund would be just sufficient to meet the costs in the first cycle. But if the fund is to meet the costs of all cycles, we must invest £x now and have £x left after meeting the costs in the first cycle. To have £x in three years time, we must invest $x(1.1)^{-3} = 0.7513x$ now. So it must follow that if £x is the amount invested now,

$$x = 0.7513x + 5421$$
$$x - 0.7513x = 5421$$
$$x = \frac{5421}{1 - 0.7513}$$

$$= £21,797$$

In other words, if we invest £21,797 now at 10% per annum, then the interest would be sufficient to pay the running costs and replace the vehicle every three years.

No doubt this seems rather complicated to you, and if we check that our calculation for the three year replacement cycle is correct, then you will probably understand the concepts better.

Sum invested	£21,797
Interest in year 1	2,179.7
	£23,976.7
less year 1 running costs	1000
	£22976.7
Interest in year 2	2297.67
	£25274.37
less year 2 running cost	1050.00
	24224.37
Interest in year 3	2422.44
	26646.81
less year 3 running cost	1150.00
	25496.81
Less replacement cost	3700.00
	£21796.81 = £21,797.

So we see that after meeting all costs during the three year period, our capital fund invested is left intact. Thus, the interest earned by this fund would be sufficient to replace the vehicle on a three year cycle for ever. Generalising, if we wish to replace an asset every n years, and we can invest at a rate r.

$$\text{Perpetual replacement fund} = \frac{\text{Discounted total cost}}{1 - (1 + r)^{-n}}$$

Table 16.7 shows the perpetual replacement fund for each replacement cycle. The smallest perpetual replacement fund occurs with a seven year cycle, so the optimum replacement period for the vehicle is seven years. Notice that using discounting techniques rate than the average cost method suggests that we postpone replacement by one extra year.

Year	$(1.1)^{-n}$	Discounted Total Cost	Perpetual Replacement fund
1	0.9091	2273	25006
2	0.8264	4008	23008
3	0.7513	5421	21797
4	0.6830	6466	20397
5	0.6209	7316	19298
6	0.5645	8157	18730
7	0.5132	9066	18623
8	0.4665	9999	18742
9	0.4241	10991	19085
10	0.3855	12065	19634

Table 16.7

Evaluation of Comparable Assets

In the chapter on investment evaluation, we examined the net present value method for determining which of a number of alternative investments we should select. However, we examined running costs only, and did not consider the problem of replacing the asset. Now with assets such as motor vehicles and machinery, replacement costs will play an important part in the evaluation process. In such cases, we should use perpetual replacement funds as our criterion for selecting between competing assets.

In the last section, we determined a replacement strategy for a motor vehicle – let us call this vehicle a Type 1 vehicle. As an alternative, the firm could use a Type 11 vehicle. Now the Type 11 vehicle has higher running costs, but its replacement costs are lower.

Year	1	2	3	4	5	6	7	8	9	10
Running cost	1500	1550	1650	1900	2100	2350	2750	3100	3600	4000
Replacement cost	1100	1700	2200	2700	3100	3400	3500	3550	3600	3700

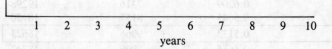

Diagram 16.04

291

Diagram 16.4 illustrates the essential differences between the two types of vehicle. We have already calculated the perpetual replacement funds for a Type 1 vehicle, and we must now do likewise for a Type 11 vehicle

Year	$(1.1)^{-n}$	Running Cost	Discounted Running cost	Total Running cost	Replacement Cost	Discounted Total Cost	Perpetual Replacement Fund
1	0.9091	1500	1364	1364	1100	2364	26006
2	0.8264	1550	1281	2645	1700	4050	23329
3	0.7513	1650	1240	3885	2200	5537	22267
4	0.6830	1900	1298	5183	2700	7028	22169
5	0.6209	2100	1304	6487	3100	8412	22189
6	0.5645	2350	1327	7814	3400	9733	22349
7	0.5132	2750	1411	9225	3500	11021	22640
8	0.4665	3100	1446	10671	3500	12327	23106
9	0.4241	3600	1527	12198	3600	13724	23832
10	0.3855	4000	1542	13740	3700	15166	24681

Table 16.8

A glance at table 16.8 shows that a Type 11 vehicle should be replaced every 4 years as this minimises the size of the perpetual replacement fund. Table 16.9 summarises the difference between the two types of vehicle, and we must conclude that a Type 1 vehicle is preferred as it involves a smaller perpetual replacement fund

Type of Vehicle	Replacement Cycle	Perpetual Replacement Fund
Type 1	7 years	£18,623
Type 11	4 years	£22,169

Table 16.9

To conclude this chapter on replacement, let us assume that the firm has a fleet of Type 11 vehicles which are two years old. Clearly, the firm will wish to change to a Type 1 vehicle − but it does not follow that the vehicle will be replaced immediately. Suppose we assume that a Type 11 vehicle costs £5000 we can then calculate the resale price at the end of each year by subtracting the replacement cost from £5000.

Year	1	2	3	4	5	6	7	8	9	10
Replacement cost	1100	1700	2200	2700	3100	3400	3500	3550	3600	3700
Resale cost	3900	3300	2800	2300	1900	1600	1500	1450	1400	1300

We can measure by how much the vehicle is depreciating on a year-by-year basis if we find its fall in value each year. This is done in table 16.10.

Year	Value at start of year	Value at End of year	Depreciation
1	5000	3900	1100
2	3900	3300	600
3	3300	2800	500
4	2800	2300	500
5	2300	1900	400
6	1900	1600	300
7	1600	1500	100
8	1500	1450	50
9	1450	1400	50
10	1400	1300	100

Table 16.10.

So we see that 2 year old vehicles have passed their maximum period of depreciation and we are now entering a more economic phase of their lives. It would appear to make sense, then, to hold on to the Type 11 vehicles for a few more years yet before changing to Type 1. What is more to the point, however, is that because we have made the decision to switch to a Type 1 vehicle, we can ignore all future replacement costs on Type 11 vehicles.

Let us examine again the running costs on a Type 11 vehicle

Year	1	2	3	4	5	6	7	8	9	10
Running cost	1500	1550	1650	1900	2100	2350	2750	3100	3600	4000

Suppose we decide to keep the Type 11 vehicle for 2 more years, then it follows that we will meet running costs of £1650 and £1900 during those years (remember that the Type 11 vehicle is 2 years old). To meet these running costs the amount we must invest now at 10% per annum is

$$1650 \times 0.9091 + 1900 \times 0.8264 = £3070$$

Also, in 2 years time we will need £18,623 to set up a perpetual replacement fund for a Type 1 vehicle, and to obtain this sum the amount we must invest now at 10% per annum is

$$18,623 \times 0.8264 = £15,390$$

So the present value of changing to a Type 1 vehicle in 2 years time is

$$15,390 + 3070 = £18,460$$

Table 16.11 shows the present value of changing to a Type 1 vehicle in 1,2,3 etc., year's time, and examining this table we see that the existing vehicle should be kept for 1 more year as this is the period with the lowest present value −

Age of Type 11 vehicle (yrs)	Years before replacement	$(1.1)^{-n}$	Running cost	Discounted running cost	P.V of perpetual replacement fund	P.V. of changing to type 1.
3	1	0.9091	1650	1500	16930	18430
4	2	0.8264	1900	1570	15390	18460
5	3	0.7513	2100	1577	13991	18638
6	4	0.6830	2350	1605	12720	18972
7	5	0.6209	2750	1707	11536	19495

Table 16.11

to change in 1 year's time would cost equivalently less now than for any other period. Notice that although this is the optimum period for changing, it would be an economic proposition to hold on to the Type 11 vehicle for up to 2 more years. It is not until the third year that the present value of changing to Type 1 (£18,638) exceeds its perpetual replacement fund (£18,623).

Exercises to Chapter 16

16.1   A firm has 100 lathes, each with ten cutting edges, that require replacement on a fairly regular basis. The following life distribution of blades is available

Life in weeks	1	2	3	4
% failures	10	30	50	10

Assuming that initially all 1000 blades were installed together, and that failed blades are replaced at the end of the week, estimate the weekly replacements each week for the first ten weeks.

16.2   For the blades in 16.1, suppose that group replacement costs £5 per blade and individual replacement costs £8 per blade. Find the group replacement cost and steady-state individual replacement cost.

16.3   For the blades in 16.1 find the mixed-strategy replacement cost and hence deduce the optimal replacement strategy.

16.4   Suppose the life distribution of a certain component is as follows:

Life in month	1	2	3	4	5
% failures	15	25	35	15	10

If initially 500 components were installed, and failed components are replaced at the end of the month, estimate the monthly replacements for ten months.

16.5   If group replacement costs £4, and individual replacement costs £6 per component, find the group replacement cost and steady-state individual replacement cost for the component in 16.4.

16.6   Find the mixed-strategy replacement cost for the component in 16.4 and hence deduce the optimal replacement strategy.

16.7   A machine cost £6,500. Its resale value and running costs over the next ten years are

Year	1	2	3	4	5	6	7
Resale Value	£5000	£4100	£3300	£2600	£2000	£1600	£1300
Running Costs	£3000	£3100	£3200	£3400	£3600	£3900	£4200

Year	8	9	10
Resale Value	£800	£600	£500
Running Costs	£4500	£4900	£5300

Using average costing, after how many years should the machine be replaced?

16.8   Assume money can be invested at 10% per annum. After how many years should the machine in 16.7 be replaced?

16.9   Assume money can be invested at 20% per annum. How would this affect your answer to 16.8?

16.10   A machine cost £9,500. Its resale value and running costs over the next ten years are

Year	1	2	3	4	5	6	7
Resale Value	£7500	£6600	£5800	£5100	£4500	£4000	£3600
Running Costs	£2000	£2200	£2400	£2600	£2800	£3000	£3200

Year	8	9	10
Resale Value	£3300	£3100	£3000
Running Costs	£3400	£3600	£3800

Using average costing, after how many years should the machine be replaced?

16.11   Assuming money can be invested at 10% per annum, after how many years should the machine in 16.10 be replaced? Which is the better buy: the machine in 16.7 or the machine in 16.10?

16.12   Suppose we have a machine as described in 16.7, and the machine is two year's old. After how many years should we switch to the machine described in 16.10?

16.13   A machine cost £8,000. Its resale value and running costs over the next ten years are

Year	1	2	3	4	5	6	7
Resale Value	£5500	£4600	£3800	£3100	£2500	£2000	£1600
Running Costs	£1500	£1700	£1900	£2100	£2300	£2500	£2700

Year	8	9	10
Resale Value	£1300	£1100	£1000
Running Costs	£2900	£3100	£3300

Using average costing, after how many years should the machine be replaced?

16.14   Assuming money can be invested at 10% per annum, after how many years should the machine in 16.13 be replaced? Which is the better buy: the machine in 16.10 or the machine in 16.13?

16.15   Suppose we have a machine as described in 16.10, and the machine is three year's old. After how many years should we switch to the machine described in 16.13?

Chapter Seventeen

Network Analysis 1: Project Planning

We all know that if a project is to be undertaken efficiently, it must be well planned, especially if a number of people are engaged on the project. All too often, people work in isolation, quite ignorant of what other people working on the same project are doing. It is the task of management to co-ordinate efficiently the efforts of such people. In the past, planning has not been so important as it is today as projects were less complex – the rule of thumb method would work quite well. However, as projects have become more complex, management researchers have turned their attention increasingly to systematic planning. Consider the complexity of producing the prototype Concorde or an Apollo moonshot, and you will soon recognise the need for systematic planning. Shortly after the Second World War, researchers evolved a method called Network Analysis. The impact of this method has been quite dramatic, largely because it is applicable to such a wide variety of projects. It has been used to plan production projects, servicing projects, research projects, sales projects and military projects.

Network Symbols

How does the method work? Well the first stage of analysis is to divide the project into a number of different *activities*. An activity is merely a particular piece of work identifiable as an entity within the project. If, for example, the project under consideration, is the servicing of a motor car, then one of the activities would be 'check the brakes for wear'. Now an activity within a network is represented by an arrow, with the description of the activity written on it viz:

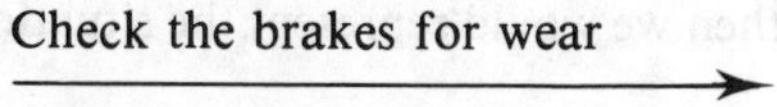

Check the brakes for wear

Diagram 17.01

In addition to activities, we must also identify events. Events mark the point in time when an activity is complete and the next activity can be started. Events are represented by circles.

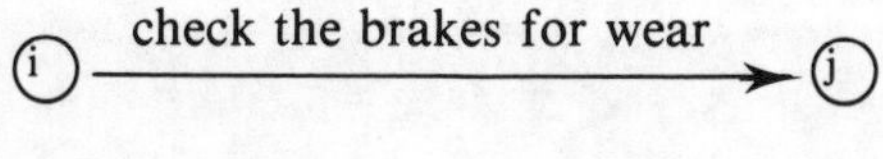

(i) —— check the brakes for wear —→ (j)

Diagram 17.02

The event ⓘ represents the point in time when the car is ready to have its brakes tested.

So far, we have not attempted to define a network and this we must now do. A network is a convenient method of showing the logical sequence of activities in a project. Suppose that in a certain project there are two activities A and B, and activity B cannot be started until activity A is completed. Using the network symbols, these activities can be represented like this.

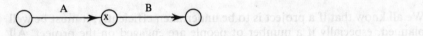

Diagram 17.03

The event ⓧ represents the point of time when activity A is completed, but it also represents the point of time when activity B can begin. We can conclude that the diagram above is a true representation of the situation when activity B depends upon activity A. Now of course it is quite likely that two or more activities are dependent upon the same activity. The situation when neither activity D not E can start until activity C is complete would be represented like this.

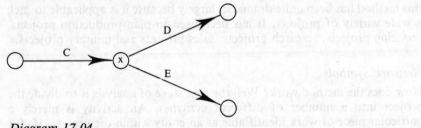

Diagram 17.04

The event X represents the point of time when activity C is completed, and also the point of time when activities D and E can start, so the diagram clearly shows that D and E depend upon C. Also, it is likely that an activity depends upon more than one other activity. If activity H cannot start until activities G and F are both complete, then we would represent the situation like this:

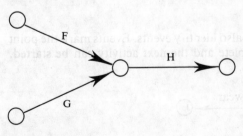

Diagram 17.05

Precedence Tables

You will probably have realised by now that the first task of network analysis is to sort out the logical sequence of activities, and we can summarise the logical sequence in a so-called "precedence table". In this table we list all the activities and their immediately preceding activities.

Activity	Preceding Activity
B, C and D	A
E and F	B
G	E
H	F
J	C
K	D
I	G and H
L	I, J and K

Constructing a precedence table is often the most difficult part of project analysis. Can you imagine how difficult it would be to construct a precedence table if the project involved the construction of a Polaris submarine? Obviously, the construction of a precedence table is, in essence, a team activity: all the experts involved in the project must be consulted.

Once we have compiled the precedence table we can begin to draw the network, and the first stage is to represent the relationships by a series of subnetworks.

Diagram 17.06

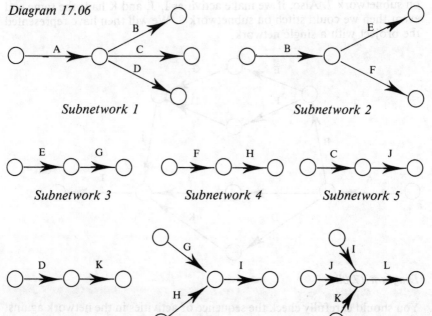

Subnetwork 1

Subnetwork 2

Subnetwork 3

Subnetwork 4

Subnetwork 5

Subnetwork 6

Subnetwork 7

Subnetwork 8

We can now attempt to join the sub-networks together and form a single network. However, one important rule must be observed; there must be just *one* start event and just *one* end event. We can stitch together the first six subnetworks into a single network like this:

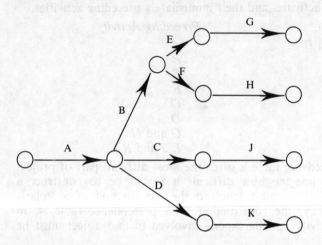

Diagram 17.07

If we make activities G and H have the same end event, then we can stitch on subnetwork 7. Also, if we make activities I, J, and K have the same end event then we could stitch on subnetwork 8. We will then have represented the project with a single network.

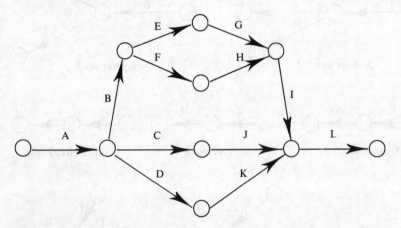

Diagram 17.08

You should carefully check the sequence of activities in the network against the sub-networks and precedence table. Of course, you can omit the sub-networks if you wish and attempt to draw the complete network directly from the precedence table. Whichever way you do it, you will seldom draw the network correctly the first time you try.

The "ij" Event Numbering Rule

If the network above consisted of real rather than imaginary activities, then a description of each activity would be written above each arrow. Now it is convenient to use a coding system to describe a particular activity, and we do this by numbering the events according to the 'ij rule'. The rule states that the event at the end of an activity must be assigned a greater number than the event at the beginning of an activity.

There is no single way of numbering the events, for the 'ij rule' allows considerable latitude. One numbering system that obeys the rule is:

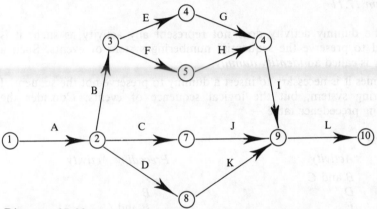

Diagram 17.09

but of course there are many others. We can now describe activity A (remember that in fact it may have quite a lengthy description) by its 'ij numbers 1 – 2.

Dummy Activities

If activities are to be described by their 'ij numbers, then it is essential that no two activities have the same numbers. Now this can present some difficulty: consider the following extract from a project's precedence table.

Example 2

Activity	Preceding Activity
B and C	A
D	B and C

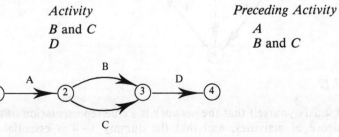

Diagram 17.10

Now this network does show a logical sequence of activities, but we cannot accept it, as activities *B* and *C* both have the same '*ij*' number. We overcome this problem by introducing a *dummy activity,* which is represented by a broken line.

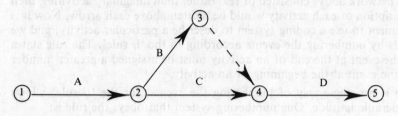

Diagram 17.11

Now the dummy activity does not represent any activity as such: it is inserted to preserve the sequential numbering system of events. Such a dummy is called an *identity dummy.*

Sometimes it is necessary to insert a dummy to preserve not the sequential numbering system, but the logical sequence of events. Consider the following precedence table –

Example 3

Activity	Preceding Activity
B and *C*	*A*
D	*B*
E	*B* and *C*
F	*D* and *E*

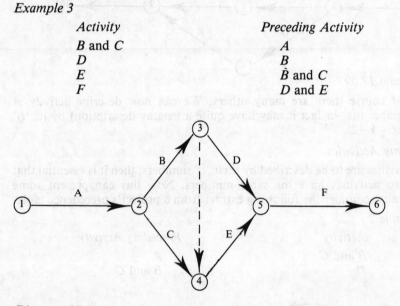

Diagram 17.12

You should satisfy yourself that the network is a true representation of the logical sequence of activities, and that the dummy 3 – 4 is essential to preserve the logical sequence.

In the last section, we stated that a network has just one start event and one end event, and it is sometimes necessary to use dummy activities to ensure that this is so. The network below illustrates this point.

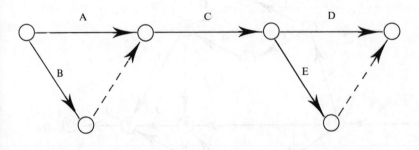

Diagram 17.13

It would be useful at this stage to state some rules so that we can decide when it is necessary to use dummies.

1. If an activity occurs in the right hand column of a precedence table but not in the left-hand column, it cannot depend upon another activity having been completed. Hence, it must be a 'starting activity'. If there is more than one start activity you *may* need dummies.

2. If an activity occurs in the left-hand column of precedence table but not in the right-hand column, then it must be an end activity. If there is more than one end activity you may need dummies.

3. If any activity occurs more than once in the right-hand column then you *will* need to introduce dummies. If the activity occurs n times, then $(n - 1)$ dummies will have to be drawn from its end event.

The precedence table of a certain project looks like this:

Activity	Preceding Activity
B, C and D	A
E and F	B
G	E
H	F
I	G and H
J	G, H, C and D
K	D
L	I, J and K

Firstly, we note that there is only one starting activity. Both *G* and *H* occur twice, so a dummy will be needed from the end event of both these activities. The network will look like this.

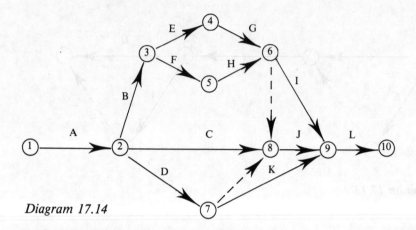

Diagram 17.14

Let us suppose that the network describes the activities in a manufacturing process. The network clearly shows that activities *B, C* and *D* can all be started together as long as we have sufficient resources to do so. Let us assume that we can easily obtain all the resources that we need. Later we can drop this assumption. Now let us assume that the project is such that the only resource needed is labour, and that all the labour available is equally capable of performing any activity. The time taken to complete each activity is known

Activity	A	B	C	D	E	F	G	H	I	J	K	L
Time (hrs.)	3	4	5	6	2	1	7	4	3	5	6	2

How long will the project take? To answer this, we must examine all the routes through the network. Can you see that there are seven possible routes? Let us list each and find the time taken.

Route	Time	
A B E G I L	$3+4+2+7+3+2$	= 21 hrs.
A B E G Dummy *J L*	$3+4+2+7+0+5+2$	= 23 hrs.
A B F H I L	$3+4+1+4+3+2$	= 17 hrs.
A B F H Dummy *J L*	$3+4+1+4+0+5+2$	= 19 hrs.
A C J L	$3+5+5+2$	= 15 hrs.
A D Dummy *I L*	$3+6+0+5+2$	= 16 hrs.
A D K L	$3+6+6+2$	= 17 hrs.

The project cannot be completed in less than 23 hours. This is determined by the longest route through the network – called the *critical path*. Activities on this route must be completed on time otherwise the total project time will lengthen; (i.e. the activities have critical times). You should realise that it would be very difficult to calculate the total project time without first drawing the network. Try to find the total project time just using the precedence table and you will realise how true this is!

Most networks will be much more complicated than the one we have examined, and it will be tedious to identify all the routes. In fact it is more than likely that some routes will be overlooked. A more efficient method is to use *the earliest event times* i.e. the earliest time that each event can occur. We divide the circle showing the event into three parts like this:

A is the event number,
B is the earliest event time.

We start at 1 and arbitrarily assign to it a start time of zero. Event two occurs when activity A is complete, so the earliest event time is 0 + 3 = third hour.

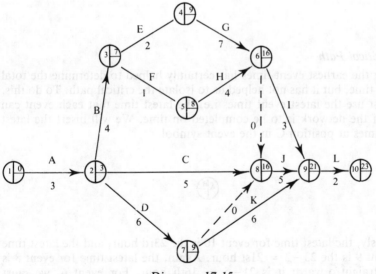

Diagram 17.15

Likewise we can deduce that

the earliest even time for event 3 is 7 hours (activity B complete)
the earliest event time for event 4 is 9 hours (activity E complete)
the earliest event time for event 5 is 8 hours (activity F complete)
the earliest event time for event 7 is 9 hours (activity D complete)

Now let us consider event 6. This cannot occur until both activity G and activity H are complete.

Activity G is complete after $9 + 7 = 16$ hours is the earliest.
Activity H is complete after $8 + 4 = 12$ hours at the earliest.

So the earliest time for event 6 is the 16th hour.

For event 8, the earliest time would be either $16 + 0 = 16$ (dummy activity $6 - 8$ complete — remember that it is not an activity as such and so cannot occupy any time) or $3 + 5 = 8$ (activity C complete) or $9 + 0 = 9$ (dummy activity $7 - 8$ complete). Clearly, the earliest time for event 8 is the 16th hour. Continuing in this way for all the other events, we finally reach the end event 10 which has an earliest time of 23 hours. Clearly, the earliest time for the end event must be the same as the total project time. Using this method to find the total project time is more efficient and (as we shall see later) is essential to further analysis of the network.

The Critical Path

Finding the earliest event times has certainly helped to determine the total project time, but it has not helped us to isolate the critical path. To do this, we must use the latest event times i.e. the latest time that each event can occur if the network is to be completed on time. We will insert the latest event times at position C in the event symbol.

Obviously, the latest time for event 10 is the 23rd hour, and the latest time for event 9 is the $23 - 2 = 21$st hour. Again, the latest time for event 8 is quite straightforward: it is $21 - 5 = 16$th hour. For event 6, we must consider the two following activities $6 - 8$ and $6 - 9$. If activity $6 - 8$ is to be complete on time, then event 6 has a latest time of $16 - 0 = 16$th hour. If activity $6 - 9$ is to be complete on time then event 6 has a latest time of $21 - 3 = 18$th hour. Can you see that if the project is to be complete on time the event 6 has the 16th hour as its latest time? Continuing in this way, we can obtain the latest times for all the events.

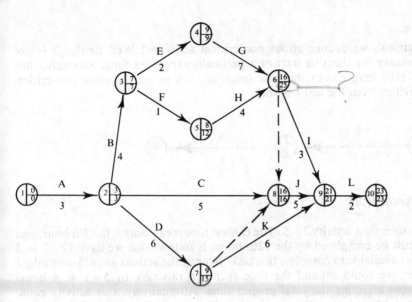

Diagram 17.16

Think back to critical activities — they must be started on time, otherwise the total project time will lengthen. What does this imply? Each event on the critical path must have the same earliest and latest times. Using this fact we can easily identify the critical path in the above network — but beware! The method is not infallible. Consider the network below.

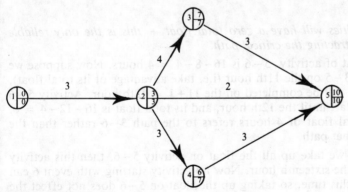

Diagram 17.17

If we state the critical path contains those events which have the same earliest and latest times, then we would isolate two paths:

    1 – 2 – 3 – 5
and 1 – 2 – 5

Are they both critical paths?

Float

What can we deduce about non-critical activities? Well firstly, it is not necessary for them to start at a particular, specified time. Secondly, they can take longer than the time specified. Let us extract some non-critical activities from the last network.

Diagram 17.18

Consider first activity $3-5$. The earliest time it can start is the 7th hour, and it must be completed by the 12th hour. It follows that we have $12-7 = 5$ hours available to complete this task. Now as the activity should only take 1 hour, we could expand the time spent on this task by $5-1 = 4$ hours without affecting the total project time. Alternatively, this activity could start 4 hours late without affecting the total project time. This 4 hours latitude we have on activity $3-5$ is called its *total float*. *We can define total float as time available for an activity minus expected activity duration,* or using i as the start event and j as the end event.

> latest time for event j
> minus earliest time for event i
> minus activity duration

Critical activities will have a zero total float − this is the only reliable method of extracting the critical path.

The total float of activity $5-6$ is $16-8-4 = 4$ hours. Now suppose we start activity $3-5$ on the 11th hour (i.e. take advantage of its total float), then this task will be completed on the $11+1 = 12$th hour. Activity $5-6$ now cannot start until the 12th hour, and its total float is $16-12-4 = 0$. Thus, the total float of 4 hours refers to the path $3-6$ rather than the activities on that path.

Now suppose we take up all the float on activity $5-6$, then this activity must end on the sixteenth hour. Now no activity starting with event 6 can begin before this time, so taking up the float on $5-6$ does not effect the following activities. The float on $5-6$ then, is essentially different to the float on $3-5$. We say that activity $5-6$ has a *free float* of 4 hours. Thus, total float affects following activities, whereas free float does not.

We can calculate free float by taking

> earliest time for j
> minus earliest time for i
> minus duration of ij

In this particular network free float (where it exists) is always the same as total float. However, this need not be so. Consider the following network

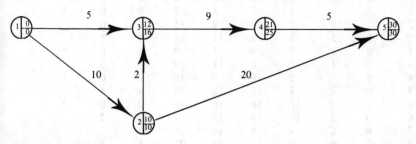

Diagram 17.19

Activity 1 – 3 has a free float of 12 – 5 – 0 = 7, but its total float is 16 – 5 – 0 = 11.

Project Summary Tables

Table 17.1 shows a standard format summary of our network. The first two columns lists the *ij* numbers of all the activities together with their estimated times. For any activity, we can pick up the earliest start and latest end like this:

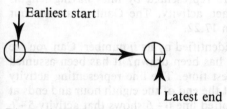

Diagram 17.20

Let us take activity F as an example.

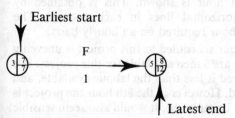

Diagram 17.21

The earliest start is day 7, so the earliest end is day 7 + 1 = 8. The latest end is on day 12, so the latest start is on day 12 – 1 = 11. We can calculate total float either by subtracting earliest start from latest start, or by subtracting earliest end from latest end. Free float is calculated as in the previous section.

Start Event	End Event	Time	Earliest Start	Earliest End	Latest Start	Latest End	Float Total	Float Free	Critical
1	2	3	0	3	0	3	0	0	*
2	3	4	3	7	3	7	0	0	*
2	7	6	3	9	9	15	6	0	
2	8	5	3	8	11	16	8	8	
3	4	2	7	9	7	9	0	0	*
3	5	1	7	8	11	12	4	0	
4	6	7	9	16	9	16	0	0	*
5	6	4	8	12	12	16	4	4	
6	8	0	16	16	16	16	0	0	*
6	9	3	16	19	18	21	2	2	
7	8	0	9	9	16	16	7	7	
7	9	6	9	15	15	21	6	6	
8	9	5	16	21	16	21	0	0	*
9	10	2	21	23	21	23	0	0	*

Table 17.1

Gantt Charts: 'Loading' the Network

So far, our analysis has ignored the supply of resources that are available to work on a project. Let us continue to analyse the same project, and assume that we require one man per activity. Allocating resources to the project is called 'loading the network', and this is usually done with a *Gantt Chart*. On a Gantt chart, the activities are represented by lines having lengths proportional to the duration of each activity. The Gantt chart for our project would look like the diagram 17.22.

Each activity on the Gantt chart is identified by its *ij* number. Can you see the assumption on which the chart has been drawn? It has been assumed that each activity starts at its earliest time. The line representing activity $5-6$ shows that the activity starts at the end of the eighth hour and ends at the end of the twelfth hour. The dotted line $6-6$ shows that activity $5-6$ must be completed at the end of the 16th hour at the latest. The dotted line shows the total float of each activity. At the foot of each column, the number of men required for that hour is shown. This is obtained by counting the number of solid horizontal lines in each column. The histogram shows the amount of labour required on an hourly basis.

The histrogram shows that the labour scheduled to this project is unevenly distributed. It also shows that there are 3 men available for this project. For most of the time, the labour required is less than the labour available, and the project is said to be underloaded. However in the 8th hour the project is overloaded, and this overload must be removed. It would also seem sensible to smooth the histogram as much as possible.

Obviously, we must concentrate on activities that have float, and as activities with free float do not affect other activities, we will consider them first. Activity $7-9$ has a free float, and if we put this forward one hour, the gaps in the histogram in the 16th hour will be filled. This, however, will leave another gap at the 10th hour. We can fill this gap and remove the

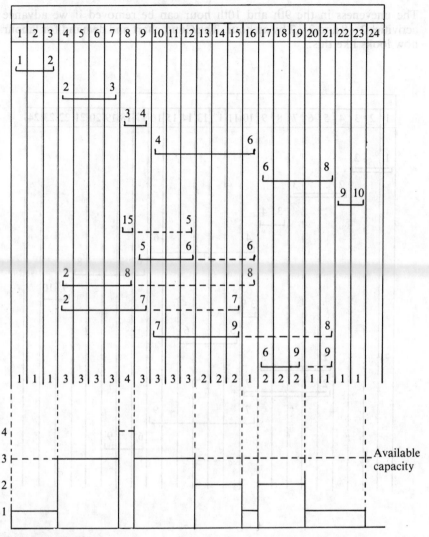

Diagram 17.22

overload in the eighth hour by advancing activities $3-5$ and $5-6$ by two hours. This removes the overload, but does not smooth the histogram as the demand for labour is now like this:

Hour	Labour required
0 – 3	1 man
4 – 8	3 men
9 – 10	2 men
11 – 14	3 men
15 – 19	2 men
20 – 23	1 man

The unevenness in the 9th and 10th hour can be removed if we advance activities 2 – 8 and 2 – 7 by an hour. The Gantt chart and demand for labour now looks like this:

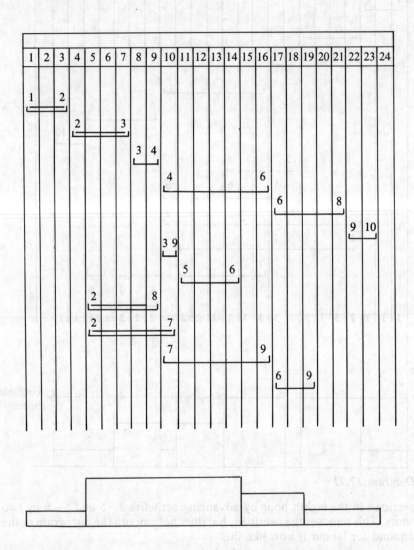

Diagram 17.23

We can now state exactly how labour will be scheduled to the project. One man can be instructed to work on the critical path. A second man will be required from the 5th to the 14th hour, working on activity 2 – 8, 3 – 5 and 5 – 6.

Progress Charts

The Gantt Chart can be used effectly to show how a project is actually progressing, and we do this by drawing a line above the activity symbol which is proportional to the amount of work completed. Suppose, for example that the Gantt Chart in diagram 17.23 represents the state of the project at the end of the 8th hour. We can conclude that activity $3-4$ should be 50% complete but that it has not yet been started.

Activity $2-7$ should be 83.33% complete − in fact it has been completed. This interpretation begs the question as to whether it is possible to transfer labour to the critical path, as the project time is in danger of lengthening. Used in this way, the Gantt chart is an important element of project control.

Dealing with Uncertainty

So far, we have assumed that the activity times can be accurately estimated. In practice, such estimates will be liable to error, so three estimates are often made. An estimate that we shall call estimate a assumes that nothing goes wrong, and so is an estimate of the shortest time that the activity could take. An estimate that we shall call estimate b assumes that everything that can go wrong does go wrong, so estimate b is an estimate of the longest time that the activity could take. Finally, an estimate that we shall call c is the most likely time for the activity − the estimate that would occur most frequently if the activity was repeated many times. We can combine the three estimates to give the expected time (te) like this:

$$te = \frac{a+b+4c}{6}$$

An estimate made in this way is called a weighted average − it places more emphasis on the c estimate than on the other two estimates. Now as te is an estimate, it is subject to error, and the extent of the error is measured by the standard deviation.

$$\text{Standard deviation of estimate} = \frac{b-a}{6}$$

Suppose the following estimates have been made for a four activity project.

Activity	shortest time	longest time	most frequent time	expected time	standard deviation
A	4 days	10 days	6 days	6.33 days	1 day
B	6 days	14 days	9 days	9.33 days	1.33 days
C	5 days	8 days	6 days	6.16 days	0.5 days
D	7 days	13 days	11 days	10.67 days	1 day

If the four activities occur in sequence, then we can estimate the time for the project by adding together the individual expected times.

$$6.33 + 9.33 + 6.16 + 10.67 = 32.5 \text{ days.}$$

Now we cannot add the individual standard deviations in order to obtain the standard deviation for the project, but we can add their squares

$$\text{standard deviation for project} = \sqrt{(1)^2 + (1.33)^2 + (.5)^2 + (1)^2} = 2.007 \text{ days.}$$

If we assume that the activity times are normally distributed, then we can be more than 95% sure that the project will be completed in less than

$$\text{expected time} + 2 \times \text{standard deviation}$$

So we could quote a completion time for the project of $32.5 + 2 \times 2.007 = 36.514$ days.

Decreasing the total project time

Sometimes it is possible to reduce the time spent on activities by drafting in extra resources, though of course this would increase the cost. Consider the example in table 17.2. Here, the ij numbers are given, so drawing the network will be much easier. Normal time is the time taken if usual procedures are adopted, whereas minimum time is the time taken if extra resources are drafted in

Task	Normal Time (days)	Minimum Time (days)	Cost of Extra Resources	Equivalent cost per day
1–2	5	4	£150	£150
2–3	9	5	£360	£90
2–4	8	6	£60	£30
3–4	0	0	0	0
3–6	4	2	£20	£10
4–5	8	7	£80	£80
5–6	0	0	0	0
5–7	4	2	£140	£70
6–7	6	3	£180	£60
7–8	2	2	0	0
			£990	

Table 17.2

Firstly, let us draw the network assuming normal procedures are adopted

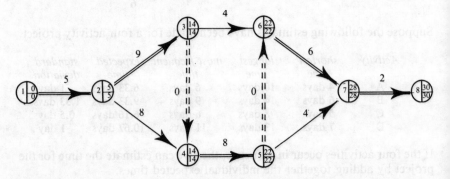

Diagram 17.24

Now let us assume that the extra resources are used, and insert the minimum times on the network.

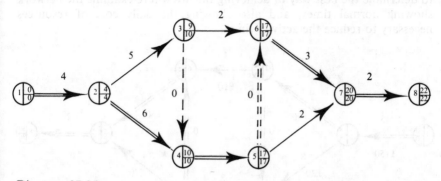

Diagram 17.25

Notice that the critical path (marked by the double lines) has changed. Drafting in extra resources has reduced the project time by 8 days, but it has increased cost by £990. But need cost increase by this much? Surely, it is not necessary to reduce non-critical activities to a minimum! Activity 5 – 7 cannot start before day 17 nor finish after day 20 – it could take 3 days without increasing the project time. Instead, then, of decreasing activity 5 – 7 from 4 days to 2 days, we can decrease it from 4 days to 3 days, and assuming that the cost increase is proportional to the time reduction, we would save 180/3 = £60. We could adjust the other non-critical activities in a similar fashion. Activity 3 – 6 could take 17 – 9 = 8 days without affecting the total project time – it could return to its 'normal' time of 4 days, saving £20 on resources. Likewise, the available time for 2 – 5 is 10 – 4 = 6 days, and if sufficient resources are allocated to achieve this a further £90 could be saved. A little thought, then, has reduced additional resources cost by 60 + 20 + 90 = £170, and the minimum time could be achieved for an extra outlay of 990 – 170 = £820.

The minimum time at minimum cost network shows that all activities except 3 – 6 are now critical.

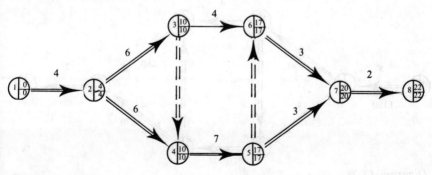

Diagram 17.26

Sometimes it is necessary to achieve a target time, and it is desirable to achieve the target time at minimum cost. Suppose the target time is 25 days, to determine the best way of achieving this we will re-examine the network showing normal times, and also showing the daily cost of resources necessary to reduce the activity times.

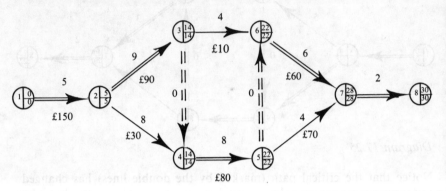

Diagram 17.27

To achieve a project time of 25 days, we must reduce the critical path by 5 days. The cheapest activity to reduce is activity $6-7$, which we can reduce by 3 days at a cost of £60 per day. However, if we were to reduce $6-7$ by 3 days, the time for the project would not also be reduced by 3 days unless we also reduce activity $5-7$ by one day. So to reduce the project time by three days using activity $6-7$ would cost £60 per day for the first two days and £130 for the third day. For the moment we shall reduce activity $6-7$, and hence the project time, by two days. The next cheapest activity to reduce is activity $4-5$ which can be reduced by one day for an outlay of £80. We now require to reduce the critical path by a further two days. Activity $2-3$ can be reduced by 4 days at a cost of £90 per day, but if we reduce this activity by more than one day we must also reduce activity $2-4$ if the project time is also to be reduced. For the moment, then, we will reduce activity $2-3$ by one day.

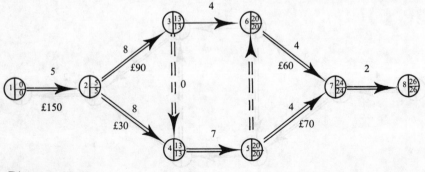

Diagram 17.28

So far, we have managed to reduce the project time by 4 days, and this has cost us $2 \times £60 + £80 + £90 = £290$. To achieve the target time of 25 days, we must reduce the critical time by one more day. We have three ways of achieving this.

a) reduce $1-2$ at a cost of £150

b) reduce $2-3$ and $2-4$ at a cost of $£90 + £30 = £120$

c) reduce $5-7$ and $6-7$ at a cost of $£70 + £60 = £130$

Option b) is the cheapest, and a target time of 25 days can be achieved for a minimum outlay on extra resources of $£290 + £120 = £410$.

Exercises to Chapter 17

17.1 The '*ij*' numbers and durations of activities in a certain project are

ij No.	Duration
$1-2$	3
$2-3$	4
$2-4$	5
$2-6$	6
$3-4$	3
$3-5$	2
$4-7$	4
$5-7$	0
$5-8$	5
$6-7$	0
$6-8$	1
$7-8$	3

Draw the network and deduce the total project time.

Prepare a summary chart for the project.

17.2 The '*ij*' identifications and durations of the tasks in a particular project are as follows:

'*ij*' Number	duration (days)
$1-2$	3
$1-4$	1
$1-5$	3
$2-3$	4
$2-6$	5
$3-6$	2
$4-6$	0
$4-7$	4
$5-7$	0
$5-8$	5
$6-7$	2
$7-8$	6

Find

a) The earliest event times and latest event times

b) The shortest time to complete the project

c) The total float and the free float for each activity.

Explain how the analysis would be modified to account for uncertainty in the duration of the tasks.

17.3 Label the activities in the last question from A to J (do not label the dummies). Now derive a precedence table for the project.

17.4 Suppose that the labour available to work on the project discussed in the text was as follows:

two men up to the end of the 11th hour

three men from the 11th to 23rd hour

Redraw the Gantt Chart to take account of the supply of labour.

17.5 Now suppose that only two men are available: the project time will have to increase. Schedule resources to the activities so that the increased total project time is a minimum.

17.6

Activity	Preceding Activity
B, F, I, J, K, L	A
C	B
D	C
E	D
G	F
M	L
N	M
H	D, G, I, J
O	E, H, K, N.

Draw the network of this project.

17.7 The activities referred to in question 6 have the following estimated durations

Activity	A	B	C	D	E	F	G	H	I	J	K	L	M	N	O
Days	5	10	5	2	3	8	1	12	5	5	10	2	10	6	5

Insert these times on your network and so deduce the earliest and latest event times. What is the total project time? What is the critical path?

17.8 Prepare a summary chart for the project, and find the total and free float for each activity. What would be the effect of activity E taking 9 days longer than expected?

17.9 Each activity requires one man, except activity B. This activity requires one man for one day at its start, and one man for one day to complete the activity. Draw the Gantt Chart on the understanding that each activity starts at its earliest possible time, and obtain the resource profile.

17.10 The labour availability for this project is – three men to the end of day 18, and two men thereafter. Can the project be completed on time?

17.11 At the end of day 14, activity L is just complete (it has taken one day longer than expected). If activity K is also just complete, what would you recommend?

17.12 You assistant has been given the task of analysing a project. He derives the following precedence table.

Activity	Preceding Activity
B, C and D	A
E	B
F	C and G
G	D and H
H	F
I	E
J	F
K	D and H

He is having difficulty with this task. Identify the difficulty and advise him where the fault lies.

17.13 Acme Ltd. supplies generating equipment on rental, and is responsible for servicing the equipment. Every five years, the equipment needs a major overhaul, and the engineers can accurately predict the times taken for the various tasks involved. These times can be reduced by drafting extra resources to the tasks, and the following details are available.

Task	Normal Time (days)	Cost of Normal Time (£)	Minimum Time (days)	Cost of Minimum Time (£)
1 – 2	18	8,000	14	10,400
1 – 3	8	6,000	6	7,000
1 – 4	7	7,000	5	8,000
2 – 7	10	6,000	6	9,400
3 – 4	0	0	0	0
3 – 5	9	8,000	6	9,800
4 – 6	11	9,000	7	10,200
5 – 6	6	3,000	5	3,400
6 – 7	9	10,000	7	11,600

The reduction in time and increase in cost is directly proportional.

Find the minimum time for completing the project and recommend a course of action to complete the project in the minimum time and at minimum cost.

17.14 For the project in question 13, recommend a course of action to complete the project in 26 days.

17.15 For the project in question 13, assume that the time for activity 2 – 7 could vary between 6 and 14 days, though 4 days could still be saved by spending on extra £3,400. Target time for completion is 30 days, and a £6,000 penalty will be imposed if this time is exceeded. Recommend an appropriate course of action.

Chapter Eighteen

Network Analysis II

In the last chapter, we used networks to analyse and control projects. We would not wish to leave you with the impression that this is the sole use of networks. After all, networks are an extremely important tool of analysis, and can be applied to a wide range of business problems. If you think carefully, you will realise that tree diagrams, which we used to great effect when considering probability and decision analysis, form another example of network techniques.

In this chapter, we will extend our knowledge of network techniques by considering three further applications.

The Minimum Spanning Tree

Supavision P.L.C. has won a licence to supply cable T.V. to a certain metropolitan district, and is considering the most effective way to route the cables. It would not be feasible to connect every household to the studio of Supavision directly, and so it is intended to set up a number of relay stations within the district, and connect each household to the nearest relay station. Each relay station would then need connecting to the studio. The local planning officer has approved the site of 5 relay stations, and the network below gives location details.

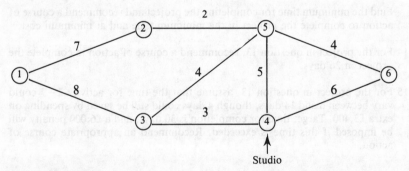

Diagram 18.01

The circles, (called nodes), give the locations of the relay stations, and node 4 gives the location of the studio (node 4 is called the source node). The lines represent possible connections between the nodes, and the number of the lines represent the distance, in kilometers between the nodes. We can see, then, that 3 kilometers of cable would be necessary to connect the relay station at node 3 to the studio. We can also see that it is not possible to connect all the relay stations to the studio directly — for example connecting the relay station at node 2 would involve routing through other relay stations. Supavision requires to know the network that connects the relay stations to the studio using the minimum length of cable — the so-called minimum spanning tree.

We can solve this problem by arbitrarily selecting a node, and we will select node 4. We now assume that node 4 is connected into the system (which, of course it must be as it is the studio) and put a cross through this node.

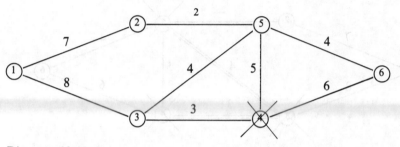

Diagram 18.02

The first stage is to identify all the nodes that can be connected directly to node 4, noting the distances in each case

Route	Distance
4 – 3	3 Km
4 – 5	5 Km
4 – 6	6 Km

The shortest route is 4 – 3, so we will connect node 3 to node 4. We indicate this on our network by marking this route with a double line, and as node 3 is now connected, we put a cross through this node.

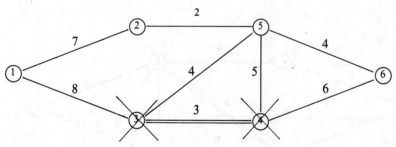

Diagram 18.03

The second stage is to identify all the unconnected nodes that can be linked directly to the connected nodes, in each case noting the distance. We then link in the node with the shortest distance, again marking it with an X.

Connected Node	Unconnected Node	Distance
3	1	8
3	5	4 ◄——— minimum.
4	5	5
4	6	6

Connecting node 5 to node 3 we have.

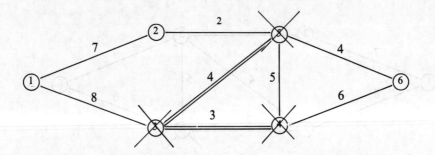

Diagram 18.04

We now repeat the second stage until all the nodes are connected.

Connected Node	Unconnected Node	Distance
3	1	8
4	6	6
5	2	2 ◄——— minimum.
5	6	4

Connecting node 2 to node 5

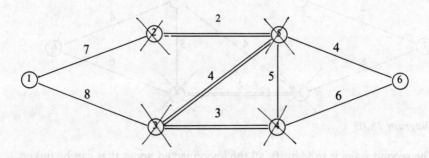

Diagram 18.05

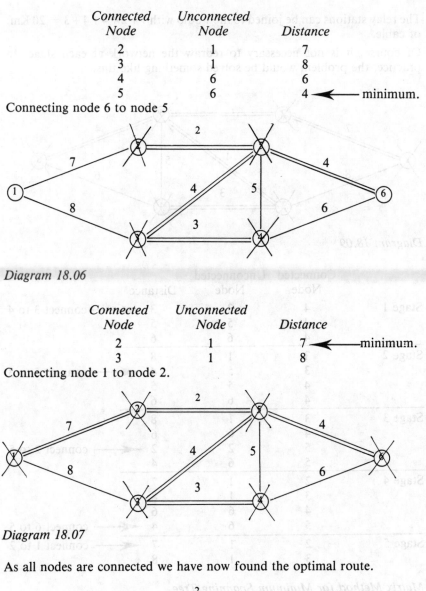

Connected Node	Unconnected Node	Distance
2	1	7
3	1	8
4	6	6
5	6	4 ← minimum.

Connecting node 6 to node 5

Diagram 18.06

Connected Node	Unconnected Node	Distance
2	1	7 ← minimum.
3	1	8

Connecting node 1 to node 2.

Diagram 18.07

As all nodes are connected we have now found the optimal route.

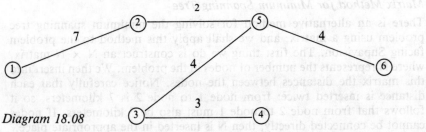

Diagram 18.08

The relay stations can be joined to the studio with $7 + 2 + 4 + 4 + 3 = 20$ Km. of cable.

Of course, it is not necessary to redraw the network at each stage. In practice, the problem would be solved something like this.

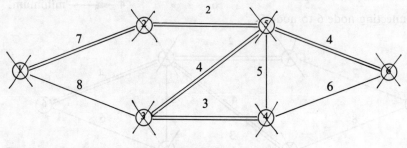

Diagram 18.09

	Connected Node	Unconnected Node	Distance	
Stage 1	4	3	3	◄── connect 3 to 4
	4	5	5	
	4	6	6	
Stage 2	3	1	8	
	3	5	4	◄── connect 5 to 3
	4	5	5	
	4	6	6	
Stage 3	3	1	8	
	4	6	6	
	5	2	2	◄── connect 2 to 5
	5	6	4	
Stage 4	2	1	7	
	3	1	8	
	4	6	6	
	5	6	4	◄── connect 6 to 5
Stage 5	2	1	7	◄── connect 1 to 2
	3	1	8	

Matrix Method for Minimum Spanning Tree

There is an alternative method for solving the minimum spanning tree problem using a matrix, and we shall apply this method to the problem facing Supavision. The first thing we do is construct an N × N matrix, where N represents the number of nodes in the problem. We then insert into this matrix the distances between the nodes. Notice carefully that each distance is inserted twice: from node 1 to node 2 is 7 kilometers, so it follows that from node 2 to node 1 must also be 7 kilometers. If nodes cannot be connected directly, then N is inserted in the appropriate place.

	To						
	1	2	3	4	5	6	
1	N	7	8	N	N	N	
2	7	N	N	N	2	N	
3	8	N	N	③	4	N	← connected.
From 4	N	N	3	N	5	6	
5	N	2	4	5	N	4	
6	N	N	N	6	4	N	

We now procede in a similar fashion as in the previous method. We arbitrarily select a node and assume it is connected. Last time we selected node 4, the studio, so this time we will select a different node. Let us start with node 3. We mark the third row as 'connected' and strike out the third column. We now scan the connected row, determine the minimum distance from node 3, and circle this minimum distance. We can see, then, that the nearest node to node 3 is node 4, so we will connect node 3 to node 4.

	To						
	1	2	3	4	5	6	
1	N	7	8	N	N	N	
2	7	N	N	N	2	N	
From 3	8	N	N	③	4	N	← connected
4	N	N	3	N	5	6	← connected
5	N	2	4	5	N	4	
6	N	N	N	6	4	N	

We can complete the solution to this problem by continuing in the same way i.e.

Step 1. Scan the connected rows (ignoring the numbers struck out) and find the minimum value. Circle this minimum value. If the minimum value occurs more than once, then arbitrarily select one of them.

Step 2. Strike out the column containing the minimum value.

Step 3. Mark as "connected" the row with the same number as the column you have just removed.

Step 4. If all the rows are connected (i.e. all columns struck out) then stop.

Step 5. Go to step 1.

Applying these rules, our route to the solution would be as follows.

	To						
	1	2	3	4	5	6	
1	N	7	8	N	N	N	
2	7	N	N	N	2	N	
From 3	8	N	N	③	④	N	← connected
4	N	N	3	N	5	6	← connected
5	N	2	4	5	N	4	← connected
6	N	N	N	6	4	N	

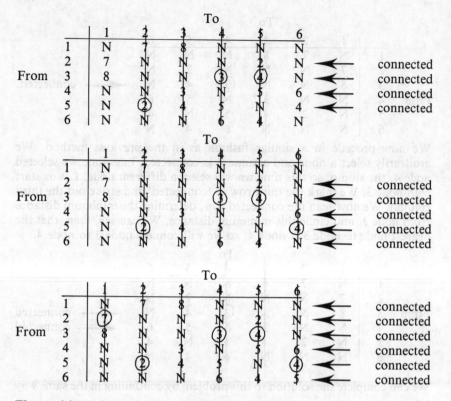

		To					
		1	2	3	4	5	6
	1	N	7	8	N	N	N
From	2	7	N	N	N	②)	N	← connected
	3	8	N	N	③	④	N	← connected
	4	N	N	3	N	5	6	← connected
	5	N	②	4	5	N	4	← connected
	6	N	N	N	6	4	N

		To					
		1	2	3	4	5	6
	1	N	7	8	N	N	N
	2	7	N	N	N	2	N	← connected
From	3	8	N	N	③	④	N	← connected
	4	N	N	N	N	5	6	← connected
	5	N	②	N	5	N	④	← connected
	6	N	N	N	6	4	N	← connected

		To					
		1	2	3	4	5	6
	1	N	7	8	N	N	N	← connected
	2	⑦	N	N	N	2	N	← connected
From	3	8	N	N	③	④	N	← connected
	4	N	N	3	N	5	6	← connected
	5	N	②	4	5	N	④	← connected
	6	N	N	N	6	4	5	← connected

The position of the circles indicate the minimum spanning tree i.e. $2-1$, $5-2$, $3-4$, $3-5$, $5-6$. You should notice that this result agrees precisely with the solution we obtained by examining the network directly. We have redrawn the matrix at each iteration for illustrative purposes only, whereas in practice only one matrix need be used.

Shortest Route Problem

A haulage company, based at town A makes regular deliveries to 5 towns, B, C, D, E, and F. The network below shows the distances between the towns (in kilometers).

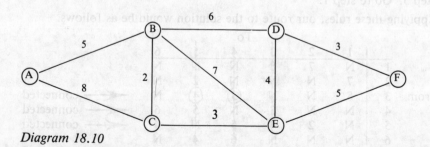

Diagram 18.10

The company wishes to know the shortest routes between town A (the source node) and all the other towns. As you might expect, problems such as this are called "shortest route" problems. Now you may be thinking that there is no difference between shortest route problems and the minimum spanning tree, but there is an important difference. With the minimum spanning tree, we are attempting to minimise the route that joins all of the nodes to the source node, but with the shortest route problem we are attempting to minimise the distance of each node from the source node. To appreciate this difference, let us again examine the solution to the problem facing Supavision.

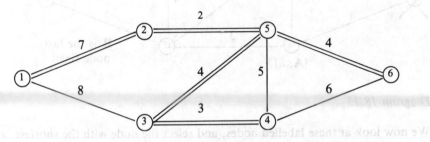

Diagram 18.11

Suppose this is a solution to the shortest route problem, finding the shortest route from each node to node 4. According to this solution, the shortest route from node 4 to node 6 is 4 → 3 → 5 → 6, a distance of 11 kilometers. But this cannot possibly be correct, as the direct distance from node 4 to node 6 is only 6 kilometers! Clearly, we need a different method for solving shortest route problems.

The method we will use is as follows. When the minimum distance of any node from the source has been found, we will cross out that node like this: ⊗. Also, each node in turn will be labelled something like this

[C, 10].

The symbol C represents the last node visited, and the number 10 represents the distance from the source node. We start by crossing out the source node A. Node A is then said to be "fixed".

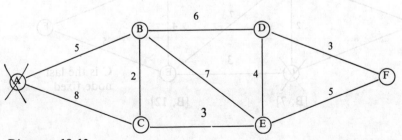

Diagram 18.12

326

We now find the distance from the source node to all nodes that can be reached directly from A (i.e. the distances to nodes B and C). This enables us to label nodes B and C.

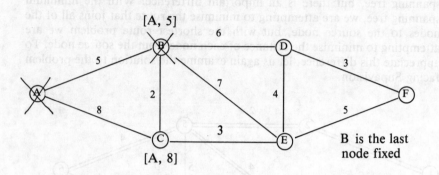

Diagram 18.13

We now look at these labelled nodes, and select the node with the shortest distance (node B). The route to node B has now been fixed, and we can cross out this node. We now examine all the nodes that can be reached directly from node B – the last fixed node. Examining the network we can see that it is possible to reach town D directly, from town B. If we take this route, then the distance from A would be 5 + 6 = 11 Km. So we label town D with [B, 11]. Likewise, we label town E with [B, 12]. You should also notice that it is possible to reach node C directly from node B, and the distance from the source is 5 + 2 = 7 Km. However, the label attached to C tells us that if we go directly from A to B the distance is 8 Km. Hence, the route A → B → C, is shorter than the direct route A → C, so we re-label node C with [B, 7]. The network now looks like this:

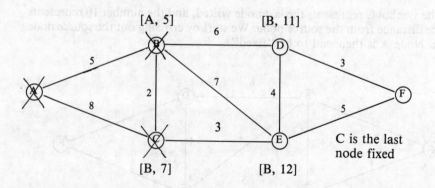

Diagram 18.14

As C now has the shortest route of all the nodes that have not yet been fixed, we have fixed the route to node C. The only node that can be reached directly from node C, the last fixed node, is node E, and the distance is $7 + 3 = 10$ Km. As this is less than the distance in node E's Label, we relabel node E with [C, 10].

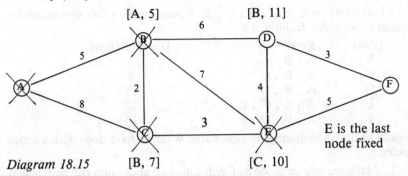

Diagram 18.15

Node E has the shortest route so we have fixed the route to node E. We now label node F with [E, 15], and as the route to D via E is $10 + 4 = 14$ Kms, we do not change the label for D.

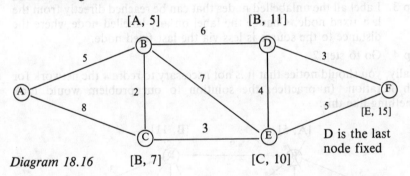

Diagram 18.16

Finally, we fix node D and re-label node F with [D, 14]. We have now reached the optimum solution as all the nodes are fixed.

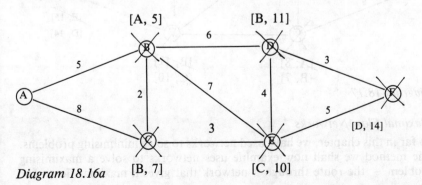

Diagram 18.16a

To find the route to a particular town, we apply the backtracking principle. Take, for example, the route to town E. Reading the labels, we can see that

We visit C before E
We visit B before C
We visit A before B,

so the best route to E is A , B , C , E. Routes to the other towns can be deduced in a similar fashion, i.e.

Town	Route	Distance (Km)
B	A , B	5
C	A , B , C	7
D	A , B , D	11
E	A , B , C , E	10
F	A , B , D , F	14

It would be useful to attempt to summarise what we have doen with a series of rules.

Step 1. Mark the source mode as fixed. Label all nodes that can be reached directly from the source node.

Step 2. Fix the labelled node with the shortest route to the source. If all labels are fixed then stop.

Step 3. Label all the unlabelled nodes that can be reached directly from the last fixed node. Change the label on any labelled node where the distance to the source is less via the last fixed node.

Step 4. Go to step 2.

Finally, you should notice that it is not necessary to redraw the network for each iteration. In practice, the solution to our problem would look something like this:

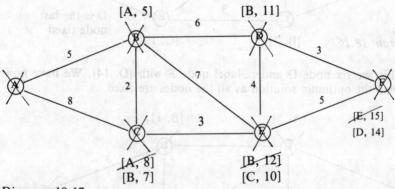

Diagram 18.17

Maximal Flow Networks

So far in this chapter, we have used networks to solve minimising problems. The method we shall now examine uses networks to solve a maximising problem − the route through a network that gives a maximal flow. The most obvious applications of this method would be to achieve an optimal flow of liquids or goods through a system of pipelines. However, you should note that the method can also be used to achieve an optimal flow of information (for example, the optimal flow of information through a telephone system, or through an interactive computer network). We will illustrate the method by examining the flow of crude oil through a network of pipelines thus:

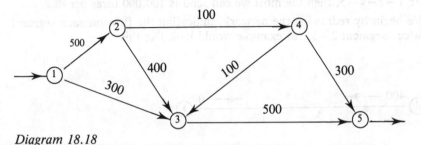

Diagram 18.18

The nodes represent geographical locations and the arrow represents the pipelines, showing the direction of flow. The numbers written on the arrows show the maximum capacity each pipleline can cope with per day in thousand litres — so it is possible, for example, to pump 300,000 litres per day from node 4 to node 5. We will assume that node 1 represents the port, and oil enters the network from node 1 — the *source*. We will also assume that node 5 represents the refinery and crude oil leaves the network at this point — the so-called *sink*. The problem we will set ourselves is to determine the maximum daily flow of oil from node 1 to node 5, and determine which route this flow of oil should take. Nodes 2, 3 and 4 represent *intermediate* towns between the port and refinery.

If you examine this network carefully, then you might conclude that it is constructed rather strangely. If you examine node 4, then you can see that the maximum flow into this node is 100,000 litres per day. However, the maximum flow out of this node is 400,000 litres per day. Does this, then, indicate poor planning? Not necessarily — it may be that node 4 is also a port receiving 300,000 litres daily directly from the oilfield. Likewise, examining node 3 we see that the maximum flow of oil into node 3 is 800,000 litres per day whereas the maximum flow out of this node is a mere 500,000 litres! But perhaps it is desired on some occasions to remove 300,000 litres per day at node 3 (oil may be stored at this node, or perhaps used for some other purpose). We will note these points but retain our objective of maximising the flow between node 1 and node 5.

Before we examine the method of achieving maximal flow, two important points should be noted. We have drawn the network in such a manner that there is only one entry point (node 5) and only one exit point. Assuming that there are no leakages within the network, it follows that the amount of oil entering at node 1 must be the same and the amount that leaves at node 5 — what goes in must come out. This is the *law of conservation of flows,* and it applies equally well to any node in the network. For example, if 500,000 litres per day flow into node 2, then 500,000 litres per day must flow out of this node. The second point to notice follows from the law of conservation of flows. Let us call any route from node 1 to node 5 an arc, and any individual pipeline on that arc a segment. It follows that the maximum flow of oil through an arc is determined by the segment with the smallest flow capacity. It is easy to see that if we send oil from node 1 to node 5 using the arc $1 \to 2 \to 4 \to 5$, then the most we can send is 100,000 litres per day.

We begin by redrawing the network, indicating the flow on each segment twice. Segment $2 - 3$, for example would look like this

Diagram 18.19

The arrows indicate the direction of the flows, and the numbers indicate flow capacity. The flow from 2 to 3 is called the forward flow, and the flow from 3 to 2 is called the reverse flow. So the complete network would look like this.

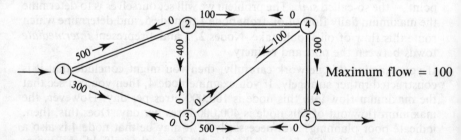

Diagram 18.20

We now select an arc between node 1 and node 5, and here we have chosen $1 \to 2 \to 4 \to 5$. We examine the forward flows on this arc, and the smallest forward flow determines the maximum flow through this arc. We note, then that 100,000 litres per day is the most we can send through this arc. To show that we will use this arc, we will subtract 100 from the forward flows on each segment of the arc. The forward flow on segment $1 - 2$, for example, will now be 400, showing that we could if we wished send an extra 400,000 litres per day through this segment. We will also add 100 to each reverse flow on the arc. Now this does not appear to make sense, but more of this later! Our network now looks like this:

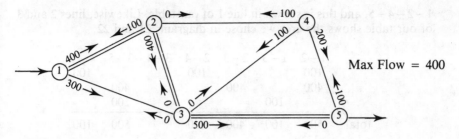

Max Flow = 400

Diagram 18.21

Examining this network for another arc from node 1 to node 5, we can see that it is possible to send a maximum flow of 400,000 litres per day along the arc 1 → 2 → 3 → 5. Subtracting 400 from all the forward flows, and adding 400 to all the reverse flows of the segments on this arc we have

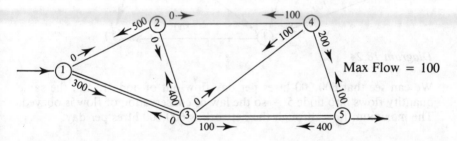

Max Flow = 100

Diagram 18.22

It is possible to send 100,000 litres along arc 1 → 3 → 5, so we subtract 100 from all forward flows, and add 100 to all reverse flows on this route.

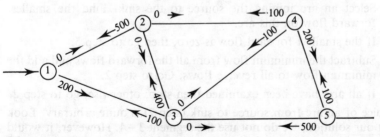

Diagram 18.23

We have now fully used the flow capacity of this network. Whichever arc we examine, we will reach a segment on that arc with a zero forward flow, and this indicates that segment must be used in another arc. We can now summarise our results in a table to determine the maximal flow through the network. In diagram 20 we sent 100,000 litres per day through the arc

1 − 2 − 4 − 5, and this is shown in line 1 of our table. Likewise, lines 2 and 3 of our table shows the arcs we chose in diagrams 21 and 22.

	1 − 2	1 − 3	2 − 3	2 − 4	3 − 4	3 − 5	4 − 5
	100			100			100
	400		400			400	
		100				100	
total	500	100	400	100		500	100

We can now transfer the total sent through each segment on the network.

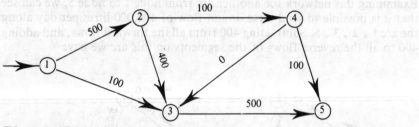

Diagram 18.24

We can see that 600,000 litres per day flow out of node 1, and the same quantity flows into node 5 − so the law of conservation of flow is obeyed. The maximum flow through the network is 600,000 litres per day.

Using reverse flows

Let us now summarise the method for solving maximal flow networks with a few simple rules

Step 1. Mark the forward flow and reverse flow on each segment within the network.

Step 2. Select an arc joining the source to the sink. Find the smallest forward flow on this arc.

Step 3. If the smallest forward flow is zero, then go to step 5.

Step 4. Subtract the minimum flow from all the forward flows and add the minimum flow to all reverse flows. Go to step 2.

Step 5. If all arcs have been examined then stop: otherwise, go to step 2.

The choice of an arc from source to sink (step 2) is quite arbitrary. Look again at our solution; we do not use the segment 3 − 4. However, it would have been quite possible to select an arc using this segment − for example, the first arc selected could well have been 1,2,4,3,5. Now if our solution to this problem is right (and it is), then we know that segment 3 − 4 should not be used. We can now explain why reverse flows are inserted on maximal flow networks. We can use reverse flows to "undo" any arc selected that would not lead to a maximal flow. To see how this works, we shall now rework our example, selecting the (non-optimising) arc 1,2,4,3,5 first.

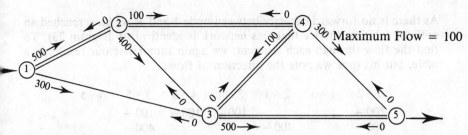

Diagram 18.25

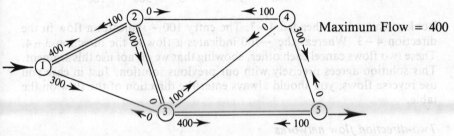

Diagram 18.26

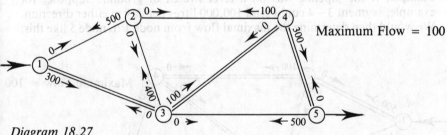

Diagram 18.27

This route uses the reverse flow on segment 3 – 4. The network now looks like this.

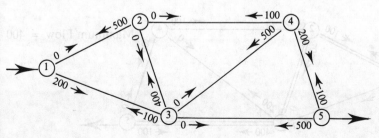

Diagram 18.28

As there is no forward capacity between node 1 and 5, we have reached an optimal solution (notice that this network is identical to diagram 23). To find the flow through each segment, we again summarise our results in a table, but his time we note the direction of flow.

1 – 2	1 – 3	2 – 3	2 – 4	4 – 3	3 – 5	4 – 5
100→			100→	100→	100→	
400→		400→			400→	
	100→			←100		100→
500→	100→	400→	100→	0	500→	100→

Look at the column headed 4 – 3. The entry 100→ indicates a flow in the direction 4 – 3. Whereas the ←100 indicates a flow in the direction 3 – 4. These two flows cancel each other, showing that we do not use this segment. This solution agrees precisely with our previous solution. Just in case you use reverse flows, you should always enter the direction of the flow on the table.

Two-direction flow networks

Sometimes it will be possible to use a segment in either direction – for example, if the pipeline was on a level stretch of ground. Suppose, for example, segment 3 – 4 could send 100,000 litres per day in either direction. We would then determine the maximal flow from node 1 to node 5 like this:

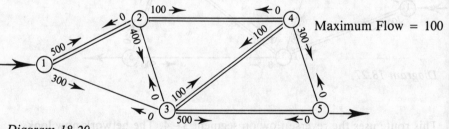

Maximum Flow = 100

Diagram 18.29

Notice that we have marked 100 in either direction for segment 3 – 4.

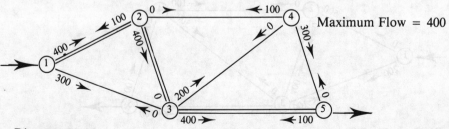

Maximum Flow = 400

Diagram 18.30

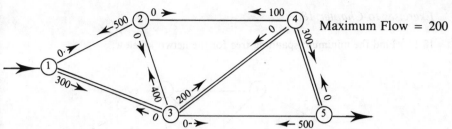

Maximum Flow = 200

Diagram 18.31

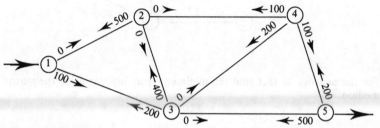

Diagram 18.32

1 – 2	1 – 3	2 – 3	2 – 4	4 – 3	3 – 5	4 – 5
100→			100→	100→	100→	
400→		400→			400→	
	200→			←200		200→
500→	200→	400→	100→	←100	500→	200→

Again the only column requiring explanation is column $4 - 3$. In the first row we send 100,000 litres from 4 to 3 and in the second row we send 200,000 litres from 3 to 4, 100,000 of which is to 'undo' our first flow. The net effect, then, is that 100,000 litres per day will be sent from 3 to 4, and the final network looks like this:

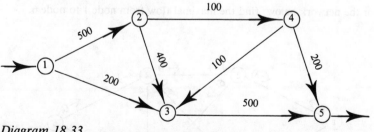

Diagram 18.33

The maximal flow from node 1 to node 5 is 700,000 litres per day, so if segment $3 - 4$ can flow in either direction, the total flow can be increased by 100,000 litres per day.

Exercises to Chapter 18

18.1 Find the minimum spanning tree for the network below.

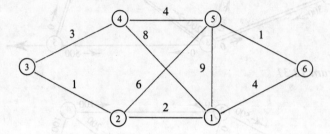

18.2 For the network in 18.1 find the minimum spanning tree using the matrix method.

18.3 In the network below find the shortest routes from town A to all the other towns

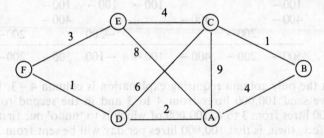

18.4 for the network below, find the maximal flow from node 1 to node 6.

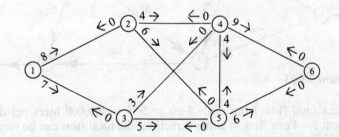

18.5   Find the minimum spanning tree for the network below

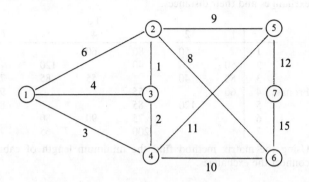

18.6   For the network in 18.5, find the minimum spanning tree using matrix methods.

18.7   In the network below find the shortest routes from town A to all other forms.

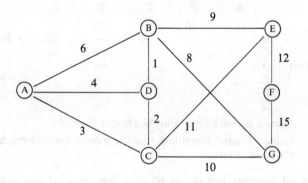

18.8   In the network below, find the maximal flow from node 1 to node 7.

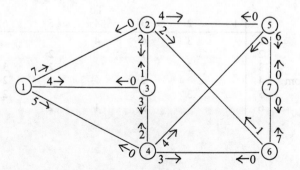

18.9 A telephone company has planning permission to build telephone exchanges in seven locations. The table below lists the possible connections between exchanges and their distances.

		To						
		1	2	3	4	5	6	7
	1		50	80	60			
	2	50		40		120		
	3	80	40		55	85	75	200
From	4	60		55			90	
	5		120	85			80	65
	6			75	90	80		75
	7			200		65	75	

Using the matrix method find the minimum length of cable that would connect the exchanges.

18.10 Draw the network for example 18.9, and from the network deduce the minimum spanning tree.

18.11 A travelling salesman (based at town A) must visit each of six towns returning to base after each visit. The table below gives the distance between the towns.

		To						
		A	B	C	D	E	F	G
	A	–	20	15	25	–	–	–
	B		–	10	–	20	40	–
	C			–	8	–	–	30
From	D				–	–	–	20
	E					–	9	6
	F						–	12
	G							–

1. Draw a network illustrating the routes available.

2. Using a suitable algorithm, find the shortest routes from town A to all the other towns.

18.12 An oil company receives its oil at a port (node 1) and pumps it along pipelines to the refinery (node 7). Pumping stations are located at nodes 2 through 6. The table below indicates the flow capacities (in million litres). Find the maximal flow between node 1 and node 7.

		To						
		1	2	3	4	5	6	7
	1		3	6	4			
	2			1		2		
	3		2			2	3	4
From	4		2			2		
	5		3	1			2	8
	6			2	1	2		7

Chapter Nineteen

Time Series Analysis

The time series take a variable and examines the way in which its magnitude has fluctuated over a period of time. We might, for example, consider the way in which output of a particular firm has varied year by year. Why should we do this? Whenever we are interested in planning, we must make forecasts of what is likely to happen in the future. Now, however complicated the technique we use, our judgement will depend to a large extent on what has happened in the past. Thus, a reliable analysis of what has happened in relevant fields in recent years is a first step in obtaining a reliable estimate of what is likely to happen in the future. Any housewife will tell you that tomato prices are likely to rise during particular months of the year, and to fall during other months. How does she know? Merely on the basis of past experience. Can we undertake a simple analysis of more complex problems to predict the future more reliably and more precisely?

The Trend

Suppose we consider the following series:

Output of A.B.C. Ltd. (Million Tons)

Year	Output	Year	Output	Year	Output
0	68	6	140	12	250
1	100	7	200	13	170
2	120	8	230	14	320
3	177	9	180	15	230
4	100	10	280	16	210
5	80	11	200	17	330

Looking at figures presented in this way will give us little information. Two things are obvious however. Figures of output show that although there have been very marked fluctuations year by year, there is a general upward rise in the figures. Moreover, certainly from year 8 to year 17 the figures tend to show a peak output every second year, followed by a fall in the intervening years.

This becomes much more apparent if you look at the graph of this time series in Diagram 19.1. The general rise in output can be clearly seen. This general tendency of figures to move in a given direction is known as the *trend*. In Diagram 19.1, the trend has been shown as a linear, or straight line trend. In other series we examine the trend will vary its direction, at first rising and then falling, or vice versa. Such a trend is curvilinear (see

Daigram 19-3). An important characteristic of such trends is that they change direction slowly over time, and so, barring catastrophes, the continuation can be sketched in from a careful examination of the existing trend line.

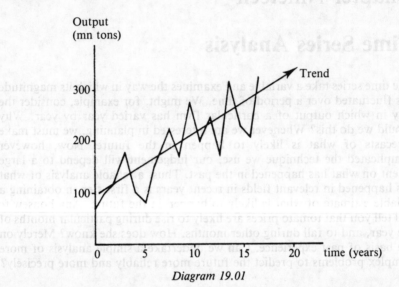

Diagram 19.01

Much more obvious in Diagram 19-1 is the succession of rises and falls in output occurring at regular intervals. Even to look at this graph suggests a certain pattern of behaviour in output in year 18. What is it?

Formal analysis of such a series can reveal much more useful data about what may happen in the future.

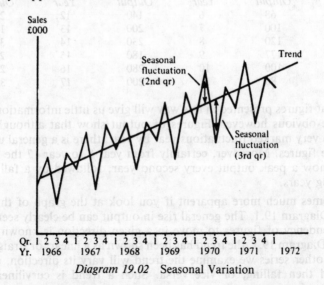

Diagram 19.02 Seasonal Variation

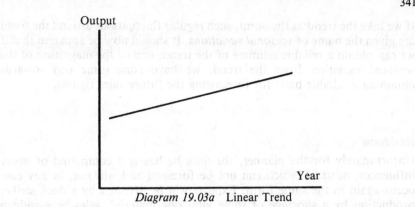

Diagram 19.03a   Linear Trend

Seasonal Variation

Many series are of such a nature that the figures become more significant when they are analysed on a monthly or quarterly basis rather than annually. Most economic series are like this. Sales, for example, show marked variations throughout the year. Everyone knows that sales tend to rise at Christmas or that more swimsuits are likely to be sold in summer than in winter. But if such fluctuations occur, are they sufficiently regular to be predictable? If they are, then we must try to ascertain the direction and probable magnitude of the swing. Diagram 19.2 shows hypothetical

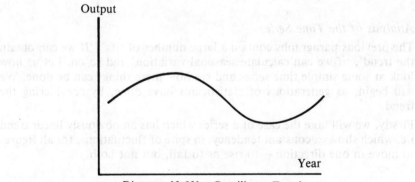

Diagram 19.03b   Curvilinear Trend

sales data plotted quarterly over a period of years. The data show a remarkable regularity. Every year there are two sales peaks, in the second and fourth quarter, while every year sales slump in the third quarter. The pattern is regular enough for us to predict that the same thing will happen in future years.

If we take the trend as the norm, such regular fluctuations around the trend are given the name of *seasonal variations*. It should now be apparent that if we can obtain a reliable estimate of the trend, and of the magniture of the seasonal variation from the trend, we have gone some way towards obtaining a reliable basis for forecasting the future sales figures.

Residuals

Unfortunately for the planner, the data he has is a compound of many influences, most of which can not be foreseen and will not, in any case occur again in the same form. Exports will be affected by a dock strike, production by a shortage of some vital raw material, sales by a sudden change in taxation. Thus the figures we have can be broken down into *trend & seasonal variation & residuals*.

By their very nature residual influences are chance happenings and are not amenable to analysis. Does this mean that we should ignore residual influences? No planner can afford to ignore a factor which might make nonsense of his forecasts!

The importance of the residuals lies in this. If over the years residual influences have had a minimal effect on the figures, we can use our forecasts with some degree of confidence that they will not be unduly affected by external events. But if the data has been affected regularly and to a large degree by residual factors, then we must use our forecasts with caution.

Analysis of the Time Series

The previous paragraphs contain a large number of 'ifs'. 'If we can obtain the trend', 'if we can calculate seasonal variation' and so on. Let us now look at some simple time series and see how these things can be done. We will begin, as generations of statisticians have done, by considering the trend.

Firstly, we will take the case of a series which has an obviously linear trend i.e. which shows a constant tendency, in spite of fluctuations, for all figures to move in one direction – to rise or to fall, but not both.

The Linear Trend

A good example of figures showing a linear trend is the series showing the value of consumer durable goods bought. It is an important series for the firms producing such goods, but its importance does not end here. As all sales are valued at year nine prices a change in standards of living can be measured by the number of cars, washing machines, refrigerators etc. we are buying.

Consumer Expenditure on Durable Goods
(£ million at Year 9 prices)

Year		Year		Year	
1	965	6	1370	11	1842
2	849	7	1334	12	1821
3	952	8	1411	13	1908
4	1113	9	1703	14	1977
5	1328	10	1853	15	1818

Can you estimate the trend line? This is obviously difficult with such complex figures. How can we be sure that this is the trend line that best describes expenditure on durable goods? To be safe we should calculate the equation of the trend line from the original data rather than rely on intuition.

What do we mean by the line that best fits the data? Clearly a straight line $y = mx + c$ cannot pass through all the points and we need some criterion for calculating m and c. You will note that the points will deviate from the line, and conventionally we fix the line in such a position that the sum of the squares of the deviations from the line is a minimum. Armed with this criterion, we can now calculate the least squares line of best fit.

The Least – Squares Trend Line

Initially, consider the simple example shown below. Copy the points on a sheet of graph paper, and draw in what you think is the line of best fit. Later, you can draw in the line based on the least squares criterion and compare with your estimate.

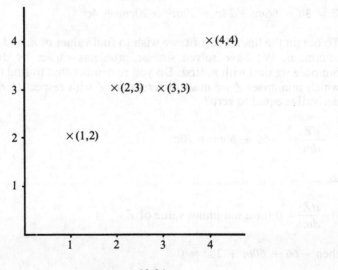

Diagram 19.04

Let us first ask by how much does the point (1,2) deviate from the line you have drawn. Now its equation in general form is $y = mx + c$. This point has $x = 1$, so the value of y on your line is

$$m + c$$

and the deviation of the point (1,2) from $m + c$ is

$$2 - (m + c) = 2 - m - c$$

and the square of the deviation is

$$(2 - m - c)^2$$

i.e. $4 - 4m - 4c + m^2 + cm + c^2$.

We can repeat this process for the points on the line where x equals 2, 3, and 4. It would be better to tabulate the results.

x	y	deviation	deviation squared
1	$m+c$	$2-(m+c)$	$4 - 4m - 4c + m^2 + 2cm + c^2$
2	$2m+c$	$3-(2m+c)$	$9 - 12m - 6c + 4m^2 + 4cm + c^2$
3	$3m+c$	$3-(3m+c)$	$9 - 18m - 6c + 9m^2 + 6cm + c^2$
4	$4m+c$	$4-(4m+c)$	$16 - 32m - 8c + 16m^2 + 8cm + c^2$
		adding . . .	$38 - 66m - 24c + 30m^2 + 20cm + 4c^2$

If Z is the sum of the square of the deviations, then

$$Z = 38 - 66m - 24c + 30m^2 + 20cm + 4c^2$$

To obtain the line of best fit, we wish to find values of m and c to make Z a minimum. We have solved similar problems earlier by differentiation. Suppose we deal with m first. Do you remember that to find the value of m which minimises Z we must differentiate Z with respect to m and put the derivative equal to zero?

$$\frac{dZ}{dm} = -66 + 60m + 20c$$

as

$$\frac{dZ}{dm} = 0 \text{ for a minimum value of } Z$$

then $-66 + 60m + 20c = 0$

or $30m + 10c = 33$ . . . . (1)

However we also wish to find the value of c which minimises Z. Differentiating Z with respect to c gives

$$\frac{dZ}{dc} = -24 + 20m + 8c$$

For a minimum value of Z $\quad \frac{dZ}{dc} = 0$

hence $-24 + 20m + 8c = 0$

or $10m + 4c = 12 \ldots \ldots (2)$

The problem now boils down to this: if we wish to find the values m and c in the line which (according to the least square criterion) best fits the points, we must find values of m and c which fit both equations (1) and (2). In other words, we must solve the simultaneous equations

$30m + 10c = 33$
$10m + \ \ 4c = 12$
Which gives $m = 0.6$, $c = 1.5$.
The line is $y = 0.6x + 1.5$.

You can now draw this line on your graph and compare it with your estimate.

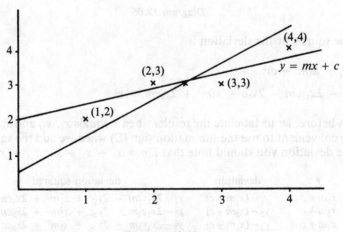

Diagram 19.05

The Normal Equations

The method is not difficult, but will become tedious if we have a large number of co-ordinates, or (worse) when the co-ordinates are not integers. What we need is a general method for finding the least squares line of best fit without have to square the deviations.

346

Let us suppose that the line $y = mx + c$ is the best fit to the points P_1, P_2, P_3, P_n, whose co-ordinates are (x_1y_1), (x_2y_2), (x_3y_3), . . . (x_ny_n),. Working in the same way as before, the value of y on this line when $x = x_1$ is

$$x_1m + c$$

and the deviation of the point (x_1y_1) from the point on the line is

$$y_1 - (x_1m + c) = y_1 = x_1m - c$$

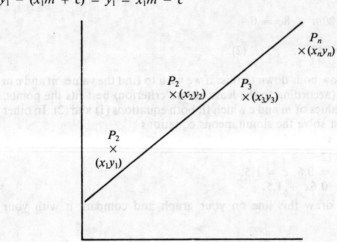

Diagram 19.06

and the square of the deviation is

$$(y_1 - x_1m - c)^2$$

i.e. $y_1^2 - 2x_1y_1m - 2y_1c + x_1^2m^2 + 2x_1cm + c^2$

As before, let us tabulate the results when x equals x_2, x_3, and x_n. It will be convenient to use the summation sign (Σ) when we add the square of the deviation you should note that $\Sigma x = x_1 + x_2 + x_3 \ldots + x_n$.

x	y	deviation	deviation squared
x_1	x_1m+c	$y_1-(x_1m+c)$	$y_1^2 - 2x_1y_1m - 2y_1c + x_1^2m^2 + 2x_1cm + c^2$
x_2	x_2m+c	$y_2-(x_2m+c)$	$y_2^2 - 2x_2y_2m - 2y_2c + x_2^2m^2 + 2x_2cm + c^2$
x_3	x_3m+c	$y_3-(x_3m+c)$	$y_3^2 - 2x_3y_3m - 2y_3c + x_3^2m^2 + 2x_3cm + c^2$
x_n	x_nm+c	$y_n-(x_nm+c)$	$y_n^2 - 2x_ny_nm - 2y_nc + x_n^2m^2 + 2x_ncm + c^2$
		Adding . . .	$\Sigma y^2 - 2m\Sigma x\Sigma y - 2c\Sigma y + m^2\Sigma x^2 + 2cm\Sigma x + nc^2$

If Z is the sum of the squares, then

$$Z = \Sigma y^2 + 2m\Sigma x\Sigma y - 2c\Sigma y + m^2\Sigma x^2 + 2cm\Sigma x + nc^2$$

Differentiating Z with respect to m gives

$$\frac{dZ}{dm} = -2\Sigma x\Sigma y + 2m\Sigma x^2 + 2c\Sigma x$$

putting the derivative equal to zero

$$-2\Sigma x\Sigma y + 2m\Sigma x^2 + 2c\Sigma x = 0$$
$$\Sigma x\Sigma y = m\Sigma x^2 + c\Sigma x \ldots \ldots (1)$$

Differentiating Z with respect to c gives

$$\frac{dZ}{dc} = -2\Sigma y + 2m\Sigma x + 2nc$$

Again, putting the derivative equal to zero

$$-2\Sigma y + 2m\Sigma x + 2nc = 0$$
$$\Sigma y = m\Sigma x + nc \ldots \ldots \ldots (2)$$

We can find the values of m and c in the least squares line of best fit by solving simultaneously equations (1) and (2). They are called the Normal Equations. Earlier we found the line of best fit from first principles. Let us now find the line using the Normal Equations.

x	y	x^2	xy
1	2	1	2
2	3	4	6
3	3	9	9
4	4	16	16
$\Sigma x = 10$	$\Sigma y = 12$	$\Sigma x^2 = 30$	$\Sigma xy = 33$

Substituting these values in the Normal Equations.

$$\Sigma xy = m\Sigma x^2 + c\Sigma x$$
$$33 = 30m + 10c$$
$$\Sigma y = m\Sigma x + nc$$
$$12 = 10m + 4c$$

This method gives the same equations as previously.

Most people dislike solving simultaneous equations, but few find it difficult to substitute values in a formula. Most examples that you will meet involve solving equations far more cumbersome than the above. We could re-arrange the normal equations to give general values for m and c. This, in fact, involves solving the Normal Equations. First let us write Normal Equation (2) this way:

$$nc = \Sigma y - m\Sigma x$$

and divide by n

$$c = \frac{1}{n}(\Sigma y - m\Sigma x)$$

We can now write this value for c in normal equation (1).

$$\Sigma xy = m\Sigma x^2 + \frac{\Sigma x}{n}(\Sigma y - m\Sigma x)$$

Now remove the bracket.

$$\Sigma xy = m\Sigma x^2 + \frac{\Sigma x\Sigma y}{n} - \frac{m(\Sigma x)^2}{n}$$

$$m\Sigma x^2 - \frac{m(\Sigma x)^2}{n} = \Sigma xy - \frac{\Sigma x\Sigma y}{n}$$

thus

$$m = \frac{\Sigma xy - \dfrac{\Sigma x\Sigma y}{n}}{\Sigma x^2 - \dfrac{(\Sigma x)^2}{n}}$$

We can find a value for m by substituting in the formula above, and a value for c by substituting in the formula obtained earlier, i.e.

$$c = \frac{1}{n}(\Sigma y - m\Sigma x)$$

In the four points example we considered earlier, we found that $\Sigma x = 10$, $\Sigma y = 12$, $\Sigma x^2 = 30$, $\Sigma xy = 33$. Substituting in the formula for m

$$m = \frac{33 - \dfrac{12 \times 10}{4}}{30 - \dfrac{(10)^2}{4}}$$

$$= \frac{3}{5}$$

$$= 0.6$$

Now substituting in the formula for c.

$$c = \frac{1}{4}(12 - 0.6 \times 10)$$

$$= 1.5$$

Which agrees with the results found from first principles.

EXAMPLE 1

x	1	2	3	4	5	6	7
y	1	2	6	7	10	16	21

Find the least squares line of best fit.

x	y	x^2	xy
1	1	1	1
2	2	4	4
3	6	9	18
4	7	16	28
5	10	25	50
6	16	36	96
7	21	49	147
$\Sigma x = 28$	$\Sigma y = 63$	$\Sigma x^2 = 140$	$\Sigma zy = 344$

Hence, $\Sigma x = 28$, $\Sigma y = 63$, $\Sigma x^2 = 140$, $\Sigma xy = 344$.

$$m = \frac{\Sigma xy - \dfrac{\Sigma x \Sigma y}{n}}{\Sigma x^2 - \dfrac{(\Sigma x)^2}{n}}$$

$$m = \frac{344 - \dfrac{28 \times 63}{7}}{140 - \dfrac{(28)^2}{7}}$$

$$= \frac{92}{28}$$

$$= 3.29$$

$$c = \frac{1}{n}(\Sigma y - m\Sigma x)$$

$$c = \frac{1}{7}(63 - 3.29 \times 28)$$

$$= -4.16$$

The equation is $y = 3.29x - 4.16$.

Using an Origin

We can now use the expressions for m and c to find the straight line trend of the time series. However, we would welcome any further simplification of the method. We can use an *origin* to find the straight line of best fit. Suppose we calculate the deviations x' from an origin 4 and y' from an origin 7, then the tabulations would look like this:

x'	y'	$(x')^2$	$x'y'$
-3	-6	9	18
-2	-5	4	10
-1	-1	1	1
0	0	0	0
1	3	1	3
2	9	4	18
3	14	9	42
$\Sigma x' = 0$	$\Sigma y' = 14$	$\Sigma(x')^2 = 28$	$\Sigma x'y' = 92$

We can now substitute the above values in the expression for m

$$m = \frac{92 - \dfrac{(0 \times 10)}{7}}{28 - \dfrac{0}{7}}$$

$$= \frac{92}{28}$$

Which is the same value that we obtained previously from m. To find c, we must convert $\Sigma x'$ into its true value Σx, and $\Sigma y'$ into its true value Σy. This presents no difficulty. Consider first $\Sigma x'$: it was obtained by subtracting 7 values from an origin 4. Thus the true value of Σx is:

$$7 \times 4 + 0 = 28$$

Likewise the true value Σy is

$$7 \times 7 + 14 = 63$$

The values Σx and Σy can now be used to calculate c as before.

You should notice that when we took 4 as an arbitrary origin for $\Sigma x'$ this made $\Sigma x' = 0$, and considerably simplified the calculation of m.

Let us again state the expression for m

$$m = \frac{\Sigma xy - \dfrac{\Sigma x \Sigma y}{n}}{\Sigma x^2 - \dfrac{(\Sigma x)^2}{n}}$$

Now if $\Sigma x' = 0, \dfrac{\Sigma y' \Sigma y}{n} = 0$, and $\dfrac{(\Sigma x')^2}{n} = 0$.

hence $m = \dfrac{\Sigma x'y'}{\Sigma(x')^2}$

Under what circumstances would $\Sigma x' = 0$? Only one condition must be fulfilled: we choose the arithmetic mean $\bar{x}$ as the origin. Moreover, in a time series we can number the time periods as consecutive integers, which makes the mean easily obtainable by inspection. The only difficulty is that if there is an even number of time periods, then neither the mean nor the deviations will be integers. To overcome this, all examples you will have to work in this book will have an odd number of time periods.

EXAMPLE 2

We now have sufficient information to fit a trend line to the data on consumer expenditure. We can take an origin 8 to simplify the calculations.

x'	y	$x'y$	$(x')^2$
-7	965	-6755	49
-6	849	-5094	36
-5	952	-4760	25
-4	1113	-4452	16
-3	1328	-3984	9
-2	1370	-2740	4
-1	1334	-1334	1
0	1411	0	0
1	1703	1703	1
2	1865	3730	4
3	1842	5526	9
4	1821	7284	16
5	1908	9540	25
6	1977	11,826	36
7	1818	12,726	49
0	22,256	23,242	280

$$m = \frac{\Sigma x'y}{\Sigma (x')^2}$$

$$= \frac{23,242}{280} = 83$$

$\Sigma x' = 0, n = 15,$

hence $\Sigma x = 15 \times 8 + 0 = 120$

$$c = \frac{1}{n}(\Sigma y - m\Sigma x)$$

$$= \frac{1}{15}(22,256 - 120 \times 83)$$

$$= 820$$

The equation of the trend line is

$$y = 83x + 820$$

y is expenditure, x is time period.

The data and regression line are plotted in diagram 19.7.

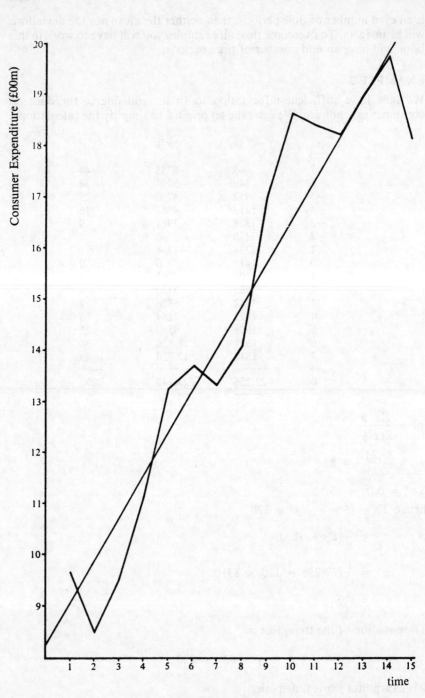

Diagram 19.07

Curvilinear Trends

Most of the time series you will meet in practice will probably not have a linear trend like those in the last section. This is because most aspects of our life are governed to some extent by the periodic upswing and down-swing of activity that the economist calls the trade cycle. If you own shares you will know that for some periods of time share prices will rise. But ultimately something happens and the trend turns gradually into a period of falling prices. The same sort of thing happens with employment, with output, with sales, and with most aspects of industrial life.

It is of course possible to derive normal equations for the curvilinear trend, but the method is complex; certainly too complex for an introductory course. You will find it far easier, and in many ways just as useful to obtain such trends by the use of what we call 'moving averages'.

What is a moving average? Quite simply it is obtained by selecting a number of consecutive values of the variable, say five, and averaging them so that the magnitude of the variations of the individual items is reduced. Then to obtain the second point on the trend line you do the same thing with the next set of five figures. But beware! The second set of five figures is not numbers 6 to 10, but numbers 2 to 6; and the third set 3 to 7 and so on. Each average we obtain then consists of four figures from the previous group plus one new one.

Let us take a simple example and calculate the five year moving average to illustrate the method.

EXAMPLE 3

Unemployment

Year	% Unemployed	5 Year Total	5 Year Average = Trend
1	2.0		
2	1.6		
3	1.3	7.2	1.44
4	1.1	6.6	1.32
5	1.2	7.1	1.42
6	1.4	8.0	1.60
7	2.1	8.5	1.70
8	2.2	8.8	1.76
9	1.6	9.4	1.88
10	1.5	9.8	1.96
11	2.0	9.2	1.84
12	2.5	9.0	1.80
13	1.6	9.0	1.80
14	1.4		
15	1.5		

These figures are plotted in diagram 8, and you can see how the moving average smooths out the fluctuations.

You will naturally have many questions to ask about the above calculation. Why did we choose a five year moving average, and not a three, or four or

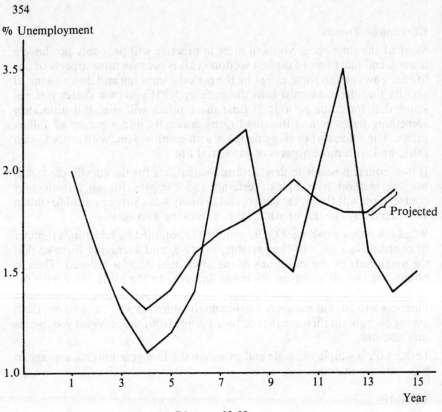

Diagram 19.08

seven year one? There is no hard and fast rule to help you choose the right one. The correct one is the one that smooths out the fluctuations best, and only trial and error can prove this. But a good working rule is to assess the period between consecutive peaks or consecutive troughs and use this period. Do this and you will not go far wrong. We chose a five year average above because it is known that the post-war cycle in unemployment is about five years.

What about the trend figure for year 1 and year 2? A weakness of this method is that they can not be obtained from the data as given. Because it is an average, by convention we place our trend figure in the centre of the group to which it refers. But this leaves a gap at the beginning and at the end of the series. Can you see why it is easier to choose for your moving average period an odd number of years?

If you look again at the graph in diagram 8, you will notice an odd thing. Although the cycles are well marked with peaks and troughs, there is a tendency for the figures to rise. Our trend is not merely curvilinear about a static value, but itself slopes upwards. The recessions show a tendency to get more severe, and the booms to be not quite so good.

The Analysis of Seasonal Variation

Analysis of long term trend has its place in business forecasting when long range planning is on the agenda. But in business, as in chess, the most important consideration is the very next move. Not what are we going to do next year, but what are we going to do next quarter, or even next month? If you think about it, most businesses show a marked variation in the level of activity within the space of a year. As an analyst you must know how to examine such data in order to find out if the pattern produced is regular enough to enable you to say that it is predictable behaviour. It is this pattern within the year that seasonal analysis examines. We will confine our attention here to a quarterly behaviour pattern, but you must remember that often a monthly pattern can be detected. Fortunately the process of analysis does not change.

Consider the expression seasonal variation. Variation implies a movement away from a point of reference or norm, and the first step in analysis is to establish that norm. It seems logical to accept the trend of a series as the reference point and accepting this we may define a seasonal variation as a movement away from the trend. Is it obvious to you that we cannot have a seasonal pattern in which all variations are above, or all are below the trend? In fact if we assess both the magnitude and direction of the seasonal fluctuations, those above the trend should cancel out those below the trend.

The Trend of a Quarterly Series

EXAMPLE 4

Let us consider the following series.

Quarterly Sales of Fertilizer
('000 tons)

Quarter \ Year	1	2	3	4	5
1	48	50	68	93	84
2	52	46	34	56	61
3	16	22	26	16	29
4	35	40	35	45	48

There is here a marked seasonal pattern of sales and on first inspection it appears that this is regular enough to justify analysis. So let us firstly calculate the trend line using the method of moving averages. Out first problem is that since this is a quarterly series we must use a four quarterly moving average. Now as you know, the moving average figure must be placed opposite the centre of the group of figures to which it relates. But this would place our trend between the second and third quarters, in which position we cannot use it. To overcome this problem we use a device known as 'centering'. Having totalled successive groups of four quarters we then add each of these totals in pairs and divide the result by eight. Thus the trend is centred against a quarter and can be related to it. An example will make this clear. Taking the first few figures of our table we proceed as follows.

Year	Qtr.	Sales	4 Qtr. Total	8 Qtr. Total	Moving Average
1	1	48			
	2	52			
			151		
	3	16		304	38
			153		
	4	35		300	37.5
			147		
2	1	50			
	2	46			

Our first 4 quarterly total is the sum of Quarters 1 – 4 of Year 1; our second the sum of the last three quarters of year 1 and the first quarter of year 2, and so on. These are placed between the second and third quarters of year 1, and between the third and fourth quarters of year 1 respectively. To centre the figures we take successive pairs of totals. (Remember this means the first and second totals, the second and third totals and so on.) Thus we have a new figures, placed at the centre of the group to which it relates i.e. opposite to a particular quarter in our series. The new total is the sum of eight quarters and so to obtain the trend we must divide by eight.

The complete calculation is done below, but before looking at it try to calculate the trend of this series for yourself.

Year	Qtr.	Sales	4 Qtr. Total	8 Qtr. Total	Moving Average	Deviation (x – Trend)
1	1	48				
	2	52				
			151			
	3	16		304	38.0	– 22.0
			153			
	4	35		300	37.5	– 2.5
			147			
2	1	50		300	37.5	+12.5
			153			
	2	46		311	38.9	+ 7.1
			158			
	3	22		334	41.7	– 19.7
			176			
	4	40		340	42.5	– 2.5
			164			
3	1	68		332	41.5	+26.5
			168			
	2	34		331	41.4	– 7.4
			163			
	3	26		351	43.9	– 17.9
			188			
	4	35		398	49.7	– 14.7
			210			
4	1	93		410	51.2	+41.8
			200			
	2	56		410	51.2	+ 4.8
			210			
	3	16		411	51.4	– 35.4
			201			
	4	45		407	50.9	– 5.9
			206			
5	1	84		425	53.1	+30.9
			219			
	2	61		441	55.1	+ 5.9
			222			
	3	29				
	4	48				

If you look at the trend you will see that it is generally rising but there is one peculiarity – a very sharp increase in the trend figure for the 4th quarter of year 3. What do you think could have caused this?

Seasonal Variation

How can we now proceed to the calculation of seasonal variation? Remembering that it is the deviation from the trend line it is a simple matter to obtain the actual deviations. But remember that in taking deviations we use (original figures minus trend) and you must be sure to get the signs right.

These deviations are now listed as follows:

	1	2	3	4
			− 22.0	− 2.5
	+ 12.5	+ 7.1	− 19.7	− 2.5
	+ 26.5	− 7.4	− 17.9	− 14.7
	+ 41.8	+ 4.8	− 35.4	− 5.9
	+ 30.9	+ 5.9		
Total	+ 117.7	+ 10.4	− 95.0	− 25.6	
Average	+ 27.9	+ 2.6	− 23.75	− 6.4	= .35
Adjustment	− .09	− .09	− .09	− .09	
S.V.	+ 27.8	+ 2.5	− 23.8	− 6.5	

The direction of the seasonal fluctuation is immediately apparent from the sign of the deviation. In the first and second quarters sales rise above trend, and in the third and fourth quarters they fall below it.

The expected magnitude of the fluctuations is the average of the deviations shown in a particular quarter. You may wonder at this but remember that our deviations include residual influences. Since these are random and may affect figures upwards or downwards it is reasonable to eliminate a large part of their impact by averaging over a period of time.

A word on the adjustment. Seasonal fluctuations from a trend are of such a nature that upswings cancel downswings exactly and so the total of our quarterly averages should be zero. In fact we are left with + 0.35 (a very small figure) and this can be eliminated by subtracting 0.09 $\left(\dfrac{0.35}{4}\right)$ from each quarterly average.

Rounding to one place of decimals our results show that in quarter 1 we expect sales to be 27.8 (thousand tons) above trend, in quarter 2, 2.5 (thousand tons) above. Conversely in quarters 3 and 4 we expect sales to be 23.8 and 6.5 (thousand tons) below trend.

Knowing these expectations, if we can project an accurate trend line it is possible to forecast sales for each quarter of year 6. Draw the graph of the trend line and do this.

Trend Fitting

You will appreciate that with large figures this method can be cumbersome, it is often easier to calculate the equation of the trend line (providing it is linear) by the method you learned earlier in this chapter.

EXAMPLE 5

Let us take one more example of this. We will examine the quarterly movement of receipts from taxation on currect account. Such a series will show marked fluctuations from quarter to quarter. Can you understand why? The majority of government taxation revenue is paid in the first quarter of the year, i.e. the last quarter of the fiscal year. We would expect a large positive seasonal variation in this quarter. The magnitude of the upswing becomes immediately apparent if you look at the series graphed in diagram 9.

Receipts from Taxation (Current Account)
£m

		Quarter			
		1	2	3	4
	1	3757	2276	2647	2596
	2	3995	2683	2975	2722
Year	3	4407	3054	3389	3338
	4	4811	3552	3781	3737
	5	5289			

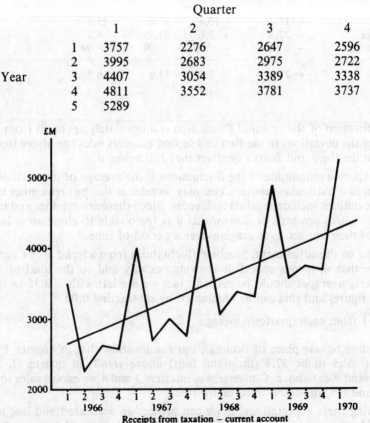

Receipts from taxation – current account

Diagram 19.09

Now fit a linear trend to this series by the method of least squares.

Year	Qtr.	x	x'	y	$x'y'$	$(x')^2$	Trend	Deviation
1	1	1	−8	3757	− 30,056	64	2674	+ 1083
	2	2	−7	2276	− 15,932	49	2773	− 497
	3	3	−6	2647	− 15,882	36	2872	− 225
	4	4	−5	2596	− 12,980	25	2971	− 375
2	1	5	−4	3995	− 15,980	16	3070	+ 925
	2	6	−3	2683	− 8049	9	3169	− 486
	3	7	−2	2975	− 5950	4	3268	− 293
	4	8	−1	2722	− 2722	1	3367	− 645
3	1	9	0	4407	0	0	3466	+ 941
	2	10	+1	3054	3054	1	3565	− 511
	3	11	+2	3389	6778	4	3664	− 275
	4	12	+3	3338	10,014	9	3763	− 425
4	1	13	+4	4811	19,244	16	3862	+ 949
	2	14	+5	3552	17,760	25	3961	− 409
	3	15	+6	3781	22,686	36	4060	− 279
	4	16	+7	3737	26,159	49	4159	− 422
5	1	17	+8	5289	42,312	64	4258	+ 1031
		153		59,009	148,007	408		
					− 107,551			
					40,456			

$$m = \frac{\Sigma x'y'}{\Sigma(x')^2} = \frac{40,456}{408} = 99.16$$

$$c = \frac{1}{n}[\Sigma y - m\Sigma x] = \frac{59,009 - 99.16 \times 153}{17}$$

$$= \frac{43770.2}{17} = 2574.17$$

$$y = 99.16x + 2574.72$$

For each of working we will take this as

$$y = 99x + 2575$$

		Quarter			
		1	2	3	4
	1	+ 1083	− 497	− 225	− 375
	2	+ 925	− 486	− 293	− 645
	3	+ 941	− 511	− 275	− 425
Year	4	+ 949	− 409	− 279	− 422
	5	+ 1031			
		+ 4929	− 1903	− 1072	− 1867
Average		+ 986	− 476	− 268	− 467	= − 225
Adjustment		+ 56	+ 56	+ 56	+ 56
S.V.		+ 1042	− 420	− 212	− 411

Forecasting

You may wonder why we stopped the series in year 5 quarter one rather than complete the year. The reason is that we wished to use the results for forecasting and you would not be convinced of the usefulness of the method unless you can see that the forecast is fairly close to the actual figures.

To predict the figures for the second quarter of years we firstly predict the trend from our equation $y = 99x + 2575$ and then adjust for our calculated seasonal variation. Thus we have

$x \times m + $ S.V.
$19 \times 99 - 420 = 4357 - 420 = 3937$
The actual figure was 4130

We can list the predicted figures from our calculations and compare with the actual figures taken from the Bank of England Quarterly

Year	Qtr.	Trend	+	S.V.	=	Prediction	Actual
5	2	4357		− 420		3937	4130
	3	4456		− 212		4244	4271
	4	4555		− 411		4144	4164
6	1	4654		+ 1042		5696	5540

The error in the forecast figurs is rather high for the second quarter of year 5 but is still less than 5%, which when you remember that no allowance has been made for changes in tax rates and allowances is not a bad result.

Series with Seasonal Variation Eliminated

Most published statistics you will see are printed with seasonal variations eliminated from the figures. The underlying purpose of this is to enable us to concentrate on the general trend without being misled by seasonal influences.

To obtain such a series is quite simple. If the seasonal variation is positive, performance is raised above trend by seasonal factors and we must reduce the actual figures by the amount of the seasonal variation. If seasonal variation is negative we increase the figures by the amount of seasonal variation. Taking the last few quarters of our tax receipts series we would eliminate seasonal variation as follows:

		S.V.	Tax Receipts	Adjustment	With S.V. Eliminated
Year 4	1	+ 1042	4811	− 1042	3769
	2	− 420	3552	+ 420	3972
	3	− 212	3781	+ 212	3993
	4	− 411	3737	+ 411	4148
Year 5	1	+ 1042	5289	− 1042	4247

You will notice that although seasonal variations are calculated as deviations from trend, eliminating them does not give us the trend figure. Try to reason out from what you know why this should be so.

361

Exercises to Chapter Nineteen

19.1 Use the equation of the trend line derived in example 2 to predict the position of the trend in years 16, 17, 18 and 19.

19.2 Find from first principles the least square line $y = mx + c$ that fits the points (1,4) (3,4) (3,3) (4,2) (5,2).

19.3

x	=	1	2	3	4	5	6	7
y	=	1.5	4.5	6	11	14.5	16.5	18

Fit a straight line $y = mx + c$.

19.4 Find the least squares trend line of the output of ABC Ltd, ignoring the data for year 1.

19.5 The following table shows the growth in the use of private transport. Calculate the least squares regression line and hence forecast the figure for year 10.

Year	1	2	3	4	5	6
Passenger miles (millions)	38	42	47	54	59	60
Year	7	8	9			
Passenger miles (millions)	78	82	89			

19.6 The following table shows the number of passengers leaving a British airport on package holidays in recent years. Fit a straight line trend to the data by the method of least squares and hence estimate the growth of traffic during the years 15 and 16.

Year	1	2	3	4	5	6	7
No. of passengers (thousands)	79	106	124	143	152	180	210
Year	8	9	10	11	12	13	
No. of passengers (thousands)	242	257	309	396	453	488	

19.7 The price of a government security and Bank Rate tend to vary inversely. The following figures show the average Bank Rate (R) for a number of years and the corresponding price of the security (C). Find the regression equation of C upon R and use it to estimate the price of the security when Bank Rate is 8%

R	C	R	C	R	C
3.7	56	4.5	56	2.0	83
4.0	57	3.9	56	3.7	58
5.0	55	3.0	67	4.6	56
4.7	55	5.5	54	4.0	55
2.0	74	2.0	76	2.4	74
2.5	67	2.0	72		

19.8 Sales of a particular commodity are collected over a period of years and the results summarised below. Graph the original data and superimpose the trend.

Sales — (all home branches)
(ten thousands)

Quarter ended

		Mar.	June	Sept.	Dec.
	1	295	329	344	325
	2	301	315	265	368
Year	3	350	386	262	405
	4	383	419	281	432
	5	393	436	302	449

19.9 You are informed that in the company whose sales figures are given in question 19.8 the need for part time employees is in the exact ratio of fluctuations in the level of sales. It is not desired to employ more than is necessary but orders must be met. What advice would you give to the personnel department regarding the employment of part time labour?

19.10 The annual abstract of statistics shows that until recently, there was an excess of male births over female births. The relevant data is given in the following table:

Excess of males over females per 1000 females born

Year	Excess of Males	Year	Excess of Males	Year	Excess of Males
1	60	8	41	15	46
2	52	9	42	16	55
3	51	10	44	17	56
4	49	11	43	18	54
5	44	12	44	19	56
6	47	13	49	20	51
7	45	14	50	21	56

Fit a trend to the above data by the method of moving averages.

19.11 Quarterly sales of a certain car (in thousands) are as follows:

Year		1	2	3	4	5
Quarter	1	66	68	86	111	102
	2	70	64	52	74	79
	3	34	40	44	34	47
	4	53	58	53	63	66

Compute the trend by the method of moving averages, and estimate the seasonal variations in sales. Rewrite the series with Seasonal Variation eliminated.

19.12 Using the data of question 19.11 fit a trend to the data by the method of least squares and estimate the seasonal variation from this calculated trend. Compare your results with those obtained in question 19.11, and comment on any differences. (Omit the last quarter of year 5).

Answers to exercises

1.1   115 pesetas = £0.78, 236 pesetas = £2.20, 428 pesetas = £2.89.

1.3 $m = \dfrac{74 - 45}{7 - 3} = \dfrac{32}{4} = 8$, $y = 8x + 21$

1.5   Maximum turning point when $x = -1$, minimum when $x = +1$.

1.7
when $x =$	2	1	0	9	$a+1$	-5
$y =$	7	0	-5	112	$a^2 + 6a$	0

2.2   For both inequalities to hold, $y < -3$.

2.4 $-2 < x < 8$.

2.6   Produce 10 standard and 5 de luxe models at a profit of £12.50.

2.8   Solution is feasible, with greatest quantity obtained by mixing 20 gallons of A with 12 gallons of C and 34 gallons of B.

2.10   To minimise cost, use 6 lorries. Maximum number of casting moved (1080) if 6 lorries and 3 vans used.

2.12   Utilise 8 Bees and 3 Wasps at a minimum cost of £11,200.

2.14   Blend 15 lbs of Vito with 45 lbs of Slam at a profit of £285.

3.2 $mx^2 - c$ has a minimum value, $c - mx^2$ has a maximum value.

3.5   Average cost per mile $= £0.000005x + \dfrac{25.4}{400} + \dfrac{180}{x}$

6000 miles per annum minimises cost per mile at 12.35p.

3.6 $\dfrac{ds}{dr} = 4\pi r - \dfrac{800}{r^2}$ $r = 3.993$, $h = 7.989$ cm.

3.8   Total revenue $= 80Q - 2Q^2$
TR maximised when $Q = 20$.

3.10   Cost $= \dfrac{100000}{q} + \dfrac{0.001q}{4}$
Cost minimised when $q = 20,000$
order every two weeks.

4.1   Order batches of 20 every two weeks.

4.2   Annual saving by taking up discount $= £371.69$.

4.5 Approximately, discount required is 1.5p or 3.75%.

4.8 To minimise cost, produce batches of 1790 (approx) which would cost £26,117 annually. Cheaper to produce than to buy.

4.10 Stock 12 magazines per week, average profit is 109.75 pence.

4.12 712.

5.1 a) $\begin{pmatrix} 3 & 5 & 2 \\ 7 & 1 & 0 \\ -2 & 7 & -1 \end{pmatrix}$ c) $\begin{pmatrix} 1 & -7 & -2 \\ -1 & 1 & 2 \\ 2 & 1 & -3 \end{pmatrix}$ e) $\begin{pmatrix} -2 & 12 & 5 \\ 5 & 21 & 6 \\ 20 & -6 & -6 \end{pmatrix}$

5.3 a) $\begin{pmatrix} 11 & 9 \\ 6 & 10 \\ 7 & 14 \end{pmatrix}$ c) not possible   e) not possible g) $\begin{pmatrix} 93 \\ 66 \\ 84 \end{pmatrix}$

i) not possible.

5.5 $\begin{pmatrix} -1 & 2 & 0 \\ 2 & -2 & -1 \\ 0 & -\frac{1}{2} & \frac{1}{2} \end{pmatrix}$

5.7 $\begin{pmatrix} a \\ b \\ c \end{pmatrix} = \begin{pmatrix} 3 \\ 4 \\ 6 \end{pmatrix}$ $\begin{pmatrix} a \\ b \\ c \\ d \end{pmatrix} = \begin{pmatrix} 1 \\ 2 \\ 3 \\ 4 \end{pmatrix}$

5.9 $T = \begin{pmatrix} \frac{3}{2} & 1 \\ \frac{3}{4} & \frac{5}{2} \end{pmatrix} \begin{pmatrix} 10 \\ 45 \end{pmatrix} = \begin{pmatrix} 60 \\ 120 \end{pmatrix}$

5.11 $R = \begin{pmatrix} 240 & 0 \\ 0 & 300 \end{pmatrix}$, $P = \begin{pmatrix} 160 & 80 \\ 0 & 300 \end{pmatrix}$, $Q = \begin{pmatrix} \frac{2}{3} & \frac{4}{15} \\ 0 & 1 \end{pmatrix}$

$S = \begin{pmatrix} 200 & 40 \\ 150 & 150 \end{pmatrix}$, $T = \begin{pmatrix} \frac{5}{6} & \frac{2}{15} \\ \frac{5}{8} & \frac{1}{2} \end{pmatrix}$

6.1 $\begin{bmatrix} 0 & 0 & 1 & -9 & 2 & 6 \\ 0 & 1 & 0 & 3 & -1 & 6 \\ 1 & 0 & 0 & -2 & 1 & 8 \\ \hline 0 & 0 & 0 & 2 & 1 & 64 \end{bmatrix}$

6.3 $\begin{bmatrix} 0 & \frac{2}{5} & \frac{1}{5} & 0 & 1 & 26 \\ 0 & \frac{9}{5} & -\frac{3}{5} & 1 & 0 & 0 \\ 1 & \frac{2}{5} & \frac{1}{5} & 0 & 1 & 36 \\ \hline 0 & 40 & 40 & 0 & 0 & 7200 \end{bmatrix}$

6.5 $\begin{bmatrix} 1 & \frac{2}{3} & \frac{1}{12} & 0 & 0 & 400 \\ 0 & \frac{10}{3} & -\frac{1}{3} & 1 & 0 & 800 \\ 0 & \frac{1}{3} & -\frac{1}{12} & 0 & 1 & 4600 \\ \hline 0 & \frac{7}{6} & \frac{11}{24} & 0 & 0 & 2200 \end{bmatrix}$

6.7
$$\left[\begin{array}{cccc|c} 1 & 0 & ^6/_{15} & -^1/_5 & ^{11}/_5 \\ 0 & 1 & -^1/_5 & ^3/_5 & ^7/_5 \\ \hline 0 & 0 & 35 & 25 & 405 \end{array}\right]$$

6.9
$$\left[\begin{array}{ccccccccc|c} 0 & 0 & 0 & 1 & -^1/_3 & -^4/_3 & 0 & 0 & -^{11}/_3 & 10 \\ 0 & 0 & 0 & 0 & ^2/_3 & -^1/_3 & 0 & 1 & ^1/_3 & 26 \\ 0 & 0 & 0 & 0 & -^1/_3 & ^2/_3 & 1 & 0 & ^4/_3 & 32 \\ 1 & 0 & 0 & 0 & -^1/_3 & ^2/_3 & 0 & 0 & ^4/_3 & 42 \\ 0 & 1 & 0 & 0 & ^2/_3 & -^1/_3 & 0 & 0 & ^1/_3 & 36 \\ 0 & 0 & 1 & 0 & 0 & 0 & 0 & 0 & -1 & 10 \\ \hline 0 & 0 & 0 & 0 & ^8/_3 & ^2/_3 & 0 & 0 & ^7/_3 & 434 \end{array}\right]$$

6.13
$$\left[\begin{array}{ccccccc} 36 & 3 & 0 & 1 & ^5/_4 & -^1/_4 & ^7/_4 \\ -1 & ^1/_4 & 1 & 0 & -^1/_{16} & ^1/_{16} & ^1/_{16} \\ \hline 96 & 0 & 0 & 0 & 10 & 2 & 26 \end{array}\right]$$

6.14
$$\left[\begin{array}{ccccccc} 0 & 1 & 0 & ^3/_4 & -^3/_{10} & -^1/_5 & ^7/_{20} \\ 1 & 0 & 0 & -^1/_4 & ^1/_2 & 0 & ^7/_4 \\ 0 & 0 & 1 & 0 & -^1/_5 & ^1/_5 & ^2/_5 \\ \hline 0 & 0 & 0 & ^{15}/_2 & 67 & 18 & 583^1/_2 \end{array}\right]$$

7.2

		To				
		a	b	c	d	e
	A	43	65	31		
From	B			24	40	10
	C	32				

7.3 either

		To			
		a	b	c	d
	A	30	15	20	
From	B	15			10
	C		10		

or

		To			
		a	b	c	d
	A	45	15	5	
From	B			15	10
	C		10		

7.7

		To				
		B'ham	Man	Leeds	Bristol	Notts
	S'hamp	77			38	
From	Thames	9		35		51
	Mersey		26	27		
	Milford		48			

7.9   51 units of Southampton output is stored.

7.11

		To			
		a	b	c	d
	A		35	20	10
From	B		25		
	C	10			

7.13

	Red	Blue	Green	Yellow
Semi	55		30	
Fully		40		20

7.14 Maximum profit = £13,050 per 100 vehicles.

8.1 A to III
B to II
C to I
D to IV

8.3 Southampton to Oxford, Bristol to Taunton, Birmingham to Northampton, Nottingham to York, Shrewsbury to Preston.

8.4 D to I
C to II
B to III

8.7 $A \to C \to B \to D \to E \to A$, cost £23.

8.9 $A \to E \to B \to C \to D \to A$, cost £141.

8.11 Carlisle $\to$ Preston $\to$ Bristol $\to$ Cambridge $\to$ Lincoln $\to$ Carlisle.
Distance 703 miles.

9.1 $V = \begin{pmatrix} 9/2 & 2 \\ 3/2 & 2 \end{pmatrix} \begin{pmatrix} 12 \\ 12 \end{pmatrix} = \begin{pmatrix} 78 \\ 42 \end{pmatrix}$

9.3 $V = \begin{pmatrix} 3 & 4/5 \\ 0 & 4/3 \end{pmatrix} \begin{pmatrix} 240 \\ 150 \end{pmatrix} = \begin{pmatrix} 840 \\ 200 \end{pmatrix}$

9.5 $V = \begin{pmatrix} 18 & 10 \\ 8/5 & 2 \end{pmatrix} \begin{pmatrix} 0 \\ 20 \end{pmatrix} = \begin{pmatrix} 200 \\ 40 \end{pmatrix}$

9.7

Country	Consumption	Imports	Exports	Autonomous Spending	Income
A	245	17.5	37.5	85	350
B	245	37.5	17.5	170	375

9.9

Country	Consumption	Imports	Exports	Autonomous Spending	Income
A	198⅓	14⅙	14⅙	85	283⅓
B	85	14⅙	14⅙	56⅔	141⅔

9.11

Country	Consumption	Imports	Exports	Autonomous Spending	Income
A	456	60.8	60.8	152	608
B	969	60.8	60.8	646	1615

M.P.I. for B = $\dfrac{60.8}{1615}$ = 0.0376

10.2 $4/11$.

10.4 b(i) 0.6591   b(ii) 0.2866
c(i) 0.08   c(ii) 0.52   c(iii) 0.2.

10.6 i) $\frac{1}{3}$ ii) $\frac{1}{36}$ iii) $\frac{91}{216}$ iv) $\frac{7}{15}$, $\frac{1}{15}$.

10.8 a) $\frac{1}{12}$ b) $\frac{1}{2}$ c) $\frac{1}{4}$ d) $\frac{1}{2}$.

10.10 a) 0.03, b) 0.33

10.12 a) 0.8938, b) 0.1025

10.14 i) 0.5838, ii) 0.05.

10.16 0.52   0.6425.

10.18 i) $\frac{5}{12}$, $\frac{1}{4}$, $\frac{1}{3}$.
  ii) $\frac{11}{80}$.
  iii) $\frac{5}{24}$.
  iv) $\frac{2}{5}$.
  v) $\frac{9}{10}$.
  vi) $\frac{20}{33}$, $\frac{8}{33}$, $\frac{5}{33}$.

10.20 b) 0.6513, 44:

10.22 i) 0.0165, ii) 0.0179.

10.24 a) $\dfrac{64}{132600}$ b) $\dfrac{16}{5525}$

10.26 P (article has both defects) = 0.3.

11.1 Maximax: buy C, Maximin: buy B, Minimax: buy C.

11.3 EVPI = 140,000 − 85,000 = £55,000.

11.5 Maximax: stock 16, Maximin: stock 10, Minimax: stock 12.

11.7 Newsagent never makes a loss, decision is repeatable, so use E.M.V.

11.9 If p = probability that expenditure is increased, 400,000 P + 100,000 (1 − p) − 50,000 > 129,687, p > 0.2656.

11.11 Maximax: buy allied
Maximin: buy guided, if system replaced do not expand.

11.13 £0.3672m.

12.1 Saloons: $\frac{3}{11}$, Hatchbacks: $\frac{8}{11}$.

12.3 a) i) $\frac{37}{72}$
  ii) $\frac{37}{192}$
  b)   manual $\frac{3}{11}$, white collar $\frac{8}{11}$.

12.5 a) Capitalist 266⅔
Democrat 433⅓
Workers 500

   b) Workers: ⅔
Democrats: ⅓

12.7 b) 900, 1200, 1500
   c) i) 825, 1100, 1675
     ii) $\pi_1 = \frac{1}{4}$, $\pi_2 = \frac{1}{4}$, $\pi_3 = \frac{1}{2}$.

12.9 Fundamental Matrix $\begin{pmatrix} \dfrac{20}{17} & \dfrac{10}{17} \\[2mm] \dfrac{6}{17} & \dfrac{20}{17} \end{pmatrix}$

$$B = \begin{pmatrix} \dfrac{29}{51} & \dfrac{22}{51} \\[2mm] \dfrac{65}{102} & \dfrac{37}{102} \end{pmatrix}$$

12.11 Fundamental Matrix $\begin{pmatrix} \dfrac{24}{11} & \dfrac{6}{11} \\[2mm] \dfrac{8}{11} & \dfrac{24}{11} \end{pmatrix}$

$$B = \begin{pmatrix} \dfrac{4}{11} & \dfrac{7}{11} \\[2mm] \dfrac{5}{11} & \dfrac{6}{11} \end{pmatrix}$$

Recruit 16 dayworkers, 18 nightworkers.

13.1 23 boxes sold, total unsatisfied demand = 11, closing stock at end of simulation = 2.

13.3 Total cycle length = 278 days, total holding cost = £245.60, 28 stockouts.

13.5

Day	1	2	3	4	5	6	7	8	9	10	11	12	13	14	15	16
Idle Time	0	1	2	3	1	0	0	2	0	2	2	0	5	0	0	0
Waiting Time	2	0	0	0	0	0	0	0	1	0	0	2	0	2	0	3

13.7 Introduce extra service point at end of the 18th period. Queues would rapidly vanish.

13.9 A second cashier would be needed after 12 mins 40 secs.

13.11
Car	1	2	3	4	5	6	7	8	9	10
Waiting Time	0	1	2	4	2	0	1	1	3	5

13.13 Total sales $= 91$, total unsatisfied demand $= 6$, Closing stock $= 0$.

14.1 $S = 3250 (1.11)^7 = £6747.65$.

14.3 $(1 + r)^6 = \dfrac{5776}{3265}$, $r = 0.0997$ or 9.97%.

14.5 $S = 9500 (1.12)^{12} + \dfrac{-800(1.12)^{12} - (-800)}{0.12} = £17,705$

14.7 a) £23,380 b)i) £3,108 ii) £2,850.

14.9 £1,356.

14.11 $£125,000 \times 0.07 = £8750$

Market price $= 125,000(1.1)^{-4} + \dfrac{8750[1 - (1.1)^{-4}]}{0.1} = £113,112$

15.2 Payback period $= 2.5$ years
NPV $= £340.88$
NPV at $r = 0.28 = £1012.80$, NPV at $0.29 = £993.16$, IRR $= 28.65\%$.

15.4 PV $= £11,666.40$, so borrow and invest.

15.6 PV i) $= £12,000$, ii) £13,210.45, iii) £13,112.20, iv) £10,222.10 so choose iv).

15.8 PV $= £5,294.60$ IRR $< 12\%$, so do not purchase.

15.10 a) NPV $= -£52.18$, not viable.
b) NPV $= £44.28$, viable.
c) NPV $= -£253.82$, not viable.

16.1
Week No.	1	2	3	4	5	6	7	8	9	10
replaced	100	310	561	299	363	438	358	379	400	377

16.3
Strategy	Weekly cost
Group	£5,000
Individual	£3,076.80
Mixed on 3 week cycle	£2,760

16.5 Average Life $= 2.8$ months. Steady state failures 178.6. Cost of individual replacement $= £1,070.40$.

16.7 Replace after 4 years, average cost $= £4,150$.

16.9 Replace at the end of the 7th year: perpetual replacement fund $= £18,754$.

16.11 Replace at the end of the 8th year, perpetual replacement fund = £31,428.

16.13 Replace after 5 or 6 years, average cost = £3,000.

16.15 Keep machine 1 more year. (PV = £26,751).

17.1	Total Float	0	0	2	5	0	3	0	5	3	5	7	0
	Free Float	0	0	2	0	0	0	0	5	3	5	7	0

17.3

Activity	Preceding Activity
D + E	A
F	D
G	B
H	C
I	B, E + F
J	C, G + I

17.5 Total project time will lengthen to 27 days.

17.7 Total project time: 39 days Critical Path 1,2,3,4,5,8,12,13.

17.9 Maximum no. of men required = 6 men on 6th day.

17.12 F, G and H form a loop.

17.13 Minimum time: 24 days.

17.15 Cheapest way of ensuring target not exceeded.
reduce 1 − 2 to 14 days
reduce 2 − 7 to 8 days

18.1

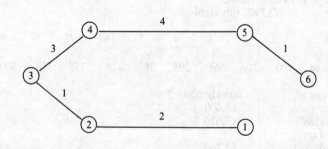

18.3	Town	Route	
	B	A − B	4
	C	A − B − C	5
	D	A − D	2
	E	A − D − F − E	6
	F	A − D − F	3

18.4

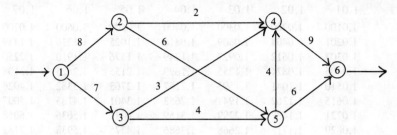

18.9

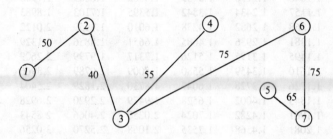

18.11

Town	Route	Distance
B	A – B	20
C	A – C	15
D	A – C – D	23
E	A – B – E	40
F	A – B – E – F	49
G	A – C – D – G	43

18.12 Max. Flow = 13.

19.1 2148, 2231, 2314, 2397.

19.3 $y = 2.93x - 1.43$.

19.5 $y = 6.367x + 28.61$, forecast is 92.28.

19.7 $C = 88.97 - 7.42R$
Forecast price for R = 8% is 29.6.

19.9 SV = 6, 38, −76, 37.

19.11 SV = 28, 2.5, −24, −6.5.

Compounding Tables for R = .01 to R = .07

	1.01	1.02	1.03	1.04	1.05	1.06	1.07
1	1.0100	1.0200	1.0300	1.0400	1.0500	1.0600	1.0700
2	1.0201	1.0404	1.0609	1.0816	1.1025	1.1236	1.1449
3	1.0303	1.0612	1.0927	1.1249	1.1576	1.1910	1.2250
4	1.0406	1.0824	1.1255	1.1699	1.2155	1.2625	1.3108
5	1.0510	1.1041	1.1593	1.2167	1.2763	1.3382	1.4026
6	1.0615	1.1262	1.1941	1.2653	1.3401	1.4185	1.5007
7	1.0721	1.1487	1.2299	1.3159	1.4071	1.5036	1.6058
8	1.0829	1.1717	1.2668	1.3686	1.4775	1.5938	1.7182
9	1.0937	1.1951	1.3048	1.4233	1.5513	1.6895	1.8385
10	1.1046	1.2190	1.3439	1.4802	1.6289	1.7908	1.9672
11	1.1157	1.2434	1.3842	1.5395	1.7103	1.8983	2.1049
12	1.1268	1.2682	1.4258	1.6010	1.7959	2.0122	2.2522
13	1.1381	1.2936	1.4685	1.6651	1.8856	2.1329	2.4098
14	1.1495	1.3195	1.5126	1.7317	1.9799	2.2609	2.5785
15	1.1610	1.3459	1.5580	1.8009	2.0789	2.3966	2.7590
16	1.1726	1.3728	1.6047	1.8730	2.1829	2.5404	2.9522
17	1.1843	1.4002	1.6528	1.9479	2.2920	2.6928	3.1588
18	1.1961	1.4282	1.7024	2.0258	2.4066	2.8543	3.3799
19	1.2081	1.4568	1.7535	2.1068	2.5270	3.0256	3.6165
20	1.2202	1.4859	1.8061	2.1911	2.6533	3.2071	3.8697

Compounding Tables for R = .08 to R = .14

	1.08	1.09	1.10	1.11	1.12	1.13	1.14
1	1.0800	1.0900	1.1000	1.1100	1.1200	1.1300	1.1400
2	1.1664	1.1881	1.2100	1.2321	1.2544	1.2769	1.2996
3	1.2597	1.2950	1.3310	1.3676	1.4049	1.4429	1.4815
4	1.3605	1.4116	1.4641	1.5181	1.5735	1.6305	1.6890
5	1.4693	1.5386	1.6105	1.6851	1.7623	1.8424	1.9254
6	1.5869	1.6771	1.7716	1.8704	1.9738	2.0820	2.1950
7	1.7138	1.8280	1.9487	2.0762	2.2107	2.3526	2.5023
8	1.8509	1.9926	2.1436	2.3045	2.4760	2.6584	2.8526
9	1.9990	2.1719	2.3579	2.5580	2.7731	3.0040	3.2519
10	2.1589	2.3674	2.5937	2.8394	3.1058	3.3946	3.7072
11	2.3316	2.5804	2.8531	3.1518	3.4785	3.8359	4.2262
12	2.5182	2.8127	3.1384	3.4985	3.8960	4.3345	4.8179
13	2.7196	3.0658	3.4523	3.8833	4.3635	4.8980	5.4924
14	2.9372	3.3417	3.7975	4.3104	4.8871	5.5348	6.2613
15	3.1722	3.6425	4.1772	4.7846	5.4736	6.2543	7.1379
16	3.4259	3.9703	4.5950	5.3109	6.1304	7.0673	8.1372
17	3.7000	4.3276	5.0545	5.8951	6.8660	7.9861	9.2765
18	3.9960	4.7171	5.5599	6.5436	7.6900	9.0243	10.5752
19	4.3157	5.1417	6.1159	7.2633	8.6128	10.1974	12.0557
20	4.6610	5.6044	6.7275	8.0623	9.6463	11.5231	13.7435

Compounding Tables for R = .15 to R = .21

	1.15	1.16	1.17	1.18	1.19	1.20	1.21
1	1.1500	1.1600	1.1700	1.1800	1.1900	1.2000	1.2100
2	1.3225	1.3456	1.3689	1.3924	1.4161	1.4400	1.4641
3	1.5209	1.5609	1.6016	1.6430	1.6852	1.7280	1.7716
4	1.7490	1.8106	1.8739	1.9388	2.0053	2.0736	2.1436
5	2.0114	2.1003	2.1924	2.2878	2.3864	2.4883	2.5937
6	2.3131	2.4364	2.5652	2.6996	2.8398	2.9860	3.1384
7	2.6600	2.8262	3.0012	3.1855	3.3793	3.5832	3.7975
8	3.0590	3.2784	3.5115	3.7589	4.0214	4.2998	4.5950
9	3.5179	3.8030	4.1084	4.4355	4.7854	5.1598	5.5599
10	4.0456	4.4114	4.8068	5.2338	5.6947	6.1917	6.7275
11	4.6524	5.1173	5.6240	6.1759	6.7767	7.4301	8.1403
12	5.3503	5.9360	6.5801	7.2876	8.0642	8.9161	9.8497
13	6.1528	6.8858	7.6987	8.5994	9.5964	10.6993	11.9182
14	7.0757	7.9875	9.0075	10.1472	11.4198	12.8392	14.4210
15	8.1371	9.2655	10.5387	11.9737	13.5895	15.4070	17.4494
16	9.3576	10.7480	12.3303	14.1290	16.1715	18.4884	21.1138
17	10.7613	12.4677	14.4265	16.6722	19.2441	22.1861	25.5477
18	12.3755	14.4625	16.8790	19.6733	22.9005	26.6233	30.9127
19	14.2318	16.7765	19.7484	23.2144	27.2516	31.9480	37.4043
20	16.3665	19.4608	23.1056	27.3930	32.4294	38.3376	45.2593

Compounding Tables for R = .22 to R = .28

	1.22	1.23	1.24	1.25	1.26	1.27	1.28
1	1.2200	1.2300	1.2400	1.2500	1.2600	1.2700	1.2800
2	1.4884	1.5129	1.5376	1.5625	1.5876	1.6129	1.6384
3	1.8158	1.8609	1.9066	1.9531	2.0004	2.0484	2.0972
4	2.2153	2.2889	2.3642	2.4414	2.5205	2.6014	2.6844
5	2.7027	2.8153	2.9316	3.0518	3.1758	3.3038	3.4360
6	3.2973	3.4628	3.6352	3.8147	4.0015	4.1959	4.3980
7	4.0227	4.2593	4.5077	4.7684	5.0419	5.3288	5.6295
8	4.9077	5.2389	5.5895	5.9605	6.3528	6.7675	7.2058
9	5.9874	6.4439	6.9310	7.4506	8.0045	8.5948	9.2234
10	7.3046	7.9259	8.5944	9.3132	10.0857	10.9153	11.8059
11	8.9117	9.7489	10.6571	11.6415	12.7080	13.8625	15.1116
12	10.8722	11.9912	13.2148	14.5519	16.0120	17.6053	19.3428
13	13.2641	14.7491	16.3863	18.1899	20.1752	22.3588	24.7588
14	16.1822	18.1414	20.3191	22.7374	25.4207	28.3957	31.6913
15	19.7423	22.3140	25.1956	28.4217	32.0301	36.0625	40.5648
16	24.0856	27.4462	31.2426	35.5271	40.3579	45.7994	51.9230
17	29.3844	33.7588	38.7408	44.4089	50.8510	58.1652	66.4614
18	35.8490	41.5233	48.0386	55.5112	64.0722	73.8698	85.0706
19	43.7358	51.0737	59.5679	69.3889	80.7310	93.8147	108.8904
20	53.3576	62.8206	73.8642	86.7362	101.7211	119.1446	139.3797

Compounding Tables for R = .29 to R = .35

	1.29	1.30	1.31	1.32	1.33	1.34	1.35
1	1.2900	1.3000	1.3100	1.3200	1.3300	1.3400	1.3500
2	1.6641	1.6900	1.7161	1.7424	1.7689	1.7956	1.8225
3	2.1467	2.1970	2.2481	2.3000	2.3526	2.4061	2.4604
4	2.7692	2.8561	2.9450	3.0360	3.1290	3.2242	3.3215
5	3.5723	3.7129	3.8579	4.0075	4.1616	4.3204	4.4840
6	4.6083	4.8268	5.0539	5.2899	5.5349	5.7893	6.0534
7	5.9447	6.2749	6.6206	6.9826	7.3614	7.7577	8.1722
8	7.6686	8.1573	8.6730	9.2170	9.7907	10.3953	11.0324
9	9.8925	10.6045	11.3617	12.1665	13.0216	13.9297	14.8937
10	12.7614	13.7858	14.8838	16.0598	17.3187	18.6659	20.1066
11	16.4622	17.9216	19.4977	21.1989	23.0339	25.0123	27.1439
12	21.2362	23.2981	25.5420	27.9825	30.6351	33.5164	36.6442
13	27.3947	30.2875	33.4601	36.9370	40.7447	44.9120	49.4697
14	35.3391	39.3738	43.8327	48.7568	54.1905	60.1821	66.7841
15	45.5875	51.1859	57.4208	64.3590	72.0733	80.6440	90.1585
16	58.8079	66.5417	75.2213	84.9538	95.8575	108.0629	121.7139
17	75.8621	86.5042	98.5399	112.1390	127.4905	144.8043	164.3138
18	97.8622	112.4554	129.0872	148.0235	169.5624	194.0378	221.0236
19	126.2422	146.1920	169.1043	195.3911	225.5180	260.0107	299.4619
20	162.8524	190.0496	221.5266	257.9162	299.9389	348.4143	404.2736

Discounting Tables for R = .01 to R = .07

	1.01	1.02	1.03	1.04	1.05	1.06	1.07
1	.9901	.9804	.9709	.9615	.9524	.9434	.9346
2	.9803	.9612	.9426	.9246	.9070	.8900	.8734
3	.9706	.9423	.9151	.8890	.8638	.8396	.8163
4	.9610	.9238	.8885	.8548	.8227	.7921	.7629
5	.9515	.9057	.8626	.8219	.7835	.7473	.7130
6	.9420	.8880	.8375	.7903	.7462	.7050	.6663
7	.9327	.8706	.8131	.7599	.7107	.6651	.6227
8	.9235	.8535	.7894	.7307	.6768	.6274	.5820
9	.9143	.8368	.7664	.7026	.6446	.5919	.5439
10	.9053	.8203	.7441	.6756	.6139	.5584	.5083
11	.8963	.8043	.7224	.6496	.5847	.5268	.4751
12	.8874	.7885	.7014	.6246	.5568	.4970	.4440
13	.8787	.7730	.6810	.6006	.5303	.4688	.4150
14	.8700	.7579	.6611	.5775	.5051	.4423	.3878
15	.8613	.7430	.6419	.5553	.4810	.4173	.3624
16	.8528	.7284	.6232	.5339	.4581	.3936	.3387
17	.8444	.7142	.6050	.5134	.4363	.3714	.3166
18	.8360	.7002	.5874	.4936	.4155	.3503	.2959
19	.8277	.6864	.5703	.4746	.3957	.3305	.2765
20	.8195	.6730	.5537	.4564	.3769	.3118	.2584

Discounting Tables for R = .08 to R = .14

	1.08	1.09	1.10	1.11	1.12	1.13	1.14
1	.9259	.9174	.9091	.9009	.8929	.8850	.8772
2	.8573	.8417	.8264	.8116	.7972	.7831	.7695
3	.7938	.7722	.7513	.7312	.7118	.6931	.6750
4	.7350	.7084	.6830	.6587	.6355	.6133	.5921
5	.6806	.6499	.6209	.5935	.5674	.5428	.5194
6	.6302	.5963	.5645	.5346	.5066	.4803	.4556
7	.5835	.5470	.5132	.4817	.4523	.4251	.3996
8	.5403	.5019	.4665	.4339	.4039	.3762	.3506
9	.5002	.4604	.4241	.3909	.3606	.3329	.3075
10	.4632	.4224	.3855	.3522	.3220	.2946	.2697
11	.4289	.3875	.3505	.3173	.2875	.2607	.2366
12	.3971	.3555	.3186	.2858	.2567	.2307	.2076
13	.3677	.3262	.2897	.2575	.2292	.2042	.1821
14	.3405	.2992	.2633	.2320	.2046	.1807	.1597
15	.3152	.2745	.2394	.2090	.1827	.1599	.1401
16	.2919	.2519	.2176	.1883	.1631	.1415	.1229
17	.2703	.2311	.1978	.1696	.1456	.1252	.1078
18	.2502	.2120	.1799	.1528	.1300	.1108	.0946
19	.2317	.1945	.1635	.1377	.1161	.0981	.0829
20	.2145	.1784	.1486	.1240	.1037	.0868	.0728

Discounting Tables for R = .15 to R = .21

	1.15	1.16	1.17	1.18	1.19	1.20	1.21
1	.8696	.8621	.8547	.8475	.8403	.8333	.8264
2	.7561	.7432	.7305	.7182	.7062	.6944	.6830
3	.6575	.6407	.6244	.6086	.5934	.5787	.5645
4	.5718	.5523	.5337	.5158	.4987	.4823	.4665
5	.4972	.4761	.4561	.4371	.4190	.4019	.3855
6	.4323	.4104	.3898	.3704	.3521	.3349	.3186
7	.3759	.3538	.3332	.3139	.2959	.2791	.2633
8	.3269	.3050	.2848	.2660	.2487	.2326	.2176
9	.2843	.2630	.2434	.2255	.2090	.1938	.1799
10	.2472	.2267	.2080	.1911	.1756	.1615	.1486
11	.2149	.1954	.1778	.1619	.1476	.1346	.1228
12	.1869	.1685	.1520	.1372	.1240	.1122	.1015
13	.1625	.1452	.1229	.1163	.1042	.0935	.0839
14	.1413	.1252	.1110	.0985	.0876	.0779	.0693
15	.1229	.1079	.0949	.0835	.0736	.0649	.0573
16	.1069	.0930	.0811	.0708	.0618	.0541	.0474
17	.0929	.0802	.0693	.0600	.0520	.0451	.0391
18	.0808	.0691	.0592	.0508	.0437	.0376	.0323
19	.0703	.0596	.0506	.0431	.0367	.0313	.0267
20	.0611	.0514	.0433	.0365	.0308	.0261	.0221

Discounting Tables for R = .22 to R = .28

	1.22	1.23	1.24	1.25	1.26	1.27	1.28
1	.8197	.8130	.8065	.8000	.7937	.7874	.7812
2	.6719	.6610	.6504	.6400	.6299	.6200	.6104
3	.5507	.5374	.5245	.5120	.4999	.4882	.4768
4	.4514	.4369	.4230	.4096	.3968	.3844	.3725
5	.3700	.3552	.3411	.3277	.3149	.3027	.2910
6	.3033	.2888	.2751	.2621	.2499	.2383	.2274
7	.2486	.2348	.2218	.2097	.1983	.1877	.1776
8	.2038	.1909	.1789	.1678	.1574	.1478	.1388
9	.1670	.1552	.1443	.1342	.1249	.1164	.1084
10	.1369	.1262	.1164	.1074	.0992	.0916	.0847
11	.1122	.1026	.0938	.0859	.0787	.0721	.0662
12	.0920	.0834	.0757	.0687	.0625	.0568	.0517
13	.0754	.0678	.0610	.0550	.0496	.0447	.0404
14	.0618	.0551	.0492	.0440	.0393	.0352	.0316
15	.0507	.0448	.0397	.0352	.0312	.0227	.0247
16	.0415	.0364	.0320	.0281	.0248	.0218	.0193
17	.0340	.0296	.0258	.0225	.0197	.0172	.0150
18	.0279	.0241	.0208	.0180	.0156	.0135	.0118
19	.0229	.0196	.0168	.0144	.0124	.0107	.0092
20	.0187	.0159	.0135	.0115	.0098	.0084	.0072

Discounting Tables for R = .29 to R = .35

	1.29	1.30	1.31	1.32	1.33	1.34	1.35
1	.7752	.7692	.7634	.7576	.7519	.7463	.7407
2	.6009	.5917	.5827	.5739	.5653	.5569	.5487
3	.4658	.4552	.4448	.4348	.4251	.4156	.4064
4	.3611	.3501	.3396	.3294	.3196	.3102	.3011
5	.2799	.2693	.2592	.2495	.2403	.2315	.2230
6	.2170	.2072	.1979	.1890	.1807	.1727	.1652
7	.1682	.1594	.1510	.1432	.1358	.1289	.1224
8	.1304	.1226	.1153	.1085	.1021	.0962	.0906
9	.1011	.0943	.0880	.0822	.0768	.0718	.0671
10	.0784	.0725	.0672	.0623	.0577	.0536	.0497
11	.0607	.0558	.0513	.0472	.0434	.0400	.0368
12	.0471	.0429	.0392	.0357	.0326	.0298	.0273
13	.0365	.0330	.0299	.0271	.0245	.0223	.0202
14	.0283	.0254	.0228	.0205	.0185	.0166	.0150
15	.0219	.0195	.0174	.0155	.0139	.0124	.0111
16	.0170	.0150	.0133	.0118	.0104	.0093	.0082
17	.0132	.0116	.0101	.0089	.0078	.0069	.0061
18	.0102	.0089	.0077	.0068	.0059	.0052	.0045
19	.0079	.0068	.0059	.0051	.0044	.0038	.0033
20	.0061	.0053	.0045	.0039	.0033	.0029	.0025

Index

380